THE GOLDEN BOOT

THE GOLDEN BOOT
Football's Top Scorers

MARK METCALF
& TONY MATTHEWS

AMBERLEY

Front cover image courtesy of Leslie Millman
Back cover image courtesy of Paul Days

First published 2012

Amberley Publishing
The Hill, Stroud
Gloucestershire, GL5 4EP

www.amberleybooks.com

British Library Cataloguing in Publication Data.
A catalogue record for this book is available from the British Library.

ISBN 978 1 4456 0532 6

Typesetting and Origination by Amberley Publishing.
Printed in Great Britain.

Introduction

To become your club's leading goalscorer is a fine achievement ... to finish a campaign as the top division's champion marksman is a real honour ... and over the years some of the game's greatest-ever forwards have been number one while at the same time, there have been several top-class strikers who have never headed the charts, at club or division level.

All serious and knowledgeable soccer enthusiasts know that League football has been played since 1888 and this book is all about those star-studded, powerhouse centre-forwards, those hard-shooting, aggressive inside-men and the out-and-out, all-action strikers who have notched enough goals, important or not, to become top marksman in the First Division/Premiership competitions.

We know that the game has changed dramatically over the course of time, but whatever level you play at, whether it be against weak or strong, moderate or impressive opponents, the ultimate aim is to kick or head the ball past the 'keeper to claim a goal.

Going back to the start of League action, to season 1888/89, when only twenty-two games were played by each of twelve clubs, the strike-force of double-winners Preston North End, John Goodall and Jimmy Ross, finished first and second in the scoring charts. And this achievement of two players from the same club taking the top two spots on their own has never occurred since!

Blackburn's Jack Southworth was also a prolific marksman during the late 1880s and early 1890s, as were Sunderland's Johnny Campbell and Jack Devey of Aston Villa. In fact, Southworth topped the list of goalscorers twice in four seasons, Campbell was leading scorer on four occasions while Devey never finished top, claiming the runner-up spot three times.

In the mid-1890s Steve Bloomer (then of Derby County) began making his mark, as did Fred Wheldon (Aston Villa).

Black Country-born Bloomer, who was missed by the likes of Wolves, Villa and West Bromwich Albion, remained as one of the League's champion goalscorers for almost a decade and then, from 1905 to the outbreak of the First World War, eleven different players headed the scoring charts in top-flight League football, among them Bolton Wanderers and Newcastle's Albert Shepherd, who also finished runner-up twice, David McLean (Sheffield Wednesday) and Bertie Freeman (Everton).

The trend of there being a different player ending the season as top scorer continued after the hostilities when, from 1920 to 1931, eleven players finished as leading marksman, one of them the legendary Dixie Dean of Everton, along with the Sunderland duo of Charlie Buchan and David Halliday, Ted Harper of Blackburn, Tom 'Pongo' Waring of Aston Villa and Vic Watson of West Ham.

Dean, who bagged a staggering 60 League goals out of the 102 scored by the Merseyside club in 1927/28 – a record which will never be beaten – became the first player to top the charts twice since Bloomer (1903/04) when he netted forty-four in 1931/32, and then, quite surprisingly in quick succession, Jack Bowers of Derby County (1932/33 and 1933/34) and

Everton's Tommy Lawton (1937/38 and 1938/39) both doubled-up before the Second World War.

The first player to head the scoring charts twice after the war was Jimmy Greaves (for Chelsea in 1958/59 and Spurs in 1962/63). Before that, some brilliant centre-forwards had finished 'top of the tree' in the First Division charts, among them Stan Mortensen (Blackpool), Nat Lofthouse (Bolton), Ronnie Allen (West Brom) and John Charles (Leeds).

Greaves went on to finish top man four more times – in 1962/63, 1963/64, 1964/65 and 1968/69 – and is the only player so far to have been leading scorer in First Division football on six separate occasions.

During the 1970s and early 1980s, several other internationals had the honour of being the First Division's champion goalscorer: Roger Hunt (Liverpool), George Best (Manchester United), West Brom's top marksman of all-time, Tony Brown, Francis Lee (Manchester City), Malcolm Macdonald (twice), Bob Latchford (Everton), Frank Worthington (Bolton) and Kevin Keegan.

These were followed, up to the introduction of the Premiership in 1992, by Gary Lineker – the only player so far to have achieved the feat with three different clubs, Leicester City, Everton and Spurs – Ian Rush (Liverpool), Clive Allen (Spurs), Alan Smith (Arsenal) and Ian Wright (Crystal Palace).

In the nineteen seasons of Premiership football, Alan Shearer (with Blackburn Rovers twice and Newcastle United once) has became the first player to head the scoring list on his own three seasons running: 1994–97 inclusive. Thierry Henry (Arsenal) equalled that feat between 2003 and 2006 and the Frenchman also topped the charts in 2001/02.

Chelsea's Didier Drogba was champion marksman in 2006/07 and again in 2009/10, and one interesting fact is that nine foreign-born players have finished as leading scorer in the Premiership since 1998 – some of them jointly. They are Dwight Yorke, Ruud van Nistelrooy, Henry, Drogba, Jimmy-Floyd Hasselbaink, Cristiano Ronaldo, Nicolas Anelka, Dimitar Berbatov and Carlos Tevez.

It's a wonderful feeling to score a goal, especially if it's a late winner in a major cup final or the one that clinches promotion or a League title, and over the last 111 seasons of First Division/Premiership football (1888–2011) some of the world's greatest footballers have done just that – as well as claiming the honour of being champion goalscorer in the top flight of English League football. Read and enjoy the stories of these goalscoring superstars.

TM & MM

ALDRIDGE, JOHN (LIVERPOOL)

Season: 1987/88
Goals scored: 28 (out of 87); 18 home, 10 away
Percentage: 32.1 per cent
Runner-up: Brian McClair (Manchester United), 24 goals
Liverpool were League Champions

Liverpool knew they were losing their chief striker, Ian Rush, to Juventus at the end of the 1986/87 season and needed a proven and experienced replacement. That player was John Aldridge, who even bore a physical resemblance to Rush.

He had been signed by Reds' manager Kenny Dalglish from Oxford United for £750,000 in January 1987 and cut his teeth with the club as Rush's partner, filling a position previously occupied by his boss Dalglish and fellow striker Paul Walsh.

Aldridge played in ten League games at the end of that season as Liverpool ended the year trophyless, including a Wembley defeat to Arsenal in the League Cup final, for which he was ineligible.

By the time of his transfer to Anfield, Aldridge had already scored fifteen goals for Oxford in twenty-five games. He made his debut for the Reds as a second-half substitute against Aston Villa and scored his first goal for his new club a week later, a 60th-minute strike which beat Southampton 1-0 at Anfield.

Aldridge quickly demonstrated to the fans that he could cope with the pressure of replacing Rush. Indeed, after Rush had left, Aldridge went on to score twenty-six goals in what turned out to be a magnificent season for Liverpool, including a strike in each of the first nine games.

Linking up with new signings Peter Beardsley and John Barnes to form one of the most exciting attacking lines in Liverpool's history, the team suffered only two defeats in the League all season. They remained unbeaten for the first twenty-nine matches and went on to clinch the 1988 League title in style, finishing nine points clear of their nearest rivals, Manchester United, although the gap between Liverpool and the Old Trafford club was considerably wider for most of the season.

Aldridge was handed the number 8 shirt for the 1987/88 season, as Dalglish felt that giving him the number 9 (previously worn by Rush) would put the pressure on him. In fact, the number 9 shirt went to winger Ray Houghton, who had, coincidentally, been Aldridge's team-mate at Oxford. It should be noted, however, that Aldridge actually favoured the number 8 as it was the number worn by his hero, Liverpool's World Cup legend Sir Roger Hunt.

The goals flowed thick and fast for Aldridge straight from the off in August 1987.

He got off to a flier with a 9th-minute opener in a 2-1 win at Arsenal, struck home a penalty in a 4-1 victory at Coventry and fired home another spot-kick in the 1-1 draw at West

Ham before, as expected, he netted in his first home game against his former club Oxford United, which Liverpool won 2-0.

His third successful penalty followed in a 3-2 win over Charlton; he then put Liverpool 2-0 up at Newcastle on their way to a resounding 4-1 victory; fired in his first Liverpool hat-trick in 32 minutes (including two more spot-kicks) in a 4-0 home win over Derby, added another from the 12-yard mark in his next game, another 4-0 win, this time over Portsmouth, and claimed his sixth penalty success when QPR became Liverpool's third successive 4-0 victims.

Aldridge was on fire at this juncture ... but he was only an efficient helper during the next three games, before getting back on track with a first-half special in a 1-1 draw at Old Trafford. Off target in a stalemate with Norwich, he returned to goalscoring form in late November with a fine strike against Watford (won 4-0), missed out at Tottenham (won 2-0) and fired home hard and low another penalty in a 2-1 win over Chelsea.

He was kept quiet during mid-December but bounced back on Boxing Day by scoring in a 3-0 win at his former employers, Oxford. He then netted twice (one a routine penalty) in yet another 4-0 win, this time over Newcastle, followed up with Liverpool's second in their sixth 4-0 victory at home to Coventry on New Year's Day and was on target in a 2-0 victory over Arsenal a fortnight later.

Goalless at Charlton (won 2-0) and West Ham (0-0), he got back on track with Liverpool's second in a 4-1 win at Watford but was injured at Portsmouth soon afterwards, forcing him to miss the next three games, including a 1-0 Merseyside derby defeat at Goodison Park (Liverpool's first set-back of the season), before returning to score against Wimbledon (won 2-1) and do likewise again from the spot in another defeat, this one at Nottingham Forest (2-1).

Admitting he wasn't fully fit, Aldridge, although not on target, played his part in a thrilling 3-3 draw with Manchester United at Anfield early in April, before going out and scoring twice in a crushing 5-0 home victory over Nottingham Forest.

He raced onto Beardsley's 30-yard defence-splitting pass before lifting the ball over Steve Sutton's head in the 37th minute to make it 2-0 and with two minutes remaining, he glided the ball home after some smart work by Nigel Spackman.

He then netted just twice more, in successive 1-1 home draws with Southampton and Luton, to end the campaign with a League tally of twenty-six goals – making him the First Division's top marksman, two ahead of Brian McClair (Manchester United).

Earlier in the season, Aldridge had scored both goals in Liverpool's FA Cup semi-final victory over Nottingham Forest, one a memorable volley from an outstanding team move.

Everyone knew he was also an efficient penalty-taker, but a predictable one at that, which led to his season, and that of Liverpool, ending in heartbreak.

In the FA Cup final, Wimbledon led 1-0 midway through the second half, when Liverpool were awarded a spot kick after Aldridge himself was fouled.

Dons' 'keeper, Dave Beasant, had anticipated that Aldridge would drive his spot-kick to his left, the way he had sent all his penalties that season, scoring every time.

Aldridge, as predicted, hit his spot-kick to Beasant's left, but it was just too near the 'keeper, who dived to keep the ball out, thus becoming the first goalie to save a penalty in the FA Cup final at Wembley.

Aldridge's failure was his first penalty miss for Liverpool. He was substituted shortly afterwards as Wimbledon held on to win 1-0, causing a major upset.

The following season was tough and eventful for Aldridge. Rush had failed to settle in Italy and Liverpool negotiated a cut-price deal to bring him back to Anfield.

This led to natural speculation that Aldridge would be surplus to requirements, but manager Dalglish disproved this by regularly playing the two strikers together, despite reservations that both players were stylistically too similar to be strike partners, and indeed, it was Aldridge who enjoyed the better form during the season as Rush struggled to re-acquaint himself with his familiar surroundings.

In the annual Charity Shield match against Wimbledon at Wembley at the start of the 1988/89 season, Aldridge mildly laid his FA Cup ghosts to rest by scoring both goals in a 2-1 win. He maintained his hot scoring streak while Rush often had to content himself with a place on the bench. In the first League game of the season, he scored a hat-trick in a 3-0 away win over Charlton Athletic and later grabbed another treble in the 5-0 home win over Luton and went on to finish the season as the club's top scorer again, this time with a total of twenty-two goals in the League, eight in the FA Cup, two in the League Cup and two in the Charity Shield, for an overall tally of thirty-four.

On 15 April 1989, crushes on the terraces at the FA Cup semi-final at Hillsborough left ninety-four Liverpool fans dead (the final death toll was ninety-six) and Aldridge, as a native Liverpudlian and boyhood supporter of the club, was deeply affected by the tragedy.

He attended every funeral he could and publicly contemplated giving up the game. Ultimately, he returned to the fray and scored two goals in the re-arranged semi-final (once again against Nottingham Forest) at Old Trafford as Liverpool won 3-1. He courted controversy with the own goal scored by Forest defender Brian Laws and was criticised for ruffling the distraught player's hair and laughing in celebration.

Aldridge fully redeemed himself for his penalty failure a year earlier by scoring in the FA Cup final at Wembley against Merseyside rivals Everton after just four minutes with his first touch of the ball. Ironically, it was Rush who ultimately sealed the win when he replaced Aldridge and scored twice in extra time to earn Liverpool a 3-2 victory.

The League and FA Cup double, achieved by Liverpool in 1986 but denied to them by Wimbledon in 1988, was again possible in 1989, with a deciding League game against Arsenal to come at Anfield.

Disappointingly, especially for Aldridge, the Gunners stole the points and the title with a 2-0 victory, courtesy of Michael Thomas's injury-time goal. Aldridge sank prostrate on to the turf, inconsolable, when the final whistle sounded, and reacted angrily when Arsenal defender and Irish team-mate David O'Leary helped him to his feet.

Aldridge scored 65 goals in 106 appearances for Liverpool before leaving Anfield for the Spanish club Real Sociedad for £1m in September 1989. Two years later, he returned to England to sign for Tranmere Rovers for £250,000. He was appointed player-manager at Prenton Park in April 1997 and retired as a player in June 1998, but continued as boss until April 2001. After that he entered BBC and TV as a match summariser.

Born in Liverpool on 18 September 1958, Aldridge played for South Liverpool and Newport County before joining Oxford United for £78,000 in March 1984.

During his professional career, he scored 412 goals in 739 appearances for his four Football League clubs. He also netted twenty-one times for Real Sociedad and struck nineteen goals in sixty-nine full internationals for the Republic of Ireland.

A Welsh Cup winner with Newport in 1980, he helped Oxford win the Second Division title in 1985 and the League Cup twelve months later before going out and doing the business for Liverpool. At 39 years and 227 days, he is the oldest player ever to appear at senior level for Tranmere (against Wolves in May 1998).

ALLEN, CLIVE (TOTTENHAM HOTSPUR)

Season: 1986/87
Goals scored: 33 (out of 68); 18 home, 15 away
Percentage: 52 per cent
Runner-up: Ian Rush (Liverpool), 30 goals
Spurs finished third

Clive Allen was born in Stepney, East London on 20 May 1961, the son of ex-Tottenham Hotspur forward Les Allen, who was a member of Bill Nicholson's legendary team which completed the double in 1960/61, with the FA Cup success occurring exactly two weeks before Allen junior's birth. He is also the brother of former professional Bradley Allen and cousin of manager Martin Allen and ex-West Ham and Spurs midfielder Paul Allen.

Allen, who holds the unique distinction of playing for more London-based football clubs than any other footballer in history, had a long professional career which spanned seventeen years, from 1978 to 1995, during which time he scored 232 goals in 485 appearances, including a record 49 for Spurs in 1986/87, when he was also voted 'Footballer of the Year'.

Allen was certainly outstanding during that 1986/87 campaign when, as they say, everything he touched turned to gold, or rather goals!

Wearing the number 7 shirt but playing through the middle with Mark Falco, he began with a hat-trick in an opening-day 3-0 win at Villa Park and 48 hours later scored again in the 1-1 home draw with Newcastle. After three blank games he then struck six goals in a fortnight, five in the League, including braces at Leicester (won 2-1) and at home to Everton (2-0).

On 11 October he fired in a second-half winner at Liverpool and followed up with his eleventh League goal of the season, at home to Sheffield Wednesday (1-1).

Five more League goals followed in November and seven in December, including three twos in a week at Chelsea (2-0), at home to West Ham (4-0) and at Coventry (lost 4-3).

Allen ended the first half of the season with twenty-three League and five League Cup goals to his name. He personally was firing on all cylinders, but Spurs were not! They were lying in sixth place in the First Division table, having slipped down to twelfth at one point.

Unfortunately Allen had a poor January (no League goals) but he was back on track with a vengeance in February, rattling in a couple in a resounding 5-0 home League win over Leicester and notching a hat-trick in a League Cup-tie against West Ham to steer Spurs into the semi-finals. Two of his goals against the Hammers were scored from close range – from crosses by Nico Claesen and cousin Paul. His other was a well-struck penalty past Phil Parkes.

One more League goal was scored in March – a penalty winner against his former club, QPR – and in April, when Spurs were on course to reach both the FA Cup and League Cup finals, he netted his second League hat-trick in a 3-0 win over Norwich, tucked away winners at Sheffield Wednesday (1-0) and at home to Charlton (also 1-0), while his goal in a 4-1 Villa Park win over Watford helped take Spurs through to the FA Cup final.

Unfortunately Spurs couldn't make it a Cup final double – despite three goals from Allen, they were beaten in a replay in the League Cup semi-final by arch-rivals Arsenal.

Allen scored his thirty-third League goal of the season in the fortieth game, a 4-0 home win over Manchester United, but then, after getting off to a flier with a strike in the second minute of the FA Cup final against Coventry City, he was thwarted by Steve Ogrizovic as Spurs were defeated 3-2 by the Sky Blues at Wembley.

So, for Allen and his haul of forty-nine goals scored, there were no prizes at club level – only the Footballer of the Year trophy for his bold and brave efforts as Spurs' ace marksman of 1986/87.

As a youngster Allen represented Havering Schools, Essex Schools and London Schools before joining Queens Park Rangers as an apprentice in June 1976, turning professional in September 1978. In June 1980 he was transferred to Arsenal for £1.25 million but never played a senior game for the Gunners, whom he left with a matter of days, joining Crystal Palace, also for £1.25 million.

In June 1981 he returned to Loftus Road for £700,000 (the highest fee paid by a British club for a teenager at that time), and three years later was recruited by Tottenham Hotspur, again for £700,000, in August 1984. He spent his best years at club level at White Hart Lane, where he played until March 1988, when sold to the French club Bordeaux for £1 million.

Sixteen months later, he returned to England to sign for Manchester City at £1.1 million; he switched to Chelsea for £250,000 in December 1991, diverted through London to West Ham United for £250,000 in March 1992 and after brief spells with Millwall and Carlisle United during the 1995/96 season, he retired and became Tottenham Hotspur Youth Development coach in August 1995. He has since twice acted as caretaker-manager, in 2007 and 2008, and has also served as assistant-manager. He has also been engaged as a Sky TV football analyst and, surprisingly, played American football for London Monarchs in the NFL Europe.

He was rewarded with five full caps for England and also played in four Schoolboy, four Youth and three U21 internationals and represented the Football League. As a member of Bobby Robson's squad for the tour of South America in the summer of 1984, he made his senior debut as a second-half substitute in place of Tony Woodcock against Brazil (when John Barnes scored that magnificent goal) and also played against Uruguay and Chile. He won his last two caps in 1987 and 1988 against Turkey (when he had a goal disallowed) and Israel.

ALLEN, RONNIE (WEST BROMWICH ALBION)

Season: 1954/55
Goals scored: 27 (out of 76); 15 home, 12 away
Percentage: 35.5 per cent
Joint runners-up: Johnny Hancocks (Wolverhampton Wanderers) and Jim Glazzard (Huddersfield Town) with 26 goals each
Albion finished seventeenth

Having netted 40 goals in 156 appearances for Port Vale whom he joined in 1944, Ronnie Allen was transferred to West Bromwich Albion on 2 March 1950 for £20,050, a club record fee for the Baggies at the time.

A scorer on his First Division debut two days later, to secure a 1-1 draw against Wolverhampton Wanderers in front of 60,945 spectators, which remains a record for a League game at The Hawthorns, he never looked back, becoming one of Albion's greatest-ever marksmen.

Only 5 feet 8 inches tall (1.73 m) and weighing barely 11 stone (70 kg), Allen was initially a right-winger, but as time passed by he emerged as one of the best centre-forwards in the game, yet gained only five England caps – simply because there were several other great strikers around at the same time, including Nat Lofthouse, Stan Mortensen and Tommy Taylor.

Between his debut day and May 1954 (just over four years) Allen scored 105 goals, including the penalty winner against his former club, Port Vale, in the 1954 FA Cup semi-final and two in the final against Preston North End, which Albion won 3-2.

The Baggies came within four points of completing the double in 1953/54, finishing runners-up in the First Division to Wolves, Allen contributing twenty-seven goals, one behind his striker-partner Johnny Nicholls, who himself was just one goal behind the Division's top marksman, Jim Glazzard (Huddersfield Town).

Twelve months on, and this time it was Allen who took the honour of being top scorer in Division One, bagging twenty-seven goals in forty-two games in 1954/55. He also notched a hat-trick in an FA Charity Shield draw with Wolves.

After failing to hit the net in the opening two away defeats at Sunderland and Newcastle, Allen's first goal of the season was made by Irish international Reg Ryan and it helped beat a strong Arsenal side 3-1 at The Hawthorns.

Allen then went out and scored in each of the next nine competitive games (six won, three drawn).

He fired home a beauty with his left foot from fully 25 yards in a 4-2 revenge victory over Newcastle (his favourite club, against whom he had scored five times the previous season and actually went on to grab a total of eleven overall) and after taking Ray Barlow's long pass in his stride, he netted with sweet aplomb to earn the points at Sheffield United (2-1). In Albion's next game at Goodison Park, he had three efforts saved before guiding home Ryan's mistimed shot with a cheeky back-heeler to clinch a 2-1 victory over Everton.

Allen's ninety-ninth League goal for Albion came from a tap-in after Preston North End's 'keeper had dropped George Lee's cross from the left in a 2-0 home win in mid-September and his 100th came up in a 3-3 home draw with Everton four days later, a thumping volley from Joe Kennedy's downward header. He then struck again shortly afterwards, whipping in Wilf Carter's cross from the right.

Soon afterwards, Allen struck both goals in a 2-0 win at Burnley – his first was thumped high into the net with immense power, his second a smart turn and shot from right-winger Frank Griffin's inch-perfect pass.

He then opened the scoring in the twelfth minute with a powerful drive from 25 yards which deflected into the net off Stan Milburn to set Albion on their way to an exciting 6-4 home win over newly-promoted Leicester City.

Four days after this ten-goal thriller, Albion shared another eight goals in a 4-4 Charity Shield draw with Wolves at Molineux when Allen claimed one of his nine hat-tricks for the club.

Back in the League, Allen scored a brilliant individual goal after a 50-yard run in a 3-3 draw at Chelsea. He followed up by flicking in a low cross-shot from Lee in a 3-2 home defeat by Aston Villa, netted with two crisp right-footed drives from crosses by debutants Alec Jackson and Allan Crowshaw in a solid 3-1 win at Charlton, and despite struggling with an injury, he managed to blast home a penalty to sew up a 2-0 home victory over Manchester United.

Early in December, Albion were outplayed at Portsmouth and trailed 6-0 before Allen popped in a late consolation goal and it wasn't a good Christmas either, as the Baggies lost 3-2 at Cardiff despite another fine goal from Allen.

In a New Year's Day draw at Arsenal (2-2), Allen scored with an 8-yard toe-poke and soon afterwards was on target again in another 2-2 draw, this time with Burnley at The Hawthorns. However, he then missed a penalty as Charlton dumped Albion out of the FA Cup, but the striker was back on the goal-trail with two goals in a 4-2 home defeat by Chelsea on a snow-covered Hawthorns pitch in early March. His first was a clinical finish from Ken Hodgkisson's square pass and his second a superb chip over the head of 'keeper 'Chick' Thomson.

Allen's last six goals of the season all came in April. He slipped in the rebound after Lee's shot had been blocked and struck home a low drive from Carter's pass in the 4-2 win at Bolton ... blasted in Stuart Williams' pass in a 3-1 revenge victory over Portsmouth ...

whipped in two wonderful left-footers from exquisite passes by wing-halves Barlow and Jimmy Dudley in a 2-1 home win over Huddersfield ... and rounded things off by shooting through a crowd of players in a last-match 2-1 defeat at home by Tottenham.

It had been a terrific season for Allen, but not so good for Albion, who finished in seventeenth place, only five points off relegation.

Allen continued to score goals – notching another 99 to bring his total to 234 in 458 games for Albion in 11 years. He left The Hawthorns for Crystal Palace in March 1961 and after retiring in May 1965 he became coach of Wolves, taking over as manager in 1966. Later manager of Athletic Bilbao, Sporting Lisbon and Walsall, he returned to The Hawthorns as a scout before taking over as Albion boss in 1977. He left after just six months in office to take over the Saudi Arabia national team and after managing Panathinaikos, he had a second spell in charge at The Hawthorns (from 1981) before quitting football on a full-time scale basis in 1983, although he did remain with Albion as a part-time coach until 1985, actually playing in his last game as a late substitute against Cheltenham Town at the age of sixty-six.

Allen, who was born in Fenton, Stoke-on-Trent on 15 January 1929, died in Great Wyrley near Walsall on 9 June 2001.

ANELKA, NICOLAS (CHELSEA)

Season: 2008/09
Goals scored: 19 (out of 68); 9 home, 10 away
Percentage: 28 per cent
Runner-up: Cristiano Ronaldo (Manchester United), 18 goals
Chelsea finished third

Nicolas Anelka recovered from missing the final penalty in the 2008 UEFA Champions League final against Manchester United to finish as the Premier League's top scorer the following season. Pushed out to the wing or employed as a substitute when he arrived from Bolton at a cost of £15 million in January 2008, the Frenchman had struggled to get on the scoresheet, scoring just twice by the end of the season.

However, with Didier Drogba missing through injury at the start of 2008/09, Anelka grabbed his chance to show his considerable goalscoring talents, thus ensuring he was retained in a more attacking role when the Ivory Coast international returned to full fitness.

With Brazilian manager Luiz Felipe Scolari taking charge for the first time, Anelka took just 26 minutes to open his account as FA Cup holders Portsmouth were swept away 4-0 at Stamford Bridge. Out-jumping David James, he headed the ball into the net.

His second came in the fourth match. Eastlands Stadium was bouncing on the back of the news that Manchester City had been taken over by mega-rich Arabs, but Chelsea demonstrated that Anelka's former employers still had a long way to go to be considered title challengers. Anelka had hit 46 goals in 103 matches for the Manchester side before moving to Fenerbahce during the 2004/05 season, and on 69 minutes he capped a marvellous performance by his current side by hitting their third. Put clean through by an inch-perfect Joe Cole pass, he gave 'keeper Joe Hart no chance, making it 3-1.

Coming on as a substitute at Stoke, Anelka again wrapped up the match, striking a first time shot past Thomas Sorensen in a 2-0 win. Having hit Chelsea's second at home to Aston Villa, Anelka continued his impressive away form by scoring his side's second in a 3-0 win at Hull.

On the first day of November, Anelka wrapped up his first Chelsea hat-trick. Already a goal up against Sunderland, he appeared to be in an offside position when Alex found him just two yards out, doubling his tally on half time when Florent Malouda's accurate ball was flicked into an empty net. Seven minutes after the restart, when the two again combined, Anelka was able to easily beat Marton Fulop from six yards and make it 5-0.

Two more quickly followed at Ewood Park when Blackburn were lucky to lose just 2-0 as he missed a hatful of chances and saw 'keeper Paul Robinson defy him with a string of impressive saves.

His red-hot run in front of goal continued at the Hawthorns as bottom club WBA were swept away 3-0. Surging into the area, Anelka left Scott Carson no chance before another smart finish on the stroke of half-time made it 3-0. He might even have had another hat-trick, but Jonas Olsson did well to block his goal-bound effort. Anelka now had twelve in the Premier League, well on the way to beating his previous best of seventeen, recorded for Arsenal in the 1998/99 season.

Signed from Monaco for £500,000 at aged seventeen in February 1997, Anelka was one of many Gunners stars the following season when Arsene Wenger's side did 'the double', with Anelka grabbing both goals in the FA Cup final victory against Newcastle United. Seeking a larger salary, Anelka left the North London club in the summer of 1999 to join Real Madrid for a fee of £22.5 million.

Back at the Reebok Stadium for the first time since his transfer south, Anelka was again hitting the net, bagging the first in a 2-0 victory that meant Chelsea, with eleven successive away victories, had beaten Tottenham's forty-eight-year-old record in the top division. After the previous weekend's home defeat against Arsenal, it also meant a valuable three points. Meeting Bosingwa's inviting cross, his diving header gave Jussi Jääskeläinen no chance.

West Ham United provided Anelka with his 100th Premier League goal. Receiving the ball from Frank Lampard, his quick feet and sharp finish saw the ball flash past Robert Green. A draw, though, against their London rivals was not the result Chelsea needed as they sought to recapture the title from Manchester United, especially as when the two sides then met at Old Trafford, the away side were insipid, failed to have a decent effort at goal and left well beaten 3-0. When another poor performance then followed at Liverpool in a 2-0 defeat, it was clear there were problems, one of which was Anelka had stopped scoring. The result was that with Manchester United now well clear in the League, Chelsea's chances of lifting silverware now lay in the Cups, European and FA.

In the FA Cup, Anelka hit his second hat-trick of the season in a 3-1 away win at Watford, thus impressing Scolari's replacement in the hot seat, Guus Hiddink. Then, after squeezing past Juventus in the last sixteen and Liverpool in the quarter-finals, Chelsea found themselves facing Barcelona in the last four of the UEFA Champions League.

Having drawn 0-0 in Camp Nou, Chelsea were favourites to make it back to the final, especially when Michael Essien fired them ahead at Stamford Bridge. The home side couldn't grab the decisive second, but should have been awarded a penalty on 82 minutes when Anelka's neat flick was clearly handled by Gerard Pique in the box. Deep into injury time, the Spaniards struck when Andres Iniesta hit a superb equaliser, firing home from the edge of the box to take his side off to play Manchester United in the final. Anelka had been denied the chance to add to the Champions League winner's medal he'd earned at Real Madrid in 2000, when he scored in both semi-finals against Bayern Munich and also played in the final.

Despite their disappointment, Chelsea maintained the fine form they had shown under Hiddink, and none more so than Anelka, who hit three goals in the final three League games of the season. His final one came at Sunderland, when he flashed a powerful drive well out of the reach of Fulop. With nineteen League goals he had become the fifth Chelsea player to finish as top scorer in English football's top League during a season, and although he failed to net in the following match, he still picked up his second FA Cup winner's medal as Chelsea beat Everton 2-1 in the final.

ARCHIBALD, STEVE (TOTTENHAM HOTSPUR)

Season: 1980/81
Goals scored: 20 (out of 72); 12 home, 8 away
Percentage: 27.7 per cent
Joint top scorer with Peter Withe (Aston Villa)
Spurs finished tenth

In his first season at White Hart Lane (1980/81), Scottish-born striker Steve Archibald struck up a marvellous rapport with Garth Crooks.

A record signing by manager Keith Burkinshaw from Aberdeen, he settled in immediately and quickly became a firm favourite with the Spurs supporters.

A slim but instinctive goalscorer, the blond-haired Archibald was a strong runner, razor-sharp inside the penalty area and had an unquenchable thirst for goals.

Taking over from Chris Jones at inside-right (number 8), he made his Spurs debut in a 2-0 home win over Nottingham Forest on 16 August 1980 before netting his first goal for the club in a 4-3 mid-week victory at London rivals Crystal Palace.

Spurs then had a rough, six-match winless League run when the team scored only three goals and played out three successive 0-0 draws, although Archibald did grab his first League Cup goal for the club in a 3-1 win over Orient.

Thankfully, things changed in early October with a 3-2 win at Stoke, Archibald netting the second goal. An identical scoreline followed at home to Middlesbrough, Archibald again on target, this time with the winner, but successive defeats away at Aston Villa and Manchester City saw Spurs slip down to a mid-table position.

From late October until mid-November, Spurs were unbeaten in five League games, Archibald scoring a total of seven goals ... two in a 4-1 home win over Coventry, another couple (one of them a real cracker) to earn a point at Everton (2-2), the opener in a 4-2 double clinching home win over Crystal Palace, and a third brace in the first-half of an excellent 3-0 victory at Nottingham Forest, again one of them a sublime effort.

Argentinian World Cup winners Ossie Ardiles and Ricky Villa and Glenn Hoddle were doing their utmost to create chances for Archibald and Crooks – and gradually Spurs were getting the right blend together.

However, three successive League defeats and elimination from the League Cup knocked the stuffing out of the team, but the introduction of Graham Roberts at the back steadied the ship and Spurs regained their form with wins over Manchester City (2-1) and Ipswich Town (5-3), Archibald scoring in both games.

He then found the net in a thrilling 4-4 Boxing Day home draw with Southampton, scored in a 2-2 encounter at Norwich twenty-four hours later and was then the hero of

White Hart Lane when his two-goal salvo saw off Arsenal in the North London derby. He scored in each half to gun down the Reds!

A week later, he scored his first FA Cup goal of his career when Spurs beat Hull City in round four.

After netting a point-saver at home to Leeds United (1-1), in a 2-1 defeat at Leicester and in the 3-1 Cup win over Coventry City, Archibald's goals dried up. Some people said he looked 'out of sorts' and, in fact, he managed only one more League goal in the next eleven outings but did find the net, crucially, in the FA Cup semi-final draw with Wolves before the end of the season.

Boss Burkinshaw, though, knew that Archibald was a key player for the team and he played his part in Spurs' 3-2 Centenary FA Cup final replay victory over Manchester City. In the eighth minute his shot was blocked by 'keeper Joe Corrigan, but Villa followed up to score. He then got a vital touch on the ball to enable Crooks to level things up at 2-2 before Villa scored a memorable individual match-winner.

Archibald was born in Glasgow on 27 September 1956.

After playing intermediate football with Crofoot United and Fernhill Athletic and having one outing with East Stirling, Archibald came to prominence as a midfielder with Clyde before being converted into a brilliant striker after signing for Aberdeen, where he forged a prolific partnership with Joe Harper.

After helping the Dons clinch the Scottish Premier Division in 1980, he moved south to Tottenham Hotspur for £800,000. He spent four years at White Hart Lane, during which time he netted 78 goals in 189 first-class appearances, helping Spurs win the UEFA Cup (his decisive penalty conversion beating Anderlecht in a shoot-out), two FA Cup finals and the League Cup, scoring against Liverpool in the 1982 final.

In 1984 he joined Barcelona for £1.25m. He became a popular figure at Camp Nou, winning La Liga, until restrictions on fielding foreign players led to him being excluded from the squad in favour of Gary Lineker and Mark Hughes. He was loaned out to Blackburn Rovers before making a surprise return to Scottish football with Hibernian. After a brief spell back in Spain with RCD Espanyol, he linked up with St Mirren and was influential in bringing former Barça team-mate Victor Muñoz to the Paisley club.

Later in his eventful career, Archibald had a trial with Reading and assisted Ayr United, Fulham, Clyde, again, East Fife (as player-manager) and Home Farm (Ireland).

Overall, he netted almost 200 goals in more than 450 club appearances, as well as gaining twenty-seven full and four U23 caps for Scotland, scoring four senior goals.

In 1996, he quit football and retired to his home in Spain for the next few years, working on a number of business interests, including that of a football agent.

In the summer of 2000, he surprisingly re-emerged in Scottish football when he mounted a bid to buy financially troubled First Division club Airdrieonians. He took over the running of the club, inserted himself as manager and did well, but ultimately failed to conclude the purchase of the club, leading to his departure in March 2001. Airdrieonians subsequently went out of business in May 2002, although a new club – Airdrie United – was formed and took over from Clydebank in the Scottish League.

Archibald now lives with his family (and friends) in sunny Spain.

ASTLE, JEFF (WEST BROMWICH ALBION)

Season: 1969/70
Goals scored: 25 (out of 58); 20 home, 5 away
Percentage: 43 per cent
Runners-up: Joe Royle (Everton) and Peter Osgood (Chelsea),
with 23 goals each
Albion finished sixteenth

Centre forward Jeff Astle was absent from eight League games
during the 1969/70 season, yet still went on to score twenty-five
goals for West Bromwich Albion, whose next highest scorer
was Colin Suggett with twelve.

The Baggies certainly missed Astle between early August and 6 September. He was
suspended for the opener at Southampton and sat out six of the next seven matches with a
knee injury. Without him, Albion looked rudderless in attack and won only two games in a
month and scored just eight goals. But when the Nottingham-born striker returned, initially
for a League Cup tie at Villa Park, when he headed in the winner and took a battering from
man-marker Bruce Rioch, who was normally an attacking midfielder who went on to play for
Scotland, Albion's overall performances on the field improved dramatically.

An inspired Astle found the net on a regular basis, netting fifteen times before the end of
the year, eleven in the League and four in the League Cup, helping Albion qualify for their
third final in five seasons.

After this, his form, particularly at The Hawthorns, was brilliant, scoring a staggering
twenty-three goals in twenty-two competitive games on home soil (twenty in the League).

Six feet tall, strong and mobile, very capable on the ground, and one of the best headers of
a football in the entire country, Astle scored seven times with his head in 1969/70 ... and he
laid on six more goals for his colleagues with deft flicks and knock-ons. Awkward to mark,
Everton's Brian Labone thought he was the best centre forward he had ever faced, while
Bobby Moore was never at ease when Astle was around.

In the home League game with West Ham on Boxing Day, Astle dragged the England
skipper all over the pitch. Although he only scored once with a glancing header from Bobby
Hope's corner, he had two more efforts saved by goalkeeper Bobby Ferguson and also struck
the outside of a post when he got the better of Moore following a swift move down the
Hammers' right flank.

Albion manager Alan Ashman, like his predecessor Jimmy Hagan, often adjusted the
team's tactics to accommodate their good fortune of having a striker who was tremendously
effective in the air. This meant getting the ball forward as quick as possible, often in the
air, so that it could be knocked down for the likes of Suggett and Tony Brown, who were
also hovering around, sniffing out a goal scoring opportunity. Tactically, it worked in a lot
of games – it was unfortunate that Albion's defenders were not always up to their job of
preventing the opposition from scoring at the other end of the field.

Albion played some exciting football, producing fine displays against many of the top
teams. They beat reigning champions Everton 2-0, Astle scoring with a superb left-foot
volley after a 40-yard measured pass by Doug Fraser ... defeated Manchester United 2-1 ...
clipped third-placed Chelsea 3-1 when Astle thumped a powerful header past Peter Bonetti
... and drew twice with Liverpool.

On 22 November 1969, Astle reached a milestone in his time with Albion, scoring his 100th League goal for the club in a 3-0 home win over Sheffield Wednesday. He reacted quickest to smash the ball home after Asa Hartford's shot had almost split the crossbar in two.

Ten days into the New Year, Astle scored his last hat-trick for Albion, in a thrilling 3-2 victory over First Division new boys Crystal Palace at The Hawthorns. This treble took 'The King' (as he was affectionately known by his fans) to the top of the Division's scoring charts, where he would remain for the rest of the season.

He notched his twenty-fifth League goal (and his thirtieth overall) on the very last day of the season at Stoke – and what a remarkable one it was, scored after only 15 seconds' play. Astle kicked off, Hartford received his pass and returned it to Astle, who was just 10 yards inside the Stoke half with his back to goal. With Denis Smith closing him down from behind, he suddenly produced an overhead kick, sending the ball sailing over Gordon Banks' head and into the net. 'I was amazed when I turned and saw the ball lying in the back of the net,' said the striker.

The most disappointing game for Albion during the course of season was the League Cup final. Despite an early headed goal by Astle – which gave him the honour of becoming the first player to score in both an FA Cup and League Cup final at Wembley – Albion lost 2-1 after extra-time to Manchester City.

In the summer of 1970, after a poor performance in the Home International against Scotland, Astle went to Mexico for the World Cup finals. He had an excellent build up, scoring the winner in a pre-tournament friendly against Columbia 'B' and then netting four times against Liga University. But unfortunately, when it mattered most, he missed a great chance to score against Brazil in a vital group three game in Guadalajara, screwing his shot wide when faced with an open goal. With England a goal down, he was introduced to the action by Alf Ramsey with half an hour to go, and within minutes found himself one and one with the Brazilian goalkeeper.

Said the Albion man after the game: 'I had all the time in the world ... I could have taken the ball up to Felix and just slipped it past him. Instead I chose to hit it first time and sent it past the far post.'

For the records, if Astle had equalised, the point gained would still have seen England finish second in the group and they would still have met West Germany in the quarter-finals.

Born in Eastwood, Nottingham on 13 May 1942 – in the same street as the writer D. H. Lawrence, author of *The Rainbow, Sons and Lovers* and, notoriously, *Lady Chatterley's Lover* – Astle joined Notts County as an amateur in 1957, turned professional in 1960 and joined Albion for £25,000 in September 1964. He remained at The Hawthorns for ten years, during which time he scored a total of 174 goals in 361 first-class appearances, helping Albion win the League Cup (1966) and the FA Cup (1968) while also being voted 'Midland Footballer of the Year' in 1968. He was capped five times by England and also represented the Football League.

After leaving The Hawthorns in 1974, Astle played for Hellenic FC (South Africa) before drifting into non-League football, eventually retiring in 1977. He later ran his own industrial cleaning business and became an entertainer with his own 'Road Show'. Sadly, 'The King' died in Burton-on-Trent on 20 January 2002; Staffordshire coroner Andrew Haigh concluded it was from brain injuries (dementia/footballers' migraine) caused by repeatedly heading a ball during his 20-year career.

BERBATOV, DIMITAR (MANCHESTER UNITED)

Season: 2010/11
Goals scored: 21 (out of 78); 17 home, 4 away
Percentage: 27 per cent
Joint top scorer with Carlos Tevez (Manchester City)
Manchester United were Premier League Champions

It was Dimitar Berbatov's goals in the first half of the 2010/11 season that helped set up Manchester United for a record-breaking nineteenth championship success at the end. By then, he'd long since lost his first team place to new man Javier Hernandez, the Mexican being preferred by Sir Alex Ferguson to play up front with Wayne Rooney. Yet while the younger pairing certainly had too much for most Premier League defences, that wasn't the case when they came up against the magical Barcelona in the Champions League final where, in particular, Hernandez's inability to keep possession suggested Ferguson had erred by not including the more technically gifted Berbatov, at the very least on the substitutes' bench.

It was Berbatov who put Manchester United on track for the title when he scored the opening goal in the first match. New boys Newcastle United had held out until the 33rd minute, when Paul Scholes found Berbatov. Steadying himself, he accurately drilled a powerful shot into the far corner. Inspired, Manchester United ran out comfortable winners 3-0.

It was the same result when West Ham came to Old Trafford. This time, Berbatov scored the third when his perfectly executed volley flashed past Robert Green. His next goal, away to Everton, also had a touch of class about it. Superbly controlling a long pass from Scholes, Berbatov's sublime touch took him clear of defender Sylvain Distin before he buried the ball beyond Tim Howard.

In the next League match Berbatov did even better, becoming the first Manchester United player to score three times against Liverpool in over six decades. First, he nodded home a Ryan Giggs corner, before stretching the lead when he forced home Nani's right wing cross. Then, after Steven Gerrard appeared to have rescued a point, Berbatov had the Old Trafford crowd dancing deliriously when he headed John O'Shea's cross home on 84 minutes.

In late November Berbatov became only the fourth player, after Andy Cole, Alan Shearer and Jermain Defoe, to score five goals in a Premier League match. He'd failed to even make the bench the previous weekend for the game against Wigan, but opened the scoring on 71 seconds at home to Blackburn Rovers on his return. Then, when Pascal Chimbonda's wayward backpass ended at his feet, he swept it home to make it 3-0 on 31 minutes.

His second hat-trick of the season came soon after half-time, when Nani tore apart the away defence to leave Berbatov with an easy finish. His fourth, and United's sixth, came on 60, before on 70 minutes he beat Paul Robinson for his fifth.

Over Christmas Berbatov scored three times, hitting both his side's goals in a 2-0 win at home to Sunderland before scoring in a 1-1 draw at Birmingham City. A Darron Gibson pass saw him move inside Liam Ridgewell before beating former team-mate Ben Foster. Berbatov now had fourteen Premier League goals for the season. Yet even though Rooney, his playing partner, was struggling to hit the net, there were already signs that Berbatov's place in the side was under severe threat, especially after Hernandez rose from the bench to score the winner at the Hawthorns on New Year's Day.

Berbatov nevertheless continued to show impressive form in front of goal and on 22 January he scored his third hat-trick of the Premier League season as Birmingham were crushed 5-0 at Old Trafford. Opening the scoring after just 2 minutes, he was presented with a simple second by Rooney before Giggs ripped the away defence apart to leave Berbatov with an easy third.

Three days later, Manchester United were struggling as the game at Bloomfield Road entered the final quarter with Blackpool 2-0 up. The introduction of Hernandez for a disappointing Rooney saw the away side surge forward, and on 72 minutes Berbatov reduced the arrears before Hernandez made it 2-2. Most sides would probably have settled for that, but Champions are made of sterner stuff and when Scholes delivered a wonderful pass, Berbatov blasted home to make it 3-2.

Despite the result, Manchester United were playing poorly away from home, and in the next match at Molineux they lost 2-1 against strugglers Wolves. Come the following match at home to Manchester City, Berbatov was on the bench and he started from there at Wigan, where Hernandez's double helped ensure a 4-0 success. And when the Mexican scored both his side's goals in a 2-1 success to move past Marseille in the Champions League, it was clear he had replaced Berbatov as Ferguson's choice as partner for Wayne Rooney.

Four days later, Manchester United seemed set to lose out on two points with Bolton hanging on to a 0-0 draw at Old Trafford with only three minutes remaining. Jonny Evans had been sent off when Jussi Jaaskelainen failed to hold Nani's long-range effort and substitute Berbatov followed up to ensure all three points. It was his twentieth Premier League goal of the season, and arguably his most important.

His final goal came a few weeks later when, from a marginally offside position, he collected Nani's pass before beating Fulham's Mark Schwarzer in a 2-0 victory. Despite this, Berbatov was not selected to start the next five League games as Manchester United moved to clinch the title, although he was on the pitch as an 80th-minute substitute at Blackburn in the 1-1 draw that sparked wild celebrations at the end. Selected against Blackpool in the final League game of the season, he was left off the bench in preference to Michael Owen for the Champions League final against Barcelona.

BEST, GEORGE (MANCHESTER UNITED)

Season: 1967/68
Goals scored: 28 (out of 89); 17 home, 11 away
Percentage: 31 per cent
Joint top scorer with Ron Davies of Southampton
Manchester United finished second

Good as he undoubtedly was, few would have bet at the start of the 1967/68 season on George Best finishing as equal top scorer in the First Division come the season's end. It was true that the lightly built Irishman had a good eye for a goal, but even so, with a total of just twenty-nine League goals in the previous three campaigns, it was a tall ask to expect a twenty-one-year-old playing at outside right to compete at putting the ball into the back of the net with the likes of strikers Jimmy Greaves and Geoff Hurst – or Denis Law. Indeed, it took Best seven games to open his League account in a 1-1 draw away at Sheffield Wednesday, and while he then grabbed two against Spurs, he only had three after eleven matches.

Things, though, began to change in November, and at Anfield on the 11th he ran the Liverpool defence ragged to score twice in a 2-1 win. He'd been asked to play inside left after Law had been suspended for six weeks following an earlier sending-off in the season, and while no-one suggested that once he was again available the Scotsman should remain in the stands, it was clear that Manchester United had a more than adequate replacement if need be.

Four weeks later, with Law still out, Best had, prior to scoring both United's goals in a 2-1 win against WBA at Old Trafford, also grabbed the all-important second in another 2-1 win, this time against Sarajevo in the second leg of the European Cup second round, the first tie having finished goalless. Joining him on the scoresheet against the Yugoslavians was John Aston, playing just outside Best and finally winning over a previously critical home crowd.

When Law returned, Best was back at outside right, but he now had his shooting boots on and two more followed in a 4-0 defeat of Wolverhampton Wanderers. It was the same a few weeks later, when he blasted two thunderbolts as Sheffield Wednesday were beaten 4-2.

He then scored a much talked-about goal when Spurs visited Old Trafford in the FA Cup. Pat Jennings had, earlier in the season, become the first, and to date only, 'keeper to score at Old Trafford when his long-range kick deceived Alex Stepney in the Charity Shield match that kicked off the season. Perhaps it was Best's way of getting his own back, or maybe he just wanted to have a laugh at his International colleague's expense, but after blocking Jennings' clearing kick, he looped the ball back over the 'keeper and into the empty net, to the cheers of the watching crowd. Best then scored in the following three League games, such that after twenty-nine games he had eighteen goals.

With Matt Busby's side through to the last four of the European Cup and just ahead of local rivals Manchester City at the top of the table, his goals were taking United ever closer to a record-breaking season. Liverpool, though, put a spoke in the wheels by winning 2-1 at Old Trafford, but with Best again scoring, he now had twenty-one.

It became twenty-three the following weekend as relegation-threatened Fulham were easily beaten at Craven Cottage 4-0. Best was, many years later, to join the London side, where for a few short weeks he and Rodney Marsh drew large crowds to watch some seriously entertaining football matches.

George Best finished equal top scorer with Southampton's Ron Davies in Division one in 1967/68. Here he rises to head home the first of his six goals against Northampton Town in the FA Cup on 7 February 1970.

With three games remaining, United were in pole position to win the league, but even though Law scored twice at the Hawthorns, they were heavily beaten 6-3 by WBA to give the advantage to City in the title run-in. It was to prove Law's final game of the season, a cartilage operation taking him into hospital, from where he was to watch the European cup final come the season's end.

In his absence Best was kept at outside right, but still managed to score a hat-trick in a 6-0 hammering of Newcastle before he hit his twenty-eighth League goal of the season against Sunderland in a match that was lost 2-1 as City claimed the title at St James' Park the same afternoon.

Best wasn't finished, though. Four days later, he helped Manchester United to a 3-3 draw in Madrid to knock Real out 4-3 on aggregate in the European Cup semi-final. Two weeks later at Wembley, in the Final and with United drawing 1-1 with Benfica, Best picked up the ball, dipped his shoulder to whisk away from his marker before sending 'keeper Henrique the wrong way and striding through to sweep United back into the lead. Five minutes later, the Cup was won when first Brian Kidd and then Bobby Charlton, with his second of the evening, added further goals to give United an unassailable 4-1 lead.

United's success and Best's part meant he was voted as European and English Footballer of the Year for the 1967/68 season.

George Best is arguably the greatest player ever to play for Manchester United and in a career shortened by alcoholism, he represented the club on 466 appearances, during which time he scored 178 goals. In addition to winning the European Cup, he also collected two First

Division Championship medals in 1964/65 and 1966/67. Best made thirty-seven international appearances for Northern Ireland. George Best died aged fifty-nine in November 2005.

BLISSETT, LUTHER (WATFORD)

Season: 1982/83
Goals scored: 27 (out of 74); 21 home, 6 away
Percentage: 36.4 per cent
Runner-up: Ian Rush (Liverpool), 24 goals
Watford finished second

Luther Blissett established himself in Watford's first team under manager Graham Taylor during the 1977/78 season, when his six goals in thirty-three games helped the Hornets gain promotion to the old Third Division. Another twenty-one goals followed in 1978/79, when the Vicarage Road club won a place in Division Two.

Among Watford's top marksmen over the next three seasons, he bagged nineteen more League goals in 1981/82, when the Hornets clinched a place in the top flight for the first time in the club's history.

Blissett and his team-mates then made the headlines in 1982/83 by surprising many of their rivals in the First Division and, in fact, briefly topped the League in the autumn before finishing runners-up to Liverpool, as well as qualifying for the UEFA Cup.

In Watford's first ever season of top flight football, Blissett finished as the First Division's top goalscorer, with twenty-seven goals. And not too many players have achieved that feat!

In the opening three games of the 1982/83 season Blissett wore the number 4 shirt, playing just behind strikers Gerry Armstrong and Ross Jenkins, with Nigel Callaghan and John Barnes the two wide men.

Watford won their opening two games (at home to Everton and away at Southampton), but lost the third at Manchester City. Blissett, who failed to score in those fixtures, got off the mark with a first-half penalty in a 2-1 victory over Swansea in game four before following up with a brace in a 3-1 win over West Brom four days later. And the three points gained took the Hornets to the top of the table.

Two weeks later, Watford went goal-crazy against Sunderland, whipping the Wearsiders 8-0 at Vicarage Road. Blissett was outstanding, scoring four times and having a hand in another.

The Hornets were leading through two Nigel Callaghan goals before Blissett scored his first – slipping the ball right-footed past Chris Turner from a long forward pass.

It was 4-0 at the break (after Ross Jenkins had tapped in) and early in the second-half Blissett, unmarked, rose to make it 5-0 with a towering header from Nigel Callaghan's inviting right-wing cross. Jenkins comfortably added a sixth before 'Man of the Match' King Luther bounded in at the far post to bury Steve Terry's high cross for goal number seven, and following a throw-in near the right-hand corner flag, he rounded off a superb display by nipping between two static defenders to roll in goal number eight. It was great stuff ... but only 16,744 fans were inside Vicarage Road to see the goal-spree.

In the next game, his first-half goal earned a point at Birmingham (1-1), but he failed to hit the target against Norwich City (2-2), Aston Villa (lost 3-0) and Coventry City (0-0) before scoring in a 3-2 defeat at Notts County.

In November, Watford won all their four League games, beating Tottenham Hotspur 1-0 at White Hart Lane, Stoke City 1-0 and Brighton 4-1, both at home, and Arsenal by 4-2 in a thrilling contest at Highbury.

Blissett fired in two penalties in the win over Brighton to bring his tally for the season to a healthy twelve.

Unfortunately, the Jamaican-born forward then went through a tough period, failing to score in any of the next eight League games, four of which ended in defeats, although he did win his first full England cap, celebrating with a hat-trick in a 9-0 thumping of the hapless part-timers from Luxembourg at Wembley.

Thankfully, he bounced back with his first club goal for two months to seal a 2-0 home win over Southampton in late January, struck twice in a 3-1 win at Swansea and netted his fourth goal in three games as Aston Villa were beaten 2-1.

After another two blank outings, he whipped in his second top-flight hat-trick in a 5-3 home win over Notts County in mid-March, following up ten days later with two excellent finishes to see off Birmingham City 2-1.

At this juncture, Liverpool were pulling clear at the top of the table, but Watford were bang on course to take second spot, and from their last eight games Graham Taylor's team

accumulated thirteen points, ending with a 3-1 home victory over the champions from Anfield.

Blissett scored seven goals in those last eight matches – two in a 4-1 win over Luton, well-struck penalties against Nottingham Forest (lost 3-1) and Arsenal (won 2-1), two more at Sunderland (2-2) and the winner against Liverpool, for whom it was manager Bob Paisley's last match.

There is no doubt that Blissett – who also netted six 'other' goals to finish with an overall total of thirty-three – and Watford had an excellent season.

Having moved to the Italian giants AC Milan for £1 million in the summer of 1983, Blissett missed the 1984 FA Cup final defeat by Everton, but he was back at Vicarage Road for the 1984/85 season, re-signed for £550,000, only to leave the Hornets again a third of the way through the 1985/86 campaign for AFC Bournemouth in a £60,000 deal. He then returned to boost the Hornets once more in August 1991, recruited for £40,000. By now, though, he was slowly on the way down – his legs weren't quite so active, but he still managed to pop in a few goals.

After a loan spell with West Bromwich Albion (October–November 1992), he moved to Bury on a free transfer in August 1993 and thereafter assisted Derry City in Ireland (on loan, September 1993), Mansfield Town (free, December 1993), Southport (on loan, March–May

1994), Wimbourne Town (briefly), Fakenham Town (as player-coach, August 1994, retiring as a player, May 1995); Watford (assistant-manager/coach, February 1996), York City (coach, May 2002–May 2003), Portsmouth (coach, seasons 2003/05) and finally Chesham United (manager, February–April 2006).

He quit football to concentrate on his involvement with the Windrush Motorsport project/Le Mans twenty-four-hour race, but surprisingly returned with Hemel Hempstead Town (as a coach, March 2010).

As mentioned earlier, Blissett's England career started well, with three goals against Luxembourg in December 1982, becoming the first black player to net for England at senior level, and also this remains the highest score for a European Championship match.

He went on to win fourteen caps, but only started five times for his country. He also gained one B and four U21 caps.

Unfortunately, his move to AC Milan coincided with a total draining of confidence from the target-man and the tabloids nicknamed him 'Luther Miss-it.' But he put that behind him and went on playing – and scoring goals at top-class level – for another decade.

At club level, he scored almost 300 goals in close on 700 appearances, 213 coming in 584 League games. He remains to this day Watford's all-time record appearance-maker and goalscorer.

Blissett was born in Falmouth, Jamaica on 1 February 1958 and initially joined Watford as an apprentice in the summer of 1973, turning professional in July 1975.

BLOOMER, STEVE (DERBY COUNTY)

Season: 1896/97
Goals scored: 24 (out of 70); 15 home, 9 away
Percentage: 34 per cent
Runner-up: Fred Wheldon (Aston Villa), 18 goals
Derby finished third

Season: 1898/99
Goals scored: 24 (out of 62); 16 home, 8 away
Percentage: 38.7 per cent
Runner-up: Jack Devey (Aston Villa), 21 goals
Derby finished ninth

Season: 1900/01
Goals scored: 24 (out of 55); 17 home, 7 away
Runner-up: Sam Raybould (Liverpool), 17 goals
Derby finished eleventh

Season: 1903/04
Goals scored: 20 (out of 58); 15 home, 5 away
Percentage: 34 per cent
Runner-up: Arthur Green (Notts County), 19 goals
Derby finished fourteenth

Derby County's greatest footballer, who, with 352 top flight goals, lies second to Jimmy Greaves in the list of all-time scorers at English football's highest level. His twenty-eight goals in twenty-three internationals was at the time an England record.

Steve Bloomer moved to Derby as a child and his impressive record in the Derbyshire Minor League with Derby Swifts soon brought him to the attention of Derby County, one of the twelve founders of the Football League in 1888.

After hitting four goals in a friendly match Bloomer made his debut, aged eighteen, at Stoke in September 1892 and three weeks later hit his first League goal in a match against WBA. Ten more were to follow as the season progressed, with Bloomer starting to form an almost telepathic relationship with John Goodall (see earlier). The following season Bloomer, who was then capped for the first time, upped his scoring rate to eighteen, and in 1895/96 he netted twenty times. It helped Derby finish as League runners up, their highest placing so far.

After such a high placing, there were real hopes that the East Midlanders might go one better and capture the title. John Goodall's younger brother Archie was playing well at centre-half and with England international Jack Robinson in goal, Derby had a solid defence. However, the 1896/97 season started poorly, with one point from six.

The fourth game was against Wolves at the Baseball Ground, and those present saw Bloomer at his very best. Initially, it looked like the away 'keeper, Bill Tennant, was going to deny him, making a series of fine saves, but on 20 minutes the Derby maestro hit home a powerful shot from 20 yards. A second soon followed and 'the wonderful form displayed by Bloomer in the first half was maintained on resuming, and he raced away unaided and scored splendidly' reported the *Cricket and Football Field*. He scored a fourth just before the end.

The following weekend, Bury, backed by 200 fans on a special train, arrived in Derby with great hopes. Heavy rain made conditions difficult, but Bloomer seemed to almost dance on the wet surface. Bury's 'keeper, Archie Montgomery, had a brilliant match, and despite conceding five first half goals, he was warmly applauded when he resumed between the sticks on the restart. Having already netted twice, Bloomer recorded his hat-trick, collecting the ball close to the touchline before coming inside and hitting a shot that fizzed inside the near post as Derby won 7-2.

Blackburn Rovers also suffered a heavy thumping at the Baseball Ground in November 1896. Bloomer scored the third in a 6-0 win, but was overshadowed by Jimmy Stevenson, who scored four times. Derby's centre forward might even have threatened Bloomer as the league's top scorer, but a two-month injury lay-off saw him miss ten games to end the season with fourteen goals.

On Christmas Day, WBA were beaten 8-1, with Bloomer grabbing his third hat-trick of the season. Early in the New Year, Derby made the long trip up to Wearside to face Sunderland. With Derby already 1-0, there was a moment of real magic. Beating the immortal Sunderland captain Hughie Wilson for pace, Bloomer cut in and as Peter Boyle came towards him, the Derby man sent a low shot between the full-back's legs, leaving a stunned Ted Doig helpless.

The Sunderland 'keeper was a great one though, and three weeks later he proved it in the return fixture, constantly defying Bloomer in what at times seemed a personal duel between the English and Scottish internationals. In the event, only one goal was scored – Doig, fisting out Hugh McQueen's cross, was beaten when Bloomer returned the ball beyond him.

With Bloomer in such magnificent form, Barnsley St Peters' excitement about playing in the FA Cup first round against Derby must have been mixed with a certain degree of fear. The Yorkshire side battled to the very end, but with Bloomer grabbing his fourth hat-trick of the season, they were ultimately beaten 8-1. Bloomer scored his fifth hat-trick in the next round as Derby beat Bolton 4-1. After such successes, there was therefore real disappointment when Everton beat Derby 3-2 in a thrilling semi-final match watched by 25,000 at the Victoria Ground, Stoke. Derby were to go on and finish the season in third place, with Bloomer having scored thirty-one times, of which seven were in the FA Cup.

Derby started the 1898/99 season still smarting from having lost to local rivals Nottingham Forest in the FA Cup final at the end of the previous campaign. Bloomer had equalised for his side on 31 minutes, showing good aerial ability to head Joe Leiper's expertly placed free kick out of the reach of Dan Allsop. It was the England international's sixth FA Cup goal of the campaign, and twenty-second of the season. Derby, however, played poorly and were beaten 3-1.

Bloomer's first of the new season came in a 1-1 draw with WBA, while his first double came at Wolves in a 2-2 draw. The following weekend, only 7,000 were inside the Baseball Ground for the visit of Everton. It proved to be some match, finishing 5-5, although at 5-3 down with just 5 minutes to go, Derby looked well beaten. Having reduced the arrears with a penalty, Bloomer then sprang Everton's offside trap to drive home the equaliser.

However, with his side struggling, they were even more grateful for his goal scoring prowess as winter kicked in, the Derby inside forward hitting the net in four consecutive games to ensure that five points were gained.

The Wednesday had beaten Derby 3-1 early in the season, but on 21 January 1899 they were to be blown away by the irrepressible Bloomer. Having hit three in the first 20 minutes to help put Derby five up, he then raced away to leave the Sheffield defenders trailing in his wake before hitting the sixth. Billy MacDonald and he then played a series of fine passes that ended with Bloomer blasting home the seventh goal of the game, his fifth. Then, 'From [Harry] Allen's centre Bloomer shot in the eighth in great style.' [*Cricket and Football Field*] Six goals, and Wednesday were thrashed 9-0.

Woolwich Arsenal were to do better in the FA Cup, but not by much. Bloomer thrilled the 25,000 Londoners who came to the game, hitting two in a 6-0 win. It was the start of another Cup run, and playing Stoke in the semi-final, Bloomer hit three more goals as Derby moved forward to face Sheffield United in the final. Played at the Crystal Palace before 74,000, Derby took a first half lead through John Boag but faded badly in the second to lose 4-1. For once, Bloomer was not at his best, with Sheffield United's Ernest 'Nudger' Needham winning their personal duel. Bloomer's disappointment with the FA Cup was to last a lifetime as in 1903, when Derby made it back to Crystal Palace, he was injured. Badly missing his influence, Derby suffered a record Cup final defeat, losing 6-0 to Bury.

Bloomer hit six FA Cup goals during the 1898/99 season, bringing his season's total to thirty.

With John Goodall having left Derby in 1899, the side was now a fading one. Unlike other seasons, there was also no Cup run to keep the crowds coming to the Baseball Ground. Derby were to score only fifty-five goals in the season, and almost half came from Bloomer. In 1899/1900 he had finished with nineteen goals, second in the scorers' chart, and by increasing his total to twenty-four, he moved back to top spot.

He began the season in great form by scoring in the first four matches. Sunderland's James Crawford had arrived and the pair combined well on the Derby right. In the first game, Bloomer scored the only goal of the match against Bolton. At home to Notts County, Crawford and Bloomer linked up to create the opening goal and when the outside right sent over a corner in the second half, Bloomer headed the winning goal.

Against Sheffield United he scored his only hat-trick of the season, finishing off a fine move with a simple chance for his first. He then headed McQueen's cross home and after Johnny May had added a third, Bloomer finished off the scoring after a great Dick Wombwell run and pass. Bloomer then scored four goals in Derby's next two games and hit a further double against Bolton at Christmas. The first, on 18 minutes, came 'when Bloomer was found by Blackett and cut inside to beat Woolfall and Brown before putting the ball out of the reach of Waller.' He was to score a last minute penalty, his second of the season, as the home side ran out 4-0 winners.

His twenty-fourth and final goal of the season came in the last League game when he headed a Davis cross home for the opener in a 3-2 victory against the Wednesday.

Having seen Derby lose heavily in the 1903 FA Cup final and having hit 'just' twenty-seven League goals combined in the 1901/02 and 1902/03 seasons, Bloomer started the 1903/04 season in determined fashion. Joe Warrington started on the right with him, but later in the season he was to be replaced by Toby Mercer. Neither combination was to work out.

Bloomer scored on the first day of the season as Small Heath were easily beaten 4-1, with Billy Richards getting two. It was, however, to be another six games before he scored again, in a 2-2 draw with Middlesbrough.

It was the same result in the following home game. Derby were aiming to gain their revenge for the thrashing they had received in the Cup final and after Bloomer added the second, they led Bury 2-0 at half time. With the Bury 'keeper Hugh Monteith off the pitch with a broken rib, the Lancashire side rolled their sleeves up and grinded out a 2-2 draw that pushed Derby further down the table and when three consecutive defeats then followed, relegation was now a possibility after a run of no victories in eleven games.

There was, therefore, a small crowd of just 5,000 for the match against Sunderland in late November. The pitch was very heavy after torrential overnight rain. Those present saw a resumption of the Doig-Bloomer battles of the past, the 'keeper defying Bloomer with some great saves from the start of the match. However, on 25 minutes, when Derby were awarded their first penalty of the season, Bloomer broke the deadlock and then, just before half-time, he added his second with a fifteen-yard effort to ensure Derby ran off 3-0 to the good. Come the end of the match, Derby had two precious points in a 7-2 victory, with Bill Hodgkinson having become the side's first player to hit three during the season.

Bloomer soon joined him as Stoke were beaten 5-0 on Boxing Day and with their improved form, Derby made an impressive start in the FA Cup. Portsmouth were beaten 5-2 in the first round, with Bloomer grabbing two. He then scored the only goal in the second round second replay against Wolves before his effort in the quarter-finals against Blackburn Rovers helped his side make it through to the last four with a 2-1 win. Against Second Division Bolton in the semi-finals Derby played poorly and were beaten 1-0, the Lancashire side going on to lose in the final, beaten by a single Manchester City goal from Billy Meredith.

Meredith and Bloomer had thrilled a 10,000-strong crowd earlier in the season, when after the latter had headed home the first goal, Meredith later scored City's second equaliser before, with 5 minutes remaining, creating the winning goal for Billy Gillespie. Bloomer's goal came in the middle of a four-match scoring run and one of the five he scored during it was at Notts County. He'd spurned an earlier opportunity, showing he was human after all by missing a penalty, but on 28 minutes he got his revenge with a powerful drive that Rowland Pennington had no chance of saving. This was just one of Bloomer's twenty League goals that season, without which Derby would probably have been relegated for the first time in the club's history as they finished just two points above relegated Liverpool.

Steve Bloomer was again Derby's top scorer the following season, with thirteen League goals, but was to be sold to Middlesbrough for a fee of £750 in the following campaign. He scored four times against Woolwich Arsenal in January 1907 and did well for 'the Boro' during his four seasons there, with 61 goals in 125 League goals. He returned to Derby in 1910, where he continued to score goals, playing his last match against Burnley on 31 January 1914 aged forty years and eleven days. He had scored 352 League goals and 36 goals in the FA Cup, which with his 28 England goals meant a career total of well over 400.

For England, Bloomer scored twice on his debut against Ireland in 1895, and by scoring in all his first ten appearances, created a record that is unlikely to be beaten. On 18 March 1896 Bloomer scored five goals against Wales, and also netted four against the same opposition five years later. Bloomer twice scored late equalisers for his country in matches against Scotland and also captained the side on one occasion.

In 1914 Bloomer went to coach in Germany, where he was interned during the First World War. After the war he played with, and coached, the Rams reserves, then coached abroad before returning to the Baseball Ground as a general assistant. He died in April 1938.

BOWERS, JACK (DERBY COUNTY)

Season: 1932/33
Goals scored: 35 (out of 71); 23 home, 12 away
Percentage: 49 per cent
Runners-up: George Brown (Aston Villa), Cliff Bastin (Arsenal),
Jack Ball (Sheffield Wednesday), Billy Hartill (Wolverhampton
Wanderers), with 33 goals each
Derby finished fifteenth

Season: 1933/34
Goals scored: 34 (out of 76) 24 home, 10 away
Percentage: 44.7 per cent
Runner-up: George Hunt (Tottenham Hotspur), 32 goals
Derby finished seventh

After a short spell with Scunthorpe [and Lindsey] United, Jack Bowers signed for Derby
County in May 1928, aged twenty. He first made the Rams first team on 2 February 1929 and
in a taste of things to come, scored in a 2-1 win against Bolton Wanderers, the winners of
the FA Cup that season.

Yet with England International Harry Bedford continuing to score regularly, it wasn't
until the start of the 1930/31 season that Bowers took the regular centre-forward spot, with
Bedford eventually moving to Newcastle United. Manager George Jobey was assembling a
fine side and Bowers was to be its goal-scoring king.

Having sat out the first nine games of the season, his chance came before a 29,783 Baseball
Ground on 11 October 1930 against the side that was to go on to dominate English Football
in the 1930s, Arsenal, the eventual League winners that season. The Gunners went home
beaten 4-2, and the following weekend Newcastle United were routed 5-2 at St James' Park,
with Bowers grabbing Derby's fifth in a match where wing man Sammy Crooks was the
star.

Especially fast, Crooks played for Derby for twenty years, and in addition to creating
numerous goals for others, he was noted for cutting inside from right wing to shoot for goal.
This was clearly effective, as he scored 102 League goals for Derby. Crooks's skills on the
right were to be superbly complemented from March 1932 by the arrival of Hull City's 'Dally'
Duncan on the left, and the two were to create many of Bowers's goals over the next few years.
This included the two the centre-forward scored against the reigning champions, Everton, on
15 October 1932, as reported by that evening's *Liverpool Express* Football Edition:

> The ball went to Duncan, who rounded Britton and centred from the line. Bowers was there
> to head through, Sagar having no chance ... then Crooks contributed a dazzling run and
> passed back for Bowers to beat Sagar.

With the country deep in recession following the Wall Street crash of the previous year, there
were only 12,000 present at the Baseball Ground on a bitter December day in 1930 when
Chelsea came calling. The Pensioners' 'keeper, MacIntosh, was to enjoy a difficult afternoon
as Bowers employed a direct style to ram home four goals in a 6-2 win. By March, with
fifteen goals in his last six games, Bowers was closing in on Derby's goal-scoring record in

a single season, needing just four more to equal it when Bolton visited the Baseball Ground on the 7th. After knocking home a penalty, he 'scored a beauty, hooking the ball into the top corner direct from a right wing centre ... there is nothing to beat his direct methods, and he worries every defence he comes up against by never easing up for one moment.' [*Derby Evening Telegraph*, 09/03/1931]

Come the season's end, Bowers had grabbed thirty-seven, enough most years to finish top of the Division One scorers' charts, but Aston Villa's 'Pongo' Waring also had a marvellous season and ended up with a magnificent forty-nine.

In the 1931/32 season, Bowers showed that his was now a name to be feared by opposing defenders with twenty-five more League goals, making him again Derby's top scorer for the season. It was, however, the following two seasons when he was to really make his mark, with eighty goals, including sixty-nine in the League, earning him the top scorer's spot in 1932/33 and 1933/34.

In the first season, he hit thirty-five League goals as Derby finished seventh. Bowers also contributed eight goals in the FA Cup as Derby reached the semi-finals, where they lost to Manchester City. This was the only round in the Cup run in which Bowers failed to score, as he finished the season with a total of forty-three goals from forty-seven matches. This remains Derby's goal-scoring record.

Sunderland in particular suffered at Bowers's hands, or rather legs and head! Early in the season he had the simple task of tapping home Derby's second at Roker Park after Crooks had cut open the Sunderland rearguard. Then, on 4 February 1933, he hit all three goals in a 3-0 win at the Baseball Ground. This is how he did it:

It was not until the 61st minute that Derby got their 1st goal when the powerful Bowers drove in a shot from 20 yards. Thorpe obviously thought the ball was going wide for he made not the slightest effort to save. Eight minutes later Bowers scored a really splendid goal. He cleverly evaded two tackles before sending a powerful swerving shot past Thorpe and just inside an upright. With the very last kick of the game Bowers turned in a centre from the right to complete his hat trick. [*Northern Mail*]

Sunderland were back at the Baseball Ground exactly a month later, a quarter-final FA Cup tie drawing almost treble the numbers of the League game, up from 12,000 to a then-record crowd of 34,218. Those present witnessed a remarkable game, in which Derby roared into a two-goal lead on 19 minutes, only to fall behind at 2-3 on 31 minutes. Bowers had a difficult time in the game in trying to lose his marker, Jock McDougall, but when he did so, four minutes later the ball was in the back of the net for the equaliser. By the end, neither side could be separated in an eight-goal thriller and with Wearside in a Cup frenzy, Roker Park was packed to the rafters for what remains Sunderland's record crowd at 75,118. Derby, with a Peter Ramage goal, won 1-0 only to lose out to Manchester City in the semi-final.

After starting the following season with a disappointing defeat away at Middlesbrough, Derby faced the FA Cup holders, Everton. The home side were losing 1-0 with a minute left when 'a Derby defender nipped in and fed Duncan on the left. Duncan cut in and crashed in a low centre. Bowers shot out a leg and the ball flashed to the back of the net. What a cheer went up.' How Everton must have hated both Duncan and Bowers, and they had even more reason to do so when Derby thrashed them 3-0 at Goodison Park on 1 January. Duncan had opened the scoring in the first minute, and then, on 47 minutes, 'Bowers neatly headed a goal from the centre made by Duncan' reported the *Liverpool Post and Mercury*.

In early December, Bowers had scored twice with his head in a 5-1 home victory over Sheffield United, one goal apiece coming from crosses supplied by Duncan and Crooks. However, just to prove he could, if need be, do it himself, Bowers scored a lovely goal from the edge of the area in a 1-1 draw with Newcastle on 20 January 1934, and hit another two in the following weekend's FA Cup fourth-round tie against Wolves that attracted a record Baseball Ground crowd of 37,727.

One of Brooks's finest games for Derby came against Spurs on Saturday 7 April, when he was up against Arthur Rowe, later to become famous as a manager for developing the Spurs 'push and run' style of play that swept all before them at the start of the 1950s. Derby won 4-3 and Bowers scored all his side's goals.

First he drove home Crooks's cross and then, after Spurs had equalised through a Willie Evans penalty, he restored the lead by finishing off a lovely Groves through-ball. Joe Nicholls in the Spurs goal then denied him a hat-trick by saving his header on the line, and when Jimmy McCormick scored it was 2-2 at half-time.

Bowers's third saw him speed away from Rowe to finish off Ralph Hann's pass with a fierce, low drive which sailed into the corner of the net. Four minutes later Bowers, accepting a pass from Ramage, crashed the ball into the net from the edge of the penalty area, and immediately afterwards he sent in two more great shots, which, however, were well held by Nicholls.

Bowers scored his final League goal of the season against Aston Villa on 21 April, when he headed home on 85 minutes. With thirty-four League goals, he thus became only the second player to finish as the league's top scorer in consecutive seasons.

His form during the season had inevitably brought him to the attention of the England selectors and he was awarded his first international cap against Ireland at Windsor Park, Belfast on 14 October 1933. Bowers scored England's third goal in the 60th minute in a 3-0 victory. He retained his place for the next match against Wales on 15 November, but failed to score as England went down 2-1, allowing Wales to claim the British Home Championship title.

Bowers kept his place for the game against Scotland and scored in the 85th minute as England defeated the Scots 3-0. It was to prove his final international appearance, because on 29 September 1934, Bowers suffered a serious knee injury against Spurs that effectively curtailed his Derby career.

His recovery was slow, although in 1935/36 his thirty goals for the Reserves helped Derby to the Central League championship. He returned to the side for the start of the 1936/37 season and on 5 September 1936, Derby were losing 4-1 at home to Manchester United when Bowers struck with four goals in an amazing 15-minute spell (between the 64th and 79th minute) to give his side a spectacular 5-4 victory.

Nevertheless, Bowers was by now no longer the first-choice centre-forward, Derby having signed, during his absence for injury, Hughie Gallacher, and in November 1936 he joined Second Division Leicester City, where he scored thirty-three League goals in just twenty-seven games to finish as top scorer in the division and assist 'the Foxes' to the title.

Bowers later returned to the Baseball Ground to hold the position of assistant trainer from 1945 to 1965. He died on 4 July 1970.

BOYER, PHIL (SOUTHAMPTON)

Season: 1979/80
Goals scored: 23 (out of 65); 20 home, 3 away
Percentage: 35.4 per cent
Runner-up: David Johnson (Liverpool), 21 goals
Saints finished eighth

Phil Boyer was born on 25 January 1949 in Nottingham and attended Musters Road School. In August 1965, he joined Derby County, turning professional in November 1966. However, Rams' manager, Brian Clough, allowed him to leave the Baseball Ground for York City in July 1968 for £3,000 without having made a first team appearance.

He scored 34 goals in 125 appearances for the 'Minstermen', while also playing an important role in creating opportunities for fellow striker Ted MacDougall, with whom he later partnered at three other clubs.

In December 1970, Boyer teamed up again with MacDougall at Bournemouth. And between them they helped the Cherries win promotion.

However, when manager John Bond took charge of Norwich City in November 1973, he quickly recruited Boyer and MacDougall and a year later the Canaries were back in the top flight, and also reached the 1975 League Cup final, which they lost 1-0 to Aston Villa at Wembley.

The Boyer/MacDougall partnership was not quite so prolific at Norwich (although at a higher level), but nevertheless they still bagged their fair share, 'Supermac' cracking in thirty-five in 1974/75.

During his time with Norwich, Boyer struck 40 goals in 137 appearances, won two England U23 caps and one full cap, in a 2-1 victory over Wales in March 1976, making him the East Anglia club's first England international.

In August 1977, Lawrie McMenemy, who was building a Southampton team to gain promotion back to Division One, signed Boyer for £130,000 and once again paired him up with MacDougall, who had joined the Saints a year earlier.

Boyer had the task of replacing Mick Channon (the First Division's top-scorer in 1973/74), who had been sold to Manchester City. And he enjoyed an excellent first season at The Dell, netting seventeen goals in forty-one League games, rapping in doubles against Burnley, Notts County, Bristol Rovers and Blackburn Rovers, all at home. And together with MacDougall's fourteen, he helped Southampton gain promotion to the top flight as runners-up in Division Two in his first season in the red and white kit.

Although he played in every League game, Boyer struggled for goals against the better teams in Division One in 1978/79, scoring only seven times. He lost his strike partner MacDougall, who had returned to Bournemouth in November 1978, and in mid-March, Boyer was again a League Cup final loser, this time against Nottingham Forest.

Then, in 1979/80, everything came up roses for Boyer. He notched twenty-three goals in forty-two League games to finish as the First Division's leading scorer. One interesting factor is that he scored in every home game from 1 September to 29 December (ten games, sixteen goals).

Without doubt, his most memorable game was on 10 November 1979, the day when Saints gained revenge over Nottingham Forest for that Cup final defeat, beating them 4-1 at The Dell.

Forest, the reigning European champions, were unable to cope with Boyer and Channon (who had returned to the club four months earlier) and suffered their worst defeat since Clough took charge four years earlier. They had a chance of saving a point when Garry Birtles brought them back into the match at 2-1 in the 56th minute, but Boyer struck twice in seven minutes to complete a memorable 4-1 victory. Boyer's second goal completed a five-man, six-touch move and the shot left goalkeeper Peter Shilton stranded from Channon's measured cross.

Before then, Boyer had scored a decisive goal in a superb 3-1 home win over Liverpool on 1 September and netted a smart opener in a brilliant 5-2 home victory over Tottenham Hotspur a fortnight later. Channon, in fact, assisted in all five goals.

Two weeks on, and he struck a wonderful hat-trick (including a penalty) in a 4-0 romp over the club that released him eleven years earlier, Derby County. And just ten days after that he blitzed Crystal Palace with another treble as Saints won 4-1 in front of their own supporters.

At this juncture, the team was playing well; so too was Boyer, who hit the net in successive home games against Coventry City and Leeds United, but his strikes were to no avail, as both ended in defeats.

Then came that wonderful performance against Clough's Forest, after which Boyer struggled for a while to hit the target, scoring just three times in the next eight games, two in a 3-1 home win over Stoke City on 1 December.

He got back on track in mid-December with a first-half winner against Everton, opened the scoring in a 2-0 victory over Bolton and was on target with his first away goal of the season in the 1-1 draw with Liverpool at Anfield. Saints jumped up to third place in the table with this point – their highest League placing ever – but almost immediately – and unaccountably – Boyer's goals dried up again ... and this time the drought was much longer!

He managed only one goal (in a 5-1 win over Brighton) in ten matches between 19 January and 29 March. He hadn't been playing badly, far from it. He set up plenty of chances for his colleagues, but the ball wouldn't run kindly. In fact, Saints scored only ten League goals in twelve games after that big win over Brighton, Boyer netting just once, in the 1-1 draw at Arsenal. That was his twentieth League strike of the season and his last three efforts all came in one match, the penultimate fixture of the season, when Bristol City were thumped 5-2 at the Dell.

Kevin Keegan arrived at Southampton in July 1980 and despite being a firm favourite with the fans, Boyer departed, ironically to Manchester City (Channon's former club), three months later. In his three and a bit seasons at The Dell, he made 162 appearances and netted 61 goals.

City paid £220,000 for Boyer's services, but his career at Maine Road was blighted by injury and he only made a handful of appearances and suffered the heartbreak of missing the 1981 FA Cup final.

In February 1982, Boyer joined the Hong Kong club for Bulova on loan. Later with Grantham, Horwich RMI, Stamford and Shepshed Charterhouse, he returned to Grantham as player/assistant-manager in 1985/86 and then served as manager at Harrowby United before quitting football in 1990.

Since then, Boyer has worked as a bank courier and has scouted for Northampton Town and Blackpool.

Note: As strike-partners, Boyer and MacDougall together scored a total of 195 goals.

BROWN, ARTHUR (SHEFFIELD UNITED)

Season: 1904/05
Goals scored: 22 (out of 64); 11 home, 11 away
Percentage: 34 per cent
Runner-up: Sandy Turnbull (Manchester City), 19 goals
Sheffield United finished sixth

Brown, signed from Second-Division Gainsborough Trinity in May 1902 as a seventeen-year-old, had finished within two goals of Steve Bloomer at the end of the 1903/04 season, during which he was capped at aged 18 years and 327 days old. Not until Duncan Edwards made his debut in April 1955 was anyone younger to play for England during the twentieth century.

A precocious talent, Brown's main strengths were his opportunism in front of goal and a powerful, accurate shot. The latter was amply demonstrated in his second and final match for England in February 1906, when he 'took a fine pass from Albert Gosnell splendidly and scored' reported the *Daily Mirror*. Despite beating Ireland 5-0 the press were unimpressed, with the *Mirror* reporting, 'The England forwards were individualists rather than combined attacking force.' Brown was not given a third chance.

Brown arrived at Bramall Lane with United as current FA Cup holders. It was the second time in four years that the steel city side had achieved the feat and followed a first-ever Championship success in 1897/98. Yet the side were already past their best and the most successful period in the club's history was at an end.

Brown scored five goals in his first season, and after a successful second he was quickly on the scoresheet in the third with a goal in the second game away to Wolves. In the fourth, at home to Small Heath [Birmingham City], he failed to make the most of a couple of openings in the first period, but also found Nat Robinson in goal in fine form. However, there was nothing the 'keeper could do when, after making a great save, the ball ran loose and Brown was quickest to it and rolled it home for a 2-1 win.

Away to Middlesbrough, Brown scored an excellent goal, reported in the *Sheffield Telegraph* as follows: 'Brown, getting the ball in midfield, tricked both Jones and Agnew in the prettiest of styles and then drawing Williamson out of his goal he put the ball into the net with a carefully judged shot. It was as good a goal as Sheffield United have scored.' It was also enough to give his side both points.

At Ewood Park Brown was again the star, shooting home with his left foot in the first half and applying a deft header in the second as Blackburn Rovers were beaten 4-2. Brown was injured the following weekend during the match with Nottingham Forest, but still was able to push the ball home for his eighth goal of the season.

The following weekend, United were a goal down at half-time in the local derby match with Wednesday, but showed who was boss by playing superbly in the second to win 3-1. Brown pushed his side ahead, earning his team-mates' congratulations because 'he was severely hampered but struggled on before managing to get in his shot.'

On Boxing Day 1905, Brown scored a hat-trick in a 5-2 Bramall Lane success against Stoke City. A header made it 3-0, a looping shot 4-1, until just before half-time, 'Brown, seizing the ball on the half-way line with the visiting defence lying well up the field, ran right through before shooting wide of Jack Whitley.'

Two days later Brown scored twice in a 4-0 home hammering of Woolwich Arsenal. After a first-half goal, he'd thrilled the crowd with an overhead kick from a Bert Lipsham cross that saw the ball flash narrowly wide of James Ashcroft's post before accepting a Leng cross to put the ball into the net for his fifteenth League goal of the season. When he netted at Derby from close in three days later, Brown was already up to sixteen with half the season still to play.

The Sheffield centre forward was unable to keep his fine run going, managing just the one goal throughout January and February, and only two in March. On 1 April, United beat Nottingham Forest away much more comfortably than the 2-1 scoreline would suggest. Brown scored his twenty-first goal of the season and, reported the *Telegraph*, 'made a good pivot'. One week later he scored his final goal of the season as United, with a 4-2 win, recorded a League double over Wednesday.

Brown was to continue to score goals for Sheffield United over the following three seasons, with a total of fifty in the league. One of the sides to suffer at his boots was Sunderland, against whom he scored four times in October 1907. And it was to the Wearsiders that he moved for a then-world record fee of £1,800 during the summer of 1908.

Although he was still only twenty-three, it was clear his best years were already behind him and little more than two years later, and after twenty-three goals in fifty-five appearances, he moved south to Fulham before rounding off his career with an uneventful season at Middlesbrough in 1912/13. Brown died in his hometown of Gainsborough in June 1944.

BROWN, TONY (WEST BROMWICH ALBION)

Season: 1970/71
Goals scored: 28 (out of 58); 15 home, 13 away
Percentage: 48 per cent
Runner-up: Martin Chivers (Tottenham Hotspur), 21 goals
Albion finished seventeenth

Surprisingly, Tony Brown reached his peak at a time when West Bromwich Albion began to wane.

In 1970/71, having lost in the League Cup final to Manchester City the season before, the Baggies finished seventeenth in Division One, and it is true to say that if it hadn't been for the goals scored by the 'Bomber' then The Hawthorns club may well have been relegated.

Sharp and snappy, with a stunning right-foot shot, Brown fed off one of the finest headers of a ball in the game, Jeff Astle, and aided by the dashing wing-play of Clive Clark and the scheming and passing ability of Bobby Hope, he topped the Division's scoring charts with twenty-eight goals, a magnificent return for the Oldham-born attacking midfielder, whose best seasonal goal-return in League competition prior to that was the seventeen he scored in both 1965/66 and 1968/69.

His haul in 1970/71 included two hat-tricks – the first in a 3-1 Boxing Day home win over Tottenham Hotspur and the second in a 4-3 victory over Manchester United at the Hawthorns in March. Two of his efforts against Spurs were superb right-footers, fired past the diving Pat Jennings, and similarly, two of his strikes against United were also cracking shots which 'keeper Alex Stepney had no chance of saving.

Brown also scored braces in the 3-3 draw at Nottingham Forest, in a 5-2 home win over Stoke City – one being a thumping 25-yard drive which flew high past Gordon Banks' right hand – in the 2-2 draw in the return fixture with Spurs, and in the 2-1 home victory over Huddersfield Town, one of his shots almost ripping through the back of the net.

He struck decisive winners in home games against Derby County (2-1) and Burnley (1-0), and smashed in beauties in a 3-3 draw at Everton and the 1-1 showdown at Liverpool.

Brown was also integral in one of football's most controversial incidents. He was in the Albion team, without an away win all season, which took on Leeds United, apparently destined for the Championship.

Needing a win to pull clear of Bertie Mee's Arsenal side, Don Revie's team trailed 1-0 to a first-half Brown goal when a poor ball from Norman Hunter cannoned off an Albion player and squirted into the Leeds half, where Baggies striker Colin Suggett was loitering at least 15 yards offside.

More in hope than expectation, Brown chased after the ball and headed towards goal. Immediately, linesman Bill Troupe raised his flag. So transparent was the offence that there was a moment of suspended animation while players on both sides waited for referee Ray Tinkler to blow his whistle. He failed to do so and an almost apologetic Brown continued on towards the Leeds goal before squaring for Astle, who also looked offside, to execute a simple tap in past a stranded Gary Sprake. Astle, smirking and still half expecting the referee to see sense, jogged back to the halfway line.

Albion and their supporters celebrated as the Leeds fans rioted on the pitch, but the goal was allowed to stand. Allan Clarke scored for Leeds late on, but Albion held on to win 2-1 and there is no doubt that that decision of almost baroque incompetence cost Don Revie and Leeds dearly, as they were pipped to the title by a single point!

Brown's all-round, and certainly vital performances in 1970/71 earned him England recognition. He was included in the squad for the Home Internationals and was selected for the second of the three games at home to Wales. It turned out to be a disappointing debut for the Albion player as a much-changed England team failed to gel and produced little football of note in a grim 0-0 draw.

Brown had one clear chance early on, but headed over and was then deemed offside as Francis Lee slammed home the ball home in another rare attack.

Alf Ramsey would never give Brown another chance, and neither would his successors. The merits of Brown's England claims can be argued forever without a satisfactory answer being reached, but it is certainly hard to argue his case ahead of players like Bobby Charlton, Martin Peters, Tony Currie and Colin Bell.

Instead of pitching in to England's cause, Brown remained a vital cog in West Bromwich Albion's plans. Under new manager Don Howe, the maturing midfielder became more of a fulcrum in the team, which was slowly being transformed, and with Astle on his way out the Bomber's goals became more important than ever.

He struck another seventeen in 1971/72, but then, in a struggling side which suffered relegation, he netted only twelve out of thirty-eight in 1972/73. However, playing at a lower level, he bagged nineteen in 1973/74, twelve the following season and ten in 1975/76, which included a last-day winner at Oldham which clinched promotion for Johnny Giles' team.

Back in the top flight, Brown struggled for a while and notched only six League goals in 1976/77, but was back on song in 1977/78 with nineteen, and under Ron Atkinson in 1978/79 he fired in ten, becoming Albion's record goalscorer of all-time in the process with a fine effort in a 3-1 win at Leeds in mid-October.

In his last full season at The Hawthorns, 1979/80, Brown managed just two League goals to bring his club tally in the competition to 218, a record which still stands today.

Born in October 1945, Brown joined Albion as an apprentice in April 1961 and turned professional in September 1963. He made a scoring League debut against Ipswich Town that same month and went on to net a total of 279 goals for Albion in 720 first-class appearances (both club records). He was also an expert from the spot, netting fifty-one penalties for the Baggies (in all games), some of them crucial.

Voted 'Midland Footballer of the Year' on three occasions, in 1969, 1971 and 1979, he twice represented the Football League and won both the League Cup (1966) and FA Cup (1968) during his twenty-year stay at The Hawthorns. On leaving Albion in October 1981, he joined Torquay United, played next for Jacksonville Teamen/NASL (for whom he had played for on loan twelve months earlier) and finally served Stafford Rangers, retiring in April 1983. He returned to Albion as a coach in 1984 and later held a similar position with Birmingham City. Now resident in Walsall, he is a match summariser on a local radio station and has his own column in the West Bromwich Albion club programme.

BUCHAN, CHARLIE (SUNDERLAND)

Season: 1922/23
Goals scored: 30 (out of 72); 23 home, 7 away
Percentage: 42 per cent
Runner-up: Tommy Roberts (Preston North End), 28 goals
Sunderland finished second

One of football's most legendary names, Buchan's feat in finishing at the top of the Division One scorers' chart in the 1922/23 season was remarkable because he was an inside rather than a centre forward. And as we shall see, what is also surprising was that it was the use of his head, rather than his undoubted ball-playing skills, which helped him top the list.

Buchan had come pretty to close to being at the summit ten years previously, notching twenty-seven in Sunderland's Championship winning side that only just, by losing to Aston Villa in the FA Cup final, lost out on becoming the first side in the twentieth century to do 'the double'. Sheffield Wednesday's David MacLean had finished as leading scorer with thirty, a total Buchan was to match in 1922/23.

Sunderland had finished in twelfth place the previous season and determined to do better, the Wearsiders had again spent heavily to bring in, among others, England International Warney Cresswell at a record £5,500 fee and two Scottish internationals in Michael Gilhooley and Jock Paterson.

There was, therefore, disappointment when the season started badly, with only one victory in the first five games, during which Buchan scored just the once, seizing on a slip by Liverpool's Tom Bromilow to put Sunderland ahead at Anfield in a game the home side won 5-1.

Bolton Wanderers were to capture the Cup at Wembley come the season's end, but when they appeared at Roker Park in September 1922 they were unlucky enough to face Buchan at his very best. Combining superbly with his other four forwards, he constantly got between the two Bolton fullbacks, Johnson and Thirkell, to exploit the acres of space behind Parker, the centre-half. Come the game's end, he'd put four in the Bolton net. At 6 feet tall, Buchan was always dangerous in the air, and two had come from headers. The Plumstead-born forward might have even ended up with a couple more, Dick Pym making two great diving saves to keep the final score down to 5-1.

Buoyed by their success Sunderland, were to quickly race up the table, Buchan playing a full part by notching eight goals in the following seven games. He was to again show how clever he was in the air in the game against Cardiff City in mid-October 1922, deftly flicking a corner kick beyond the reach of Tom Farquharson to give the home side both points.

The following weekend, Buchan was at Stamford Bridge to play a game of real quality, pulling the ball down and bringing his colleagues into the game. He scored on five minutes with a toe-poke past Howard Baker, who'd finish sixth at the 1920 Olympics in the High Jump, and then when Chelsea failed to mark him at a corner fifteen minutes later, he again headed home as Sunderland went on to win 3-1.

His display had again alerted the national papers to Buchan's quality and there were calls for Buchan to be considered for his fifth England cap. The First World War had undoubtedly restricted his number of England appearances, but so too had his unwillingness to accept his meagre rations as a professional footballer, Buchan being a keen member of the committee that ran the Association Footballers' Union, which sought improved pay and conditions.

The Sunderland forward had also argued with a member of the FA selection committee following his debut in February 1913, a game in which Ireland caused a sensation by winning 2-1 after Buchan had opened the scoring. In the event, Buchan did eventually win a fifth cap when, late in the season, he captained England in Paris in a 4-1 victory in which he scored after 35 minutes. He was to add one further cap, when in the following season he played at Wembley for the first time in a 1-1 draw with Scotland. The match was watched by 37,250 people.

As 1922 came to a close Sunderland were flying, and although Newcastle beat their local rivals at St James' Park, it was the Wearsiders' only defeat in nineteen games when they travelled south to face Birmingham at St Andrews on 6 January 1923. Buchan had already scored eighteen League goals, but this time it was his role as a schemer that was to ensure both points were captured. In particular, the first of two for Paterson was courtesy of a piece of individual brilliance, Buchan taking the ball around the home defence before squaring it for an easy chance for the centre forward.

When Sunderland next travelled south, it was to face Huddersfield Town and a tight game was heading towards a goalless draw when on sixty minutes, 'Buchan trapped the ball smartly with one foot and then fired in a first time shot with the other which completely beat Taylor. It was a masterful piece of football indeed and it was regarded by the 30,000 spectators as one of the best efforts seen at Leeds Rd this season.' (*Newcastle Daily Chronicle*)

Buchan was putting his side in with a chance of the title, with Sunderland now competing with Liverpool at the top of the table, especially as five points were gathered from the next six. There was therefore real disappointment when two defeats in three followed, and it was only thanks to Buchan's two efforts against Preston that a third was avoided, with a 2-2 draw.

He was again in wonderful form when Sunderland played in London, creating a host of chances for his fellow forwards, and just when it looked like none would be taken, Paterson, for once left unmarked by Spurs' Charlie Walters, was left to tap in Buchan's pulled-back pass with just 12 minutes remaining. With a game in hand, Sunderland were now just four points behind Liverpool with six matches still to play. Victory at home to Sheffield United was therefore vital in a midweek match.

The home side started brilliantly, and none more so than Charlie Buchan, hitting two in the first 17 minutes, including a by now trademark header from a corner. However, the Blades' forwards were razor sharp they and were soon level, only for Buchan to score a great goal by running at the away defence before hitting a shot that 'keeper Gough never had any real chance of saving. Little good it was to do Sunderland, though, when another equaliser soon followed and when Sheffield United added two further goals, it was a sorry home side that limped off, beaten 5-3.

Buchan's hat-trick had taken him to top spot in the scorers' list, but it was of little consolation as, barring a real slump, the title was now Liverpool's. That certainly was the case when two defeats in the next three games followed and although Sunderland recovered to win the final two matches, they finished in second place, six points off the top.

Buchan ensured he finished with thirty League goals in the final home game of the season when he hit two past Cyril Spiers in the Villa goal. The reporter for the *Newcastle Daily Chronicle* noted that 'what was remarkable with these efforts was that both were scored with his feet. Buchan has not been known to secure two goals without one coming from his cranium in the present season.'

Buchan was to remain at Sunderland before moving back 'home' to play for Herbert Chapman's Arsenal side between 1925 and 1928, picking up a second FA Cup losers medal when the Gunners lost 1-0 to Cardiff City in 1927. His transfer was remarkable in that in an attempt to resolve the deadlock over the fee, the Sunderland manager Bob Kyle, seeking £4,000, agreed to let Buchan move for a fee of £2,000, plus £100 a goal the following season – he scored twenty-one times and Sunderland thus received an overall total of £4,100. Buchan, on retirement, was to become one of the best-known names in sports journalism, replicating off the pitch his awesome skills on it.

CAMPBELL, JOHN (SUNDERLAND)

Season: 1891/92
Goals scored: 32 (out of 93); 21 home, 11 away
Percentage: 34 per cent
Runner-up: Jack Devey (Aston Villa), 29 goals
Sunderland were Football League Champions

Season: 1892/93
Goals scored: 30 (out of 100); 17 home, 13 away
Percentage: 30 per cent
Runners-up: Fred Geary (Everton) and Jimmy Hannah (Sunderland), with 19 goals each
Sunderland were First Division Champions

Season: 1894/95
Goals scored: 21 (out of 80); 11 home, 10 away
Percentage: 26 per cent
Runners-up: Harry Hammond (Sheffield United) and Harry Bradshaw (Liverpool), with 17 goals each
Sunderland were First Division Champions

By finishing as top scorer three times, John Campbell ranks as the first of English football's truly prolific goal-scoring merchants. It was Campbell who turned the 1890s Sunderland side into a great one, deserving of the title 'The Team of All the Talents', with title successes in 1891/2, 1892/3 and 1894/5.

Campbell, who stood 5 feet 9 inches tall, had in 1889 caught the eye of one of Sunderland's financiers during a friendly with Scottish Cup winners Renton. The Wearsiders were seeking entry to the Football League and were assembling a formidable team. High-profile friendlies had drawn large crowds and when pitched in an election battle against the league's bottom club, Stoke City, Sunderland obtained more votes and joined the Football League for the 1890/91 season.

It didn't take long for Campbell to get his name on the scoresheet, scoring in Sunderland's second game, against Wolves, and then in the seventh game of the season, he became the first Sunderland player to score four goals in a League game as Bolton Wanderers were hammered 5-2. Sunderland finished in a respectable seventh place. Campbell had missed just one of the twenty-two League games and had netted eighteen times.

Sunderland started the following season at home to Wolves. The away side had taken an early lead when Campbell scored his first of the season, when he powerfully headed John Murray's free kick past Billy Rose. His second was a real beauty, giving Rose no chance, with a powerful drive from around 20 yards. It was enough to turn the game and in the second period Sunderland attacked strongly, with Campbell's colleague James Millar, a fine inside forward who later won the Scottish League on two occasions with Rangers, scoring a hat-trick in a 5-2 win.

Penalty kicks had only been introduced at the start of the season and on 24 October 1891, John Campbell became the first to score one for Sunderland when he stroked the ball past WBA's Bob Roberts in a match that was won 4-0, and in which he scored three times.

Darwen were struggling at the bottom of the League when they arrived at Newcastle Road on 12 December 1891. Sensing an opportunity, the home side pressed from the kick-off. Campbell's two helped Sunderland record a 7-0 victory that cut the gap on leaders Bolton to five points. When victory at Everton on Christmas Day followed, Campbell getting the second, it was clear the Wearsiders were now title contenders.

The following day, Sunderland played Wolves away. The Molineux side had only lost once at home, and with Sunderland's reputation growing, there was a healthy crowd of 12,000 present. The away side had a fine afternoon, and when news of their 3-1 victory was received back on Wearside, there was 'jubilation as this match was regarded by many as a particularly hard fixture and the result was most satisfying'. (*Newcastle Daily Chronicle*)

Sunderland were now just two points behind leaders Bolton and despite Campbell's absence through injury, when the sides met it was Sunderland who won 4-1. Back against new League leaders Preston North End, Campbell scored in a game that, despite a heavy snowstorm, attracted the season's biggest gate so far – 12,000. Another 4-1 home victory was the fans' reward for having risked the elements.

Aston Villa had put Sunderland out of the FA Cup, but travelled north after losing to near neighbours WBA in the final. Another 12,000-strong crowd packed out Newcastle Road to witness a cracking encounter, and when the Villa centre forward Jack Devey equalised in the 85th minute, it seemed Sunderland might be denied top spot. However, 3 minutes later, John Hannah struck a famous winner that had the 'crowd going wild. When the final whistle blew Sunderland had snatched a famous victory and were sitting proudly at the top of the league.' (*Chronicle*)

Therefore, 2 April 1892 was a big day for a club playing only its second League season. Victory at home to Stoke would set up manager Tom Watson's side for the title. Campbell was clearly determined to start the match quickly. On 2 minutes, he 'got possession to spin round and bang in a lightning shot that that flew past Rowley's despairing dive to put Sunderland one up'. His second, on the stroke of full-time, confirmed the home side's superiority in a 4-1 win that meant they could afford to lose two of their remaining four fixtures and still win the League Championship.

At home to Blackburn Rovers, Campbell was in fine form, hitting the opener with a powerful drive on 8 minutes. It was the first of four as Sunderland virtually confirmed the title in a 6-1 demolition. Three more followed in a 7-1 victory at Darwen before the season was completed when Sunderland won 2-1 at Turf Moor, Campbell scoring once. Champions Sunderland had scored ninety-three times in twenty-six matches with Campbell striking thirty-two, three ahead of Villa's Jack Devey.

Sunderland were favourites to make it two in a row when the 1892/93 season got under way with a 6-0 hammering of Accrington. Campbell opened the scoring and added another two by the end. The Scotsman was also first on the score sheet the following weekend, in a 2-2 home draw with Notts County. Having hit six in their first away game, Sunderland repeated the feat in the second at Aston Villa. Again, Campbell was in fine form, scoring his side's second on five minutes. It came in the following fashion - 'The game had hardly been restarted when J. Campbell got possession and cleverly beat Cowan to lash in a hotshot that left Dunning helpless.' (*Newcastle Daily Chronicle*) He added a second as Sunderland won 6-1.

Campbell was now playing the best football of his career; two more goals followed against Blackburn Rovers, including a twenty-yard 'hot-shot' that flew past the famous 'keeper Herbie Arthur. When he then scored against Stoke City the following weekend, it meant he'd put the ball into the net in all five Sunderland games so far, to record nine goals. Absent from the scorers' list at Everton, Campbell then took the opportunity to grab six in the next two home games, including a hat-trick in what was then Sunderland's record League victory, 8-1 against WBA.

Away to Sheffield Wednesday Sunderland took the lead when 'Campbell got possession just over the halfway line and set off for the Wednesday goal. As he closed the range he unleashed a surprise snapshot that flew past Allan to open the scoring.' Despite the advantage, Sunderland faded and lost their first game of the season 3-2. Campbell had now scored fifteen times in nine games. By early December, his total was up to twenty.

Newton Heath, the league's new boys, had remarkably beaten Wolves 10-0, but were struggling at the bottom. Nevertheless, the draw of watching Sunderland was enough to attract a record crowd of 15,000 to Heath's North Road ground on 4 March 1892. The away side did not disappoint them and after Campbell swept home the opening two in the 24th and 25th minutes, Sunderland continued their search for goals, winning 5-0 by the end, with the Sunderland centre-forward running off with another hat-trick to his name. When he then notched another double in the following match at home to Derby County, his overall total had risen to twenty-eight.

It became thirty when bottom club Newton Heath made the return journey. It would have needed a miracle for Preston North End to overtake Sunderland at the top. Ten points behind and with five games remaining, the Lancashire side also needed Sunderland to lose their remaining three games. There was never any chance of that happening, especially once John Hannah swept the ball home on eleven minutes. A 6-0 home win confirmed that the Championship would be returning to Wearside. Campbell got two, his second a 'grand shot' just before the end of the game.

The result gave Sunderland a chance of becoming the first side ever to score a hundred League goals in a season, and after drawing 1-1 away at Derby they did just this by winning 3-2 at Turf Moor, with John Harvey grabbing the final and 100th League goal of the season. Of these, John Campbell had scored thirty.

After narrowly losing out to Aston Villa in the 1893/94 season, during which Campbell, with eighteen goals, found himself outscored by Millar, Sunderland began the 1894/95 season with a bang. With Campbell scoring three times, Sunderland stormed to their then-record victory, 8-0 against Derby County.

In the third game of the season, Sunderland travelled to face the champions, Aston Villa. One down, they were brought back into the game when:

> Campbell caught Cowan and Elliott completely by surprise when he suddenly checked back and drove a magnificent low shot past Wilkes from 20 yards for an equaliser. Although the goal was against the home side it was warmly applauded by the sporting home crowd. It was enough to help Sunderland win the game 2-1, an important marker for the season to come.

When Sunderland went on to beat WBA 3-0, with Campbell opening the scoring, the Wearsiders had begun the season with maximum points from four games. By the time Campbell grabbed his seventh League goal of the season, Sunderland were on fifteen points from eighteen and racing towards their third title in four seasons. His eighth in a 4-0 victory over Bolton Wanderers came as follows: 'Moments later Campbell tried a shot from 20 yards that struck Somerville. Catching it on the rebound Campbell let fly with a shot that flew well out of Sutcliffe's reach and high into the net to put Sunderland 3-0 up.'

Against Liverpool, Campbell spun on a loose ball in a 3-2 home victory that helped ensure Sunderland had twenty from a possible twenty-four points. Amazingly, when Sunderland then won the next game 7-1 at home to Small Heath, Campbell was absent from the scorers. It didn't take him long in the following game, scoring in the first minute as Sunderland beat Blackburn Rovers 3-2.

Sunderland's early season form was, however, on the wane and after beating WBA on Boxing Day, the following four games yielded just three points. Campbell failed to score in these games and his name was also absent from the list of scorers at home to Nottingham Forest on 5 January as the game entered the final quarter of an hour with the away side 2-1 to the good. Defeat and Villa would go top.

> But cometh the hour, cometh the man when 'out of the blue' Sunderland grabbed an equaliser. Scott and Hannah swept upfield and passed to Campbell who was almost 30 yards out. He let fly with an absolute beauty that flew straight as an arrow into the top corner of the net to level the scores after 75 minutes. (*Newcastle Journal*)

It was clearly his best goal of the season, and definitely his most important, as a revived Sunderland then journeyed to Molineux to beat Wolves 4-1, with guess who grabbing a couple? Two more followed at the Victoria Ground, Stoke in a 5-2 victory. The first was a darting 60-yard run that left defenders trailing behind him before a fine finish beat Clawley.

Sunderland were at the top of the table as they looked forward to the start of the 1895 FA Cup. Playing Fairfield at home was new territory, but the unknowns from Manchester proved no threat and were hammered 11-1, a victory that remains Sunderland's record victory to this day. Campbell failed to score!

He was, though, on the scoresheet as Sheffield United were beaten 2-0. He then scored Sunderland's second in an important 3-1 win over the Wednesday that established a four-point gap at the top of the table. Sheffield United, though, showed there was still work to do when they thrashed Sunderland 4-0 at Bramall Lane.

Two weekends later, after suffering a disappointing FA Cup semi-final defeat to Aston Villa, Sunderland faced a tricky fixture at Olive Grove. And when Alec Brady equalised for Wednesday just after half time, the away side were looking for inspiration. It came from John Harvey, who, making space, found Campbell on 54 minutes, who smartly drove the ball home to ensure a 2-1 success.

Two days later, Sunderland were faced with another difficult encounter, away at Anfield against Liverpool. Campbell opened the scoring and Sunderland squeezed to a 3-2 victory in what all the papers agreed afterwards had been a brilliant match, enjoyed in particular by away fans who'd journeyed to the game on a train special.

Still, with Everton refusing to concede the title, Sunderland faced a third tricky away match on 13 April 1895, this time at Turf Moor. Backed by a travelling following numbering a total of three, Sunderland gave each of them of them a goal to cheer. Campbell didn't score, but it meant that when the away side ran off, the title was as good as theirs as Everton were four points behind. With the teams set to play each other the following weekend, Sunderland knew that even a draw would end the contest.

Such was the clamour to watch the match that far too many people were allowed into the Newcastle Road ground, which was packed beyond its agreed 18,000 capacity, with the gate later given as 20,000.

With Sunderland determined to finish the season in style, Everton had done well to stay with them at 1-1 when, with just ten minutes left, 'Campbell got possession near the halfway line beat Holt cleverly and set off towards the Everton goal. As Arridge and Kelso dashed across to try to check his run Campbell steadied himself and then let fly with a tremendous shot from 15 yards. Hillman seemed to be taken by surprise, was late with his dive and the ball flew past his left hand and crashed into the net to restore Sunderland's lead. It was a great goal even by Campbell's standards and the crowd roared their approval.'

Campbell had scored the winning goal to clinch the title, Sunderland's third in four seasons, in which he had personally triumphed by finishing as the league's top scorer – again!

Campbell played another two seasons for Sunderland before signing for Newcastle United in May 1897 and helping the Magpies to win promotion the following season. Campbell remains the fifth-highest goalscorer in Sunderland's history, with 150 goals in just 215 appearances. He was just thirty-six when he died in June 1906. Surprisingly, Campbell never received international recognition for Scotland.

CAMPBELL, JOHNNY (ASTON VILLA)

Season: 1895/96
Goals scored: 26 (out of 78); 17 home, 9 away
Percentage: 33.3 per cent
Runner-up: Steve Bloomer (Derby County), 20 goals
Villa were League Champions

Johnny Campbell was a wonderfully gifted and clever inside or centre-forward. He was brave, aggressive when required, possessed plenty of tricks, and above all had an instinctive knack of scoring goals.

Not in anyway a battering ram – as a lot of players in his position tended to be described in Victorian Days – he was a deft, clever forward who used his intelligence to manoeuvre himself into scoring positions. He had exceptional balance, close control and dribbling skills, and above all, he was totally committed to playing football, often dragging himself off his sick bed to turn out for his club. In fact, in one game he had both knees heavily strapped up, while also suffering from a migraine.

He had done remarkably well north of the border before moving south to join Aston Villa in the summer of 1895. And as soon as he set foot inside the Birmingham club's ground at Perry Barr, everyone knew they had signed someone special!

Campbell had a superb first season with Villa, helping them lift the First Division title for the second time in three years. Not only did the likeable Scot top the scoring charts, he was also the First Division's leading marksman, with a total of twenty-six goals.

After a relatively quiet first game for Villa, a 1-0 home win over neighbours West Bromwich Albion, he burst into life with a four-timer in his second game as Villa thumped Small Heath 7-3 in the 'second city' derby. He scored with two flashing right-foot drives, a glancing header from Charlie Athersmith's curling centre and a tap in after Steve Smith's shot had cannoned off a defender. Campbell also helped set up two goals for Devey.

A fortnight later, Campbell scored his fifth goal of the season against Derby County (won 4-1), followed up with smart efforts in away draws at Blackburn Rovers and West Brom, and in successive home wins over Everton and Sunderland before hitting the net again when Villa completed the double over Small Heath with a 4-1 win at Muntz Street.

Absent for four games during October and November, he was back in action in early December with two goals in a 4-3 defeat at Preston. He then clinched a 2-0 home win over Bolton Wanderers with a stinging right-footer and bagged braces in victories over Bury (2-0) and Stoke (2-1). One of his strikes against the Potters was a brilliant individual effort.

Surprisingly, Campbell was goalless in his next four games – and it wasn't for the want of trying, as he struck the woodwork in a 1-0 home win over Preston and the 3-1 victory at Sheffield Wednesday.

On 22 February, with the Championship race hotting up, in-form Villa defeated Stoke 5-2 in their return game, Campbell bagging his second hat-trick for the club. It had been a closely-fought encounter for an hour, but then Campbell got going, two of his goals coming after some smart inter-play involving Bob Chatt and Devey.

A draw at Bolton and a home win over Sheffield Wednesday, when Campbell scored another 'fine goal', was followed by a 5-3 defeat by Bury, but by winning their last two matches at Nottingham Forest (2-0), with Campbell on target again, and at home to Wolves (4-1), when Campbell scored twice, including a thumping effort from outside the area, the Championship trophy came back to Villa.

After helping Aston Villa emulate Preston North End's feat of completing the League and FA Cup double, Campbell decided to return to his first love, Celtic, who paid £70 for his signature. In 1898 he gained a Scottish League Championship winner's medal, and two years later collected his second.

After scoring a total of 113 goals in 215 senior appearances during his two spells with Celtic, he moved to Third Lanark in August 1903, and in his first season helped the now-defunct Scottish club win the title.

Campbell eventually retired from competitive football in April 1906 at the age of thirty-four. He had scored a grand total of 141 goals in 264 club games and 4 in 12 internationals. He also represented the Scottish League on four occasions and played three times for a Glasgow Select XI, scoring another three goals.

No relation to the J. M. Campbell who played for Sunderland and Newcastle United between 1890 and 1898, but a cousin of fellow Scottish international John Campbell, who starred for Partick Thistle, Blackburn Rovers, Rangers, West Ham United and Hibernian in the late 1890s/early 1900s, J. J. Campbell was born in Govan, Glasgow on 12 September 1871. A prolific goalscorer in local football with St Alexandra's and Glasgow Benburb, he signed professionally for Celtic in May 1890, and in his first full season scored over fifty goals at various levels, including twelve in one reserve team game. At the end of the 1891/92 season, he scored twice in Celtic's 5-1 Scottish Cup final victory over Queen's Park.

Campbell gained the first of his 12 Scotland caps in a 5-1 win over Ireland in March 1893, and the following month was in the team beaten 5-2 by England. A year after helping the Bhoys win back-to-back Scottish League Championships, Campbell surprised people by leaving Glasgow in May 1895, joining a fine Villa side where he teamed up with some brilliant forwards, including John Devey, Dennis Hodgetts, Athersmith and Stephen Smith.

He remained in Scotland for the rest of his life, passing away in Glasgow on 2 December 1947.

CHADWICK, WILF (EVERTON)

Season: 1923/24
Goals scored: 28 (out of 62); 22 home, 6 away
Percentage: 45 per cent
Runner-up: Tommy Roberts (Preston North End), 26 goals
Everton finished seventh

Inside-left (and occasionally centre-forward) Wilf Chadwick joined Everton at the age of twenty-one, and after a handful of reserve team games, made his senior debut for the Merseysiders in March 1922 against Bradford City, celebrating the occasion by netting twice in a 2-0 win over the Bantams.

Chadwick hit one more goal that season (in the return game with Bradford) and was the club's joint leading scorer the following season with thirteen, but in 1923/24 he was not only Everton's top marksman, but he also headed the First Division charts when he netted twenty-eight times in League action, plus twice more in the FA Cup.

For Chadwick, this feat was extraordinary ... for he admitted that he was not an out-and-out goalscorer. 'I create goals rather than score them,' he said.

In the four seasons since the Great War, Everton had finished sixteenth, seventh, twentieth and fifth in the First Division and had scored only 255 goals in 168 League games. But out of the blue, Chadwick had an inspired campaign in 1923/24, bagging almost 50 per cent of his side's goals, and he admitted that he should have scored more!

Described as being 'sprightly with good skills and a powerful right foot shot', he had made twenty-seven appearances in 1922/23, the last thirteen in the inside-left position ... and that's where he started from in 1923/24.

Keen and determined to make an impact from the outset, he certainly did that, scoring twice in the second game, a 2-2 draw at Burnley, following up with another brace against the Clarets in the return fixture, which ended 3-3.

After a few lack-lustre performances for both himself and the team, he bounced back with a fine goal in a 2-0 home win over Aston Villa, continued with a point-saver against champions-elect Huddersfield Town and then netted a vital first-half winner in his second Merseyside derby early in October, when Everton beat Liverpool 1-0 in front of 51,000 fans at Goodison Park.

Five goals came in the next five matches, one of them a real cracker in a 2-0 victory over Sheffield United, and after failing to score in four of the next five games, he produced a wonderful display in the home encounter with Manchester City three days before Christmas.

A week earlier, Everton had lost 2-1 at Hyde Road (City's old ground), but it was a completely different story in the return fixture at Goodison Park as the Blues romped to a 6-1 victory, Chadwick scoring four of the goals, two of them right-foot belters.

Around this time, Jack Cock was aiding and abetting Chadwick in the goalscoring ranks, and there is no doubt that the Everton duo was one of the best in the Division. It seemed that when Chadwick failed to score, Cock did, and vice-versa.

Chadwick, as do all strikers, had another lean spell between early January and mid-February without playing at all badly. He wasn't quiet for long, however, and, with the help of wingers Sam Chedgzoy on the right and Alec Troup on the left, he ended the season in great style, scoring in eight of the last twelve games.

He netted in the home and away fixtures with Chelsea, claimed a beauty in a 2-2 draw with FA Cup winners Newcastle United and almost speared the ball through the back of the net when scoring in a 5-2 win at Tottenham.

Six days after that win at White Hart Lane, Chadwick struck twice in a splendid 3-1 home victory over Arsenal, and then secured his second hat-trick of the season when Everton completed the double over Spurs with a competent 4-2 win at Goodison Park in the penultimate game of the campaign.

And, to finish off a terrific season, Chadwick duly bagged the winner against the Gunners in the final game to clinch a second 'London double' in the space of nine days.

Despite Chadwick's goalscoring exploits, Everton managed only seventh place in the table, finishing eight points behind the champions Huddersfield Town.

In 1924/25, Chadwick, troubled by a knee injury, struggled to find his form and mustered only six League goals.

Unfortunately – and perhaps surprisingly – he never really established himself as a favourite, either with the Goodison Park hierarchy or indeed the fans. He was unfairly compared to the legendary Edgar Chadwick, who had left the club some twenty years earlier, and at times with Alex Young, Bobby Parker and also Frank Bradshaw.

In the end, Chadwick was the player who effectively made way for Everton's greatest goal scorer, Dixie Dean, when he was transferred to Leeds United in November 1925.

He scored a total of 55 goals in 109 senior appearances for Everton and later played for Wolverhampton Wanderers (August 1926 – May 1929), Stoke City (for one season) and Halifax Town, eventually retiring, rather prematurely, in May 1932.

A Lancastrian, born in Bury on 7 October 1900, Chadwick joined his hometown club as a professional in October 1918, moved to Nelson in 1920 and played for Rossendale United before moving to Everton in February 1922. He died in Bury on 14 February 1973.

CHANNON, MICK (SOUTHAMPTON)

Season: 1973/74
Goals scored: 21 (out of 47); 13 home, 8 away
Percentage: 44.6 per cent
Runner-up: Frank Worthington (Leicester City), 20 goals
Saints finished twentieth

It is rare indeed for someone to reach the very top of two unrelated sporting professions, but Mick Channon has achieved it.

After scoring over 300 goals in more than 850 appearances in club football (232 of his goals coming in 717 League games), gaining 46 caps for England (21 goals) and winning FA Cup and League Cup medals during an illustrious career, he now oversees a racehorse training operation involving some 200 horses out of his West Ilsley stables, formerly owned by the Queen.

Out on the football pitch, he developed into a supreme marksman and did so, initially, with an unfashionable club, Southampton, whom he served for a total of sixteen years in two separate spells (1964–77 and 1979–82).

Born in Orcheston, Hampshire on 28 November 1948, Channon represented Salisbury and Wiltshire Schools before joining Southampton as an apprentice in March 1964, turning professional in December 1965. He made his Football League debut as a seventeen-year-old in April 1966, scoring in a 2-2 home draw with Bristol City to celebrate the occasion.

Within three years he had established himself as the Saints' number one striker, and from 1968 onwards he was one of the club's most outstanding players. He teamed up superbly with Ron Davies, both players benefitting greatly from the service provided by right-winger Terry Paine.

He took over from Davies as Saints' leading scorer in 1969/70, netting eighteen times in League and Cup. He then topped the League charts in each of the next six seasons, amassing 109 goals in the process, while finishing as the First Division's leading marksman in 1973/74 with a haul of twenty-one – this after his strike-partner Davies had left the club!

He started the campaign off with a bang, scoring in each of the first three games – in a 1-1 draw at QPR, the deciding penalty in a 1-0 win at Newcastle and the equaliser in a 2-1 home victory over Wolves. Goalless in the next three, he was injured in a 2-0 defeat at Norwich but returned within three days, only to have a poor game in a 6-2 thumping at Derby, for whom Kevin Hector bagged a hat-trick.

Thankfully he got over that disappointment, as did his team-mates, and a week later Channon netted in a 3-0 win over Sheffield United, following up with a point-saving effort at Manchester City (1-1) and the first-half penalty winner at home to Liverpool (1-0).

Over a four-week period – from 20 October to 17 November – Channon notched three more important goals – the winner at Leicester (1-0), the opener in a 2-2 home draw with Burnley and another face-saving penalty at home to Tottenham Hotspur (1-1). Unfortunately, he drew a blank as Saints slipped out of the League Cup at the hands of Norwich City.

He then had a very good December, scoring penalties in successive 2-0 home wins over Everton and Ipswich Town and also in the 4-2 defeat at Sheffield United, while claiming another spot-kick in the 1-1 draw with Coventry City at The Dell.

The team rose to fifth place in the Division during this month – the joint highest position ever in the club's history.

Four more goals followed in January, including both in a 2-2 draw with QPR and one against Bolton in the FA Cup, but he was relatively quiet in February, notching only one goal in a 3-1 win over Newcastle and missing two chances in a 1-0 home FA Cup defeat by Wrexham. Saints also crashed 7-0 at Ipswich – their joint second worst defeat ever and the best in the League by the Tractormen.

At this point in the season, Southampton were plummeting dramatically down the ladder and quickly found themselves facing a battle against relegation.

Channon's goals (and those of his colleagues) were now of vital importance, but things went from bad to worse. Only one win was recorded in thirteen League games between 23 February and 22 April. More disappointingly is that an out-of-sorts Channon scored only three times – in 1-1 home draws with Derby and fellow strugglers Manchester United (his penalty coming in the second-half) and in the 4-1 hammering at lowly West Ham, when he struck home yet another penalty, his seventh of the season.

A 2-0 defeat at Burnley in their penultimate game sent them down after spending eight years in the top flight. It was unfortunate that Saints were the first victims of the three-up, three-down rule (they finished third from bottom).

When the pressure was off, surprisingly, Saints ended on a high, beating Everton 3-0 at Goodison Park, Channon on target along with Peter Osgood (his first for the club) and Brian O'Neil.

In 1974/75, Saints, who finished just below halfway in Division Two, caused a major upset by beating Manchester United in the FA Cup final. The following season they missed out on promotion by just four points before having a fairly moderate campaign in 1976/77, after which Channon left for Manchester City for a fee of £300,000.

He spent two seasons at Maine Road, returning to The Dell in September 1979. After adding another twenty-nine goals to his tally, and having loan spells with Newcastle KB United and Gosnells City in Australia and Caroline Hills in Hong Kong, he joined Newcastle United in August 1982.

Thereafter, he played in turn for Bristol Rovers (October 1982), Norwich City (December 1982), Durban City in South Africa (loan, 1983), Miramar Rangers (1983), Portsmouth (August 1985) and Finn Harps in Ireland (from August 1986), eventually retiring in May 1987.

NB: Mick Channon's method of celebrating a goal became world famous! He would make jubilant circles with his fully stretched right arm – this became known as the 'Windmill celebration'.

CHARLES, JOHN (LEEDS UNITED)

Season: 1956/57
Goals scored: 38 (out of 72); 21 home, 17 away
Percentage: 53 per cent
Runner-up: Jackie Mudie (Blackpool), 32 goals
Leeds United finished eighth

'Gentle Giant' John Charles played only one season in the First Division before a big money move whisked him off to become one of Juventus's greatest ever stars. His departure must have come as a relief for the opposition defenders he'd battered in the 1956/57 season, in which, by scoring thirty-eight times, he ended up above the likes of Nat Lofthouse and Manchester United's Tommy Taylor at the top of the goal scorers' chart.

Born Christmas 1931, Charles was on the books of his hometown club, Swansea, when Leeds manager Major Frank Buckley persuaded the sixteen-year-old to travel north for a trial. Within weeks, a contract giving the teenager £6 a week had been signed and soon after, Charles was switched from right back to centre-half. On 19 April 1948 the youngster made his debut in a high-profile Elland Road friendly against Queen of the South, whose side included centre-forward Billy Houliston, scourge of England, and their highly-regarded centre-half Neil Franklin, who had appeared days earlier at Wembley in a 3-1 win for the Scots.

Charles did well, ensuring Leeds recorded a 0-0 draw, and his success ensured a League debut the following weekend at Ewood Park in another 0-0 game.

Leeds had been relegated in 1946/47 and hopes were high of a promotion challenge in 1949/50. In the event it was the FA Cup that provided the excitement, with Leeds only going out of the Cup in the quarter-finals, losing unluckily at Highbury 1-0 to eventual winners Arsenal in a game in which Charles was outstanding at the back. His form had been so good that he was selected to play for his country, becoming Wales's youngest player ever. Sadly, he showed he was only human by playing badly.

Leeds had another disappointing season in 1950/51, and when they faced a forward crisis prior to the game with Manchester City at Easter, Charles was moved to centre-forward. Leeds were hammered 4-1 and he hardly got a kick, but the manager must have seen something in his efforts as he was retained up front for the following day's game with Hull City, where he scored twice. It wasn't, though, to be the start of a prolonged career, as over the next couple of years Charles was still needed at the back.

A marker for the future had been placed and when he was moved back up front to score twice in a Yorkshire Cup tie against Halifax Town in October 1952, there was no going back. November 1952 saw him twice score hat-tricks – against Hull City and Brentford. Come the season's end, he had scored twenty-seven League and Cup goals in just twenty-nine games. Leeds, though, had only finished tenth and Raich Carter replaced Buckley.

Charles started the 1953/54 season by scoring four times against Notts County on the opening day. It was the opening salvo in a season of goals as Charles broke the club's individual goal-scoring record for a season with forty-two League goals. Leeds, though, had a poor season, and again ended in tenth place. Fortunately, when Cardiff came calling with a £40,000 offer for their star man, the Yorkshire club had the good sense to turn them down.

After another unsuccessful season Leeds began 1955/56 badly, losing 2-1 at Barnsley in the first match. Steady improvement throughout the season raised Peacock fans' hopes but when their favourites lost to Nottingham Forest on Easter Saturday, promotion seemed to be just out of reach. John Charles clearly had other ideas and smashed a hat-trick as Fulham were thrashed 6-1.

On the season's final day, victory at Hull would ensure a promotion party. It was Charles who provided the goals that did it, when after The Tigers levelled his earlier effort, he drove home a penalty, which, with two late goals from Harold Brook, sent Leeds up. Charles now had a chance to show what he could do at the highest level.

Leeds started impressively, beating Everton 5-1, although Charles's single effort was overshadowed by a Brook hat-trick. The Welshman then hit both as Leeds returned from the Valley victorious, and with things on the pitch going remarkably well there was every reason to anticipate a great season. However, on 18 September 1956 disaster struck when a fire consumed the Elland Road main stand. It was a body blow to a club already facing substantial financial problems.

Come the following Saturday, and with every player needing new boots, it was Charles who raised the spirits, beating Aston Villa's Nigel Sims in the 19th minute and forcing the Villa 'keeper to subsequently make a series of fine saves. Charles had scored twice against Wolves, but got one more than that against Sheffield Wednesday on 10 November. This set Leeds up nicely going into the away game at Old Trafford against reigning champions Manchester United. Charles hit a penalty but Leeds lost 3-2. Nevertheless, they remained in fourth place.

On Boxing Day, Brook grabbed a hat-trick and Charles yet another double as Leeds pulled off a memorable Elland Road triumph, winning by 5-0 against Blackpool. In a season in which he scored some great goals, Charles' best arguably came in this game. The *Yorkshire Post* reported: 'A sensational opening set the home side on their victory march, the ball travelling in 13 seconds from the kick off from Brook, Forrest and Overfield to Charles, who took the left winger's forward centre in his stride to crash the ball past Farm from the acutest of angles.'

Having started the season so thrillingly, it was perhaps no great surprise that Leeds faded in the second half of the campaign. Charles, however, was still banging the goals in, and hit his second hat-trick of the season against Yorkshire rivals Sheffield Wednesday in a 3-2 win. He'd also hit two in an amazing game at Burnden Park, charging through the middle to beat Bolton 'keeper Eddie Hopkinson with a powerful shot and heading home a Meek free kick to give Leeds a 2-1 lead in a game they eventually lost 5-3 after five goals came in the first twenty-three minutes.

Now everyone in the country wanted to see John Charles, especially as it was known that hard-up Leeds were prepared to cash in on their most prized asset by letting him move abroad, where Charles himself would be able to benefit by earning considerably more than in English football. Sunderland had struggled all season at the bottom of the First Division. On 13 April 1957, a crowd of 34,749 had seen Sunderland beat Arsenal 1-0 at Roker Park. Six days later, when Charles and Leeds were in town, close to 57,000 were present. The Welshman failed to score but had his revenge three days later, when he notched a couple as Leeds won the return 3-1.

'It was John Charles's day at Elland Road and just Sunderland's bad luck they had to meet Britain's finest footballer in his farewell match. Charles's exit was perfectly executed. He scored twice, spoon fed his wings and most of the game led Sunderland a merry dance in midfield,' the *Journal* newspaper reported.

His double meant that John Charles had hit thirty-eight League goals. No wonder that the Italian clubs with money to burn wanted him, and when it was Juventus that ended up signing him, there was no great surprise when it emerged they'd paid a world-record £65,000 transfer fee. It was to prove a wise investment, as over the following five seasons he scored almost 100 times in just 150 games, helping his club to three Italian League Championship and two Italian Cups. In 1997, during centenary celebrations, Juventus fans voted him the finest foreign footballer ever to play for their club.

Charles later returned to again play briefly for Leeds in 1962, before a further spell in Italy with Roma was followed by appearances at Cardiff City and non-League Hereford United.

Charles made thirty-eight appearances for Wales. It would have been more but, to his annoyance, he found Juventus unwilling to release him for many of his country's matches. In 1958 he starred as a member of the Welsh side that made it through to the last eight of the World Cup finals in Sweden. His absence through injury in the quarter-final match with eventual winners Brazil proved too great a handicap as the South American side, with Pele in it, squeezed through 1-0.

Sir Bobby Robson described Charles as 'incomparable' and noted that he was the only footballing great to be world-class in two very different positions.

Jimmy Greaves said, 'If I were picking my all-time great British team, or even a world eleven, John Charles would be in it.'

COLE, ANDY (NEWCASTLE UNITED)

Season: 1993/94
Goals scored: 34 (out of 82); 22 home, 12 away
Percentage: 41 per cent
Runner-up: Alan Shearer (Blackburn Rovers), 31 goals
Newcastle finished third

Rejected after making just one substitute appearance for Arsenal, Cole arrived at Newcastle from Bristol City in the spring of 1993. Manager Kevin Keegan was convinced he would be just the player to ensure promotion to the Premier League and in the event, the club record fee of £1.75 million proved money well spent as the Nottingham-born Cole struck twelve times in twelve games, including two hat-tricks against Barnsley and Leicester City, to take Newcastle back into the top flight.

With striking partner David Kelly sold to Wolves, Keegan paired Cole with Peter Beardsley, signed from Everton. The two didn't hit it off immediately and a score of 1-0 down at Old Trafford, after losing the first two matches of the season, had Mancunians taunting the travelling support with chants of 'Going Down.' It was Cole who silenced the doubters, sweeping home Nicos Papavasiliou's cross from eight yards for what Keegan predicted afterwards was going to be the first of 'a hatful of goals'.

Victory over Everton in the home game that followed was followed by two 1-1 draws, against Blackburn Rovers at home and Ipswich Town away. Cole scored both of Newcastle's goals and delighted the away fans at Portman Road by following in the footsteps of his one-time Arsenal team mate Ian Wright by producing his own celebratory jig.

Against Sheffield Wednesday, Cole's opening goal looked like not being enough as, after 77 minutes, Newcastle were a goal down. However, when Nigel Pearson slipped, Cole was on to the loose ball to drive home and, inspired by their good fortune, the home side struck through Alex Mathie and Malcolm Allen to win 4-2.

The following home game also saw Newcastle a goal down, Notts County taking an early lead in the first leg of the second-round League Cup. Cole walloped home a hat-trick in a 4-1 win, and in the return leg repeated the feat as the Magpies beat the Magpies 11-2 on aggregate. At Meadow Lane he first streaked away to finish Lee Clark's through-ball, then three minutes later, on 61 minutes, he headed Allen's cross into the net and then, on 80 minutes, he finished off a pass from John Beresford.

In between the two Cup games, he'd continued his fine form in the league, scoring both goals in the 2-0 win at home to West Ham and hitting his side's second in a 2-0 win at Villa Park.

Cole was, however, upstaged in the home game with Wimbledon when Beardsley, whose total of twenty-one League goals at the end of the season was the highest he achieved during his long career, scored a hat-trick. Cole did get the other goal in a 4-0 victory and then, after slotting home twice in a 3-1 win away to Oldham Athletic, he followed in Beardsley's footsteps with the first Premier League hat-trick of his career as Liverpool were blown away 3-0. All the goals came in the first 30 minutes, Cole finishing off crosses from Robbie Lee and Scott Sellars before completing the scoring after Lee, Sellars and Clark combined to put him in the clear.

Three weeks later, when Manchester United arrived at St James' Park, it was Cole who ensured Newcastle got a deserved point by heading home Lee's cross in a 1-1 draw.

On New Year's Day, by scoring both goals in the 2-0 home victory against Manchester City, Cole already had twenty-one Premier League goals. First, Beardsley headed a Sellars cross for him to head past Tony Coton, and then Clark's ball saw the Newcastle number 9 beat the offside trap and finish from 15 yards.

The 22nd proved enough to overcome a resilient Norwich City side at Carrow Road. Beardsley had equalised with his 200th goal in competitive football when on 79 minutes Cole, after earlier hitting the bar and post, clinched victory during a period when the away side produced some thrilling football.

Coventry also couldn't cope with the man Keegan described as 'the best in the business' when they travelled north and were beaten 4-0, with Cole grabbing another hat-trick. Just back after a two-match lay-off with a shoulder injury and described by his manager as only '60 per cent fit', Cole gave 'keeper Steve Ogrizovic a torrid time as he beat him three times in 27 minutes after the first half had ended 0-0.

Having then scored the only goal at Sheffield Wednesday, Cole was part of the Newcastle side that thrashed struggling Swindon Town 7-0 at St James' Park. Amazingly, in a season when he hit home so many goals, he failed to find the net!

It was at Liverpool that Cole equalled Hughie Gallacher and George Robledo's record of thirty-nine goals for Newcastle in a single season when, on 56 minutes, he called for the ball from Ruel Fox. Sweeping home, he danced towards the away fans at Anfield as Newcastle took an unassailable 2-0 lead. It was his thirty-second League goal of the season and after adding one more in a 5-1 thrashing of Aston Villa, he lined up to play Arsenal in the final game of the season.

After winning the Cup Winners' Cup, the Gunners were given a great reception by the Newcastle crowd. Cole wasn't so generous, hitting the opening goal just after half time. A great Beardsley run had been ended by a fabulous save by Alan Miller, but from the rebound Cole, despite falling backwards, still managed to get enough on the ball to send it back past the scrambling 'keeper for his forty-first goal of the season, thirty-four in the Premier League. Some of those watching must have thought Arsenal had been a little rash in letting him go.

Which was just what Newcastle did only weeks into 1995, when Alex Ferguson persuaded Keegan to let him move to Manchester United in a £7 million deal. There were to be some who felt Ferguson had wasted his money when Cole missed a series of golden chances on the final day of the season as United struggled to snatch a winning goal at West Ham that would have given them the title.

Cole, though, was always confident in his own ability, even after it became clear in the summer of 1996 that his manager was willing to offload him to Blackburn Rovers as part of a deal to bring Alan Shearer to Old Trafford. Ignoring his critics, he was part of a glorious side that captured all before them in 1998/99 with success in the Premier League, FA Cup and Champions League. When he did finally move to Ewood Park in 2001, he took with him another four Premier League winner's medals and one from the FA Cup. Spells with Fulham, Manchester City, Portsmouth, Birmingham City, Sunderland, Burnley and Nottingham Forest followed before he retired from playing in November 2008. Capped fifteen times for England, he failed to produce his club form and scored just the once.

CRAWFORD, RAY (IPSWICH TOWN)

Season: 1961/62
Goals scored: 33 (out of 93); 23 home, 10 away
Percentage: 35.4 per cent
Joint top scorer with Derek Kevan (West Bromwich Albion)
Ipswich Town were League Champions

Ray Crawford was a key member of Alf Ramsey's Ipswich team that won the Second and First Division Championships in successive seasons, 1960/62.

During these two campaigns, centre-forward Crawford scored 73 League goals (40 and 33 respectively in a total of 193), finishing joint top marksman in Division One in 1961/62 with the West Bromwich Albion striker Derek Kevan.

A thrustful opportunist with a real zest for the game, Crawford was aided and abetted all the way by first-class wingers in Roy Stephenson and Jimmy Leadbetter, and by two inside-forwards, Doug 'Dixie' Moran, a £12,000 buy from Falkirk who bagged fourteen goals and the evergreen Ted Phillips (twenty-eight).

Brilliant in the air, timing his jumps to perfection, he scored plenty of goals with his head, some of them crucial, while at the same time he was one of the best 'inside-the-box' poachers in the game. No defender could relax when Crawford was around!

Ipswich drew their first-ever game in the top flight 0-0 at Bolton on 19 August 1961 and lost their second and third games, by 2-1 at Burnley three days later, when Crawford scored his first goal, and 4-2 at home to Manchester City, when Crawford was twice foiled by German goalkeeper Bert Trautmann.

Ipswich's first-ever win in the top flight quickly followed when sweet revenge was gained over Burnley, who were thumped 6-2 at Portman Road, all five forwards finding the net with Crawford bagging two. This, in fact, was Ipswich's biggest League win since April 1939.

Another Crawford goal followed in Town's first away win, 3-1 at West Brom, and he was on target again a week later when Birmingham City succumbed to a 4-1 defeat at Portman Road.

Despite two Crawford goals – one an inch-perfect cross by Leadbetter – in the home game with Fulham, the visitors took both points by scoring four themselves, but fine strikes by the Ipswich star in each of the next two games helped to secure impressive victories over Sheffield Wednesday (4-1) and West Ham (4-2), all six goals in the latter coming in the second-half.

After another exquisite goal had helped set up an impressive 3-2 home win over the 1960/61 double winners Tottenham in mid-October in front of a new record Portman Road crowd of 28,778, the in-form striker surprisingly missed out in the next three games before scoring in a comprehensive 4-1 win over Manchester United, following up a fortnight later with his first hat-trick of the campaign to see off Chelsea 5-2 on a freezing cold December afternoon in Suffolk. Unfortunately, ex-England 'keeper Reg Matthews didn't have a happy day, letting in two sloppy goals, one from Crawford.

At this juncture Ipswich, third in the table, looked good, and although they crashed to a 3-0 defeat at Villa Park, they kept in touch with the leaders (Burnley) thanks to Crawford's two-goal salvo, which clinched a smart 2-1 home victory over Bolton.

Beaten 3-0 by Manchester City just before Christmas, Crawford's excellent goal was enough to beat Leicester City on Boxing Day before he played his part in the 3-0 win over West Brom as Ipswich gained their first-ever top-flight double.

Crawford's neat goal at Birmingham was all in vain, but his efforts against Everton and Fulham in the next two games helped secure 4-2 and 2-1 victories.

Going into March, with the race for honours hotting up, Crawford struck twice in a comprehensive 4-0 home win over Sheffield United and netted again soon afterwards in a 2-1 victory over United's neighbours, Wednesday.

Then, on 14 March, came the match of the season – a top-of-the-table clash between Tottenham and Ipswich at White Hart Lane. A crowd of over 51,000 saw Ipswich produce a terrific display to win 3-1, Crawford and Phillips (2 goals) doing the business.

There were ten matches to play at this stage in the season and effectively there were four teams battling it out for the First Division title – Ipswich, Spurs, Burnley (the bookies' favourites) and Everton.

After failing to score in draws with Blackpool and Nottingham Forest, Crawford bounced back with telling goals in vital wins over Leicester City (2-0) and Wolves (3-2). However, the striker missed the next game at Old Trafford due to an England call-up and he was sorely missed, Manchester United inflicting upon Ipswich their heaviest defeat since Christmas Day 1954 ... 5-0 in front of just 24,976 spectators!

Despite this battering, confidence was still high and with three of the last five games at home, Ipswich knew they had a great chance of winning back-to-back League titles.

They beat Cardiff City 1-0 to go top by a point with four games left – FA Cup finalists Burnley had six to play. But successive 2-2 draws with Arsenal at home in front of another record crowd of 30,649 and with Chelsea away meant a tense finish was in store – and so it proved.

Ipswich, though, were riding high and won their penultimate game in style, whipping the Gunners 3-0 at Highbury with a brace from Crawford.

This left them needing to win their final game at home to Aston Villa to have any chance of lifting the Championship. If they failed and Burnley won their last three games then the trophy would end up at Turf Moor.

With almost 29,000 packed into Portman Road, Ipswich played cautiously during a nervous first-half, but as news filtered through that Burnley were being held by Chelsea,

Ramsey's men turned up the throttle, drove forward and went on to win the game 2-0, with Crawford scoring both. With Burnley being held by relegated Chelsea, it was Ipswich who were crowned champions at the end of their first-ever season in top-flight football.

The partying went on for weeks after the complete outsiders, the underdogs, 'Ramsey's Rustics', the 'Ipswich Yokels' – a team that cost under £30,000 to assemble – had lifted the toughest League title in the world – and Ray Crawford, centre-forward supreme, had led the way.

Born in Portsmouth on 13 July 1936, Crawford was a junior at Fratton Park before turning professional in December 1954. After completing his National Service in Malaysia, the country for whom he played in a representative match, he returned to Portsmouth and made his League debut in August 1957, in a goalless draw with Burnley. He went on to score ten goals in twenty senior appearances for his hometown club before joining second-flight Ipswich Town for what was to prove a bargain fee of £6,000 in August 1958.

He spent five and a bit seasons at Portman Road, during which time he helped Ipswich win those back-to-back titles and netted 157 goals in 220 outings, bagging a five-timer in the process, in a 10-0 European Cup win over FC Floriana of Malta in September 1962 – the first time a player had score five goals in one game in this prestigious competition. He also played twice for England – the first player from Portman Road to do so – and twice represented the Football League (scoring twice in a 6-1 win over the Irish League in Belfast) and played for an FA XI.

He won his first cap against Northern Ireland at Wembley in November 1961, setting up Bobby Charlton to score in the 1-1 draw, and played in the next fixture against Austria, also at Wembley, in April 1962, opening the scoring in a 3-1 win. It can be argued that Crawford's brief international career was due to the fact that he was around when Jimmy Greaves was also creating a reputation as a prolific goalscorer.

Transferred to Wolves in September 1963, he netted forty-one goals in sixty-one appearances in total for the Molineux club before moving across the Black Country to rivals West Brom for £30,000 in January 1965. He failed to establish himself at The Hawthorns (seven goals in seventeen games) and as a result rejoined Ipswich for £15,000 in March 1965, remaining with the 'Tractor Boys' for another three full seasons, lifting his tally with the club to 228 goals in 354 appearances (all competitions).

Crawford joined Charlton Athletic in March 1969, but quickly dropped into the non-League with Kettering Town, only to re-enter the Football League with Colchester United in June 1970. In his only season at Layer Road he scored twenty-four goals in forty-five appearances, and, most notably, netted twice in a famous giant-killing 3-2 FA Cup fifth-round victory over Leeds United.

After accumulating 289 goals in 475 League games, Crawford quit English football in the summer of 1971, teaming up with Durban City, and in his only season in South Africa gained a Cup winner's medal and helped City finish runners-up in the League.

On his return to England, Crawford became youth-team coach at Brighton but left after Brian Clough became manager the following year. He then had two spells as coach at his former club, Portsmouth, also worked in New Zealand with FC Eden (1974) and managed non-League sides Fareham Town and Winchester City before retiring from football in 1984.

In 2007, Crawford published his autobiography, entitled *Curse of the Jungle Boy*. He now works as a summariser on BBC Suffolk, covering Ipswich Town's away matches.

DAVIES, RON (SOUTHAMPTON)

Season: 1966/67
Goals scored: 37 (out of 74); 22 home, 15 away
Percentage: 50 per cent
Runner-up: Geoff Hurst (West Ham United), 29 goals
Saints finished nineteenth

Season: 1967/68
Goals scored: 28 (out of 66); 16 home, 12 away
Percentage: 42.4 per cent
Joint top scorer with George Best.
Saints finished sixteenth

In the summer of 1966, Southampton manager Ted Bates splashed out a then-club record £55,000 for striker Ron Davies as Saints prepared to face their inaugural season in the top division of English football.

Already an established Welsh international, Davies, brought in to replace the departed George O'Brien, was exceptionally strong in the air and as good as most centre-forwards on the ground. He had already scored over 120 goals in almost 250 League games for his three previous clubs, Chester, Luton Town and Norwich City, and was as keen as anyone at The Dell to try his luck – and indeed bang in a few goals – against the First Division big boys. And he did just that.

He rattled in no fewer than thirty-seven, exactly half of Southampton's seasonal tally of seventy-four League goals, scoring in ten consecutive games to become the Division's leading marksman, finishing top of the pile, with eight more goals than England's 1966 World Cup hero, Geoff Hurst.

The first of Davies's goals for Southampton came in his third game, on 27 August 1966 at Bloomfield Road, when hosts Blackpool were defeated 3-2 in front of a crowd of 15,258. He lobbed Tony Waiters from fully 35 yards as the 'keeper came off his line. 'I couldn't believe it. I just knocked it over his head and watched it bounce into the net,' said a delighted Davies.

His second goal clinched a 3-1 home victory over Sunderland four days later and then, after a few near misses in a 3-0 defeat by Chelsea, he netted in ten consecutive League games – and he also scored a hat-trick in a 4-3 League Cup win over Plymouth Argyle.

The first goal in his ten-match run was the winner at Villa Park on 5 September and he followed that up by 'earning' a point at Leicester (1-1).

A fine effort against Liverpool at The Dell went to waste in a 2-1 defeat, which was not helped when 'keeper Campbell Forsyth broke his leg. But Davies scored beauties in the 2-2 draw at West Ham and also in the 4-2 victory at home to Sheffield Wednesday, only to see his efforts in the next three games count for nothing as Southampton lost 3-2 to Sheffield United, by the same score at Stoke, and 3-1 at home to FA Cup holders Everton.

Towards the end of October, he stunned the Elland Road faithful with the winner against Leeds (1-0) and netted twice in a revenge 3-2 home win over Stoke, one from a brilliant cross by the in-form Terry Paine.

Unfortunately, his goals in the next three matches were once again insignificant as Saints lost 4-1 at Burnley, 2-1 at home to Manchester United (in front of almost 30,000 fans) and 5-3 at Tottenham.

His last goal in his ten-match sequence came in a 2-0 home win over Newcastle on the first Saturday in December, at a time when Saints were struggling at the wrong end of the table.

It was frustrating for the supporters – and certainly for the management team and to a certain extent the strikers – for no matter how many goals Davies and his fellow front men scored, the defence would let in at least as many, and probably more, at the back!

Although Davies still kept on popping in the goals – earning a point at Manchester City (1-1), and cracking in his first hat-trick for the club in a 4-4 home draw with Leicester City – Saints won only two League games out of twelve and collected just six points out of a possible twenty-four between 10 December and 4 March. And they exited the FA Cup.

They were deep in relegation trouble – and the muddy grounds weren't helping their football. However, following the signings of goalkeeper Eric Martin and midfielder Hugh Fisher, performances improved; Davies got back on the goal trail, bagging another hat-trick in a resounding 4-0 home win over Burnley and finishing with a four-timer (including two belting headers) in a 6-2 last-match home win over demoted Aston Villa as Saints picked up six points late on to avoid the drop by just two places.

For Davies it had been a memorable season ... and he didn't finish there!

After the summer break, he started the goal rush again, going on to finish the 1967/68 season as joint top-scorer in the First Division, this time with the magical George Best.

After a tough opening game at Newcastle (lost 3-0), Saints set their season in motion with a 3-2 home win over champions-elect Manchester City on 23 August, Davies scoring twice. The Welsh superstar then netted two more in a thumping 4-0 home victory over West Bromwich Albion, and was on target in the return fixture with Manchester City (lost 4-2) before he destroyed Chelsea at Stamford Bridge with a terrific four-timer in a brilliant 6-2 victory. This win shot Saints up to sixth in the Division, but the early good form didn't last and all the team's old inadequacies were soon apparent.

In October, Leicester won 5-1 at The Dell and to add insult to injury, visiting 'keeper Peter Shilton, who would later join Saints, saw his wind-assisted punt downfield bounce over his counterpart Forsyth and into the net for his side's fifth goal.

At this juncture Davies, and indeed most his colleagues, were struggling on the field and the team as a whole continued to have mixed results right through to February. In fact, after beating Liverpool 1-0 on 16 September, Southampton won only three League games out of twenty, and once again relegation loomed.

Davies' strike partner Martin Chivers had been sold to Tottenham in late December and was effectively replaced by Mick Channon, but it was some time before 'MC' settled in.

Then, thankfully, things started to improve from mid-February onwards. Davies scored a decisive goal in a 2-2 draw at Nottingham Forest, found the net again in a 3-2 home win over Everton, struck twice in an excellent 3-0 victory at Sunderland and netted again in a 2-0 home win over Sheffield United.

He was certainly the man in form, but the defence was still wobbling, letting in six goals at Tottenham (one scored by ex-Saint Chivers) before a Davies double saw off Arsenal and another fine effort earned a point against high-flying Manchester United.

Thankfully, by picking up eight points from their last seven matches, Saints escaped relegation once again, and there is no doubt that the goals scored by Davies did the trick.

What a player – sixty-seven League goals in eighty-one League games in two seasons – plus another six in Cup football.

Over the next five seasons he netted another eighty times, finishing with a 'Saintly' record of 153 goals in 281 appearances.

On 16 August 1969, after scoring four goals, all superb headers, in a 4-1 League win over Manchester United at Old Trafford, Sir Matt Busby said that Davies had no peer in Europe.

By the mid-1970s, many clubs had learned how to cope with Davies' aerial power and he was often neutralised by defenders playing the man rather than the ball. A series of injuries reduced his effectiveness and his scoring was reduced. By 1973, he was unable to retain a regular place in the first team and was subsequently sold to Portsmouth. He later played for Manchester United, Arcadia Shepherds in South Africa, Millwall and the Los Angeles Aztecs (two spells), Tulsa Roughnecks and Seattle Sounders in the NASL before winding down an excellent career in non-League football. Davies was also capped twenty-nine times by Wales (twenty-three as a 'Saint') and appeared in three Under-23 internationals.

During his playing career, at senior level, Davies scored a grand total of 315 in 702 appearances, netting 275 times in 549 League games.

Outside football, he had a passion for fishing and a great talent for drawing caricatures, particularly footballers.

Davies, who was born in Holywell, Flintshire, on 25 May 1942, is now living in a motorhome in Albuquerque, New Mexico.

His brother, Paul, was an apprentice with Arsenal (one game) before going on to make fifty-seven League appearances for Charlton Athletic.

DAVIS, DICKIE (SUNDERLAND)

Season: 1949/50
Goals scored: 25 (out of 83); 12 home, 13 away
Percentage: 30 per cent
Runners-up: Stan Mortensen (Blackpool) and Jackie Stamps (Derby County), with 22 goals each
Sunderland finished third

Adolf Hitler's attacking ambitions delayed Birmingham-born Richard 'Dickie' Davis's League debut for Sunderland until he was aged twenty-four. He didn't get on the scoresheet away to Leeds in December 1946, but when the Wearsiders returned to Roker Park he grabbed his first League goal against Liverpool. It proved to be one of five during the season.

However, with manager Bill Murray preferring Cliff Whitelum at centre-forward, Davis was forced to bide his time at the start of the following season, being switched to inside-forward before finally appearing to make the number 9 shirt his own.

The 1948/49 season was therefore a frustrating one as Davis found himself sharing the centre-forward spot with Ronnie Turnbull in a side in which record signing 'Clown Prince' Len Shackleton was the undoubted star. Davis was missing when Sunderland sensationally crashed out of the FA Cup when beaten by non-leaguers Yeovil Town. Having scored just seven times during the 1948/49 season, there was little to suggest that Davis, standing 5 feet 8 inches tall and weighing just over 11 stones, was about to set the First Division alight at the start of the 1949/50 season.

Yet within 41 minutes of the opening match, Davis had knocked home his first of the season, and although Liverpool had beaten Sunderland 4-2 at Anfield, there was enough in Sunderland's performance to suggest they were going to have a decent season. This was confirmed in the next game at Burnley, when the sides shared four goals, one of which Davis struck home on 12 minutes. It was reward for a fine performance that had the *Journal* reporter at the game stating, 'Davis proved a constant menace to the Burnley goal. Cummings did a good job against him but could not prevent the centre forward putting in some dangerous shots.'

Shackleton was at his magnificent best when Sunderland played their first home game of the season, notching up two in a 4-2 victory against Arsenal, the Wearsiders' first against the Gunners in fourteen years. Davis failed to get on the scoresheet and after five games without a goal, he was under pressure to deliver when Sunderland ran out to play Derby at the Baseball Ground in the eighth League game of the season. When he notched up Sunderland's second just before half-time the away side seemed set to run out easy winners, but three second-half goals by the home side saw The Rams capture both points.

Sunderland's indifferent start to the season looked like it might continue when, with just 13 minutes of the home game to play against WBA, the score was tied. Then Davis, receiving a pass from Jack Stelling, pivoted sharply and shot past Jim Sanders to ensure a 2-1 victory. It was just the tonic he and his side needed, and the following weekend the man who'd guested for Aston Villa during the war was in impressive form against Manchester United at Old Trafford. First, on 9 minutes he hit a powerful shot that was going past 'keeper Jack Compton, only for Johnny Carey to get the last touch. Today such a goal would recorded as the striker's, but if Davis was disappointed he didn't show it as 6 minutes later, he eluded Allenby Chilton and met a perfect Tommy Reynolds centre first time, Sunderland eventually running off 3-1 winners.

Sunderland's next away game was at Newcastle and Davis was again to add his name to the scoresheet. There were doubts about whether his shot had crossed the line in a 2-2 draw, but there were no doubts about the quality of the finish, a back-heeler in a crowded goalmouth from 15 yards out. It was the sort of goal only a player in form would have attempted and Davis followed it up by opening the scoring in the first minute of the following weekend's 2-1 home victory against Fulham. Two further goals followed in the next game at Roker Park, a header and then a tap-in after the Charlton legend Sam Bartram inexplicably dropped a simple cross at the centre-forward's feet.

With Sunderland and Davis maintaining their form into the New Year, the Wearsiders travelled to face Birmingham City in mid-January. The Blues had in goal one of England's greatest 'keepers in Gil Merrick, but on 67 minutes he was to be left helpless by a magnificent Davis goal. Shackleton had crossed, but with the ball going away from both Davis and the goal, there seemed little danger before the Sunderland man leapt backwards to flick the ball over his head and past the startled Birmingham number one.

It proved to be a crucial match winner and with his confidence now raised to new heights, Davis struck his first hat-trick when he scored half his side's goals in a 6-1 demolition of Derby. If there was then the shock of being well-beaten 5-1 at Second-Division Spurs in the FA Cup, it was not enough to prevent Sunderland continuing their League progress.

Cup holders Wolverhampton Wanderers had a fine defence with England international Billy Wright at the centre and the man many feel is the best ever between the sticks for the Black Country side, Bert 'the Cat' Williams. Dickie Davis, though, was now in sparkling form and on 11 March 1950 he notched his second hat-trick of the season as Sunderland won 3-1 at Molineux. Centre-half Bill Shorthouse gave his much smaller opponent a right battering, but it failed to prevent him running off at the top of the First Division goal scorers'

chart with a total of twenty-three. It soon became twenty-five, as having hit the equalising goal at Fratton Park against reigning champions Portsmouth in a 1-1 draw, Dickie Davis then grabbed Sunderland's second in a 2-2 draw at the Valley, nodding home a Tommy Wright cross with just three minutes remaining.

Davis was off the scoresheet in the next two games. Both were played at Roker Park and it was the man playing at inside right, next to him, who was the star. Ivor Broadis had been Carlisle's player-manager when Sunderland had enquired about employing his services, and so he duly became the first man to transfer himself when he moved from the west to the east coast at a cost of £18,000 in January 1949. After hitting both goals in a 2-1 win against Villa, Broadis again got both goals as Middlesbrough returned down the north-east coast beaten 2-0. The result, though, had come at a cost, Davis being injured in a collision with Boro 'keeper Rolando Ugolini that saw him limp out the second half on the wing.

There were thirty-six games of the season gone and Davis had played in thirty-three of them and notched up twenty-five goals. Sunderland were just coming into form, and since losing to Stoke City at the Victoria Ground in late December had played twelve League games unbeaten, winning eight of them.

Len Duns had been a fine servant for Sunderland, playing at Wembley when Preston were beaten in the FA Cup final in 1937 and earlier collecting a League winner's medal. He hadn't, though, played a League game in over a year. Drafted in to play outside right, Sunderland reshuffled with Tommy Wright moved to play centre forward. Fulham were easily beaten 3-0 at Craven Cottage, but with Middlesbrough fighting for their lives a derby match at Ayresome Park was always going to be a difficult test. So it proved, as Sunderland went down 2-0.

The performance saw further changes in the starting line up for the must-win home game with Manchester City. Bert Trautmann twice saved one of Stelling's penalty kicks as Sunderland flopped 2-1. When Sunderland subsequently lost a third consecutive game, at Huddersfield, they were out of the title race as despite two victories in the final pair of games, it was not enough to pip holders Portsmouth for the title. Davis's absence in the last six games of the season had proved crucial and although he ended up with the honour of being the First Division top-scorer, he would surely have traded it for a League winner's medal.

Dickie Davis was to go on and make a total of 154 first team appearances for Sunderland before departing to play for Darlington in May 1954 after having hit seventy-nine goals on Wearside. The 1949/50 season was clearly the finest during his relatively short career. Sunderland were the League top scorers with eighty-three and Davis hit twenty-five of them. They included a beauty at St Andrews and two hat-tricks during a season in which Davis demonstrated his all-round goal-scoring abilities with goals from both left and right feet and his head. By finishing three goals in front of second-placed Stan Mortensen and Derby's Jackie Stamps, Davis had shown that on his day he was up there with the best.

DEAN, DIXIE (EVERTON)

Season: 1927/28
Goals scored: 60 (out of 102); 29 home, 31 away
Percentage: 61.2 per cent
Runner-up: George Beel (Burnley), 35 goals
Everton were League Champions

Season: 1931/32
Goals scored: 45 (out of 116); 33 home, 12 away
Percentage: 52.2 per cent
Runners-up: Jimmy Dunne (Sheffield United) and Dave Mangnall (Huddersfield Town), with 33 goals each
Everton were League Champions

Dixie Dean's tally of sixty League goals in one season of First Division football will never be beaten.

In 1927/28, the rough and ready, raven-haired centre-forward was only twenty-one years of age when he created this staggering record and who knows, if he had played in the three matches he missed, what sort of total he might have finished with!

Having bagged twenty-four goals during the previous season (twenty-one in the League) he was bang in form, and in the first nine games of 1927/28 scored fourteen times, including all five in a 5-2 home win over against Manchester United, further hat-tricks against Portsmouth (3-1) and Leicester City (7-1), plus braces against Birmingham, Newcastle, Huddersfield Town, Tottenham and Derby, in that order. Defenders up and down the country were struggling to cope with his power, especially in the air, where he was quite brilliant.

By January, with thirty-nine goals already under his belt, Dean had beaten Everton's club record for most goals in a season scored by a single player, previously held by Bertie Freeman (thirty-eight), and he was only four behind the Division's all-time record holder, Ted Harper (Blackburn Rovers), who netted forty-three in 1925/26.

Dean broke Harper's record on 25 February with a hat-trick in a 3-3 Merseyside derby draw at Anfield, yet with thirteen games remaining, he was still seventeen goals short of breaking George Camsell's existing record for most League goals scored in a single season of English football – fifty-nine for Second-Division Middlesbrough in 1926/27.

It was not going to be easy for the robust, hard-shooting centre-forward, especially after he suffered an uncharacteristically dry spell of four games without a goal in March and was absent from a 0-0 draw with Portsmouth.

With nine games remaining, he suddenly found himself needing to work overtime to secure the seventeen goals he required to become a record-breaker ... a big ask.

But deep down, Dean, and his colleagues, knew he could do it. He got back onto the scoring trail with a double against Derby in late March but then missed the next game due to an England call-up, before smacking in eight more goals in the next five fixtures.

But this still left him needing a staggering seven more goals from just two matches. Surely this was impossible? Not at all!

Dean stunned everyone present at Turf Moor by scoring four times in a 5-3 penultimate game win over Burnley and as a result, he then required at least a hat-trick going into the last game of the season, at home to Arsenal, on 5 May.

Everton had already been crowned First Division champions due to title rivals Huddersfield losing a few days earlier, and almost 49,000 fans packed into Goodison Park to see if Dean could reach the magical sixty-goal mark and become a legend in his own lifetime.

Things didn't go according to plan, with Arsenal scoring early on through Jim Shaw. But Dean would not be denied, and straight from the kick-off, he equalised by bundling the ball over the line following Ted Critchley's right-wing corner. One down, two to go.

With only 6 minutes on the clock, Dean dashed into the penalty area, only to be brought down by Jack Butler. No-one else dared take the spot-kick! No way. Dean grabbed hold of the ball, placed it on the ground, stepped back and, as cool as a cucumber, banged it hard and low past goalkeeper Bill Paterson – fifty-nine scored, one to go.

Arsenal, though, were not following the script, and a sliced own-goal by Everton full-back Jack O'Donnell saw the teams go into half-time level at 2-2.

Everton, playing at a frantic pace throughout the second half, pegged Arsenal back. Dean missed two chances, and as the minutes ticked by, the crowd, sensing time was running out for their hero, suddenly transformed Goodison Park into a seething cauldron.

With just 8 minutes remaining, and with a hoard of blue shirts swarming round the Gunners' penalty area like bees round a hive, Paterson turned George Martin's pile-driver away for a corner. Everyone piled into the box for left-winger Alec Troup's flag-kick and as the ball came over, up leapt Dean to power home his record-breaking sixtieth goal of the season. The fans went wild and even a late equaliser by Shaw couldn't dampen the enthusiasm or sheer delight inside the ground. Even the Arsenal players shook the hand of Dixie Dean ... the hero of Goodison Park.

After some more enterprising and thrilling seasons, Dean topped the League's scoring charts for a second time in 1931/32, when he netted forty-five goals in thirty-eight games.

Goalless in each of the opening four fixtures he played in, he sparked into life with a match-winning first-half hat-trick in a 3-1 Merseyside derby victory at Anfield in mid-September and after yet another goal against Arsenal, he whipped home his second treble of the campaign in a 5-1 win at Sheffield United. A week later, he notched a five-timer in a resounding 9-3 victory over Sheffield Wednesday, when he also assisted in goals for Tommy White and Jimmy Stein, and at the end of the month his brace helped destroy Newcastle United 8-1 at Goodison Park.

Dean, who was thriving on the high, looping crosses supplied by wingers Critchley (on the right) and Stein (left), was on top of his game as winter closed in, and on 14 November, he hammered in his second five-timer of the season as Chelsea were blitzed 7-1 in Merseyside; two of his efforts were bullet headers from inside the penalty area.

A fortnight later he was outstanding yet again, this time with four goals in the 9-2 demolition of Leicester City, and after a 'day off' in a 4-2 defeat at West Ham, he scored in four successive games up to Boxing day, including his sixth hat-trick of the season in a 5-0 home win over Blackburn Rovers.

He hit a 'smartly-taken goal' in a 5-1 win over Sheffield United and two more in a 3-1 victory at Hillsborough. With venom in his boots, he then netted twice in a 4-2 victory over Aston Villa at Goodison, whipped in yet another hat-trick in a 4-1 home romp over Huddersfield, struck a fine effort at home to West Bromwich Albion (won 2-1) and after a week off, scored his fortieth League goal of the season (and his 100th in two campaigns) with a belter in a 4-2 triumph over Grimsby.

Could he top the fifty-goal mark again? This was the question everyone was asking. Well, he came close ... scoring at Leicester (1-0), striking in another hat-trick against West Ham United (6-1) and claiming the winner against Bolton Wanderers (1-0) to finish the campaign with a total of forty-six for Everton (forty-five in the League), as well as netting once for England.

Born in Birkenhead on 22 January 1907, Dean played his early football for Laird Street School, Moreton Bible Class, Heswell and Pensby United before joining Third-Division strugglers Tranmere Rovers in November 1923.

Dean adapted to League football superbly well and went on to score twenty-seven goals in thirty games up to March 1925 when he joined Everton for a fee of £3,000, making his debut against Arsenal at Highbury before netting on his home debut a week later against Aston Villa.

A strong, dashing centre-forward with a powerful right-foot shot and blessed with exceptional heading ability, Dean was, without doubt, one of the greatest centre-forwards of his era and became an Everton legend.

He finished up as the Merseysiders' leading scorer with thirty-three goals in his first full season, but was involved in a serious motorcycle accident in Holywell in 1926, in which he suffered a fractured skull and jaw. While in hospital, he was told by doctors that he may never play football again, as they were particularly concerned about the dangers posed by heading the ball.

Dean ignored that advice and was once again Everton's top scorer in the 1926/27 season; his tally of twenty-four goals included a large number of headers!

In February 1927, Dean won his first international cap, playing for England in a 3-3 draw with Wales at Wrexham. He scored after 10 minutes and added a second before the end of the game. The following month he scored two more against Scotland (won 2-1 in Glasgow), and in May of that same year notched hat-tricks in 9-1 and 5-2 wins over Belgium and Luxembourg. In his first five internationals he struck an amazing twelve goals, adding another six in his next eleven outings.

After his record-breaking haul he was again top scorer in 1928/29 and 1929/30, and while his efforts could not save Everton from being relegated in the latter campaign, they were vitally important again in 1930/31 (forty-eight in total) as the Blues easily won the Second Division championship. During this season he scored in 12 consecutive League games and once again was the club's leading marksman.

In 1932/33, he netted twenty-nine times, once in a 3-0 FA Cup final victory over Manchester City, but secured only nine goals in twelve games in 1933/34. In fact, his whole body took a terrible hammering during his career and he suffered several spells out of the side with various injuries.

However, he was back to his lethal best in 1934/35 with a haul of twenty-seven and followed up with seventeen and twenty-seven over the next two seasons, before netting his 383rd and final Everton goal against Arsenal in August 1937, which was also his 433rd senior appearance.

He eventually left Goodison Park in March 1938, signing for Notts County. In January 1939 he ventured over to Ireland to play for Sligo Rovers, and during the early part of the war assisted Hurst FC, before retiring in April 1941. He became a licensee in Chester, a job he gave up through ill health in 1962, before working for Littlewoods Pools (Liverpool).

'Dixie was the greatest centre-forward there will ever be,' said Bill Shankly at a celebratory dinner on the day of his friend's death. 'He belongs to the company of the supremely great, like Beethoven, Shakespeare and Rembrandt.'

Matt Busby played against Dean several times. In his autobiography, he pointed out, 'To play against Dean was at once a delight and a nightmare. He was a perfect specimen of an athlete, beautifully proportioned, with immense strength, adept on the ground but with extraordinary skill in the air. However close you watched him, his timing in the air was such that he was coming down before you got anywhere near him, and he hit that ball with his head as hard and as accurate as most players could kick it.'

In 1936, Everton signed Tommy Lawton and when he set foot inside Goodison Park, Dean went up to him and put his arm round his shoulder and said, 'I know you've come here to take my place. Anything I can do to help you I will. I promise, anything at all.' At the time, Dean was thirty years old and he knew that there was not much time left for him at the top. Dean kept his promise and spent a lot of time with Lawton on the training field.

Dean was always known as Dixie ... a reference to his dark complexion and curly black hair. Surprisingly, he actually hated being called by this name and insisted that his friends and acquaintances used his real name, Bill. His biographer, Nick Walsh, argues in his book,

Dixie Dean: The Official Biography of a Goalscoring Legend (1977), that Dean felt that the term 'had connections with colour problems connected with the Southern states of America, and therefore contained an inference that he was of that origin, or half-caste.'

This is true ... As Dean left the pitch at the end of a League game in 1938, a spectator shouted out, 'We'll get you yet, you black bastard.' Dean went over to him and punched him full in the face. A policeman came running over to Dean but instead of arresting him, shook him by the hand.

Members of the Royal Family all talked about Dean's scoring exploits, and the great American baseball player Babe Ruth went out of his way to meet the Everton star on a visit to England. Later, a waxwork likeness of Dean – goalscorer extraordinaire – was put on display at Madame Tussauds.

At the end of the 1937/38 season, Dean was transferred to Notts County, in the Third Division. While at Everton he had scored 349 goals in 399 games. This included nineteen against local rivals Liverpool. He only played nine games for his new club before moving to Ireland to play for Sligo Rovers.

After retiring from football in April 1941, Dixie Dean ran a pub in Chester. He had his right leg amputated in 1976 and eventually died of a heart attack on 1 March 1980, while watching Everton play Liverpool at Goodison Park.

DIXON, KERRY (CHELSEA)

Season: 1984/85
Goals scored: 24 (out of 63); 15 home, 9 away
Percentage: 38 per cent
Joint top scorer with Gary Lineker (Tottenham)
Chelsea finished sixth

Kerry Dixon – born in Luton on 24 July 1961 – was a tall, athletic striker with pace, impressive heading ability, two good feet and, more than anything, the will to win.

He started out as an apprentice with Tottenham Hotspur, but was released before ever playing for the club. After spells with Chesham United and Dunstable Town, he got his first taste of League football with Reading, who signed him for £20,000 in July 1980. He went on to score 51 League goals in 116 appearances, including a four-timer in a 7-5 defeat at Doncaster Rovers in September 1982.

Chelsea manager John Neal recruited him from Elm Park in August 1983. Chairman Ken Bates initially hesitated when faced with the £150,000 transfer fee plus an additional £25,000 if Dixon ever played for the England national side, but relented and the deal eventually went through.

Dixon arrived at Stamford Bridge as part of Neal's radical rebuilding of the side and was joined in the same summer by winger Pat Nevin, midfielder Nigel Spackman, defender Joe McLaughlin and 'keeper Eddie Niedzwiecki.

Dixon's impact at Chelsea was immediate. He netted twice on his debut against Derby County and added thirty-two more in helping the Blues win the Second Division Championship in his first season.

Promotion was secured with a 5-0 hammering of Leeds United, in which Dixon scored three.

Striking up an impressive partnership with fiery Scot David Speedie, despite initial personal problems between the two, Dixon also linked up exceedingly well with Nevin. In fact, between them, the trio scored almost 200 goals over a three-year period.

Dixon's impact on the higher League the following season was equally impressive, scoring with a memorable volley in the opening match against Highbury in a 1-1 draw. He continued to threaten all season and certainly put the wind up some of the finest defenders in the game.

Surprisingly, Dixon failed to score in any of the next six League games (two won, two drawn, two lost), but he was back on track at the end of September with a brace in a 3-0 home win over Leicester which saw Chelsea climb to seventh in the table.

On target twice, but to no avail, in the next home game (a 3-2 defeat by Watford), Dixon quickly followed up with a flurry of six goals in a fortnight – both goals in a 2-0 home victory over Ipswich Town, his first hat-trick for the club in a 6-2 thumping of Coventry City and a consolation goal in a 2-1 reverse at Newcastle.

At this juncture in the season, Chelsea were lying halfway in the First Division table. They were still in the League Cup but home crowds had dropped to under 17,500.

Dixon was doing okay; he put Chelsea ahead against London rivals Spurs at White Hart Lane only for Mark Falco to equalise in the second-half, and a week later he netted again in a 3-1 home win over Liverpool, following up with a point-saver against Stoke City (1-1) before putting away two penalties in a 2-2 showdown at QPR.

Unfortunately, both Dixon and Chelsea had a rather disappointing run between 29 December and 9 March. The team won only two out of eight League games, lost three on the trot and went out of the FA Cup, somewhat surprisingly, to Millwall.

Dixon failed to score in eight League games, but got back on form with goals in successive wins over Watford (3-2), Sunderland (2-0) and QPR (1-0). Three more blanks followed but in the last seven matches of the season, he weighed in with five more goals, including both in a 2-1 home win over Sheffield Wednesday, the winner at WBA (1-0) and a superb effort in a 2-0 victory over Luton Town.

Dixon eventually finished up as the First Division's joint-top scorer (alongside Gary Lineker), each with twenty-four League goals, as Chelsea finished sixth in the final table.

Also in the 1984-85 season, Dixon hit a further eight goals in the League Cup as Chelsea reached the semi-finals, where they lost to Sunderland.

In his first two seasons at Stamford Bridge he scored a total of 70 goals in just 101 games.

Chelsea challenged for the title in the 1985/86 season, but Dixon suffered torn stomach muscles during an FA Cup tie against Liverpool in January, which severely hampered their chances as the weeks started to run out. They eventually finished sixth again, though Dixon did score twice in a 2-1 win over Manchester United at Old Trafford.

The injury also took away much of Dixon's pace and he was never quite the same player again. Indeed, Chelsea struggled during the next few years after a series of clashes between key players and the management saw the promotion-winning side gradually broken up.

An out-of-form Dixon was dropped and at one point could have joined Arsenal, the deal eventually collapsing after a last-minute intervention by Chelsea Chairman Ken Bates.

When Chelsea were relegated in 1988, the event ironically rejuvenated Dixon's career with the club. He scored twenty-five League goals, helping the Blues return to the top flight as champions at the first attempt. A year later he scored a further twenty-six times, including a final-day treble against Millwall, to help Chelsea claim fifth place in the table, their highest position since 1970.

He eventually left Stamford Bridge for Southampton for £575,000 in July 1992, having amassed a grand total of 193 goals in 421 appearances, making him the club's second highest goalscorer of all time behind Bobby Tambling. From The Dell, Dixon moved to Luton Town on a free transfer in February 1993, and after spells with Milwall, Doncaster Rovers (as player-manager), Watford and Basildon United, he wound down his career with managerial spells at Boreham Wood, Hitchin Town, Letchworth Town and Dunstable Town, retiring out of club football in 2006. He also spent a short time running a pub.

During his career at senior level, Dixon scored almost 280 goals in 720 club appearances (231 in 593 League games).

DRAKE, TED (ARSENAL)

Season: 1934/35
Goals scored: 42 (out of 115); 27 home, 15 away
Percentage: 36 per cent
Runner-up: Pat Glover (Grimsby Town), 34 goals
Arsenal were League Champions

Ted Drake was born in Southampton on 16 August 1912. After representing Southampton schools, he worked as a gas-meter reader and played for the town's local gasworks team before joining Winchester City, switching to Southampton as an amateur in June 1931, turning professional five months later.

He made a terrific start to his League career with the Saints, scoring a hat-trick on his debut against Swansea Town in November 1931. In truth, he never looked back, or indeed stopped scoring after that, going on to bag a total of forty-eight in seventy-three appearances for Southampton.

Arsenal manager Herbert Chapman had tried to sign Drake in the summer of 1933 but the rugged centre-forward rejected a move to Highbury, saying he was happy playing for George Kay at The Dell. His decision proved right, but in the end Arsenal got their man.

The Gunners had learned that Southampton had financial problems. As a result, new manager Joe Shaw, who had taken over from Chapman, confided with club secretary George Allison, who himself would soon become boss at Highbury, and they persuaded Drake to join the Gunners for a fee of £6,500.

Starting as he would finish, Drake scored on his Arsenal debut against Wolverhampton Wanderers on 24 March 1934, and he played his part in bringing the First Division League championship to the North London club that season by contributing seven goals.

Then, in 1934/35, no one could stop the 'mighty' Drake from scoring. He struck a club record of forty-two goals in forty-one League games (plus one more in the FA Cup). He fired in three hat-tricks in resounding wins over Liverpool (8-1), Tottenham Hotspur (5-1) and Leicester City (8-0), claimed four four-goal hauls in victories over Birmingham (5-1), Chelsea (5-2), one of his favourite teams, Wolves (7-0), and Middlesbrough (8-0), and weighed in with two braces against Blackburn (won 4-0) and Tottenham, away (won 6-0).

In fact, when Drake did score, at home or away, Arsenal rarely lost. They won fifteen and drew six of the twenty-two games Drake scored in. The only one lost was by 2-1 at Sunderland in late October, and even then he clipped the crossbar and had two fine efforts saved by the home goalkeeper, Johnny Mapson.

If he didn't find the back of the net, Drake was instrumental in setting up chances in most of the other matches. In fact, he had a hand in three of the goals in a 5-3 win over Leicester City, two when Preston were beaten by the same score and likewise when Alex James netted a hat-trick in a 4-1 triumph over Sheffield Wednesday.

His goals once again helped Arsenal to win the League title and for his noble efforts, he also won the first of five international caps for England against Italy in November 1934. The England team that day also included his Arsenal teammates Eddie Hapgood, Ray Bowden, Wilf Copping, Cliff Bastin, George Male and Frank Moss. Stanley Matthews and Eric Brook both starred on the wings, Drake scored and England won 3-2.

The following season, Drake played in England's 2-1 victory over Northern Ireland and he had a particularly good game against Aston Villa on 14 December 1935! Despite suffering from a knee injury, his manager George Allison decided to risk him. By half-time Drake had scored a hat-trick, and quickly followed up by netting three more goals in the first 15 minutes of the second half. He then hit the bar and when he told the referee it had crossed the line, the official replied, 'Don't be greedy. Isn't six enough?' No – it wasn't and in the very last minute, Drake converted a cross from Cliff Bastin to bag his seventh of the game to create an existing record for most away goals in a single game – an amazing achievement.

One of the toughest centre-forwards in the game during the 1930s, Drake never gave up, always chasing and harassing defenders. Legendary goalkeeper Frank Swift believed he was one of the best central strikers he ever faced, saying, 'There was no quarter given or asked, but it was a delight to play against him.'

Give him a through ball to chase and he'd go after it like a charging bull. He was fearless and strong, and often suffered leg injuries, quite regularly starting a game with bandages on both ankles and kneecaps.

A serious knee injury that required an operation ruled Drake out of action for ten weeks in 1935/36. Arsenal missed his goals and only finished in sixth place, behind Sunderland, but he did the business in the FA Cup final, his goal beating Sheffield United.

Drake, without a shadow of doubt, was one hell of a player ... the Arsenal fans loved him and he went on to score 230 goals in 314 first-team games for the Gunners, including 124 in 168 First Division matches and 91 in 130 Second World War fixtures.

Besides helping the Gunners clinch two League titles and the FA Cup, he was twice an FA Charity Shield winner and also collected back-to-back Football League (South) winner's medals in 1942 and 1943.

Forced to retire following a spinal injury suffered initially against Reading in March 1945, Drake immediately became coach at Highbury and was in charge of Hendon for a short time before managing Reading for five years from 1947 to 1952. After that he bossed Chelsea from June 1952 to September 1961, guiding the Blues to the Division One League title in 1955 and becoming the first man to play in and manage a League championship winning team. Then, following a lengthy period working as a turf accountant, Drake had a short spell as assistant-manager at Barcelona (1970) and also worked briefly as an insurance salesman in London before linking up with Fulham, first as reserve team manager from 1972, then as chief scout for twelve years. He was appointed a club director in 1979 and later became president. He died in Wimbledon, on 31 May 1995, aged eighty-two.

DROGBA, DIDIER (CHELSEA)

Season: 2006/07
Goals scored: 20 (out of 64); 16 home, 4 away
Percentage: 31.2 per cent
Runner-up: Benni McCarthy (Blackburn Rovers), 18 goals
Chelsea were second

Season: 2009/10
Goals scored: 29 (out of 103); 14 home, 15 away
Percentage: 28.1 per cent
Runner-up: Wayne Rooney (Manchester United), 26 goals
Chelsea were Premiership champions

Prior to joining Chelsea for £24 million in July 2004, striker Didier Drogba had scored 71 goals in 177 club appearances while playing for Le Mans (whom he joined as a professional in 1999 at the age of twenty-one), FC Guingamp (2001–03) and Olympic Marseille. Over the next five years he added a further 144 goals to his tally (in 381 outings) for Chelsea and he has also netted forty-seven times in seventy-three full internationals for Côte d'Ivoire (2002–11), giving him an overall career record, up to May 2011, of 262 goals in 631 games at club and international level.

The all-time top scorer for his country, Drogba has also netted more goals for Chelsea than any other foreign player and is currently the London club's sixth-highest goalscorer of all time.

Drogba's key attributes include his physical strength, ability in the air, and his power to retain possession of the ball. And although looking casual on the pitch at times, there is no doubt that when on form, he is one of the finest strikers in world football.

Drogba scored in his third game for Chelsea with a header against Crystal Palace in September 2004, but his season at Stamford Bridge was interrupted by a pulled stomach muscle which kept him out of action for over two months. Chelsea, though, went on to win the Premiership title and also the League Cup, Drogba scoring in the extra-time 3-2 victory over Liverpool. The Blues also reached the semi-finals of the Champions League as Drogba bagged sixteen goals in all competitions.

He started the 2005/06 campaign by scoring twice in the FA Community Shield win over Arsenal, but his reputation was marred amid accusations of cheating during a Premiership victory over Manchester City. TV replays showed that he had used his hand to control the ball before scoring the second of his two goals.

This occurred just a week after a similar incident against Fulham, where the goal was disallowed. In a post-match interview with the BBC, Drogba acknowledged that he had handled the ball and when prompted by the interviewer regarding allegations about his tendency to dive, he said, 'Sometimes I dive, sometimes I stand,' before immediately retracting his comment: 'I don't dive, I play my game.' The BBC pundits went on to suggest that he had misunderstood the question due to language barriers.

Chelsea went on to retain the League title with two games to play, thus becoming only the second team to win back-to-back championships in the Premier League era. And once again, Drogba finished with sixteen goals.

The following season – 2006/07 – was a personal success for Drogba as he hit thirty-three goals in all competitions (more than his tally in the previous two seasons combined), including twenty in the Premiership to win the Ballon d'Or. In doing so, he became the first

Chelsea player since Kerry Dixon in 1984/85 to break through the thirty-goal barrier in a season.

He started off with a goal in an opening day 3-0 Premiership win over Manchester City and after that, he scored in fifteen of his other thirty-five League appearances, as well as finding the net in League Cup, FA Cup and Champions League competitions.

Among the highlights were two stunning Premiership winners from outside the penalty area, both with thumping shots, against Liverpool (1-0 at home in mid-September) and Everton (3-2 at Goodison Park in December). He also cracked in a 93rd-minute equaliser against Barcelona in the Champions League at Camp Nou (2-2), having hit the winner in the home leg (1-0), and he then struck both goals in Chelsea's 2-1 League Cup final victory over Arsenal.

He notched two hat-tricks – the first against Watford in a 4-0 Premiership win in November, the second against Levski Sofia in the Champions League – slotted in braces against Reading (home 2-2) and Middlesbrough (home, won 3-2), and then, in his last competitive game of the season, he fired home the winning goal to beat Manchester United in the FA Cup final.

This also meant that he joined the Manchester United duo of Norman Whiteside (1983) and Mark Hughes (1994) as the only players to have scored in both English domestic finals in the same year.

In January 2007, Drogba was named the Ivorian Player of the Year, two months later he was crowned African Footballer of the Year for the first time, and soon afterwards he was voted runner-up to Cristiano Ronaldo in the PFA Player of the Year awards.

The 2007/08 season began badly for Drogba as he expressed doubts about the departure of manager José Mourinho. He was reportedly in tears when the 'Special One' told him he was leaving the club, and said, 'Mourinho's departure destroys a certain familiarity we had at the club. Many of us used to play first and foremost for the manager. Now we need to forget those feelings and find another source of motivation.'

Following these claims, Drogba told *France Football* magazine, 'I want to leave Chelsea. Something is broken with Chelsea, the damage is big in the dressing room.'

Despite having signed a four-year contract with the club in 2006, Drogba reportedly pointed out that Barcelona, Real Madrid, Milan or Inter Milan could be a possible future destination, but in the end he regretted what he had said and said he was 'now 100 per cent committed to Chelsea.'

He soon regained the trust of the board and fans, scoring in a 2-0 victory over Middlesbrough in October, against Schalke 04 in the Champions League four days later, and twice against Manchester City, giving superb performances in all.

Drogba continued scoring goals, but suffered an injury at the training ground and decided to have an operation on his knee. Out for four weeks, he missed key games against Valencia, Arsenal and Liverpool, but was fit to play in the African Nations Cup.

Upon his return, Drogba scored a goal in the 2008 League Cup final which made him the all-time leading scorer in League Cup finals with four. He also became the first player to score in three League Cup finals and the first to score in three consecutive English domestic Cup finals.

On 26 April 2008, Drogba faced controversy after a clash with Manchester United's Serbian defender Nemanja Vidić, who had to have stitches under his lip after losing a tooth in the clash.

There was discussion whether Drogba had the intention or not to injure his rival. In the end, the yellow card he had received was deemed adequate punishment by the FA.

There was more controversy surrounding Drogba in the UEFA Champions League semi-final second-leg clash with Liverpool. He was accused of diving by Anfield boss Rafael Benítez, who claimed to have compiled a four-year dossier of Drogba's 'diving' antics, but the Chelsea star hit back at Benítez in an interview.

Chelsea went on to beat Liverpool over two legs and reach their first Champions League final as Drogba became Chelsea's top scorer in all European competitions with seventeen, one more than Peter Osgood.

Unfortunately, Drogba was sent off in the 117th minute of the Champions League final for slapping defender Vidić, making him only the second player to be dismissed in a European Cup final. Chelsea went on to lose 6-5 on penalties after a 1-1 draw in extra time.

Chelsea assistant manager Henk ten Cate revealed that Drogba was due to take the vital fifth spot-kick in the shoot-out. But instead, captain John Terry stepped forward and missed after losing his footing!

Drogba suffered a string of injuries early in the 2008/09 season and in fact he struggled to regain fitness, missing several games as well as being suspended. He lost his first-team place as manager Phil Scolari favoured Nicolas Anelka.

Upon the appointment of Guus Hiddink in early February, Drogba enjoyed a rejuvenation of sorts, returning to his rich goal-scoring form with four goals in five games after the new manager took over. His revival in form helped Chelsea reach the Champions League semi-finals and also the FA Cup final victory, when he scored his sixth goal in a major final in England as the Blues beat Everton 2-1 to lift the trophy for the fifth time.

Drogba began the 2009/10 season in fine form, netting from the spot in the penalty shoot-out victory over Manchester United to clinch the Community Shield, scoring twice in a 2-1 victory over Hull City, earning a penalty (which Frank Lampard converted) in a 3-1 victory over Sunderland and bagging the opener in a 2-0 win at Fulham.

He followed up soon afterwards with his fourth goal of the campaign against Stoke City (won 2-1), added a fifth at home against Tottenham Hotspur on 20 September (won 3-0), and then claimed his 100th goal for Chelsea in a 3-1 defeat at Wigan Athletic.

Drogba was on fire and after netting an important goal in the 2-0 win over title rivals Liverpool in early October, when he set up both goals, he scored a superb glancing header in a 5-0 rout of Blackburn, bringing his tally to an impressive eight goals in eleven games.

The well-built, hard-running striker maintained his form with another terrific header in a 4-0 League Cup win over Bolton Wanderers and was on target against the same opponents in another 4-0 victory in the Premier League.

Suspended for the first three Champions League matches, Drogba started the fourth game against Atletico Madrid, scoring twice in the last 10 minutes to salvage a 2-2 draw, his second being a fine solo effort in which he beat five defenders before having his shot saved, only to react quickest and slot in the rebound.

On 29 November, Drogba scored both goals in a famous 2-1 win at The Emirates against Arsenal, the second of which was a stunning free kick from outside the box. This effort brought his tally for the season to fourteen goals (in sixteen games), and he quickly made it sixteen with two more in a 3-3 home draw with Everton.

Between 3 and 30 January Drogba was again on duty in the Africa Cup of Nations but was quickly back to scoring duties on his return against Hull City, slotting in a 40th-minute point-saver (1-1).

On 24 March, Drogba scored his thirtieth goal of the season in a 5-0 away win at Portsmouth and after netting the winner at Manchester United (2-1) in early April, he ended the season with a smart strike in a 2-0 victory at Liverpool and a second-half hat-trick, including a penalty, as Chelsea thrashed Wigan Athletic 8-0.

Not only did his twenty-nine Premiership goals help Chelsea win the title for the third time in five years, he once again won the Ballon d'Or, beating Wayne Rooney, who finished on twenty-six goals.

For Drogba, season 2010-11 was, by his own admission, not 'brilliant'. He suffered a bout of malaria for at least a month, having first complained of feeling unwell before the October 2010 international break, but the illness was only diagnosed on 8 November 2010. He also served suspension and was sidelined through injury. Nevertheless, he still netted thirteen goals in forty-one senior appearances as Chelsea finished runners-up to Manchester United in the Premiership.

Didier Yves Drogba Tébily was born in Abidjan, Côte d'Ivoire on 11 March 1978. He started playing football in earnest with Levallois FC before joining Le Mans as an amateur in 1998. He holds a French passport.

DUBLIN, DION (COVENTRY)

Season: 1997/98
Goals scored: 18 (out of 46); 12 home, 6 away
Percentage: 39 per cent
Joint top scorer with Michael Owen (Liverpool) and Chris Sutton (Blackburn Rovers)
Coventry finished eleventh
Darren Huckerby also scored 14 League goals, the pair scoring 70 per cent of Coventry's goals

Dion Dublin's potential as a goal scorer was spotted when, after leaving Norwich City without making a first-team appearance, he signed for Cambridge United and was moved from centre-half to centre-forward. Hitting the net regularly, he took the U's to successive promotions but when Cambridge failed to gain promotion to the Premier League at the end of the 1991/92 season, he was allowed to grab his chance of playing at a higher level.

Signed by Alex Ferguson for a fee of £1 million, he scored on his full debut for Manchester United only to suffer a broken leg soon after that left him out of the game for the next six months. If that was unfortunate, so too was the fact that by the time he returned Leeds had agreed to allow Eric Cantona to cross the Pennines and the Frenchman quickly established a fine relationship with Mark Hughes.

Dublin joined Coventry City for a fee of £2 million at the end of the 1993/94 season. He was to enjoy four and a half seasons at Highfield Road, during which time he scored with great regularity and became an England international.

As season 1996/97 came to a close, Coventry's thirty-year run of top-flight football looked certain to end. Having failed to win a League match in two months, the Sky Blues were given little chance away to Liverpool. At 1-1 with just seconds remaining, Dublin, who had played much of the season as an emergency centre-half, scored the all-important winner and then, on the final day of the season, he scored the first in a 2-1 win at Tottenham Hotspur that saw the Sky Blues leap above Sunderland in the table.

After such a narrow escape Coventry were determined to do better and it was Dublin and his partner up front, Darren Huckerby, lightning fast, who allowed them to do so in 1997/98 under the direction of Gordon Strachan.

FA Cup holders Chelsea provided the opening day's opposition at Highfield Road. In a thrilling game it was Dublin who was the match winner, scoring all of Coventry's goals in a 3-2 victory. He'd equalised Frank Sinclair's effort in the first half, but with 8 minutes to go they were trailing when Gary McAllister floated over a corner and Dublin showed his always impressive aerial abilities by flicking the ball past Ed de Goey. Six minutes later, Highfield Road erupted when Dublin lashed home the winner. Hopes were high but with goals hard to come by, Coventry, unable to score in their opening five away games of the season, were again in trouble.

A vital win at home to Newcastle was ruined when Robert Lee hit a wonderful 35-yard equaliser to tie the scores at 2-2 after Dublin had scored twice. His first was a bizarre goal, when after easily collecting a cross, 'keeper Shay Given forgot that the tall Sky Blues striker was behind him and when he put down the ball, Dublin slammed it into the net. Tottenham were a point below Coventry in the relegation zone when the sides met at Highfield Road in December and while Dublin failed to score, a 4-0 home win came as a welcome relief.

On 28 December, Coventry produced their best performance of the season. At home to Manchester United and 2-1 down with 4 minutes left, they were given a lifeline when Henning Berg fouled Huckerby and amid great tension, Dublin scored from the resulting penalty. Three minutes later, Huckerby sent the home fans wild as he rode four challenges before planting a low shot beyond Kevin Pilkington.

Amid strong rumours that cash-strapped Coventry were going to sell him, Dublin then scored a second-half penalty in a 2-2 draw with Arsenal. Dublin was happy at Coventry and to many people's surprise, he then turned down a move to Blackburn Rovers which would have meant a big pay-rise.

The Sky Blues were doing well at home but performing disastrously away. All that changed at the Reebok Stadium against Bolton Wanderers. Already 3-1 up, Huckerby having hit a brace, Dublin scored in the 73rd and 78th minutes for a 5-1 victory. A few days later, he and Liverpool's Michael Owen both made their debuts for England at Wembley in a match won 2-0 by Chile.

Coventry had beaten Liverpool at Anfield in the FA Cup third round, Dublin one of three scorers in a 3-1 win, and he hit both goals as Derby took the short trip home, beaten 2-0 in the fourth round, before a 1-0 victory at Villa Park gave Coventry a great chance to reach the final four, courtesy of a quarter-final home tie with Sheffield United. Dublin scored a penalty but the match went to a replay. Leading through a David Burrows goal with just 5 minutes remaining, there was heartbreak when David Holdsworth equalised and then, after extra time, Coventry lost out 3-1 on penalties.

In April, Coventry faced Liverpool at home. With England manager Glenn Hoddle at the game, Dublin did his chances of going to the 1998 World Cup in France in the summer no harm by hitting a second-half penalty.

Dublin hit his seventeenth League goal in Coventry's final home game of the season, Blackburn being beaten 2-0. It meant that going into the final game of the season, he was level with Sutton and a goal behind Owen. With Liverpool losing 1-0 at Derby, Dublin took his chance to draw level at the top when, with just 2 minutes remaining, he equalised at Everton. With Sutton scoring at exactly the same time at home to Newcastle United, it meant that Dublin tied with the Rovers man and Owen at the top of the scorers' table. It was a fine achievement and his goals had helped Coventry finish eleventh, equalling their best Premier League final position yet.

Despite his record, Dublin, after failing to score in two friendlies against Morocco and Belgium, was left out of the England World Cup squad. In late November 1998 he was to make his final appearance in an England shirt, but he again failed to hit the back of the net.

On 7 November 1998, Dublin, after again turning down Blackburn Rovers and spurning Newcastle's offer to make him Alan Shearer's partner, signed for Aston Villa for a £5.75 million fee. He started well and hit seven goals in his first three matches but in 1999 he suffered a life-threatening broken neck, the result of which has left him with a titanium plate holding three neck vertebrae together. On his return he scored a penalty in the shoot-out to help Villa overcome Bolton Wanderers in the FA Cup semi-final, but his side subsequently lost out in a poor final, beaten 1-0 by Chelsea. Dublin played in the final. After leaving Villa in 2004, he then had short spells, with mixed success, at Leicester City, Celtic and back at his first club, Norwich City. He played his final game on 4 May 2008.

ELLIOTT, GEORGE (MIDDLESBROUGH)

Season: 1913/14
Goals scored: 31 (out of 77); 21 home, 10 away
Percentage: 40 per cent
Runner-up: Danny Shea (Blackburn Rovers), 27 goals
Middlesbrough finished third

George Elliott's sporting enthusiasm saw him ignore his family's advice to go to Cambridge University, instead signing for Middlesbrough on 3 May 1909. He'd already shown enough promise that when Derby County enquired about re-signing Steve Bloomer in September the following year, Middlesbrough were happy to let him return south. Having hit four goals in his first season, Elliott proceeded to steadily up his scoring record with ten, seventeen and twenty-two League goals in the following three seasons. The Teesiders, though, had struggled in the 1912/13 season, finishing in sixteenth place in Division One. The 1913/14 was to be very different, as with Sunderland-born Elliott in rampaging form, Middlesbrough were to finish in their highest ever League placing of third.

Elliott got his goal tally off the ground by netting twice against Derby County. Having been on the end of a fine move with a ten-yard header, he banged home a 'grand goal, with the ball striking the foot of the post before going into the net', reported the *Middlesbrough Gazette*.

He went one better at Ayresome Park in the local derby with reigning champions Sunderland. It was a brilliant game played at a cracking pace, and with the result in doubt to the very end. At 0-0, 'Elliott eluded Gladwin and Ness with a pretty dribble and gave Butler no chance of saving his hard drive into the net,' reported the *Newcastle Journal*. Then, after hitting home a penalty, he brought his side back into the game at 3-4 with a close-in finish, but with the home side having lost Andrew Jackson at half time, the ten men couldn't force home a late equaliser against a Sunderland side that was more than prepared to stretch the rules to capture both points, with a late tackle leaving the Boro centre-forward injured and absent for the following three games.

Back in the side against Newcastle United, Elliott earned and scored a penalty and his two goals were enough to ensure a comfortable 3-0 victory. Debutant Walter Tinsley had been signed from Sunderland to play alongside Elliott at inside left. The two were able to form a deadly partnership, with the new man able to grab nineteen League goals in just twenty-three matches before the end of the season, including three in the following home game that saw Aston Villa beaten 5-2. 'Rarely, if ever has the five forwards that represented the club been equalled,' reported the *Gazette*.

On New Year's Day, Elliott lifted a John Carr centre high into the net for the winner in a five-goal thriller against Derby County. Two weekends later, League leaders Blackburn Rovers arrived at Ayresome Park to find Elliott in sparkling form, constantly picking up the ball to find wingers Cook and Stirling before getting on the end of their crosses to hit home all three goals in the match. It was the third time he had hit a Middlesbrough hat-trick, his first having come against Bolton Wanderers during the previous season.

'Elliott was in international form,' reported the *Gazette* and to confirm that was the case, he scored both his side's goals in a 4-2 defeat at Roker Park the following weekend. His first, and that of the game, came on 34 minutes, when 'Stirling dashed away leaving Ness trailing in his wake and from his centre Elliott scored a lovely goal', reported the *Newcastle Journal*. Towards the end, he reduced the away side's three-goal deficit with a simple finish.

Two weeks later, he might have scored a lot more than his single effort against Everton. But what a goal it was and in its reporting – courtesy of the *Liverpool Echo* – we catch a glimpse of the Boro centre-forward's assets.

> The scoring of the second point was worth going far to see, as to taking the ball there was no hesitancy and flashing between the backs, he simply rendered Fern, who made a gallant effort to arrest the lighting shot, practically helpless ... As a distributor and an opportunist, Elliott had no compare, and the honours that have come his way have undoubtedly been well merited.

Elliott's superb form brought him a place in the England line-up against Ireland in the Home International Championship. With the game being played at Ayresome Park, he was on familiar territory. Ireland were no mugs and Elliott had been part of the England side the previous season, when the Irish had won for the first time ever in games between the sides. With Liverpool's Billy Lacey in sparking form, the away side showed that the result in Belfast had been no fluke by winning 3-0. There was therefore to be no place for Elliott against Scotland at Hampden Park and when the Boro man did finally make it back into his country's colours in March 1920, he suffered the agony of losing for the third and final time.

Despite the Ireland disappointment, Elliott continued to score regularly as the 1913/14 season came to its conclusion. He hit a beauty against Manchester United, but remained just behind Danny Shea of Blackburn Rovers in the scorers' chart.

Then, at home to Sheffield Wednesday, he hit his third hat-trick of the season and when he then scored twice to help push Preston towards relegation, he had moved up to twenty-eight League goals for the season. Bashing home a late winner at Turf Moor, he moved on to thirty with a fine effort in a narrow 3-2 home defeat to Sheffield United.

Shea was to have the honour of collecting a League winner's medal, but the Blackburn man was not going to earn the title of the season's 'hot-shot' and with Tinsley scoring twice, Elliott ended the season with another goal in a 3-1 defeat of runners up Aston Villa. Reward, if that's not stretching the English language too far, came from knowing that a bonus totalling £165 could be paid to the players for finishing third, £15 per position divided by the number of games played by each player. Having missed a sixth of the season through injury and playing for England, Elliott would have lost out on £2.50.

Elliott's Ayresome Park career continued to be a fine one. It was cut short by the First World War, but in 1919/20 he again scored thirty-one League goals. When he finally quit, he left behind a record that read 365 first team appearances and 213 goals, leaving him second behind George Camsell in the list of all-time Boro scorers.

FENTON, MICKY (MIDDLESBROUGH)

Season: 1938/39
Goals scored: 34 (out of 93); 22 home, 12 away
Percentage: 36.5 per cent
Joint top scorer with Tommy Lawton (Everton)
Middlesbrough finished fourth

A prolific goalscorer, strong with both feet as well as in the air, Micky Fenton was also blessed with blistering pace and in the 1938/39 season, was regarded as one of the best centre-forwards in the country. In fact, only Tommy Lawton (Everton) prevented him from becoming an England regular.

Both players finished joint-top scorers in the First Division that season, when Lawton's goals helped his club win the championship, while Middlesbrough took fourth place, 10 points behind (59–49).

Having ended the 1937/38 season by scoring four times against West Bromwich Albion, Fenton started the new campaign off brilliantly with a goal in each of the first three games – in 3-1 wins over Manchester United and Stoke and a 1-1 draw with Aston Villa.

He missed out in the home draw with Chelsea (1-1), but was back on course at Liverpool soon afterwards, cracked in a penalty at Preston and then struck twice early in the second half of an excellent 4-0 home victory over Charlton before netting a with rasping right-footer against Leeds United.

Injury ruled him out for three games before he returned (not looking 100 per cent fit) at Everton but was right on song against Huddersfield Town, when he cracked in a hat-trick in a 4-1 home victory in mid-November.

Disappointingly for Fenton, he then produced a few below-par performances before regaining his form and confidence with a marvellous display against Blackpool on 10 December. He scored his second hat-trick of the season in a 9-2 win at Ayresome Park and knew that he should have at least netted twice more, missing the target when well-placed and only the 'keeper to beat. Wilf Mannion outscored him in this game with four goals, but for Fenton it was another 'match to remember'.

The Daily Telegraph reporter wrote, 'With beautifully timed passes to Milne and Fenton, Mannion also set the Middlesbrough forward-line playing to a blackboard technique.'

After seeing his side battered, the Blackpool manager Joe Smith said, 'I don't know of a team that could have escaped a towsing,' adding that he'd like to have Fenton in his line-up.

Fenton quickly followed up that exquisite performance with a brace at Derby (won 4-1), netted in a narrow defeat at Birmingham, scored in the return fixture with Blues (2-2), fired home a cracker in a comfortable 5-1 victory over Stoke City and weighed in with a couple as Liverpool caved in 3-0 on Teeside early in January. In this latter game, he also struck the woodwork and saw to goal-bound efforts brilliantly saved by Reds' goalkeeper Dirk Kemp.

Fenton managed only one more goal in January – against Bolton Wanderers (lost 2-1) – but claimed four in February, including two in the 3-0 win over Sunderland.

He was out of sorts and managed only two goals in March. The second, against Everton, came at 3-2 just before the break and saw Fenton crash into the post as he dashed to push the ball between the sticks. Despite being in great pain, he insisted on returning to play out the rest of the game at outside right, only to suffer further agony as Everton recovered to earn a point in a 4-4 draw, with Tommy Lawton scoring a hat-trick.

'It was resilient Everton, fighting for the championship, but we also saw a brilliant 'Boro forward line-up,' stated the *Middlesbrough Gazette*.

The injury saw him miss the following five games and as all were won, among which were an 8-2 hammering of Portsmouth, some fans suggested he wasn't missed, especially after despite scoring two on his return, 'Boro lost 5-3 at Leicester and 4-0 at Blackpool.

Fenton simply got on with the task of scoring goals by hitting both in the 2-0 final home game win over Derby. One was a penalty.

The Gazette reporter wrote, 'Against the Rams, he (Fenton) took his penalty kick in model style and scored his second goal under considerable difficulty.'

And in the final game of the season – while his late leveller against Aston Villa was not enough to keep 'Boro in third place – by finishing fourth, the players were entitled to a bonus of £110 – i.e. £10 per position, divided by the number of games played.

Fenton's final haul of thirty-four League goals was the highest in a season by a Middlesbrough player since George Camsell's tally of fifty-nine in Division Two in 1926/27 – and one feels that if he (Fenton) had played in all forty-two League games (he missed nine), then his final tally would have been well over the forty mark.

Fenton was born in Stockton-on-Tees on 30 October 1913 and began his professional career with Middlesbrough in 1932, having previously played junior football for Princess Street Juniors and South Bank East, as well as having a trial with Wolves. Indeed, he was almost ready to sign for the Molineux club but after talking with family and friends, he turned down the offer at the last minute.

He made his Football League debut, alongside Camsell, in May 1933 against Blackburn Rovers at Ayresome Park – and he celebrated the occasion by scoring in a 4-0 win. After this the pair became a lethal partnership, and over the next six years they netted almost 200 goals in competitive matches for 'Boro.

Camsell had been the club's top marksman for ten consecutive seasons from 1926/27 and 1936/37 marked the beginning of the 'Fenton era' at Ayresome Park, when he headed the scoring charts for the first time (ahead of Camsell's eighteen) with twenty-two goals in the First Division. The very next season, he netted twenty-six times – and played for England against Scotland at Wembley.

Fenton continued to annoy goalkeepers in wartime football, when he played for 'Boro and as a guest for Blackpool, Port Vale, Notts County, Rochdale and Wolverhampton Wanderers when free from duty with the RAF, with whom he served in North Africa and Egypt. In fact, between September 1939 and May 1946, he knocked in another eighty-five 'regional' goals, sixty-three for Middlesbrough alone.

After the war, despite being wanted by Everton, he continued his scoring record, finishing as Middlesbrough's top goalscorer in three successive seasons from 1946, before retiring in the summer of 1950 with a total of 162 goals to his credit in 269 first-class appearances. Fenton joined the backroom staff at Ayresome Park and remained with the club as a trainer and coach until 1965. He died in Stockton-on-Tees on 5 February 2003.

FREEMAN, BERTIE (EVERTON)

Season: 1908/09
Goals scored: 38 (out of 82); 24 home, 14 away
Percentage: 46 per cent
Runner-up: Billy Hibbert (Bury), 26 goals
Everton finished second

In February 1908, Everton, seeking an established goalscorer to play alongside Alex Young, signed the Woolwich Arsenal inside-forward Tim Coleman.

On arriving at Goodison Park, Coleman spoke highly of his Gunners teammate Bertie Freeman, who had also been scoring a few goals for the London club. Taking on board what was said, the Everton directors sent a representative to go and watch Freeman in action in a League game against Sheffield United.

On his return, the director was asked, 'Did he score any goals?'

'Yes, one, but he did nothing else,' was the reply.

However, Ernest Edwards, a *Liverpool Echo* journalist, the man who christened The Spion Kop at Anfield, subsequently convinced the Blues' board that Freeman was worth taking a chance on.

Everton agreed and within a matter of six weeks, they signed the twenty-two-year-old Birmingham-born forward for what was to prove a bargain fee of just £350.

He played in the last four games of the season and netted once (the winner against Notts County) before doing everything right in 1908/09.

He broke the First Division scoring record with a total of thirty-eight goals, seven more than the previous record of thirty-one set by Liverpool's Sam Raybould in 1902/03.

In fact, Freeman's magnificent feat was to stand until broken by the Blackburn Rovers centre-forward Ted Harper with forty-three in 1925/26.

Scoring twice in each of the opening two games of the season, in 4-0 and 2-0 away wins over his former club Arsenal and Bristol City respectively, Freeman had a mini lean spell before netting a second-half winner at Middlesbrough (3-2) and striking an excellent effort in a 6-3 home victory over Manchester City.

In the autumn of 1908 – between 10 October and 12 December – Freeman had a splendid run by scoring in ten consecutive League games. During this time, he was 'on fire', cracking in no less than seventeen goals, including hat-tricks in convincing wins over Sheffield United (5-1 away) and Sunderland (4-0 at home) and smartly taken braces in further wins over Bury (4-0) and Manchester United (3-2), and in an exciting 3-3 draw at Chelsea.

After easing up and recharging his batteries over Christmas and the New Year, Freeman struck twice more in a 5-2 win over Bristol City in early January before bagging five goals in February, including his third hat-trick of the season, against Sheffield United (won 5-1), and further efforts against Aston Villa and Bury. He then helped himself to his fourth treble of the campaign in March, clinching a hard-earned 3-2 home win over Chelsea ... the team he seemed to love playing against most of all!

Bearing down on the championship, Everton needed a good set of results from their remaining seven matches to stand any chance of winning the title ... but they had it all to do as the favourites, Newcastle United, were clear and in form at the top.

Unfortunately, only two wins were recorded during the run-in. Freeman missed the home defeat by Bradford City and was 'completely out of sorts' in the games against Blackburn Rovers,

Newcastle and Sheffield Wednesday, although he did score two excellent goals in a 5-2 double-clinching victory over rivals Liverpool and two more in a last-match 4-2 victory over Leicester.

The following season (1909/10) Freeman scored twenty-six League and Cup goals, but only added two more to his collection in 1910/11 before he departed company with the Merseyside club.

Born in Handsworth, Birmingham on 10 October 1885, Freeman was a pupil at Gower Street School, Aston and played for Gower Street Old Boys and Aston Manor before joining Aston Villa as an eighteen-year-old professional in April 1904. Eighteen months later, he was transferred to Woolwich Arsenal before signing for Everton in April 1908.

After spending three excellent years at Goodison Park – during which time he scored a total of sixty-seven goals in only ninety-four senior appearances – he switched his allegiance to Burnley, later assisting Wigan Borough, Kettering Town and Kidderminster Harriers, retiring in August 1924.

An FA Cup winner with Burnley in 1914, Freeman scored the only goal of the final against Liverpool, his effort being described as follows in the local press: 'From a throw-in on the right Nesbitt sent across to Hodgson who cleverly headed the ball to Freeman, who in a twinkling first time shot, without any pulse-beating preliminaries, shot the ball into the far corner of the net. Campbell had not the ghost of a chance.'

Freeman differed from many of his contemporaries, inasmuch that he was a ball player rather than an all-action, robust centre-forward whose League career realised 197 goals in more than 350 appearances.

He netted on his international debut for England in a 2-0 win over Wales at Nottingham in March 1909 and was on target again in the 6-1 and 2-0 wins over Ireland and Wales in February and March 1912. He also represented the Football League on four occasions.

GARRATY, BILLY (ASTON VILLA)

Season: 1899/1900
Goals scored: 27 (out of 77); 17 home, 10 away
Percentage: 28.5 per cent
Runner-up: Steve Bloomer (Derby County), 19 goals
Villa were League Champions

Billy Garraty set a new Aston Villa scoring record in 1899/1900 when, in a total of forty first-class matches, he netted thirty-one goals, twenty-seven in the League. His closest rival was his strike partner Jack Devey with eighteen (thirteen in the League) and Garraty's tally could and should have been higher, as he missed two penalties!

Nevertheless, his haul of twenty-seven in the League remains as the second highest total in any one season by a Villa player; the great Tom 'Pongo' Waring holds the record, with an amazing haul of forty-nine in 1930/31.

In 1899/1900, Billy played wonderfully well – nothing seemed to bother him. He was confident, even arrogant at times, as he took on and beat some of the best defenders in the game and scored some smashing goals. One journalist described him as being 'an industrious, never-say-die inside or centre-forward, not polished, but invaluable for his scoring proclivities'.

Taking over from George Johnson (injured) and with Devey on his right and Fred Wheldon to his left, he lined up in the opening League game of the campaign at Sunderland, and celebrated by scoring the winner (1-0). He never looked back!

In the next game in front of his own supporters, Garraty was 'on fire', scoring four times in a resounding 9-0 win over Glossop ... 'One of his efforts, struck from distance, almost tore a hole in the beak of the net,' wrote one reporter.

He took a knock in the third game (a 2-0 home defeat by neighbours West Brom) and limped along in the second half, but he was fit for the fourth League encounter, scoring in a 2-1 win at Everton.

Surprisingly – and certainly not for the want of trying – over the next ten weeks or so, he failed to score a single goal but aided and abetted his colleagues with some clever flicks, delicate chipped passes, smart headers and a lot of off-the-ball running, pulling defenders all over the place!

In fact, Garraty missed the away game at Notts County in mid-October through injury and his replacement, Johnson, bagged a hat-trick in a 4-1 victory. At that juncture, some thought his position was under threat. No chance!

He returned with confidence and although he didn't get on the scoresheet as was expected, his contribution was outstanding as Villa surged to the top of the First Division table.

On 2 December he scored his first goal for nearly three months in an emphatic 5-0 win at Preston, and later in the month claimed his second hat-trick of the season as Villa completed the double over Sunderland with an excellent 4-2 home victory.

Now bang in form and going for their fifth First Division Championship triumph in seven seasons, Villa lost only one of their last thirteen League games as they took the top prize, finishing two points ahead of Sheffield United (50–48).

Garraty scored in eight of those games. He struck both goals in a revenge 2-0 victory over West Brom, netted twice in 4-0 and 3-2 victories at Blackburn and at home to Derby, struck another treble as Notts County got hammered 6-2 (one of his right-footed strikes hitting the underside of the crossbar and one of the uprights before flying into the net), notched a vital goal in the crucial top-of-the-table 1-1 draw with Sheffield United, netted twice (one a real beauty) at Manchester City (won 2-0) and did likewise to see off Preston North End (3-1).

The reporter covering the Manchester City game for the local *Sports Argus* wrote, 'Garraty's performance was of the highest order ... he had far too much energy and power for the opposition and his incisiveness, intelligent play and judgment was quite outstanding. The best of his three goals was his second – a splendid right foot shot following smart work down the right by Athersmith and Devey.'

Surprisingly, both Garraty and the team as a whole disappointed all and sundry during the next two seasons, but things improved greatly in 1902/03 as Villa finished second in the First Division table, Garraty notching fifteen goals. He also won his only England cap in a 2-1 win over Wales at Portsmouth in the March, when he played 'up front' alongside his Villa teammate Joe Bache.

Confident and in good form, he followed up in 1903/04 with another nine League goals and the following season weighed in with eight more, while also gaining an FA Cup winner's medal when he was named 'Man of the Match' after Villa had beaten Newcastle United 2-0 in the final before a then-record crowd of 101,117 at Crystal Palace.

After scoring another twenty-one goals in 1905/06, he managed just two the following year, and at this juncture his association with Villa looked like ending. But he held in there and played well for a short time after being switched to right-half. However, he and the fans knew that his career in top-flight football was slowly coming to an end. He was fast approaching his thirtieth birthday when, in September 1908, after an eleven-year stay at Villa Park, he was transferred to Leicester Fosse for £350, having scored 112 goals in 259 senior appearances in the claret and blue strip.

He never really settled in at Leicester, failing to find the net in six appearances, and in October 1908 was sold to Second-Division West Bromwich Albion for £270. Two years later, in November 1910, after netting twenty-two times in fifty-nine games for the Baggies, Garraty moved to Lincoln City for £100, announcing his retirement, through injury, in the summer of 1911.

He returned to Villa Park as a trainer in April 1913, but fell ill with pneumonia and spent several weeks in hospital. Thankfully, he regained full health and subsequently went to work as a beer delivery driver at Ansells Brewery, remaining there until his death in Aston, Birmingham on 6 May 1931.

Born in Saltley, Birmingham on 6 October 1878 and a pupil at Church Road and Saltley St Saviour's schools (Birmingham), Garraty played for Ashted Swifts, St Saviour's FC, Highfield Villa, Lozells FC and Aston Shakespeare before joining Aston Villa as a professional in August 1897 – a few months after the Birmingham club had emulated Preston North End's feat of capturing the League and FA Cup double.

He made his League debut towards the end of the 1897/98 season, in a 1-1 home draw with Stoke, and after a long spell in the reserves, was brought back into the first team late on in 1898/99. He played supremely well, scored six goals (including a hat-trick in a thumping 7-1 win over West Bromwich Albion) in nine games and helped Villa win the First Division championship again, thus collecting his first club medal as the League title was retained.

During his time at Villa Park, Garraty was regarded as one of the great utility players of the game. Apart from his ability to score goals, he set up many more for his colleagues and there is no doubt he would have scored many more goals for Villa if he had been allowed to play as an out-and-out striker.

GLAZZARD, JIMMY (HUDDERSFIELD TOWN)

Season: 1953/54
Goals scored: 29 (out of 78); 18 home, 11 away
Percentage: 37 per cent
Runner-up: John Nicholls (West Bromwich Albion), 28 goals
Huddersfield Town finished third

After thirty-three goals in ninety-eight Second World War games, Normanton-born Glazzard scored Huddersfield Town's first League goal when football resumed in August 1946. Although he was top scorer, with eleven goals, it was a difficult season, with The Terriers only just staying up in twentieth place, and over the next few seasons they continued to flirt with relegation. In 1950/51, with the drop seemingly inevitable, the arrival of Bill McGarry from Port Vale proved an inspirational signing by manager George Stephenson. With Glazzard back in the side, six games from seven were won to complete the great escape. It was a temporary reprieve as in 1951/52, relegation finally arrived. With Stephenson gone, Stockport County's Andy Beattie became manager.

Promotion was gained in the first season. Huddersfield's defence was superb, with Jack Wheeler in goal only conceding thirty-three League goals all season, twenty-two fewer than champions Sheffield United. Up front, with thirty League goals, Glazzard finished as his side's top-scorer, with the highlight being four headed goals on 11, 33, 48 and 71 minutes respectively as Everton were beaten 8-2.

Despite his success, critics were doubtful he could repeat it in the First Division, especially as 'Gentleman Jim' was now aged thirty. With seven from a possible eight points, Huddersfield raced to the top of the league. Glazzard did not score in the first three of those games but hit a hat-trick in the fourth as Portsmouth were beaten 5-1 at Leeds Road. It was his first top-flight hat-trick.

First, he worried Jack Froggatt and when the ball ran loose, he forced it home; then, on 64 minutes, he restored Huddersfield's lead by spinning to drive home before completing his hat-trick with a goal typical of many he scored for his side, heading home a Vic Metcalfe cross. And in an exact repeat, he equalised for Huddersfield in a 2-1 defeat at Cardiff before another header put his side 2-1 up at home to Chelsea shortly after.

Then, on 19 September he again scored three times, as Sheffield United were beaten 6-3 at Bramall Lane. He had again headed home a Metcalfe cross to put his side 1-0 up on 2 minutes and he made it 3-1 when, after Metcalfe's shot was blocked, he nipped in to give Ted Burgin no chance. Pegged back in a thrilling game, he restored Town's lead at 4-3 with a neat flick over the 'keeper's head from Willie Davie's pass. Middlesbrough were next to suffer, first when he slammed the ball beyond Rolando Ugolini on eight minutes, and then 6 minutes later he forced Jimmy Watson's header home

The following weekend, he made it eight goals in three matches as Aston Villa were swept aside 4-0. His opener on 16 minutes came when Keith Jones parried Metcalfe's drive and he forced home the rebound. The second was a brilliant goal in which he finished off a fine move with a powerful drive, and then he nipped in to finish off a Davie cross to round off his hat-trick on the stroke of half-time.

Never the quickest of players, Glazzard surprised the Liverpool defence when he ran on to a fine McGarry pass and with Russell Crossley advancing, he chipped the ball home for a fine goal in a 2-0 success. The following weekend, he drew Newcastle's Ronnie Simpson before beating the 'keeper in a 2-0 away victory at Saint James' Park. On 7 November, his magnificent run in front of goal continued when he hooked the ball over his head and beyond the despairing dive of Sam Bartram to give his side the lead at Charlton Athletic.

Sheffield Wednesday were the next to suffer as he scored both goals in a 2-0 win at Leeds Road, deflecting a Davie shot just before half-time and then hitting a cracking drive well clear of Brian Ryalls' despairing dive. A header against Burnley helped his side win 3-1 before a thigh injury kept him sidelined for two matches.

Back in the side for the match with champions Arsenal, he scored two more. First with a sharp shot beyond Jack Kelsey, and then, when Metcalfe's cross sailed over the 'keeper, he headed an easy goal. Having been out injured for five out of six games, the Huddersfield centre-forward again scored twice at Stamford Bridge in a 2-2 draw. A neat finish on 19 minutes was followed by another headed goal from a Metcalfe cross. Another header, this time from a cross by England international fullback Ron Staniforth, capped a good performance in a 3-0 win at Middlesbrough.

Glazzard himself never played for England. With Nat Lofthouse, Jackie Milburn, Stan Mortensen and Ronnie Allen standing in his way it was no surprise, although in

March 1954 he did get the chance to play for England B against West Germany B in Gelsenkirchen.

Defeat in mid-March by WBA at home meant any chance of winning the title for the first time since 1925/26 disappeared, but Huddersfield continued to press for a first top three finish since 1935/36. Glazzard's 100th League goal against Sheffield Wednesday in a 4-1 win at Hillsborough was a bit of a fluke. Rising on 7 minutes, Roy Shiner's corner flew off his shoulder to lob high over Dave McIntosh to give the Terriers the lead.

On Easter Tuesday, Glazzard hit the first in a 2-1 victory against leaders Wolves, and although he failed to net in the last game of the season, a 2-1 success against Bolton Wanderers maintained Huddersfield in third place, just six points behind champions Wolves.

Having scored twenty-nine times, the *Huddersfield Examiner* quite rightly noted in their season's review, 'The man largely responsible for Huddersfield's fine season was Glazzard – his partnership with Metcalfe was amongst one of the most deadly in the country.'

Glazzard continued to score freely the following season with twenty-six League goals, including away hat-tricks at Maine Road and Molineux. Twelfth place, though, was big fall and the downward spiral continued into the next, when Huddersfield were relegated for the second time in four seasons. With eleven goals, Glazzard was again top-scorer but now aged thirty-three, his best times were behind him. In August he departed to Everton. He left having scored 153 goals in 321 matches for Huddersfield. A short spell at Mansfield Town followed an unsuccessful time at Goodison Park before he retired from football the following summer. Jimmy Glazzard died in 1995.

GOODALL, JOHN (PRESTON NORTH END)

Season: 1888/1889
Goals scored: 20 (out of 74); 12 home, 8 away
Percentage: 27 per cent
Runner-up: Jimmy Ross (Preston North End), 19 goals
Preston were League Champions and FA Cup winners

The top scorer in the inaugural Football League season was Preston North End's John Goodall, who in a race to the very end, finished with a goal more than his colleague Jimmy Ross. Not surprisingly, in a League in which each team played only twenty-two games, Preston ran away with the title, remaining unbeaten and drawing just four times.

Formed in 1881, Preston was the first club to become wholly professional. Secretary Major William Sudell had drawn on the example of sides north of the border. England and Scotland had first faced each other internationally in 1872, and the former even became the first winners with a 4-2 victory in 1873. After that, the Scots reigned supreme by deploying their players in a more balanced formation of two full-backs, three half backs and a five forward line-up. As a result, the emphasis moved away from the dribbling game, in which players waited until one of their teammates lost the ball, towards a passing one.

In this, Preston were to prove the undoubted masters and Goodall – known as Johnny All Good – was the main man, earning him the honour of being known as the first player to pioneer scientific football.

The son of a corporal in the Royal Scottish Fusiliers, Goodall was born in Westminster, London, on 19 June 1863, a quirk of fate giving him the right to play internationally for England. After leaving school, Goodall worked as an iron turner and played football whenever possible. He joined Kilmarnock Burns as a fifteen-year-old. A year later, he signed for Kilmarnock Athletic and made his senior debut in 1870.

Four years later, in 1884, he was lured south into English football – professionalism was just round the corner and thinly disguised financial arrangements were commonplace, and Goodall joined the Bolton side Great Lever. Playing his first game for the Lancashire club against Derby County, he scored five goals in a 6-0 victory.

In August Goodall switched his allegiance to Preston North End, where he developed a wonderful partnership with Jimmy Ross. It was during this season that Goodall first played for England, scoring on his debut against Wales in a 5-1 victory. He was to play fourteen times in all, scoring twelve times, including two marvellous efforts when England beat Scotland 4-1 in April 1892 – his dad must have been pleased!

Preston had opened the 1888/89 season with a 5-2 defeat of Burnley before a Deepdale crowd of 5,000. Goodall had the honour of kicking off the game, but had failed to get on the scoresheet. It didn't take him long, though, to do so in the next match at Wolverhampton Wanderers, scoring on 5 minutes. Wolves were well beaten 4-0 by the end. It was clear that the Lilywhites were already establishing themselves as the side to beat. Derby certainly gave it a good effort in the fourth game, but 2-0 down just before half-time, Preston fought back to win 3-2 with Jimmy Ross scoring twice, including an unstoppable shot from 20 yards out.

And it was Ross who proved to be the Preston match-winner the following weekend, when he became the first man to score four goals in a League game as Stoke were thrashed 7-0. Ross now had nine in the first five games and when he added another against WBA in a 3-0 victory, he looked set to finish as the top scorer in the first League season.

In the eighth game, after Accrington became the only side during the season to keep out Preston in the seventh, Goodall scored his first League hat-trick against Wolves. Even though it's now well over a hundred years ago, you can still catch a glimpse from the match report that appeared in the *Football Field* that evening of Preston's play and how good Goodall was.

> The first goal on five minutes came from some good passing between Gordon and Ross, and when the latter crossed Goodall finished the move off in some style bringing a great cheer from the 5,000 who had paid to see the action.

Leading 2-1 at half-time, Preston scored soon after the 5 minute break, when 'Edwards and Gordon then broke away with the ball to find Goodall who made it 3-1 ... Ross and Gordon combined to set up Goodall for his second to make it 4-2. The final score was PNE 5 Wolves 2 in what 'the Football Field' newspaper reported was "an excellent game."'

Goodall now had his shooting boots on, and the following weekend he again hit three as Notts County were thrashed 7-0 at their Trent Bridge ground.

When Preston had a chance to extract some revenge for Accrington having denied them victory in the first match that season, they were hanging on to a 1-0 lead when 'following some good passing between Goodall and Thomson the ball found its way to Gordon who struck a hard shot that Johnny Horne was nowhere near saving.' Preston was running away with the League and ended November by beating Bolton 5-2 away. Ross grabbed two in this game and after fifteen games he had sixteen goals, four in front of Goodall.

Goodall wasn't finished, though, and some fine passing created the opening goal for him the following weekend in a 3-0 win against Everton, in which he added his second just before the end. WBA were then thrashed 5-0 at their Stoney Lane ground, with Goodall and Ross both hitting two. Five games to go and only two between them, but when Goodall then hit the only goal in the game against Blackburn Rovers and followed it up with two against Notts County on 5 January, it pushed him to the top of the scoring charts with nineteen goals.

There were 15,000, a huge crowd in those days, at Anfield to witness Preston's penultimate game of the season. Many were hoping to see Everton become the first side to beat the League champions and at 0-0 at half time, the game could have gone either way.

However, soon after the break Preston struck and by scoring, Ross drew level with Goodall. According to the *Football Field*, the goal came when, 'Again the Preston forwards with good passing brought the ball up the field and from a pass by Goodall, immediately Jimmy Ross scored with a low shot.'

Soon after, Preston made sure of victory when, 'Goodall again rushed up the centre and after passing his opponents he lowered the home citadel a second time.'

It also, of course, put Goodall back at the top of the scorers' chart with twenty and when both players failed to score in the final League game of the season, a 2-0 victory at Villa Park, he stayed there in a side that had gone the season unbeaten in the League, winning the title by eleven points from second-placed Villa.

To top things off Preston won the FA Cup, beating Wolves 3-0 in the Final and thus winning the competition without conceding a goal. No wonder the team become known as 'the Invincibles', and in Goodall they had the ultimate playmaker and goal scorer. Goodall had scored fifty goals in only fifty-six first-class appearances for Preston. His speed over the ground, clever footwork, willingness to shoot from any distance and his accuracy in front of goal made him one of the most accurate marksmen the game of football has ever seen.

Not that such success was enough to keep him at Deepdale, as within weeks he signed for Derby County. It appears money was the main reason, as along with his brother Archie, who also signed for Derby at the same time, he was given the tenancy of The Plough pub on London Road.

Although Derby won no major trophies while Goodall was there, the side earned a reputation for being the most entertaining in the League, narrowly missing honours on several occasions. Goodall also acted as a figurehead to the young players, and in particular to another player who features heavily in this book, Steve Bloomer.

Goodall remained at Derby until 1899, when he moved to New Brighton Tower. He later joined League side Glossop North End before becoming Watford's first manager in May 1903, where he continued to play. In 1910 he became player-manager at Racing Club de Roubaix in France, and finally hung up his boots in 1913, aged fifty, as player-manager of the Welsh club Mardy. He retired to Hertfordshire and died aged seventy-eight on 20 May 1942.

GRAY, ANDY (ASTON VILLA)

Season: 1976/77
Goals scored: 25 (out of 76); 20 home, 5 away
Percentage: 33.8 per cent
Joint top scorer with Malcolm Macdonald (Arsenal)
Villa finished fourth

Regarded as one of the greatest centre-forwards ever to don the famous claret and blue strip, charismatic Scottish international Andy Gray became an instant hero at Villa Park, where his rugged, all-action style made him a firm favourite with the supporters, but not with opponents!

Signed from Dundee United for £110,000 in 1975, he netted twelve goals in thirty-three appearances in his first season with Villa and followed up with twenty-nine in his second, which saw him finish joint top (with Arsenal's Malcolm Macdonald) of the First Division charts.

Partnering Brian Little and occasionally John Deehan in attack, he was extremely powerful in the air and thrived on the tempting crosses sent over by wingers Alex Cropley and Ray Graydon, as well as the defence-splitting passes supplied by midfielder Gordon Cowans.

He opened up with two goals in a 4-0 home win over West Ham, and in the fourth game of the season he grabbed his first hat-trick in English football when Ipswich Town were defeated 5-2, following up with a goal in each of the next three games, two of which were lost 2-1, against rivals Birmingham City and QPR, and one won 2-0 against Leicester.

Two goals were then netted in a crushing 5-1 home win over Arsenal on 20 October, two more followed as Manchester United lost 3-2 at Villa Park, and before Christmas he scored once in a 2-2 draw with Coventry and twice in the 3-1 and 5-1 victories over Leeds United and reigning champions and table-toppers Liverpool respectively.

He was brilliant against Bob Paisley's team, and in truth Villa's first-half display against the Merseysiders was something to behold as they scored all five goals to blitz the visitors into submission.

Paisley said, 'We got a thumping.'

Gray opened his account as early as the 9th minute after a flowing move involving Cropley, Deehan and full-back John Robson, whose hanging cross was headed powerfully

past Ray Clemence by the rampaging Scot. Deehan scored the next two goals before John Gidman set up Little for number four, which was followed soon afterwards by Gray's second. The striker 'lost' Phil Thompson and Emlyn Hughes as he rose to meet Dennis Mortimer's cross to send a stunning header past Clemence.

This was Liverpool's heaviest League defeat since their 7-2 slaughter at Tottenham in 1963.

Gray scored once more before the end of the year (at Middlesbrough), while at the same time he was also helping Villa make progress in the League Cup.

Further goals helped gain League points off West Ham and Everton, against whom he was injured and missed three games. Surprisingly, he managed only one more goal in his next four outings before being sidelined again, only to suffer another barren spell, although he did help Villa win the League Cup (against Everton). He finished the season on a high, claiming his second hat-trick for the club in a last-match 4-0 home win over rivals West Bromwich Albion.

Such was his impact that he was voted PFA Footballer of the Year and Young Player of the Year for 1976, having gained the first of his twenty full caps for Scotland the previous year. He was on the international scene for a decade and scored seven goals for his country.

Gray netted twenty goals in 1977/78 and eight the following season before leaving Villa Park for Wolverhampton Wanderers in September 1979, signed for a record fee of £1.4 million. The goals continued to flow at Molineux, one of them being the winner in the 1980 League Cup final against Nottingham Forest.

After moving to Everton, he helped the Goodison Park club win the League, FA Cup and European Cup-winner's Cup, scoring in the finals of the last two competitions. He then returned to Villa Park for a second spell in 1985, but the club was in decline. He added a few more goals to his overall tally (ending with 78 to his name in 210 appearances) before rounding off an eventful and enterprising career with Notts County (loan), West Bromwich Albion, Glasgow Rangers (with whom he won the Skol Cup) and Cheltenham Town. He also had another season with Villa, as assistant to manager Ron Atkinson in 1991/92, before leaving the game to pursue a television career, eventually working for Sky before his dismissal, along with Richard Key, in January 2011.

Born in Glasgow on 30 November 1955, Gray started his career with Clydebank Strollers before joining Dundee United in 1973. Over the next eighteen years or so, he scored over 200 goals in more than 600 club games.

GREAVES, JIMMY (CHELSEA AND TOTTENHAM HOTSPUR)

Chelsea
Season: 1958/59
Goals scored: 32 (out of 77); 22 home, 10 away
Percentage: 41.4 per cent
Finished joint top scorer with Bobby Smith (Tottenham Hotspur)
Chelsea finished fourteenth

Season: 1960/61
Goals scored: 41 (out of 98); 28 home, 13 away
Percentage: 41.8 per cent
Runners-up: David Herd (Arsenal) and Gerry Hitchens (Aston Villa), with 29 goals each
Chelsea finished twelfth

Tottenham Hotspur
Season: 1962/63
Goals scored: 37 (out of 111); 27 home, 10 away
Percentage: 33.3 per cent
Runners-up Joe Baker (Arsenal) and David Layne (Sheffield Wednesday), with 29 goals each
Tottenham finished second

Season: 1963/64
Goals scored: 35 (out of 97); 20 home, 15 away
Percentage: 36 per cent
Runners-up: Andy McEvoy (Blackburn Rovers) and Fred Pickering (Blackburn Rovers and Everton), with 32 goals each
Tottenham finished fourth

Season: 1964/65
Goals scored: 29 (out of 87); 20 home, 9 away
Percentage: 33 per cent
Joint top scorer with Andy McEvoy (Blackburn Rovers)
Tottenham finished sixth

Season: 1968/69
Goals scored: 27 (out of 61); 18 home, 9 away
Percentage: 44.1 per cent
Runner-up Geoff Hurst (West Ham United), 25 goals
Tottenham finished sixth

Without a shadow of doubt, Jimmy Greaves has been one of the greatest goalscorers in Football League history.

Quick over the ground and blessed with an incredibly cool assurance and superb balance, he had unnerving anticipation in and around opposing penalty areas when chances presented themselves and above all, he simply knew where and when to find the back of the net!

He would ghost past a defender, sometimes two, even three, as if they were not there and then smartly tuck away his shot ... brilliant.

Like so many of his generation, Greaves (JP to his pals) was born in the East End of London on 20 February 1940, at a time when Germans and the Allies were blinking at each other during the worst winter for 100 years.

He became an avid Spurs supporter, preferring to make the trek from the East End to White Hart Lane rather than walk to the nearer Upton Park at a time when West Ham were nothing more than Second Division nonentities.

In the late 1940s and early '50s, Spurs were exciting to watch, their push and run football bringing them successive Second and First Division championship victories.

In the autumn of 1954, Greaves almost joined the Tottenham ground staff but with the threat of relegation looming, manager Arthur Rowe had second thoughts about signing an 'untried' youngster.

Disappointed, Greaves was quickly taken under the wing of one Jimmy Thompson, a one-man Pied Piper who led so many East End boys to Chelsea, including Peter Brabrook, Barry Bridges and Terry Venables.

Greaves was a smash hit in the Chelsea youth side, bagging no less than 114 goals in the 1956/57 season.

On 24 August 1957, Greaves made his senior debut for the Blues and as was to be a pattern over the course of time, he did absolutely nothing at all apart from scoring in the 1-1 draw at, of all places, Tottenham!

For 89 minutes of a game, he seemed to idle around, chatting to anyone who cared to talk back, but his instincts were razor sharp and he rarely missed the target when a chance came along.

In his first season at Stamford Bridge – despite missing six matches up to Christmas Day 1957 – he returned in style, blitzing in a four-timer in a 7-4 home victory over Portsmouth. He scored twenty-two League goals that term, and in his second netted thirty-two to finish equal top dog with Bobby Smith in Division One while also setting a new Chelsea record, surpassing Bob Whittingham's tally of thirty goals in 1910/11. Two seasons later, he once again topped the League's scoring charts with a haul of twenty-nine.

He got off to a flier in 1958/59, notching eight goals in his first three matches, including a stunning five-timer in a 6-2 home win over the reigning League champions Wolves. In mid-September he netted twice in a thrilling 6-5 victory over Newcastle, and at the end of the month struck a hat-trick in a 4-1 defeat of Nottingham Forest. He was on fire and, as so often happens, all of a sudden the goals dried up!

However, you couldn't keep 'JP' quiet for long and he returned with a brace when Leeds lost 2-0 in early November, following up soon afterwards with a clinical finish to beat Birmingham City 1-0 at the Bridge.

After some mediocre performances by his standards, Greaves had a good January and February, salvaging a point against Portsmouth (2-2) and netting in a 3-2 home win over West Ham.

By this time Chelsea were edging well clear of relegation and Greaves, although not at his best, still popped in a few goals as the season wound down, his efforts at Leicester City and Nottingham Forest, and at home to Preston, Manchester City and Everton all securing victories. Unfortunately, his two FA Cup and three Inter Cities Fairs Cup goals (for London) were all in vain.

Still only nineteen when the 1959/60 season started, Greaves was now staking a claim for a regular place in the England team as well as being Chelsea's 'pride and joy', and what a start he made to the new campaign, cracking in a hat-trick in a thrilling 4-4 home draw with Preston. Later in the season, he scored all his side's goals at Deepdale – with a minimum of fuss – as Chelsea won 5-4.

His second treble of the campaign came in a 4-2 home win over Birmingham City in mid-September but between then and his goal feast at Preston, he wasn't quite himself, netting only three times in twelve League games as Chelsea plummeted to the bottom end of the table.

Another six-week barren spell followed after Christmas, but thankfully – for club and fans alike – his goal touch returned when it mattered most and braces helped see off Fulham (4-2) and Luton Town (3-0), and also earn a point against West Brom. Late on, he netted in a 3-0 home win over Manchester City, helped salvage a draw with Nottingham Forest and beat his former club Tottenham with the only goal of the game at White Hart Lane. In the end Greaves' goals certainly did the trick, as Chelsea escaped the drop by just three points!

During the 1960/61 season footballers were increasingly restive as the Players' Union, led by Fulham's Jimmy Hill, fought to improve their wages. There was talk of a strike, but this fizzled out when the Football League conceded that the players had a case. In the meantime, Greaves could not wait – he was transferred to AC Milan for £80,000 in June 1961, but only after scoring another forty-one League goals (a club record that brought his tally up to 132 in 169 appearances for the Blues), including hat-tricks against Wolverhampton Wanderers, Blackburn Rovers and Manchester City, as well as four-timers against Newcastle at St James' Park and at home to Nottingham Forest in his final game for the Pensioners. On 3 December 1960, he also scored five times as West Brom was thrashed 7-1 at Stamford Bridge.

Greaves was never a happy chappie in Italy. The system used by his club was far too regimented. Sex was banned for three days before a match, as was alcohol. He could not bear this sort of restrictiveness and made it clear he didn't like Italian food either. In short, he was a typical British holidaymaker!

It soon became evident that Milan hierarchy was not pleased with Greaves' attitude, or indeed his performances, especially after he had hinted he wanted to return to England. Tottenham were first to make a bid, which Chelsea countered. Spurs then increased their offer, Chelsea dropped out, and in December 1961, Greaves was signed for a fee of £99,999, manager Bill Nicholson refusing to make him a £100,000 footballer. He had scored just nine times in Serie A.

Greaves' first appearance for Spurs was in a reserve game at Plymouth, but on the day of his senior debut shortly afterwards, against Blackpool at home, he scored a hat-trick (Les Allen grabbed the other two goals) in a 5-2 thrashing of the Seasiders and no-one who was present will ever forget the spectacular bicycle kick which brought him his third goal. Quite an effort, this – just ask the Blackpool goalkeeper Tony Waiters.

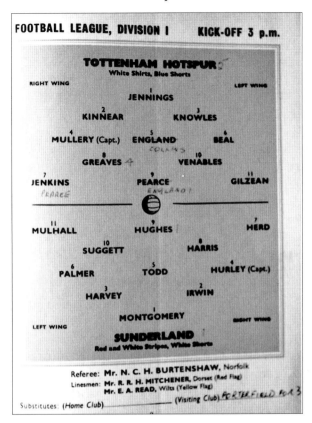

Before Greaves made his debut, Spurs' attack had been somewhat lack-lustre with Bobby Smith injured and Allen suffering a lack of confidence. Greaves came in and made one hell of a difference. He went on to score twenty-one goals in twenty-two League appearances that season, becoming a huge favourite with the fans. In fact, he almost single-handedly brought the championship back to White Hart Lane, but Spurs failed to beat Ipswich in the run-in. He did, however, gain a medal by netting a vital goal in a 3-1 FA Cup final victory over Burnley.

In his first full season for Spurs, Greaves broke the club record for scoring most League goals (thirty-seven) in one single campaign, Ted Harper (1930/31) and Bobby Smith (1957/58) having been the joint holders with thirty-six. He also topped the First Division scoring charts for the third time in five years ... and this was despite the winter being the second worst since the Second World War. Football was hard hit. Very few games were played from Boxing Day until the beginning of March, so it was amazing that Greaves was able to create this amazing record.

Six goals in the opening five matches, including a stunner in a 6-1 win over West Ham and two beauties in a 4-2 home victory over Aston Villa, set the pattern. He bagged a couple more in a tight game at Wolves (2-2) before having his best game for quite some time, certainly his best for Spurs (at that time), when Nottingham Forest was comprehensively battered 9-2 at the end of September.

He was outstanding and scored four times that afternoon. He equalised Trevor Hockey's early goal in the sixth minute from Medwin's cross and then put his side in front five minutes later from another pinpoint Medwin pass. Goals by Cliff Jones and Medwin himself then made it 5-1 before Greaves completed his hat-trick with a sixth strike on the half-hour mark.

At this juncture, many records looked endangered. But, as so often happens, Spurs felt they had done enough, eased up and managed only three more goals (to Forest's two) in the next hour, from a Les Allen penalty (51 minutes), a Jones ground shot (53) and Greaves' fourth (on 72) from Dave Mackay's measured pass. Towards the end Greaves had two more goal-bound shots well saved by Peter Grummitt, but who cared really ... this was a great win and another great day out for hot-shot Greaves.

Hat-trick number two for Greaves followed in a superb 6-2 home win over Manchester United in late October and after narrowly failing to make it three trebles with a brace and two near misses against Leicester City (won 4-0), he whipped in three snorters to see off League champions Ipswich Town 5-0 at White Hart Lane, later adding another two more to his tally (one a rare penalty) when Spurs beat the 'Tractor boys' 4-2 in the return fixture at Portman Road.

In between times, Greaves struck twice to beat Blackpool 2-0 and towards the end of the season, he did something special, a feat very few footballers over the years have achieved. He scored four goals in a game against Liverpool. It happened at White Hart Lane in mid-April, when everything he touched turned to gold as the Merseysiders were humiliated to the tune of 7-2 ... this being sweet revenge for Spurs, who had been whipped 5-2 at Anfield three days earlier.

Greaves eventually set the new – and still existing – record when he fired home in a 4-2 win over Sheffield United on 4 May 1963. Surprisingly, he then failed to score in the remaining three games, when only one point was gained. Four would have given Spurs the championship.

Spurs made history on another front in 1962/63 when they won the European Cup-winner's Cup, thrashing Atletico Madrid 5-1 in the final. The star of the night was not Greaves, who scored twice, but darting midget left-winger Terry Dyson, who ran the Spanish defence ragged.

In 1963/64, Greaves notched another thirty-five goals in forty-one League matches to once again finish as the First Division's leading marksman. He claimed four well-taken hat-tricks in resounding wins over the club he loved playing against, Nottingham Forest (4-1), Blackpool (6-1), Birmingham City (6-1) and Blackburn Rovers (4-1). He also struck twice (once from the spot) in a 4-2 win at Wolves, did likewise in the 4-2 victory at Villa Park, played his part with a splendid goal in a thrill-a-minute 4-4 draw with Arsenal at Highbury in front of a near 68,000 crowd, beat Fulham on his own (1-0), did the same thing against Stoke City (netting twice to seal a 2-1 win), tucked away the winner against Nottingham Forest (2-1) and denied West Brom victory with two fine individual efforts in a 4-4 draw at The Hawthorns.

During the second half of the season, his goals earned full points off Blackpool (2-0), Aston Villa (3-1), Arsenal (3-1), Birmingham City (2-1) and Bolton (1-0), his penalties in the games against the Gunners and Blues being so vital. He also played his heart out, scoring, but to no avail in a devastating 7-2 defeat at Burnley.

Cliff Jones (fourteen goals) and Bobby Smith (thirteen) followed Greaves home in the scoring charts that season.

And it was Jones (thirteen), Alan Gilzean (eleven) and Frank Saul (eleven) who assisted Greaves (twenty-nine) in 1964/65 when, for the second season running, he was the top striker, this time jointly with the Blackburn striker Andy McEvoy, in the First Division.

Perhaps not as strong as they had been in the previous three seasons, Spurs were perhaps relying too much on Greaves' goals ... but he did the business and the fans loved him!

Once again keeping himself free from injury – surprising, this, for a striker – this was the third season running Greaves had missed only one League game. He scored in three of the first five games, missed the sixth and then netted twice at West Ham (lost 3-2) and in home wins over Stoke City (2-1) and West Brom (1-0). Further strikes followed in home wins over Fulham (3-0), Arsenal (3-1), Sunderland 3-0, Aston Villa (4-0) and Sheffield Wednesday (3-2), in successive victories over Nottingham Forest (2-1 away and 4-0 at home) and draws at Liverpool (1-1) and Sheffield United (3-3) and at home to Everton (2-2). Into the New Year, his double helped see off the FA Cup holders West Ham (3-2), and in mid-March he netted a spanker in a 4-1 win over Blackpool before netting twice in a 5-2 roasting of Blackburn and doing likewise in a last-match 6-2 tonking of Leicester City. All good stuff as far as Greaves was concerned, but his efforts were in vain as Spurs floundered to finish sixth in the Division, their lowest placing since 1958/59.

The goals were hard to come by for Greaves in 1965/66, with only fifteen scored. He was also part of England's World Cup-winning squad, but sustained a minor injury, which let in Geoff Hurst at the quarter-final stage. The rest is history.

Greaves, in fact, had been taken ill with hepatitis B after scoring twice in a 2-1 League win over West Bromwich Albion on 30 October and did not reappear in the Spurs side until the end of January, when he converted a penalty in a 4-0 win over Blackburn Rovers.

The oddest game during the 1965/66 season was the 5-5 draw with Aston Villa. It wasn't funny at the time, however! When the second half started, Spurs held a 5-1 lead and were cruising to victory. With 10 minutes of the game remaining, Tony Hateley equalised to make it 5-5, and in the dying seconds Villa missed an open goal!

Greaves weighed in with another twenty-five League goals in 1966/67 as Spurs finished third in the League, behind Manchester United and Nottingham Forest. He also netted six goals in the FA Cup, which Spurs won by beating Greaves' former club, Chelsea in the final.

In 1967/68, Greaves scored only twenty-three League goals! He followed up, however, with a haul of twenty-seven in 1968/69 to become the First Division's top man for the sixth time – a feat never achieved before or since.

This was to be Greaves' last full season at White Hart Lane, and in the game against Leicester City in October he scored the 'best goal' of his entire career. Unfortunately there were no TV cameras to capture the moment, but those who saw it will surely agree that it was something special. 'Keeper Pat Jennings booted the ball out to the wing, where Greaves had wandered. He killed the ball dead, spun round and was away before his marker had realised where he'd gone. He glided past four defenders, even rounded the referee, drew Peter Shilton and stroked the ball into the net. Sheer perfection. He netted twice more against the Foxes in a 3-1 win.

Prior to that 'special occasion', he had already knocked in nine goals in eleven games, including a hat-trick in a 7-0 drubbing of Burnley at White Hart Lane. Soon after his exploits against Leicester, he swept home two grand efforts to beat Liverpool 2-1 in London and earned a point against Stoke City (1-1) before going goal-crazy again, this time with a four-timer in a brilliant 5-1 home victory over Sunderland on a freezing cold day in mid-November. He netted at Southampton in his next game (1-2), but after this the 'goal king' couldn't do a thing right! He was absent from the scoresheet in each of the next seven League games (only one of which ended in a victory) before obliging in a 1-1 draw with QPR. Still, the goals were at a premium – only one scored, a penalty against Ipswich Town, in his next eight outings, but he ended on a high, scoring in four consecutive matches during April, including two in a 4-3 triumph at West Brom and the winner in the London derby against West Ham (1-0).

His four FA Cup and five League Cup goals proved worthless, with defeat in the semi-final of the latter competition being something Greaves found hard to forget. In an earlier round, he had netted his first-ever League Cup hat-trick, against Exeter City (won 6-3).

After Greaves had netted eight League goals in twenty-nine games during the first two-thirds of 1969/70, Spurs' manager Bill Nicholson stunned the fans by using his champion and record goalscorer as a makeweight in a £200,000 player-exchange deal that brought Martin Peters to White Hart Lane from West Ham. Greaves had notched an amazing total of 306 goals in 440 first-team games for Spurs, including 220 in 322 League outings and 46 in 59 Cup matches.

He spent just one season with the Hammers (thirteen goals) before winding down his career with Barnet, Chelmsford City, Brentwood Town and Woodford Town, finally calling it a day in 1976. During a wonderful career, Greaves scored no less than 554 goals in 750 games for clubs and country. He netted forty-four times in fifty-seven full internationals for England (1959–67), struck thirteen in twelve U23 matches, three more for an England XI, five in ten Inter-league games, one for the Rest of The World and six in two youth internationals.

He went on to become a popular pundit, hosting the ITV Saturday lunchtime soccer programme (*Saint and Greavsie*) with ex-Liverpool star Ian St John. He also wrote a column in a national newspaper, travelled round the South-East on the after-dinner speaking circuit, appeared in the theatre and co-wrote (with the help of some expert journalists) some excellent books.

The England football team. Jimmy Greaves is second from the left in the front row. Next to him, in the middle of the front row, is Bobby Smith.

HALLIDAY, DAVID (SUNDERLAND)

Season: 1928/29
Goals scored: 43 (out of 93); 30 home, 13 away
Percentage: 46 per cent
Runner-up: Tommy Johnson (Manchester City), 38 goals
Sunderland finished fourth

David Halliday is the only player to have notched thirty top-flight goals in four consecutive seasons and his record of forty-three in 1928/29 not only earned him top-spot in the scorer's charts that season, but also makes him Sunderland's highest scorer in a single season.

The Scotsman's career straddled the change in the offside law, when, alarmed by the shortage of goals, officials changed the rules in 1925 so that a forward could only be offside if there were fewer than two, rather than three, defenders between him and the goal.

Even before the change, Halliday was already a prolific striker and had finished top scorer in the Scottish League with Dundee in 1923/24, hitting thirty-eight goals in thirty-six appearances. With such a pedigree, it was no surprise when he was lured south to Sunderland in April 1925.

The Wearsiders were looking to rebuild their side after a disappointing seventh place and Halliday's arrival marked the end of Charlie Buchan's time at Roker Park, the league's highest scorer just two seasons before moving on to play with (further) distinction at Highbury.

Halliday's role was a 'simple one' – get the ball into the goal. At 6 feet tall and 12 stone and 4 pounds in weight, he was powerful enough to give any opposing centre-half a hard time, especially as he was lightning quick and fearless in front of goal. He started with a bang, hitting ten goals in his first four games, and although he could never have hoped to keep up such a record, he had hit 106 for Sunderland in the League when the 1928/29 season got under way, with the Wearsiders one of the title favourites under manager Johnny Cochrane.

Halliday scored on the opening day, but Sunderland lost 3-1 at Burnley. Back at Roker Park he was, for once, missing his shooting boots when Blackburn came to town. Determined to put right his mistakes, Halliday then hit a hat-trick in the home game with Derby that followed.

Two more followed when Bolton travelled north, the centre-forward profiting from some lovely moves down the home right involving Bob Wallace and Johnny Lynas. After eight games he'd hit home seven goals. Sunderland, though, were struggling down near the bottom and in attempt to freshen up the side, inside right Bobby McKay was signed from neighbours Newcastle United.

The Scotsman was a bundle of tricks and a sublime passer of the ball, and was to scheme a host of goals for Halliday as the season progressed. Both men were on the scoresheet in a 5-3 defeat at Maine Road, and a few short weeks later each hit a double in a 5-2 Roker Park demolition of Newcastle, McKay playing particularly brilliantly.

Bury's defence was never going to be strong enough when Sunderland visited Gigg Lane in November, McKay and his fellow inside forward Tom McInally threading the ball between the two full-backs during a period in the game of football when three defenders in a centre-half and two full-backs was the norm. Halliday hit two and soon after, when Bury's near neighbours Manchester United journeyed to Roker Park, his rich vein of goal-scoring continued with a hat-trick in a 5-1 victory, Alf Steward twice being beaten with thundering drives. It wasn't long before a third hat-trick of the season followed, although it still didn't stop Sheffield United taking a point in a 4-4 draw.

Sunderland's David Halliday puts Newcastle 'keeper Willie Nelson under pressure on 27 October 1928 in a game in which he scored two of his forty-three League goals in 1928/29.

Arsenal were building a team that would go on to dominate English football in the 1930s, but Halliday showed they still had much to learn by scoring three times over Christmas and the New Year as Sunderland earned a draw at Highbury before hammering the Gunners 5-1 at Roker Park on New Year's Day.

When Sheffield Wednesday travelled to Roker Park, fans got the chance to compare Halliday with Jack Allen, who was competing with him for the honour of finishing as the league's top scorer come the season's end. Allen did grab a 30th-minute goal, but by then Halliday had hit two. Both came in the first 6 minutes, with a neat finish from 8 yards and a cracking 20-yard drive soon after. It might have been four, but Wednesday 'keeper Jack Brown twice reacted brilliantly during intense second-half pressure from the home side in a 4-2 win that put them in touch near the top with their defeated opponents.

Halliday's goals were putting the Wearsiders in with a chance of a first title success in sixteen seasons, especially as the following weekend, he again hit two in a 5-0 defeat of Portsmouth. Winning away from home, though, had proved difficult and so when a falling backwards Halliday headed Adam McLean's cross into the net at Leeds Road, it was a big boost as Sunderland then withstood strong pressure to win 2-1.

It meant that thousands of the side's followers travelled expectantly to St James' Park for the local derby, and although their side played well, they returned disappointed after witnessing a 4-3 defeat in a match that revealed the genius of Hughie Gallacher, who, with 3 minutes left, superbly headed a Tommy Lang cross home. Gallacher had been a major part of the previous season's Scottish side that had wiped the floor with England by winning 5-1 at Wembley, and it was his brilliance that meant Halliday never even played once for his country.

Newcastle's last-gasp winner seemed to take the wind out of Sunderland's sails in the title run-in and when only five points followed in seven matches, it meant only 10,000 were at Roker Park for the final home game of the season. That was shame, because they missed Halliday finish off with a flourish against West Ham HU, scoring another hat-trick described as follows in the *Newcastle Daily Chronicle*:

> Halliday scored a hat trick with his first goal coming after a fierce bombardment, the second when he cleverly took a pass from McInally and the third after the interval was the best of the lot. He started a dribble over 40 yards out and finally drew Ted Hufton from goal to shoot into the empty net.

The Sunderland man had blasted forty-three goals to finish at the top of the scorers' charts. Despite this success, the Scotsman had departed to Arsenal before 1929 had ended. Robert Gurney was ten years younger and his time had arrived. The local lad was, in fact, to enjoy a magnificent career at Sunderland and remains the Wearsiders' record goalscorer with 228 goals from 388 appearances. His strike rate, however, never matched that of Halliday, who scored 162 in 175 appearances.

Halliday stayed a year at Highbury before moving on to Manchester City, with later spells at Folkestone, Clapton Orient and as player-manager with Yeovil and Petters United. As a manager he was highly successful, leading Aberdeen to Championship and Cup success and Leicester City to the Second Division title. He died in January 1970.

HAMPTON, HARRY (ASTON VILLA)

Season: 1911/12
Goals scored: 25 (out of 76); 13 home, 12 away
Percentage: 32.9 per cent
Joint top scorer with Tom Holley (Sunderland) and David McLean (Sheffield Wednesday)
Villa finished sixth

Born in Shropshire on 21 April 1885, 'Appy' Harry Hampton, also known as the 'Wellington Whirlwind' because of the way he used to swing his arms around when running, was a real terror to opposing goalkeepers and defenders alike.

During the decade leading up the outbreak of the First World War, he was one of the finest centre-forwards in the game. Afraid of no one, his devil-may-care, strong, forceful, determined style was admired and appreciated by plenty, and he was one of the few players who bundled the hefty frame of Sheffield United's 22-stone goalkeeper Willie 'Fatty' Foulke over the line!

Since the day he first set foot inside Villa Park, Hampton scored goals, plenty of them. He went on to bang in no less than 242 (with a club record 215 coming in the First Division) in 376 appearances for the club between 1904 and 1920. He helped win the FA Cup twice, scoring both goals in the 1905 final victory over Newcastle United and then, in the 1913 victory over Sunderland, he dropped back to centre-half for a spell when Jimmy Harrop had to take over in goal following an injury to Sam Hardy.

In 1910, his efforts up front went a long way in Villa's race towards winning the League championship.

Hampton scored over 140 in his first seven seasons at Villa Park and then, in 1911/12, he netted a total of twenty-eight goals, topping the First Division scoring charts jointly with Tom Holley and David McLean.

He started the campaign off with his side's only goal in a 2-1 defeat at Bradford City, but was bottled up by the West Bromwich Albion centre-half Jack Manners in the second game (a 3-0 home defeat) before striking twice in a superb 4-1 victory over Woolwich Arsenal at Villa Park, one of his goals almost ripping a hole in the netting.

A week later he scored one and set up three more, two for Joe Bache, who fired a hat-trick in a thumping 6-2 win at Manchester City, before adding to his own tally in a 3-0 triumph over Everton and knocking one in at The Hawthorns when Albion were held to a 2-2 draw.

Injury forced him to miss two of the next six games; he was goalless in the four he did play in, but got back on track with two decisive finishes in a 2-2 home draw with Tottenham in mid-November.

'Appy Harry' admitted he was not 100 per cent fit, though, and looked well off the pace when failing to score in five of the next six games. However, he must have had a good Christmas dinner, returning to his brilliant best on Boxing Day with a four-timer in a tremendous 6-1 home win over Oldham Athletic, two of his goals being powerful headers from swinging crosses by Charlie Wallace.

Hampton netted only one League goal in January and failed to score at all in February, although he did manage three in the FA Cup (two coming in a 6-0 win over Walsall) before grabbing his second four-timer of the season in a 5-2 win over Bury in early March, when once again he benefited from some wonderful wing play by the impressive Wallace.

A week later, he netted twice in a 5-1 win over Notts County and then found the net in five of the last six games, including a real beauty in the 6-0 demolition of the reigning League champions Manchester United.

Ten of Hampton's twenty-five League goals came from headers and there is no doubt that he relied on high crosses driven over from deep by Villa's two exciting wingers – Wallace on the right, who scored six out of nine penalties, four of them awarded for fouls on Hampton, and Horace Henshall on the left.

Besides his club football, Hampton played four times for England, scoring on his international debut against Wales in March 1913 (won 4-3). Then, in his second game, against Scotland at Stamford Bridge a month later, he shoulder-charged the Scots' goalkeeper Jim Brownlie 'over the line' for the winning goal. The Scots weren't too pleased with the referee's decision to allow the goal, claiming a foul on the 'keeper, who was adamant that the ball had not crossed the line, and nor had he.

His other two England outings were against Wales and Scotland the following season. Hampton also represented the Football League three times, played for Birmingham against London on three occasions and starred in an international trial in 1913.

During the First World War, he also guested for Birmingham, Blackpool, Derby County, Fulham, Nottingham Forest, Reading and Stoke.

After leaving Villa Park, Hampton's sixteen goals helped second city rivals Birmingham win the Division Two title in 1921 before he went on to assist Newport County (season 1922/23) and his hometown club, Wellington Town. Retiring in 1925, he was appointed first team coach at Preston North End in season 1925/26, and after a break from the game he became trainer-coach of the colts' team at his former club, Birmingham (1934/37).

Later proprietor of the Carlton Café in Queen Street, Rhyl, Aston Villa legend Hampton was almost seventy-eight years of age when he died in Wrexham on 15 March 1963.

HARPER, TED (BLACKBURN ROVERS)

Season: 1925/26
Goals scored: 43 (out of 91); 26 home, 17 away
Percentage: 47 per cent
Runner-up: David Halliday (Sunderland), 36 goals
Blackburn Rovers finished twelfth

Born in Sheerness, Kent on 22 August 1901, Ted Harper arrived at Ewood Park in 1923 from Sheppey United on the strength of his goalscoring record in the Kent League. Critics said he looked clumsy and had no ball control, but as a goalscorer there were few better. He was quickly off the mark with eighteen goals in his first season.

In February 1925, Rovers signed Syd Puddefoot from Falkirk for £4,000. Despite being aged thirty, the ex-West Ham United favourite was a gifted playmaker whose vision and passing ability would – particularly in light of the new rules that reduced the offside trap from three to two players – carve out the sort of chances Harper could happily put away. The result was that in their first full season, Harper was to become the first player to crash through the barrier of forty goals in a League season. It remains a record no one at Ewood Park has seriously threatened since.

Harper's season hardly started with a bang, but after failing to be selected for the first three games of it – all of which Rovers lost, including a 6-2 thrashing at Roker Park – he scored a stunning five goals in his first match, aiding his side to a 7-1 win at Newcastle United. The home side had beaten Notts County heavily in the previous game and were in a confident mood before kick-off.

Few could have predicted how wonderfully the away side would play as a team, yet by half time they were already three goals up. Long before the end Harper joined the select band of players who have scored five goals in a top-flight match. He did it by staying well up the field, constantly seeking to break through Newcastle's continued use of the offside trap that a few short years earlier had been the best in the business, but was now unable to come to terms with the law changes. With Puddefoot inside him and wingers Joe Hulme and Arthur Rigby outside, Harper was presented with numerous chances and did his best to grab as many goals as possible. In the event, five wasn't too bad.

Back at Ewood, Harper then scored his first of the season there with a penalty against WBA. Two days later, at Bramall Lane, the Kent lad got his seventh of the season in a 1-1 draw.

There was a large crowd inside Ewood for the return fixture with Sunderland. They witnessed some of the qualities that had brought Rovers success at Newcastle. Puddefoot, given a roving commission, pulled the Wearsiders' defence apart and after Rigby opened the scoring, Harper added two more in the second period in a 3-0 success. Harper's nine League goals in just four matches rose to twelve in five in the next game as Cardiff were beaten 6-3 at Ewood Park.

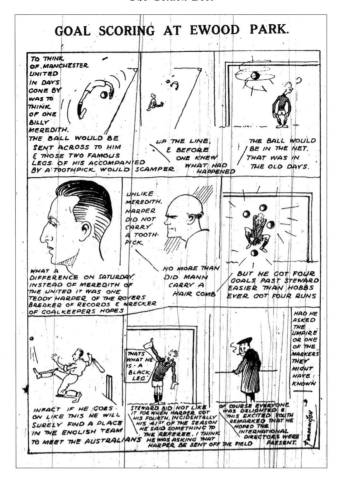

Two more in his next two games meant it was fourteen in seven. Newcastle arrived much better prepared than in the first game and shocked the home support by winning 2-1, and also stopped Harper scoring for the first time in the season. Bolton repeated the feat at Burnden Park, but Notts County were unable to and his two goals, one a penalty, took Harper's record up to sixteen in ten starts.

This rose to nineteen in eleven and as the hat-trick was at Turf Moor, there was extra joy for the Rovers fans that were able to make the short journey to Burnley. With the game tied on 60 minutes at 0-0, Harper pounced when Harold Hill and Jerry Dawson dallied over who should clear the ball. It was a typical opportunist goal, one of many the Rovers man happily picked up during his time with the club, and on 80 minutes he was again in just the right place to accept Puddefoot's pass and make it 2-0. Just before the end, he again scored to ensure his side won 3-1. A penalty at home to Leeds the following weekend made it twenty in twelve games.

At home to Everton on Christmas Day, Harper got another couple. The first, reported the *Liverpool Echo*, was 'a brilliant equaliser, Harper, after a run of many yards (in which he thrice mastered efforts by McDonald to stop him) leaving Hardy helpless with a fine shot.' It was now twenty-five in nineteen games. Three more followed in his next four matches before a temporary blip in form saw him score just twice in Rovers' next five games.

Nevertheless, with seven from the next eight games it meant that prior to kick-off against Manchester United on 10 April, he had notched thirty-seven League goals and needed just two to overtake Everton's Bert Freeman and Bolton's Joe Smith, whose thirty-eight in 1908/09 and 1920/21 respectively remained a League record. Furthermore, a hat-trick and Harper would also overtake David Brown as the top scorer in any league, the Darlington man having scored thirty-nine in the previous season's Division Three North.

Despite his successes in front of goal, the Rovers man was not even assured of finishing as Division One top scorer. Sunderland's David Halliday had already scored thirty-eight and with Harper certain to miss Rovers' penultimate game of the season to represent his country in his debut match against Scotland, he really needed to find the net.

He certainly did so, hammering home four goals in a 7-0 win. Each of his goals was greeted with special cheers, especially the second, which took him on to thirty-nine for the season.

The first was another piece of opportunism and cheeky skill, pouncing on the ball after Alf Steward had saved to drill it just inside the post as he fell backwards. Then, after beating Charlie Moore for pace, he cleverly placed the ball beyond the 'keeper. His third was similar, a brilliant run and a powerful shot, and when he touched home his fourth the crowd roared its approval. Coming off, he then learned that Halliday had failed to score against Arsenal, leaving him three ahead of the Sunderland man.

It was the perfect boost prior to his first international, but with Puddefoot alongside him it was to prove a disappointing afternoon as Scotland won 1-0 at Old Trafford. Never selected again for his country, it meant Harper never played at Wembley because when Rovers got to the FA Cup final in 1928, he had already left the previous year to join Sheffield Wednesday.

Back home for the final League game of the season, Harper struck a further two goals against Aston Villa to take his season's record to a remarkable forty-three goals in thirty-seven games.

At Sheffield Wednesday Harper scored thirteen goals in eighteen games and helped the Owls, with five goals in six games, capture the First Division title in 1928/29. He moved to Spurs in 1929 and scored sixty-two goals in sixty-three League games before returning to Lancashire with Preston in 1931. He saw out his career back with the Rovers in November 1933, before joining the club's backroom staff until 1948. He broke individual goalscoring records at Blackburn, Tottenham and Preston during his career. His Rovers record reads 177 League and FA Cup Apps, 122 goals. Ted died in Blackburn on 22 July 1959.

HASSELBAINK, JIMMY FLOYD (LEEDS UNITED AND CHELSEA)

Season: 1998/99
Goals scored: 18 (out of 62); 8 home, 10 away
Percentage: 29 per cent
Joint top scorer with Dwight Yorke (Manchester United) and Michael Owen (Liverpool)
Leeds United finished fourth

Season: 2000/01
Goals scored: 23 (out of 68); 15 at home, 8 away
Percentage: 34 per cent
Runner-up: Marcus Stewart (Ipswich Town), 19 goals
Chelsea finished in sixth place

Jimmy Floyd Hasselbaink burst onto the English football scene at the start of the 1997/98 season by scoring on his Leeds United debut against Arsenal. George Graham had signed the twenty-five-year-old Dutchman in the summer from Portuguese side Boavista for a £200,000 fee. It was to prove money well spent, as Hasselbaink was to score freely over the next two seasons before acrimoniously departing to Atletico Madrid for sixty times as much at £12 million.

Following his initial opening Hasselbaink struggled, and not until the beginning of November did he begin to rival Rod Wallace as Leeds dangerman. He'd been sent off in a League Cup match at Bristol City and his side were 3-2 down at half time against Derby County at home. Introduced at the interval, Hasselbaink rifled home the equaliser on 51 minutes and then set up the winner for fellow substitute Lee Bowyer in the 89th minute to give Leeds a remarkable win, considering they had been trailing 2-0 at one point.

Two more goals followed in the next home game, as Leeds again came from a goal down on 65 minutes to beat West Ham 3-1 and begin a charge up the table.

On 8 April, Hasselbaink hit his eighteenth and nineteenth goals of the season as Chelsea were beaten 3-1 at Elland Road, his first on just 7 minutes seeing him drift away from two defenders before letting fly with a right-foot rocket which beat 'keeper Dmitri Kharine off the inside of his left-hand post.

He then scored an 86th-minute winner at Bolton and added two more in a 3-3 draw with Coventry as Leeds confirmed a place in the following season's UEFA Cup. Hasselbaink had done his bit by hitting sixteen Premier League goals.

George Graham's appointment as Leeds manager had been controversial, as the ex-Arsenal manager had previously received a one-year ban for pocketing illegal payments from an agent and so when he walked out to join Spurs within weeks of the new season starting, the whole football world was left stunned. Assistant manager David O'Leary was asked to take a step up, with Leeds legend Eddie Gray helping him out.

Hasselbaink had opened his and Leeds' account for the season with the only goal at home to Blackburn Rovers. With turmoil off the pitch, both struggled, and it wasn't until his fifth game in charge that O'Leary saw his side take all three points, when with Hasselbaink equalising Andy Booth's early goal for Sheffield Wednesday, there was relief all round when eighteen-year-old Jonathon Woodgate headed the winner.

With confidence now flowing through the side, Leeds crossed the Pennines to beat Liverpool at Anfield, where after Robbie Fowler opened the scoring on 68 minutes, the Yorkshire side rolled up their sleeves and hit three. Hasselbaink grabbed the final two, lashing home from 15 yards for his first, and then on 86 minutes scoring a goal that combined power, pace and precision. Surging from the halfway line, he gave 'keeper David James no chance.

The Dutchman also scored a fine opening goal a few short weeks later at Old Trafford, cutting inside from the left wing to beat Phil Neville before curling a shot off the inside of the post and into the net. A depleted Leeds fell 3-2, however. When Hasselbaink then scored in a 4-0 win at home to WHU, it was his sixth in five games as Leeds moved towards the Premiership's leading pack.

It was a race Leeds couldn't maintain over the Christmas and New Year period. Hasselbaink had only scored one goal in eight games prior to kick-off at Villa Park in mid-February. He was still in confident mood, though, and had predicted he would end his barren run in the lead-up to the game. And he certainly did by scoring twice, his second a stunning curling free kick that gave Michael Oakes no chance to save it. It was just what his side needed and the 2-1 victory was the first of six consecutive wins that again pushed Leeds into a UEFA Cup spot.

So it was a raucous atmosphere when Manchester United, competing with Arsenal for the title, came to Elland Road on 25 April. The game was to finish 1-1, but not before Hasselbaink again showed a scorer's touch. Receiving a lovely through-ball from Harry Kewell, he showed just enough of the ball to Peter Schmeichel for the great Dane to think he could grab it, only for the Dutchman to whisk it away from the 'keeper and plonk it firmly in the net.

The following weekend he again scored, lashing home from 20 yards in the first minute of a 5-1 hammering of West Ham at Upton Park. He also scored the winner in Leeds' final home game of the season. Not that many home fans were that pleased, knowing that whatever the result, their favourites would finish in fourth place in the table. By beating Arsenal 1-0, their side had opened the door for hated rivals Manchester United to steal the title. Four minutes from time, Hasselbaink was on the end of a lovely Kewell cross.

Leeds, after a poor start to the season, had done remarkably well. Most of their side were aged twenty-one or under; greater glories clearly beckoned, especially if their number 9, by now adored by the Leeds fans, could be persuaded to stay on. Determined to cash in on his fame, Hasselbaink was after a substantial pay rise and when Leeds refused to make him the highest-paid player in the UK at £60,000 a week, he demanded a transfer. Atletico Madrid was happy to pay £12 million for his services and accommodate his wage request and Hasselbaink went off to Spain to try his luck.

Hasselbaink arrived at Chelsea after just a season at Atletico Madrid, where despite scoring twenty-four goals in thirty-four appearances, his side was relegated. Unwilling to play Spanish Second Division football, he moved to Stamford Bridge for a fee of £15 million.

Manager Gianluca Vialli was looking to strengthen in attack. The new man, making his debut alongside fellow new boy Mario Stanic – signed for £5.6 million – was quickly into his stride at the start of the 2000/01 season, scoring Chelsea's opening goal at Wembley as Manchester United were beaten 2-0 in the Charity Shield.

Both men then scored on their League debuts as West Ham United were beaten 4-2 on the opening day of the Premier League season. Hasselbaink's third goal of the season also came against another London team, a sweet shot that put his side ahead against Arsenal on 35 minutes in a match that finished 2-2.

Chelsea had started the season slowly and disaffected directors wanted a change. Out went Vialli and in came Claudio Ranieri, Hasselbaink's coach at Madrid. At Old Trafford the Chelsea centre-forward scored one of his finest goals for the Pensioners, chesting down the ball and letting fly with a thunderous volley that 'keeper van der Gouw admired as it whistled into the net. It was Tore Andre Flo, shortly to move to Rangers after Ranieri decided to partner summer signing Eidur Gudjohnsen with Hasselbaink, though, who rescued Chelsea by scoring two late goals in a 3-3 draw. It was the new pairing, however, with a goal apiece, who did the damage as Chelsea then hammered Gerald Houllier's Liverpool 3-0.

Coventry City was thrashed 6-1 at Stamford Bridge. Hasselbaink had gone down dramatically as he raced through on goal and when referee Stephen Lodge pointed to the spot, it was almost inevitable that Chris Kirkland, in only his second game, would see red. Hasselbaink showed little sympathy as he struck home the penalty before going on to score three more times as his speed and skill tore the away defence to shreds. It wasn't all glory, though, as in a fiery match at Goodison Park, a late elbow on Michael Ball saw the Chelsea man sent off. Chelsea lost, and for Hasselbaink a three-game ban followed. Chelsea was continuing to be unbeatable at home and when they beat Ipswich Town 4-1 in January, the returning Hasselbaink scored the fourth.

Finally, on 7 March Chelsea won their first Premier League away game of the season. It came at Upton Park, courtesy of two finely worked and finished goals from Gudjohnsen and Hasselbaink. It was three precious points in the challenge for a spot in the top six, but rivals Sunderland then threw a spanner in the works by ruining Ranieri's unbeaten home record with a 4-2 win at Stamford Bridge. There was therefore relief when Chelsea produced a marvellous performance in a 4-0 defeat of Derby at Pride Park, the away side scoring all their goals in the final quarter of the match, with Hasselbaink's single effort being upstaged by a double from Gus Poyet.

Spurs had not beaten Chelsea at home since 1987 and when Hasselbaink gave the away side the lead with a header on 29 minutes, there was only going to be one winner, Chelsea cruising to a 3-0 victory.

On 8 May, Chelsea travelled to Anfield knowing that a draw would deny Liverpool, who were facing two – the FA and UEFA – Cup finals in the coming weeks, a chance to finish in the all-important second spot that guaranteed Champions' League football the following season. Michael Owen was to grab two for the home side, but Hasselbaink was to outshine him with two spectacular efforts of his own.

With Chelsea a goal down, Hasselbaink drove forward from midfield and with the home defence backing off, he lashed a fierce, low drive from 30 yards that Sander Westerveld got his hands to but couldn't prevent entering the net.

Then, in the second half, after Owen had restored Liverpool's lead, Hasselbaink got in behind Stephane Henchoz to bury an angled drive into the far bottom corner. It was his twenty-second Premier League goal of the season and he added to his total with a fine winning effort at Maine Road. Chelsea needed only a point to confirm sixth place and a place in the UEFA Cup the following season. Drawing 1-1, they appeared happy enough to see out the season, but on 62 minutes Zola found Hasselbaink and the Dutch international drove home from just outside the area. After finishing as joint-top scorer two seasons earlier in the Premier League, Jimmy Floyd Hasselbaink had now gone one better by finishing above everyone else at the end of the 2000/01 season.

Hasselbaink was to play another three seasons at Chelsea, collecting an FA Cup runners-up medal in 2002 before moving to Middlesbrough. He left behind him an impressive strike rate, with 69 League goals in just 119 starts and 17 substitute appearances.

He continued to score regularly. He was a member of the Middlesbrough side that reached the UEFA Cup final in 2006, although Sevilla were much too strong and the North-East side lost 4-0. After scoring thirty-four goals he moved to Charlton Athletic, but scored just four goals and after further failure at Cardiff City, he retired at the end of the 2007/08 season.

Despite his goalscoring successes, Surinam-born Hasselbaink was never first choice for his adopted country, Holland. Competition was always fierce, with Denis Bergkamp, Patrick Kluivert and Ruud Van Nistelrooy among his competitors. He did well at the 1998 World Cup in France and ended his career having made twenty-three international appearances, of which only eleven were starts, scoring nine times.

HENRY, THIERRY (ARSENAL)

Season: 2001/02
Goals scored: 24 (out of 79); 12 home, 12 away
Percentage: 30.3 per cent
Runner-up: Alan Shearer (Newcastle United), 23 goals
Arsenal were League Champions

Season: 2003/04
Goals scored: 30 (out of 73); 22 home, 8 away
Percentage: 41 per cent
Runner-up: Alan Shearer (Newcastle United), 22 goals
Arsenal were League Champions

Season: 2004/05
Goals scored: 25 (out of 87); 21 home, 4 away
Percentage: 28.7 per cent
Runner-up: Andy Johnson (Crystal Palace), 21 goals
Arsenal finished runners-up

Season: 2005/06
Goals scored: 27 (out of 68); 20 home, 7 away
Percentage: 39.7 per cent
Runner-up: Ruud van Nistelrooy (Manchester United), 21 goals
Arsenal finished fourth

Thierry Henry is of Antillean heritage. His father, Antoine, comes from Guadeloupe and his mother from Martinique. He was born in Les Ulis, Essonne near Paris on 17 August 1977 and raised in a tough neighbourhood that also provided good footballing facilities.

As a seven-year-old, Henry showed great potential, prompting Claude Chezelle to recruit him to the local club CO Les Ulis. His father pressured him to attend training, although as a youngster he was not particularly drawn to football. At the age of twelve he joined US Palaiseau, but left after a year to join ES Viry-Châtillon, where he remained for two years. His coach, Jean-Marie Panza, Henry's future mentor, followed him there.

Henry impressed all and sundry with his skilful play and goalscoring prowess. So much so that in 1990 AS Monaco sent their head scout Arnold Catalano to watch Henry in action. He played a 'blinder', scoring all his side's goals in a 6-0 victory.

Catalano immediately asked him to join Monaco, never considering offering him a trial. Without hesitation Henry agreed to sign for the French club, but by doing so he had to complete a course at the elite Clairefontaine football academy.

At first the academy refused to admit Henry due to his poor school results, but after some gentle persuasion he was allowed to complete the course and eventually joined Arsene Wenger's Monaco as a youth team player.

After several excellent displays, as well as scoring a few goals, Henry duly signed as a full-time professional with Monaco in August 1994. He made his senior debut straightaway, initially appearing on the left wing, where his pace, natural ball control and skill would be more effective against a full-back rather than a sturdy, rock-like centre-half. In his first season with Monaco, he scored three goals in eighteen appearances … and after that he improved with every game.

Under the tutelage of his manager (Wenger), Henry was named France's Young Footballer of the Year in 1996, and the following season his solid performances helped the Monaco win the Ligue 1 title and the French Super Cup.

During the 1997/98 campaign, he was instrumental in leading his club into the UEFA Cup semi-finals, setting a French record in the process by scoring seven goals in the competition. By his third season, he had gained the first of his 123 full international caps (fifty-one goals scored) and was part of France's World Cup-winning team of 1998. Henry was a member of the French squad at the European Championships in 2000 and his three goals contributed to their success. Henry blotted his reputation in 2009 when he handled the ball twice in the lead-up to France's goal that took them to South Africa at Ireland's expense.

He continued to impress on the field with Monaco, and in his five seasons with the French club scored 20 League goals in 105 appearances.

Henry left Monaco in January 1999, signing for Italian giants Juventus for £10.5 million.

Unfortunately, as a winger he was ineffective against the Serie A defensive discipline in a position uncharacteristic for him, and after netting three times in sixteen outings, he left the Turin club for Arsenal in August 1999, being reunited with Arsene Wenger, who paid an estimated fee of £11 million for one of the world's great footballers.

Henry was an instant hit at Highbury, thrilling the crowds week after week. He became Arsenal's greatest-ever goalscorer, topping the Premiership charts four times in five seasons between 2001 and 2006.

Henry also became the first player to win Europe's 'Golden Boot' award two years running, in 2004 and 2005, his twenty-five goals in the latter season tying him with Diego Forlán.

Also in 2005, Henry was runner-up in the World Player of the Year poll and received the accolade of France's Sportsman of the Year.

Henry's total of twenty-four top-flight goals in 2001/02 went an awful long way in helping Arsenal complete the double. His haul included a crucial last-minute winner at home to Aston Villa (3-2), important strikes to secure 2-0 victories at Derby County, Southampton and Ipswich, and two well-taken efforts (albeit one courtesy of a blunder by his fellow Frenchman, goalkeeper Fabian Barthez) in the last 5 minutes to ensure a 3-1 home win over Manchester United.

Earlier that season, he had struck home a 43rd-minute breakthrough goal to set Arsenal on their way to a 4-0 opening day win at Middlesbrough, cracked in a point-saver against Blackburn (3-3) and slotted in two more in a 4-1 home victory over Fulham, being one of eight Frenchmen who started against the Cottagers.

Henry commenced Arsenal's 2003/04 Premiership-winning campaign with a bang, scoring in four of the first five games, including important penalties in home clashes with Everton (won 1-0) and Portsmouth (drew 1-1). Two more spot-kicks followed shortly afterwards, both of them in a 3-2 victory over Newcastle at Highbury before he stroked home a late winner to see off Chelsea (2-1).

Two first-half goals paved the way for a 4-1 win at Leeds on 1 November but he had to wait until Boxing Day before scoring again, bagging a couple in a 3-0 victory over Wolves.

Starting the year with yet another penalty conversion in the 4-1 win over Middlesbrough on 10 January, Henry found the net in eight of the next ten games, ending with a hat-trick in a superb 4-1 home victory over Liverpool on 9 April.

In between times, he scored twice at Villa Park (won 2-0), squeezed in a late winner against Manchester City (2-1) and netted the brace that beat Southampton.

Keeping his best until almost the last, Henry produced a quite brilliant individual performance against Leeds United at home in mid-April. With the Championship trophy within their grasp, the Gunners triumphed 5-0, Henry scoring four times between the 27th and 67th minutes. His opener was a penalty – his seventh of the season – and he also bagged his 150th goal in all competitions for the club.

Continuing where he had left off, Henry was on the scoresheet in six of Arsenal's opening nine Premiership games of the 2004/05 season, netting twice in the 5-3 and 4-1 home wins over Middlesbrough and Charlton Athletic respectively.

Before the turn of the year he saved a point in a 1-1 draw at Crystal Palace, scored two late goals to seal a 3-0 win over Birmingham City and netted twice more in a 2-2 draw with Chelsea at The Emirates, while also playing his part in a thrilling 5-4 north London derby win at Tottenham.

Surprisingly goalless in the first five games of 2005, he got back on track with a smart effort in a 3-1 victory at Villa Park in early February before scoring twice in the 5-1 home beating of Crystal Palace and weighing in with hat-tricks in solid home victories over Portsmouth (3-0) and Norwich City (4-1).

Unfortunately, injury and illness caused him to miss six of the last eight games and this certainly denied him the chance of topping the thirty-goal mark for the second season running as Arsenal failed to retain the Premiership trophy (losing out to Chelsea by twelve points!), but they did lift the FA Cup (on penalties against Manchester United) for the tenth time in their history, despite being without the sidelined Henry.

In the 2005/06 season, having being appointed Arsenal's captain following the departure of fellow Frenchman Patrick Vieira, Henry or 'Titi', as he is called, smashed the Gunners' all-time scoring record, held previously by Ian Wright (185 goals), with his second strike in the Champions League game against Sparta Prague in October. He also broke Cliff Bastin's club League scoring record against West Ham in February and in the very next game reached the milestone of 200 goals for the Gunners when he netted against Birmingham City.

Henry bagged a total of thirty-three goals in all competitions in 2005/06 – nine more than Dutch international Ruud Van Nistelrooy of Manchester United.

He started off by dispatching, with ease, a first-half penalty in a 2-0 opening-day victory over Newcastle and notched a brace in a 4-1 third-match thumping of Fulham, yet missed six of Arsenal's first ten Premiership games, three of which ended in defeats!

He had been sorely missed and this was evident on his return as he struck twice in successive wins over Sunderland at home (3-1) and Wigan away (3-2) while also scoring in a 3-0 victory over Blackburn.

Four goalless games followed before he netted twice in 6 first-half minutes to help dispose of Portsmouth 4-0, and then, after a disappointing Christmas and New Year, he whipped in a hat-trick when Middlesbrough crashed 7-0 at Highbury.

Out of sorts somewhat during late February, when he failed to score, Henry hit top form again in March by scoring twice in victories over Fulham (4-0 at Craven Cottage), Liverpool (2-1 at Highbury) and then, on 1 March, he was 'on fire' with a brace in the 5-0 annihilation of Aston Villa, also at Highbury.

Further goals followed against Portsmouth (1-1), Tottenham (1-1) and Sunderland (3-0) before he rounded off another excellent season with a last-day hat-trick against Wigan Athletic, one of his goals coming from yet another penalty, after which he knelt down on knees to kiss farewell to the Highbury turf that had served him so well. Or so everyone thought!

It was a false impression, as Henry turned down Barcelona and remained at the club for one more campaign, when he added a further twelve goals to his tally.

Regarded as one of the finest strikers ever to have worn an Arsenal shirt, Henry spent just seven seasons with the Gunners, during which time he rattled in no fewer than 226 goals in 370 first-class appearances, 174 of his goals coming in 254 Premiership games.

In June 2007, in what was described in the press as 'an unexpected turn of events', Henry was eventually transferred to Barcelona for £18 million, signing a four-year deal, reported to be worth around £4.6 million per season in wages. It was also revealed that the contract included a release clause of £84.9 million.

Henry cited the departure of vice-Chairman David Dein and the continued uncertainty over Wenger's future as the main reasons for leaving The Emirates, stating, 'I always said that if I ever left Arsenal it would be to play for Barcelona.'

Despite his departure, Arsenal got off to an impressive start for the 2007/08 campaign, and Henry admitted that his presence in the team might have been more of a hindrance than a help, saying, 'Because of my seniority, the fact that I was captain and my habit of screaming for the ball, they would sometimes give it to me even when I was not in the best position. So in that sense it was good for the team that I moved on.'

At Barcelona, Henry was given the number 14 jersey, the same as he had worn at Arsenal. He scored his first goal for his new club in mid-September 2007 in a 3-0 Champions League group stage win over Lyon and netted his first hat-trick in Spanish football in a La Liga victory over Levante ten days later.

Despite indicating that he was missing life 'back home' and even 'the English press', Henry remained at the Camp Nou Stadium until May 2010.

He helped Barcelona win the Copa del Rey, La Liga and the UEFA Champions League, combining with two other world superstars in Lionel Messi and Samuel Eto'o to become the most prolific trio in Spanish League history, scoring seventy-two goals between them, surpassing the sixty-six netted by Real Madrid's Ferenc Puskas, Alfredo Di Stefano and Luis Del Sol in 1960/61.

In 2009, Henry helped Barcelona win an unprecedented sextuple – Spain's Super Cup, the UEFA Super Cup and the FIFA World Cup.

A year later, with twelve months still left on his contract, Barcelona club president Joan Laporta agreed to release Henry who, in July 2010, joined the American MLS club New York Red Bulls as its second designated player, after the former Aston Villa striker Juan Pablo Angel.

In January 2011 Henry returned to his beloved Arsenal during the MLS close season to coach the club's strikers, while also keeping himself extremely fit.

NB: As players, managers and coaches all over Europe will testify, Henry's deadly finishing was matched only by his elegant style.

HOLLEY, GEORGE (SUNDERLAND)

Season: 1911/12
Goals scored: 25 (out of 58); 18 home, 7 away
Percentage: 43 per cent
Joint top scorer with David McLean (Sheffield Wednesday) and Harry Hampton (Aston Villa)
Sunderland finished eighth

Having captured the first Division title for the fourth time in 1901/02, Sunderland fans had hoped to see their side go on to greater success. Instead, they had been forced to watch with envy as near-neighbours Newcastle United became the North-East's number one club for the next nine years, with three League titles and a much-prized FA Cup success in 1910. There was some consolation for the Wearsiders' followers on 5 December 1908, when a Newcastle side that was to finish top at the season's end were hammered 9-1 by a rampant Sunderland side in which George Holley was one of two hat-trick scorers.

The County Durham lad played inside left that day, and although he'd scored four times as a centre-forward when Sunderland beat Bury 4-1 in February 1911, it was as an inside forward that he was best known prior to the start of the 1911/12 season. His debut for England had come at inside left on 15 March 1909, when he scored England's first on 15 minutes in the 2-0 defeat of Wales. Another nine caps and three goals were to follow over the next four years.

Holley had made his debut at Christmas 1904, scoring Sunderland's goal in a 1-1 away draw with Sheffield Wednesday. By the end of the season, he had added another eight to his total. It wasn't until towards the end of the 1906/07 season that he established himself in the first team.

Sunderland had experimented with Harry Low at centre-forward at the end of the 1910/11 season, but with appendicitis laying him low for the first game of the 1911/12 season, manager Bob Kyle selected Holley to play centre-forward against Middlesbrough. It was a move that paid off when 15 minutes into the new season, he scored the only goal of the game, hitting a ball that was reported to have flown 'with a great pace into the net'.

Sunderland's second game was against Blackburn Rovers, the side that were to go on and win the Division One championship come the end of the season.

At right back, Rovers had Bob Crompton, whom Charlie Buchan later described as the greatest pre-war defender in the world. It was Holley, though, who was the star this particular day, scoring on 5 and 90 minutes in a 3-0 win. He maintained his fine form away at Notts

County, when he equalised the home side's early goal with a fine effort reported as such in the *Newcastle Daily Chronicle*: 'Holley made a brilliant dash through on his own and beat Murphy and West before levelling the scores with a beautiful shot.' Sunderland, though, left empty-handed, beaten 3-1.

Holley maintained his scoring run by hitting Sunderland's equaliser in the home game with Spurs that followed. This time, the goal was the result of some pre-planning on the training ground.

Holley was fouled about 2 yards outside the penalty area, and from the free kick Sunderland levelled the scores. The goal came from a clever move by the home side, which had been tried without success earlier in the match. This time, Buchan stepped up to take the kick as Tottenham packed their goal. He jumped over the ball and Holley, following up, cracked a beautiful low shot that Lunn could not reach. (*Newcastle Daily Chronicle*)

It was now five in four for Holley and although he failed to score in the next two, he was soon back in form with another five in the next three games, so that after nine games he was already in double figures. Two had come at Bramall Lane in a 2-1 success with the first on 15: 'Best had found him with a fine centre and Holley seized on the ball to put in one of his best shots which Lievesey had no chance of stopping.' (*Newcastle Daily Chronicle*)

Despite his fine start to the season, Holley's manager was clearly still intent on moving him back to his usual inside left position, and in November signed centre-forward John Young from Bradford City.

On 16 December 1911, Holley scored what must go down as one of the greatest goals ever scored at the now long-gone Roker Park. Preston North End had never won there when the game started, and after a moment of Holley magic they were never going to do so.

The first goal came after 11 minutes and was a brilliant effort from Holley. He got the ball from Young and dashed upfield before dodging Waring, Galloway and Baker to close in on goal. Taylor rushed out to Holley's feet but Holley slipped the ball under his dive, ran round his prostrate body and fired into the net. (*Newcastle Daily Chronicle*)

Holley was to add a further goal in a 3-0 win and followed up with another double in a 3-3 draw in a local derby at Ayresome Park before again scoring twice against Notts County.

On 27 January 1912, the League champions were in town. Manchester United had captured the title twice in the previous three League seasons, and in addition to Billy Meredith up front they had a renowned half back line-up in Charlie Roberts, Dick Duckworth and Alex Bell. Little good it did them, as Holley was to exert a spell-binding 90 minutes over them from inside left.

Having already scored twice, the game was in the 52nd minute, when 'Holley got possession to score a brilliant individual goal. He got the ball in the centre circle, worked nicely into position, beat a couple of defenders and then fired in a swift low shot that Edmonds touched but could not keep out of the net.' (*Newcastle Journal*)

By the end it was 5-0, and Holley had scored four. Sunderland was nowhere near the top of the League, but they now had the league's top scorer on their books. Sadly, an injury just towards the end of the game meant he was missing for the next couple of games, and when he returned his form seemed to have disappeared such that he failed to net in four games. With four games of the season remaining, it seemed that he was set to lose out to either Villa's Harry Hampton or the Wednesday's David McLean, both fine players.

When Everton came north in early April, Holley was to play his best game since Manchester United, opening the scoring with a header and finishing things off with two decent shots from just inside the box to ensure a 4-0 victory. He now had twenty-four goals and two days later he added another goal to his considerable tally, knocking home Jackie Mordue's miss hit shot in a 1-0 home victory against Bury.

Holley's record of twenty-five goals came from thirty-six League games. In the vast majority of seasons, he would not have finished at the top of the tree with the most goals, but reading the reports on the quality of his efforts shows just how fine a season he had in 1911/12. Holley was to go on and win the League title the following season with Sunderland and might have even done the 'double' if Sunderland had not unwisely selected him when not fully fit to play against Aston Villa in the 1913 FA Cup final.

Guesting for Fulham during the war, he later had a short spell with Brighton before becoming a trainer for a decade at Wolves, and several years at Barnsley. He died in August 1942.

HUNT, ROGER (LIVERPOOL)

Season: 1965/66
Goals scored: 30 (out of 79); 18 home, 12 away
Percentage: 38 per cent
Runner-up: Willie Irvine (Burnley), 29 goals
Liverpool were League Champions

The only player to have an honorary knighthood bestowed upon him by the Anfield faithful, Roger Hunt is one of the most popular figures ever to pull on the red jersey.

The only 'Red' in England's World Cup-winning team of 1966, the exploits of hat-trick hero Geoff Hurst mean he's sadly overlooked whenever the nation reminisces about Alf Ramsey's side … and it's easy to forget that Hunt was regarded as one of the key men going into the tournament.

However, it was for his achievements at club level for which Hunt will always be remembered on Merseyside. In fact, until Ian Rush came along, he was Liverpool's all-time record goalscorer, and to this day no one has scored more for the Reds in League competition.

Without Hunt's goals, Liverpool may never have escaped the depression of life in Division Two, but with him in the forward-line the club not only regained their place in the top flight, but also became the country's top team.

Born in Goldborne, Cheshire on 20 July 1938, Hunt played his early football with Croft Youth Club, Devizes Town and Stockton Heath before being spotted by former Liverpool star Bill Jones as a twenty-one-year-old. Signed by manager Phil Taylor as an amateur in August 1949, he turned professional in July of the following year and scored on his League debut at home to Scunthorpe United – the first of 286 goals he would net for the Reds in 492 first-class appearances. He also scored seventeen goals in thirty-four games for England and represented the Football League.

New boss Bill Shankly, who succeeded Taylor in the Anfield hot seat, embarked on a mass clear-out of playing personnel, but young Hunt's position was never in jeopardy.

'Shanks' was a big admirer of the striker and immediately entrusted the 'Blonde Bomber' (as he was called around Anfield) with the responsibility of spearheading Liverpool's charge back to the top-flight.

In 1961/62, he did just that, notching a remarkable forty-one goals from forty-one games as the Second Division championship was won in style. His partnership with Ian St John has since passed into football folklore and together they went on to terrorize First Division defences.

After another decent campaign in 1962/63, when he scored twenty-four League goals, Hunt then top-scored again with thirty-one when the title came Liverpool's way in 1963/64. He followed up with another twenty-five League goals in 1964/65 and also opened the scoring in the Reds' FA Cup final victory over Leeds United.

Besides his deadly finishing, Hunt was also known for his tremendous work-rate. Fast and strong, he would run himself into the ground for the Liverpool cause and was a handful for even the most accomplished of defenders. At club level, Bobby Moore said he was one of the most difficult he ever played with, while Jack Charlton, although far better in the air, never got to grips with him on the ground.

In 1965/66, Hunt, with a haul of thirty League goals in thirty-seven outings, topped the First Division scoring charts for the first and only time in his illustrious career and his efforts helped bring the League Championship back to Anfield for the second time in three years.

He started off the campaign with two goals in a 3-1 away win at Leicester, clinching victory with an extra-special strike 10 minutes from time. Two goalless games followed against Sheffield United before he netted twice more in a 3-2 win at Blackpool. He actually equalised (at 2-2) 13 minutes into the second half before helping set up Ian Callaghan's winner with a quarter of an hour remaining.

Against West Ham, Hunt scored one of the fastest hat-tricks ever by a Liverpool player – striking his three goals in the space of 8 minutes (between the 42nd and 50th) to see off the Hammers 5-1 at Upton Park.

After bagging the winner (2-1) against Fulham shortly afterwards, Hunt was applauded off the Anfield pitch after netting twice and assisting in two other goals after Everton had been thrashed 5-0 in the Merseyside derby.

In mid-October he opened the scoring in the 26th minute of a 2-0 home win over Newcastle before weighing in with two more in a 4-0 thumping of Nottingham Forest at the end of the month, his goals coming in the 72nd and 83rd minutes, at a time when Forest were getting back into the game.

On target in each of the next three games – all won, against Sheffield Wednesday (2-0), Northampton Town (5-0) and Blackburn Rovers (5-2) – he then set Liverpool on their way to an important victory over Burnley (2-1) which saw Liverpool top the table for the first time in the season, a position they never relinquished.

Hunt then netted a 73rd-minute winner at Chelsea (1-0) and followed up with a decisive 80th-minute goal to seal a 4-2 home win over Arsenal in early December.

Surprisingly, hotshot Hunt was goalless between 18 December and 29 January, failing to score in seven League games. But he returned to form early in February with a 43rd-minute strike which sent Liverpool in at the break 2-1 up at Blackburn, a game they went on to win 4-1 ... and from this point there was no stopping the Reds' march towards the title.

A week later, Hunt rapped in his second hat-trick of the season in a 4-0 drubbing of Sunderland at Anfield, netting in the 46th, 52nd and 64th minutes with Ron Yeats knocking in the other goal just on the hour mark.

Two more goals were poached by Hunt in a 4-1 home victory over Blackpool; he struck the only goal of the game in the 65th minute to beat Spurs on 12 March and drilled in two more in a 3-0 win at Villa Park towards the end of the month.

Injury forced to him to miss five of the last six games, only playing in the penultimate fixture of the season against Chelsea at Anfield, when he scored both goals in a 2-1 win to clinch the title in front of 53,754 fans.

Manager Shankly utilised only fourteen players during the 1965/66 League season – a record for the competition. And although ousted from the FA Cup in the third round (by Chelsea), Liverpool went on to reach the final of the European Cup-winner's Cup, only to lose 2-1 after extra-time to Borussia Dortmund at Hampden Park, Hunt scoring his side's goal.

In 1966/67, Hunt scored fourteen League goals as Liverpool slipped to fifth in the League. In 1967/68, when they finished third, he notched twenty-five and in January of that season, he overtook the great Gordon Hodgson as the club's all-time leading goalscorer with a typical poacher's strike at Stamford Bridge, but the end was nigh for the Kop favourite.

Around this time, 'Shanks' had started constructing his second great side, but an ageing Hunt still found the net, bagging thirteen League goals in 1968/69 and six the following season before he bade the Reds a fond farewell by joining Bolton Wanderers for a fee of £31,000 in December 1969, retiring from the game in May 1972, when he entered the family haulage business.

Three years after leaving Anfield, Hunt returned to Liverpool for one final time for a well-deserved testimonial. The gates were locked hours before kick-off as fans clamoured to pay their respects. An astonishing gate of 56,214 was recorded, with many thousands more reported to be locked outside.

If anyone had ever doubted his popularity among Liverpudlians, they had no ground for argument after this amazing show of support.

Belated recognition for the role he played in England's finest hour in '66 finally arrived at the turn of the century when Hunt was awarded an MBE, but the event passed almost unnoticed by the Liverpool fans – because they had honoured him when it mattered most! Despite the biased opinions of members of the southern-based media, to quote a line from the famous Kop chant of his time: 'Sir Roger Hunt - was wonderful!'

KEEGAN, KEVIN (SOUTHAMPTON)

Season: 1981/82
Goals scored: 26 (out of 72); 14 home, 12 away
Percentage: 36.1 per cent
Runner-up: Alan Brazil (Ipswich Town), 22 goals
Southampton finished sixth

On 10 February 1980, Lawrie McMenemy called a press conference at the Potters Heron hotel, Ampfield, where he officially announced that the European Footballer of the Year, Kevin Keegan, would be joining Southampton in the forthcoming summer.

The news stunned the world of football, as Southampton was a relatively small club, having only recently established themselves in the top Division, but this signing showed how persuasive their manager could be, especially when Keegan captained England in the 1980 European Championships in Italy.

Keegan, who cost £400,000 from the German side HSV Hamburg, with whom he won the coveted European Footballer of the Year award twice, gained a Bundesliga

Championship winner's medal, helped the club reach the European Cup final and was voted German Footballer of the Year, made his Southampton debut in a pre-season friendly against Shamrock Rovers in July 1980 and in his two seasons at The Dell was part of a flamboyant attacking team which included Alan Ball, Phil Boyer, Mick Channon and Charlie George.

In fact, in his first campaign at The Dell, Keegan netted eleven of the team's seventy-six League goals, helping Saints claim sixth place, their highest League finish at that time.

The following season, 1981/82, Keegan was on fire, producing his best form and at the end of January, Southampton proudly topped the First Division table, but a poor run of results – only three wins from the end of February – meant a rather disappointing seventh place finish for Saints.

Keegan nevertheless bagged twenty-six out of a total of seventy-two League goals scored by the team to finish as the First Division leading marksman. He was also voted the PFA's Footballer of the Year, was awarded the OBE for services to football and was also his club's Player of the Year.

Wearing his traditional number seven shirt, previously donned with distinction by Terry Paine and then Alan Ball, he certainly started off the 1981-82 campaign with a bang, scoring in each of the first four League games, three of his efforts helping Saints beat Wolves 4-1 and Everton 1-0 and draw at Manchester City.

He then had a couple of off-days (in a 2-0 win over Middlesbrough and a 4-2 defeat at West Ham), but was back on track with two fine efforts in a second successive 4-2 reverse at Coventry before firing home his seventh goal of the season in a thrilling 4-3 home win over Ipswich early in October.

Surprisingly, despite playing exceptionally well and having several chances to increase his goal-tally, Keegan netted only five times in the next ten League games as Saints edged slowly but effectively towards the top of the First Division table.

He struck twice in a 3-1 win over Notts County, set up a 2-0 victory at Stoke, opened the scoring in a resounding 4-0 home win over Leeds United and did likewise when Manchester United were beaten 3-2 at The Dell at the start of December.

Three days after Christmas Keegan was outstanding in a 3-1 home victory over Swansea City, when he scored twice, but although producing solid displays, he once again lost his goal-touch before striking the winner at Middlesbrough on 30 January – a victory that shot Saints to the top of the Division for the first time in the club's ninety-seven-year history.

Despite being knocked out of the FA Cup (by Leicester) and the UEFA Cup (by Sporting Lisbon), Saints and Keegan bounded along in the League, losing only one of seven games between 6 February and 6 March, Keegan himself scoring another five goals, including two beauties to earn a point at Aston Villa (1-1) and a 3-1 home win over Birmingham City.

As the season approached its climax, however, Southampton found the pressure too much for them and they slipped down the table to finish seventh, which still carried the compensation of another crack at winning the UEFA Cup. They won only three of their last thirteen League games, Keegan managing just six more goals, including two in a remarkable 5-5 draw at home to Coventry in early May.

'Super Kev' finished the season with a haul of twenty-six goals, topping the list of all the marksmen in the First Division. He also bagged three more goals in Cup competitions, plus an extra eight in 'other' games.

Keegan, though, stunned the Saints' supporters by leaving the Dell for Newcastle United on the eve of the 1982/83 season. There was a lot of ill-feeling when he departed, many fans claiming they had bought season tickets on the strength of Keegan being part of manager

Lawrie McMenemy's plans, especially after he had recruited England goalkeeper Peter Shilton.

Keegan's controversial decampment upset the club big-time ... and some supporters to this day have never really forgiven Keegan for what he did, leaving so quickly and without giving any worthwhile explanation!

Keegan carried on scoring goals – plenty of them. In fact, when he retired as a player in 2005, he had netted 203 in 590 League games for his five major clubs, notching 296 in 832 club games overall, plus those at international level. Par excellence!

Born in Armthorpe, Doncaster, on St Valentine's Day in February 1951, he played for Enfield House Youth Club before signing for Scunthorpe United as a professional in 1968. After moving to Liverpool in 1971, Keegan won three First Division titles, two UEFA Cups, one FA Cup (when he scored twice in the 1974 final victory over Newcastle United), and the European Cup during his six years at Anfield.

He also gained the first of his sixty-three full England caps in 1972. He went on to play international football for a decade, netting twenty-one goals for his country.

Keegan moved to SV Hamburg in 1977 and spent three years in German football before returning to England to sign for Southampton in 1980. After leaving the Dell, he helped the Geordies gain promotion in his second season, and also had a brief spell in Australia with Blackstown City in 1985 before eventually retiring at the age of thirty-four.

In February 1992, some seven years after his final game as a player and having lived in Spain, Keegan returned to football as manager of Newcastle, replacing Ossie Ardiles. The team had been relegated from the top flight in 1989 and narrowly missed out on promotion in 1990, but in 1991 they had failed to make the play-offs and at several stages in 1991/92 had occupied bottom spot in Division Two.

He kept Newcastle up and quickly guided the club back into the Premier League as Division One champions.

Like he had done as a Southampton player, Keegan – who had seen Newcastle finish runners-up in the Premiership in 1996 – dropped another massive bombshell when, on 7 January 1997, he announced his resignation as United's manager. A club statement following his resignation read:

> Newcastle United Football Club today announce the resignation of manager Kevin Keegan. Kevin informed the board of his wish to resign at the end of the season, having decided he no longer wishes to continue in football management at this stage in his life. Following lengthy discussions of which the board attempted to persuade Kevin to change his mind, both parties eventually agreed that the best route forward was for the club to, reluctantly, accept his resignation with immediate effect.

Keegan said, 'It was my decision and my decision alone to resign. I feel I have taken the club as far as I can, and that it would be in the best interests of all concerned if I resigned now. I wish the club and everyone concerned with it all the best for the future.'

After a spell in charge at Fulham, he took charge of the England team in 1999 but resigned in the autumn of 2000, following a 1-0 defeat by Germany in a World Cup qualifier in the last game at the old Wembley Stadium.

Keegan was then named manager of Manchester City in 2001 and spent four years at the club before resigning in 2005. He was then out of football for almost three years when he returned to Newcastle for a second spell as manager in January 2008.

This time he lasted only eight months at St James' Park, resigning in early September 2008 following days of speculation regarding a dispute with the club directors.

In March 2011, Keegan was announced as one of eleven industry experts for Npower's 'What's Your Goal' campaign, designed to showcase the vast and varied roles and responsibilities found in football to an age group of twelve to sixteen and inspire them to start thinking about their future careers.

KEVAN, DEREK (WEST BROMWICH ALBION)

Season: 1961/62
Goals scored: 33 (out of 83); 24 at home, 9 away
Percentage: 39 per cent
Joint top scorer: Ray Crawford (Ipswich Town)
Albion finished ninth

Although most football enthusiasts knew he lacked finesse, Derek Kevan made up for it with pure strength and commitment, often bulldozing his way through both First Division and international defences. Referred to as 'The Tank', he certainly thrilled a lot of supporters, especially those of West Bromwich Albion, with his all-action style and his goalscoring ability.

Kevan moved to The Hawthorns in February 1953, secured from Bradford Park Avenue by manager and former Tottenham Hotspur defender Vic Buckingham for what was to prove a bargain fee of just £2,000.

The burly centre-forward completed his National Service in the Army before bedding himself in at West Brom.

He recalled, 'I was based initially at Yeovil and then at Preston and played a few games for my battalion and when on leave I also turned out occasionally for Albion's second and third teams. During this time I first met up with Don Howe and Duncan Edwards.'

Kevan, who was being coached by the former Baggies goalscoring hero from the 1930s, 'W. G.' Richardson, eventually made his Albion debut (with Howe) in a 2-0 home win over Everton in August 1955. Replacing the injured Ronnie Allen, he impressed that evening by scoring twice, but it wasn't until early in 1956/57 that he finally established himself in the first team. He stayed to become a Hawthorns legend.

Standing well over 6 feet and weighing 13 stone, Kevan was as strong as an ox and, despite his bulk, was pretty quick off the mark. Predominantly right-footed, he was exceptionally good in the air. His tank-like thunderings down the middle of the pitch gave opposing goalkeepers (and centre-halves) nightmares more than once.

During the early part of his Albion career, Kevan had classy right-winger Frank Griffin and left-half Ray Barlow to feed him with the forward pass onto which he would flourish and after they had left, Clive Clark and Bobby Hope took over as chief suppliers.

Kevan thrived on the ball placed ahead of him and given enough space, he was onto it like a flash, shooting at goal whenever possible. He didn't bother about passing to a colleague – his aim was to score for his club, and he did that regularly.

Buckingham agreed that Kevan's control was really no more than adequate at best and he tended to be a shade slow on the turn. But his presence out on the pitch always made defenders think twice, especially when the ball was pumped into the air.

After netting 110 League goals in six seasons from debut day in 1955 to April 1961, Kevan finished as joint top-scorer in the First Division in 1961/62 with future Albion centre-forward Ray Crawford, then of Ipswich Town, both players bagging thirty-three goals.

He didn't start the season off too well, claiming just one goal in his first seven games, but from mid-September onwards, with only the odd off-day here and there, he was outstanding in terms of goalscoring!

He netted with a powerful right-footer in a 4-0 win over Arsenal, powered in the winner at Birmingham (2-1) and was on target in draws against both Manchester clubs.

He scored one and made two in an exciting 4-4 draw with Nottingham Forest, flashed in a thumping header to earn a point at West Ham (3-3) and claimed his first hat-trick of the season as Albion beat Sheffield United 3-1 in mid-November.

The Blades took the lead in this game before 'The Tank' got rolling! For almost an hour, he had been in his own words, 'rubbish' ... he was having a stinker, as they say. But then it all changed for the big fella. He equalised on 58 minutes with a crisp, low shot from 12 yards after a clever dribble and cross by Alec Jackson. Then, after missing two clear-cut chances and also shaving a post, he edged Albion 2-1 in front with 3 minutes remaining, cleverly heading in another Jackson centre. Then, with time fast running out, he sealed victory by tapping home from 6 yards after 'keeper Alan Hodgkinson had palmed out a Davey Burnside ground shot.

Goals followed at regular intervals, including a 23rd-minute right-footed belter in the 1-1 Black Country derby draw with Wolves on Boxing Day and two more in resounding 6-2 and 5-1 home wins over Bolton Wanderers and Cardiff City respectively.

In the return fixture with Wolves under the Molineux floodlights, he netted with a stunning 18-yard header from Alec Jackson's right-wing cross as Albion won 5-1.

During the last month of the campaign, he was lethal, rapping home braces in 4-0, 2-1 and 2-0 wins over Chelsea, Tottenham Hotspur at White Hart Lane and Fulham before rounding off a splendid season with a four-timer in the 7-1 demolition of Blackpool at The Hawthorns on 28 April.

Netting from close range after just 30 seconds against the Seasiders, he made it 2-0 in the 7th minute, completed his hat-trick with a rasping low drive halfway through the half before adding his fourth goal (and his thirty-third of the season) 3 minutes from time, following Graham Lovett's right-wing cross.

After scoring a total of 173 goals in 291 senior games for Albion, Kevan joined Chelsea for £50,000 in March 1963. Never a happy chappie at Stamford Bridge, he left the Blues for Manchester City eight months later. He set a new scoring record for the Maine Road club of thirty League goals in 1963/64 before winding down his career with spells at Crystal Palace, Peterborough United, Luton Town, Stockport County (with whom he won a Fourth Division championship medal) and Macclesfield Town, eventually retiring in 1975 with a career record of 235 goals in 440 appearances.

Capped fourteen times by England (eight goals scored), Kevan played in the 1958 World Cup finals in Sweden. He also gained four U21 caps and represented the Football League.

Born in Ripon, Yorkshire, in March 1935 and now living in Castle Vale, Birmingham, he is a member of the West Bromwich Albion Former Players Association.

LATCHFORD, BOB (EVERTON)

Season: 1977/78
Goals scored: 30 (out of 76); 20 home, 10 away
Percentage: 39.4 per cent
Runner-up: Trevor Francis (Birmingham City), 25 goals
Everton finished third

Bob Latchford was rewarded with a cheque for £10,000 by the *Daily Express* newspaper for scoring thirty League goals for Everton in the 1977/78 season, yet the centre-forward admitted, twenty-eight years later, that he was effectively only responsible for twenty-nine of them!

In his book, entitled *30*, published in 2006, Latchford reveals that the all football statisticians – and even Everton football club – have him listed as scoring thirty League goals in that season, but his third, in a 5-1 win over QPR at Loftus Road in early October was, in fact, an own goal by defender Dave Needham.

But no-one quibbled in the end and nowadays the record books everywhere clearly state that 'Super Bob' did 'officially' find the net thirty times in 1977/78 to become the first Everton player to reach that milestone in top-flight football for thirty-nine years, since the great Tommy Lawton bagged thirty-four in 1938/39. And, in fact, he was also the first Division One player to top the thirty-goal mark in six years.

Having moved to Goodison Park from Birmingham City in February 1974 for a British record deal of £350,000 involving Howard Kendall and Archie Styles, who both switched to St Andrew's, Latchford netted seven times during the last three months of the 1973/74 season. He then followed up with nineteen, thirteen and twenty-five goals respectively during the next three campaigns before bagging an overall tally of thirty-two in 1977/78, when he was certainly one of the best centre-forwards in League football.

Big and strong, he had the uncanny knack of turning half-chances into goals and teamed up well with Duncan McKenzie in Everton's attack, although quite a few of his goals were created by winger Dave Thomas, with midfielders Andy King and Martin Dobson also feeding him the ammunition to fire!

A bustling striker in the traditional mould, Latchford, who missed the opening game of the season (a 3-1 home defeat by Nottingham Forest), failed to score in any of his first three League outings, finally getting off the mark in a resounding 5-1 victory at Leicester on 10 September.

Two more goalless games followed before he struck again in the 1-1 home draw with Manchester City on the first Saturday in October. His third goal of the season clinched a 3-1 mid-week win on a wet and greasy Goodison Park pitch over West Bromwich Albion before he went to town with a 'four-timer' in that emphatic 5-1 victory at Loftus Road. The first two were brave headers from left-wing crosses; then came that dubious third before he steered home his fourth with the utmost confidence from 10 yards.

And after this performance, his manager Gordon Lee said, 'He's the best striker in the country and England boss Ron Greenwood should take a look at him – quickly.' He did – and capped him against Italy in a World Cup qualifier a month later. This was the first of twelve appearances Latchford made for his country up to June 1979 (five goals scored).

Before collecting his first cap, Latchford scored four more League goals, netting braces in an exciting 4-4 draw with Newcastle United and in the 2-1 victory over his former club Birmingham City, both at Goodison Park. At this juncture Everton lay second in the table, three points behind Nottingham Forest.

A fortnight after celebrating victory over his previous employers, Latchford went out and grabbed his second hat-trick of the season when Coventry City were blitzed 6-0 on Merseyside ... although Sky Blues 'keeper Jim Blyth ably assisted him with one of his goals!

The in-form centre-forward then fired home a second-half winner at Chelsea (1-0) and bagged a couple in a decisive 3-0 win over Middlesbrough, but was kept in check by Pat Howard and Tony Want when he returned to St Andrew's for a 0-0 draw in mid-December.

On Boxing Day, his goal at Old Trafford was technically a consolation as Manchester United slammed Everton, but the Blues and Latchford hit back with a 2-0 home win over Arsenal on New Year's Eve.

January, though, was a bad month for both Latchford and Everton ... only one win in three League games and elimination from both domestic Cup competitions.

Thankfully, things improved in February, two Latchford goals being enough to brush aside Leicester City (2-0), but he went off injured in a 3-1 win over West Ham, causing him to miss the 1-0 defeat at Maine Road and the 3-3 home draw with his 'favourite' team, QPR.

Back in business from early March, he had played his part in a 1-0 win at Bristol City and twice came close to scoring at Norwich (0-0) before netting in each of the next four games as the championship race (with Forest) went into overdrive.

He opened the scoring in successive 2-0 home wins over Newcastle and Leeds United, stunned the 55,277 crowd at Old Trafford by striking two blows to see off Manchester United (2-1) and notched the winner against Derby County (2-1).

With six games remaining, Forest were clear favourites to win the First Division championship. Everton and arch-rivals Liverpool were still in the chase, although it would take an almighty collapse by Brian Clough's men for one of the Merseyside clubs to steal the glory.

As it was, Everton faltered badly when it mattered most, picking up only seven points out of eighteen (two wins and a draw). Liverpool claimed fourteen and Forest ten.

Latchford scored in a 3-2 defeat at Coventry and struck the penalty winner at home to Ipswich Town (1-0). This left him needing two in the final game of the season against Chelsea to reach the thirty-goal mark and collect his £10,000 prize money.

Frustrated for well over an hour as Everton dominated proceedings to go 4-0 up, he suddenly burst into life and scored the two goals required (one from the spot) to seal a 6-0 win, setting an Everton post-war record in the process as well as becoming a much richer person!

Everton (55 points) finished third in the table behind runners-up Liverpool (57) and champions Forest (64).

Latchford went on to score another 42 goals for Everton, finishing with 138 in 289 games overall. He left Goodison Park for Swansea City in July 1981 and after assisting NAC Breda (Holland), Coventry City, Newport County and Merthyr Tydfil, he retired in 1988 with a club record of 282 goals in 655 appearances.

He later worked with Birmingham City's Football in the Community department.

Born in Birmingham in January 1951, Latchford now lives in Germany with his family and makes regular trips back to England to speak on the after-dinner circuit.

His brothers, Dave (Birmingham City) and Peter (West Bromwich Albion and Celtic), were both goalkeepers.

LAWTON, TOMMY (EVERTON)

Season: 1937/38
Goals scored: 29 (out of 79); 19 home, 10 away
Percentage: 36.7 per cent
Runner-up: Dave McCulloch (Brentford), 26 goals
Everton finished fourteenth

Season: 1938/39
Goals scored: 34 (out of 88); 20 home, 14 away
Percentage: 38.6 per cent
Joint top scorer with Mick Fenton (Middlesbrough)
Everton were League Champions

In their book *The Essential History of England*, published in 2002, writers Andrew Mourant and Jack Rollin wrote, 'Lawton combined brawn and delicacy; one moment a blood-and-thunder centre-forward, the next executing some manoeuvre of wit and subtlety.'

One contemporary said that he was '... the lightest mover of any big man who ever played football', while another wrote, 'Everything was about him was a threat: from his coolness, to the jut of his head on a muscular neck that could flick a heavy ball into goal like a stone from a catapult.'

Yes, indeed, he was a great centre-forward, brilliant on the ground, absolutely supreme in the air and a constant threat to defences throughout his career ... and all this despite having flat feet!

The only player to have scored in five consecutive England internationals on two separate occasions, he still holds the best post-war strike-rate of any England forward, netting sixteen goals in fifteen appearances for his country (1946–48) ... doing so when there weren't too many under-par footballing nationals around! He also scored one of the quickest-ever goals by an Englishman, netting after just 17 seconds against Portugal in 1947.

Over a period of twenty years, from his professional debut in 1935 until his retirement in 1956, Lawton scored a total of 292 goals in 471 competitive matches, including 232 in 390 League games. He also netted almost 160 goals in 125 wartime games (152 in 114 starts for Everton), struck twenty-two goals in twenty-three appearances for England, including two fours, against Holland in 1946 and Portugal in 1947, bagged another twenty-four goals in twenty-three Wartime and Victory internationals and notched two in his three appearances for the Football League.

He also scored another 200 goals in various friendly, tour and other wartime matches. That's some record.

Tommy Lawton was born in Bolton on 6 October 1919. His father was a signalman on the Lancashire & Yorkshire Railway, his mother a weaver.

A pupil at Tongue Moor and Castle Hill schools, Bolton, he represented Lancashire Boys (playing for the North against the South in 1933) and scored a staggering 570 goals in just three seasons for his school and for weekend team Hayes Athletic. An amateur with Bolton and a trialist with Sheffield Wednesday, he also played for Rossendale United before joining Burnley as a fifteen-year-old in May 1935, turning professional in October 1936.

Lawton became Burnley's youngest ever League debutant when he played against Doncaster Rovers in March 1936 at the age of sixteen years, 174 days. Seven months later, he was the youngest ever player (at that time) to score a League hat-trick, netting three times for the Clarets against Spurs. Then, following his move from Turf Moor to Goodison Park in December 1936 for £6,500 – a record for a teenager – he became the youngest ever scorer in a Merseyside derby, obliging against Liverpool at the age of seventeen years, 362 days in October 1937.

He went on to top the First Division scoring charts in the 1937/38 season with twenty-nine goals, and the following year he helped Everton win the League championship with a haul of thirty-four goals, which saw him top the scoring charts again, this time jointly with Micky Fenton of Middlesbrough.

Remaining at Goodison Park for nine years – and having played as a wartime guest for Aldershot, Morton and Tranmere Rovers – he switched his allegiance to Chelsea for £11,000 in November 1945. After spending two years at Stamford Bridge – and falling out with manager Billy Burrell – he was transferred to Notts County for a record fee of £20,000. He helped the Magpies win the Third Division (S) championship in 1950 and following a spell at Brentford (from March 1952 to September 1953) he wound down his career with Arsenal, whom he joined in a £10,000 cash/player-exchange deal involving James Robertson.

In March 1956, Lawton was appointed player-manager of Kettering Town. A year later he took over at his former club, Notts County, before returning to Kettering for a second spell as boss in 1963, becoming a director in 1968. Thereafter, he worked as a coach and chief scout at Meadow Lane before becoming a licensee in Lowdham, Nottingham, where he lived until his death in November 1996.

Back in 1936, Lawton teamed up with the great Dixie Dean at Everton and when they first met, the legendary centre-forward put his arm round Lawton and said, 'I know you've come here to take my place. Anything I can do to help you I will. I promise, anything at all.'

Dean, thirty years old at the time, had suffered several serious injuries and knew that there was not much time left for him at top level.

Dean kept his promise and spent a lot of time with Lawton on the training ground. Gordon Watson, who played at inside left for Everton, later recalled, 'Lawton and Dean used to work together under the main stand, Dean throwing up a large cased ball, stuffed with wet paper to make it as heavy as a medicine ball.'

Six weeks after joining Everton, Lawton was introduced to the first team for an away match against Wolverhampton Wanderers, Dean being rested prior to a fifth-round FA Cup tie with Tottenham Hotspur. Lawton found it difficult playing against England's rugged centre-half Stan Cullis, but he did he manage a consolation goal 15 minutes from the end of a devastating 7-2 defeat at Molineux.

Everton drew their Cup-tie with Spurs, and it was decided to play Lawton alongside Dean in the replay. In the second minute, Lawton scored with a tremendous shot from outside the penalty area. Dean turned to his teammate Joe Mercer and said, 'Well, that's it then. That's my swan song. That's the end of it.'

Dean realised at this point that it would not be long before Lawton would take his place in the side.

After 20 minutes, Albert Geldard crossed for Dean to make it 2-0. Dean later added a third, but to no avail as Spurs scored four to go into the sixth round.

Dean and Lawton both netted in the next game, when Leeds United were thumped 7-0, and they finished the season with thirty-four and three goals to their credit respectively. This was the start of things to come.

At the beginning of the 1937/38 season, Lawton lined up again alongside Dean, but the pairing did not work, Everton failing to win a game when the two strikers played together. In early September, Dean was dropped and Lawton switched to centre-forward for the game against Manchester City. He scored in the 4-1 victory and kept his place; Dean only played in two more games for Everton before leaving the club.

After netting against the team he supported as a lad, Bolton Wanderers, Lawton celebrated with a goal in the 2-1 Merseyside derby win at Liverpool before scoring in six of the seven League games played in October and November, including an excellent strike against Leeds United (1-1). This made it five goals in eight games as Everton started to climb the table. However, on the Monday after the Leeds game, Lawton upset several players by walking into the dressing room at Goodison Park and saying, 'Morning boys.' As a result, he was thrown fully clothed into the bath!

There followed a rather lean spell in December before he returned to form with a fine goal against Blackpool (won 3-1), scored another in a competent 4-1 and double-achieving victory over Bolton and claimed braces at Leeds (4-4), and in home wins over Grimsby Town (3-2) and West Bromwich Albion (5-3).

Everton finished fourteenth in 1937/38 and Lawton ended up as top marksman, with twenty-eight goals in thirty-nine League games. The following season he finished top of the charts again, this time jointly with Fenton, an amazing achievement for someone so young, as he was still only eighteen years of age.

Lawton scored in each of the first four League games at the start of the 1938/39 campaign (all won). The fifth match was against Arsenal, the reigning League champions, at Highbury, in front of almost 65,000 fans.

After 15 minutes, Lawton laid on a goal for Alex Stevenson before powering in a second himself in the 38th minute, George Casey of the *Sunday Pictorial* describing it as 'a wonder goal'.

In the second half, Bryn Jones scored for the Gunners from 30 yards. However, Everton held on to their lead despite Lawton getting a battering from Wilf Copping.

Lawton had constantly beat the Arsenal defenders in the air and Copping warned him that he was 'jumping too high' and that he would have to be 'brought down to my level'.

As Lawton later recalled, 'Sure enough the next time we both went for a cross, I ended up on the ground, blood streaming from my nose. Copping, looking down at me, said, "Ah told thee, Tom. Tha's jumping too high!"'

Lawton's nose was broken and to make things worse, when Arsenal came to Goodison Park later in the season, Copping broke Lawton's nose again!

Charlie Buchan, writing in the *Daily Chronicle*, argued that Lawton was the main reason for Everton's 2-1 victory: '… he had a lot to do with the success; he kept the wings moving and was ever dangerous in front of goal.'

On target in the next game – a 5-1 home win over Portsmouth – Lawton had now scored in the first six matches. After a couple of goalless encounters, he got back on track with the winner over Wolves, and also found the net at Bolton before whipping in a hat-trick in a 4-0 romp over Middlesbrough at Goodison Park, one of his goals being a stupendous header, directed with enormous power and accuracy past 'keeper Dave Cumming.

Following up with two goals against both Manchester United (won 3-0) and Chelsea (won 4-1), Lawton was impressing all and sundry with his strong and clever centre-forward play. However, he didn't have much success in the scoring stakes between mid-December and mid-January, but stormed back with another fine goal in a 2-0 home win over Arsenal before hitting the target in home victories over Huddersfield Town (3-2), Portsmouth (1-0) and a 3-0 win at Liverpool.

Following another three-week spell without a goal, during which time Everton also slipped out of the FA Cup in the sixth round, Lawton was outstanding in the last two months of the campaign. He scored in a 4-0 win over Leicester, hammered home the first four-timer of his career in an eight-goal thriller with Middlesbrough at Ayresome Park (4-4 – with Cumming again the hapless 'Boro 'keeper), netted two vital goals in a 4-2 win over Birmingham, salvaged another point at home to Stoke (1-1), grabbed the winner at Sunderland (2-1) and then helped his team-mates complete the double over the Wearsiders with another smart goal in a 6-2 victory at Goodison Park.

This proved to be Lawton's last goal of the season, as one more win and a draw secured the League title ahead of Wolves.

During this excellent campaign, Lawton won his first cap for England, lining up against Wales in October. He scored in the 27th minute, but surprisingly, the Welsh won the game 4-2. Four days later, Lawton scored again in a 3-0 victory over FIFA and the following month netted in both games against Norway (4-0) and Northern Ireland (7-0).

Lawton was only twenty years old when war was declared in September 1939. At the peak of his form at the time, he continued to sparkle throughout the hostilities, scoring goals galore for Everton and England.

The British Army invited some of the best footballers to become Physical Training Instructors at Aldershot. Lawton was one of them, along with a certain Matt Busby.

On returning 'home', he continued to play for Everton before surprisingly being sold to Chelsea.

What they said about Tommy Lawton … centre-forward supreme:

In his prime, Tommy had everything – a terrific shot with either foot, strength and accuracy with his head, the perfect physique, wonderful positional sense and a quickness off the mark that was unexpected in one of his build. (Len Shackleton – Sunderland and England)

Tommy possessed a rocket of a shot, he could hit the ball equally well with either foot and was lethal in the air and, most surprisingly for a centre-forward of the time, had all the ball skill and creative prowess of the most mercurial of inside-forwards. (Stanley Matthews – Blackpool and England)

I cannot recall any centre half who could keep him in check in his international days. He was the complete centre forward. (Wilf Mannion – Middlesbrough and England)

Tommy had a wonderful knack of heading the ball from a high centre. He was marvellously equipped for the job of leading a forward line. (Stan Mortensen – Blackpool and England)

* Lawton was rewarded with a belated benefit match (Notts County v. Nottingham Forest) in 1971 and a Testimonial match at Goodison Park in 1972.

LEE, FRANCIS (MANCHESTER CITY)

Season: 1971/72
Goals scored: 33 (out of 77); 19 home, 14 away
Percentage: 42 per cent
Runner-up: Martin Chivers (Tottenham Hotspur), 25 goals
Manchester City finished fourth

The signing of Lee by City manager Joe Mercer for £60,000 from Bolton Wanderers in October 1967 was to prove a shrewd piece of business by the end of the season, as by scoring sixteen times in thirty-one appearances, Lee played a crucial part in the Maine Road side's second League Championship success. This was to be the forerunner to further trophies, as the FA Cup, League Cup and European Cup Winners' Cup were all hoisted aloft over the next three seasons by captain Tony Book. Lee had scored a vital penalty in the final of the Cup Winners Cup in 1969/70, at the end of which he finished as the club's top scorer, a position he was to fill over the next four seasons before he departed to Dave Mackay's Derby County.

Success in the Cup competitions had come at a price in the league, City having finished in mid-table in the three seasons that followed their winning of the championship. Goals, too, had become hard to come by, with only forty-seven in forty-two games in 1970/71.

In an effort to improve this, Mercer and his assistant coach Malcolm Allison had drafted in from Newcastle Lee's playing partner at Bolton, Wyn Davies. The move was to send City rocketing to the top of the scorers charts in 1971/72, with seventy-seven League goals in all, with Lee grabbing thirty-three, a figure no-one was to match for another fifteen years or beat for over two decades.

Yet despite such an achievement, Lee enjoyed his fair share of criticism, the main one being that his diving had wrongly given him far too many scoring opportunities from the penalty spot. It was enough to earn him the nickname Lee Won Pen, and more than four decades on, his name remains cited in debates about diving in football.

Lee scored his side's first goal of the season in the second game against Crystal Palace. It was a penalty and the Eagles players complained bitterly to the referee that he had dived.

Lee drove home the penalty and added his second on 26 minutes, with a brave diving header as the ball bounced around the 6-yard box following a Neil Young corner. Another penalty at Wolves soon followed, although the Molineux side took both points as City started the season poorly.

They had picked up the pace, with eight points in ten, when Southampton visited and Lee was again first on the scoresheet, with his strike partner Davies joining him in a 3-0 win. It was the first indication that a possible repeat of 1967/68 might be on, with the Saints manager Ted Bates saying afterwards, 'They deserved to win and certainly showed their speed and footballing abilities.'

Lee scored another penalty at Upton Park in a 2-0 victory. Tommy Taylor had got in a continuous battle with Davies and brought him down in the box for Lee to tuck away the first. Lee then returned the favour, threading a fine ball for Davies to sprint away to finish confidently past Bobby Ferguson. The more combative style Davies had introduced to the City side was bringing great dividends.

Ipswich was blasted away, beaten 4-0 with midfielder Mike Doyle playing flawlessly and Lee scoring the final goal with a low 20-yard shot on 50 minutes. In a four-way tussle at the top, City was starting to look like a serious title contender.

Lee scored his only hat-trick of the season against Wolves in January. The weekend was dominated by the Bloody Sunday massacre in Derry, but on the football field John Richards struck twice for his side, who on another day might even have got a point. City, though, were more deadly in front of goal and Lee's opening goal was a masterpiece from an almost impossible angle.

It marked the start of a good week for the small, stocky striker as by the Thursday, his appeal against a third booking that would have led to a lengthy ban had proved successful. Despite the fact that they were among the sides battling with City for the title, Derby's Colin Todd had given evidence on his behalf.

Against Arsenal, Lee drove home his fourteenth penalty of the season. For once, there were no accusations of diving after Pat Rice had inexplicably handled the ball. Lee added City's second in the 81st minute and when two further victories followed, his side had gone to the top of the League with just eight games left.

Despite their fine form, Malcolm Allison, who had won his personal battle with Mercer to be allowed to step up from being his assistant, decided it was time to strengthen up front and paid QPR £200,000 for the services of the talented Rodney Marsh. He had played poorly on his debut against Chelsea, in which Tommy Booth had headed a well-flighted Lee cross home for the only goal of the match.

April was to be the crucial month; City, Leeds, Derby and Liverpool all remained in with a chance of the title. But with two defeats in three days, against Stoke City and Southampton, City moved to outsiders in the race. Lee had missed the sort of chance he would normally have taken at the Dell, his 8-yard shot hitting the crossbar on 52 minutes as City trailed 1-0.

City put themselves back in with a chance when, with Marsh playing superbly, they beat West Ham 3-1 at home. Yet when Martin Buchan gave Manchester United the lead on 59 minutes at Old Trafford, there seemed little way back, but 4 minutes later Lee had scored twice to put his side 2-1 up as they moved to collect both points in a 3-1 derby success.

The goals had taken him to thirty-two in the league, beating Derek Kevan's City post-war record of thirty. Lee was happy about this, saying, 'It's good to have the record, but it would be better to have a championship medal.'

Marsh had been dropped to the bench, but he came on to make it 3-1 in the 85th minute. He stayed there against Coventry, City playing poorly and losing out when Denis Mortimer equalised on 85 minutes.

Lee scored his thirty-third goal of the season on the final day against Derby County. Again it was a penalty, when on 67 minutes Todd bundled him over and he stood back up to stroke the ball home from the spot.

Marsh had played brilliantly in a 2-0 win but it was Derby, under Brian Clough, who were to win the League for the first time in their history. By the time they repeated the feat three seasons later, Lee was in their side, scoring twelve times to capture his second League Winner's medal.

Despite this, it is for his on-field battle with Leeds legend and hard-man Norman Hunter that Lee is best remembered during his time at the Baseball Ground. Having won and scored a penalty, Lee was accused of diving and the pair set about each other, continuing to trade punches with one another after being dismissed. In 2003 the incident was named by *The Observer* as sport's most spectacular dismissal.

Lee was always noted for his fiery determination on the field, and was the first Englishman to be yellow-carded at a World Cup during the tournament in Mexico in 1970. Lee played twenty-seven times for his country, scoring ten goals. Retiring from playing in 1976, Lee became a successful businessman and continued his involvement at City becoming chairman in 1994 before stepping down four years later.

LINEKER, GARY, OBE (LEICESTER CITY, EVERTON AND TOTTENHAM HOTSPUR)

Leicester City
Season: 1984/85
Goals scored: 24 (out of 65); 17 home, 7 away
Percentage: 36.9 per cent
Joint top scorer with Kerry Dixon (Chelsea)
Leicester finished: fifteenth

Everton
Season: 1985/86
Goals scored: 30 (out of 87); 19 home, 11 away
Percentage: 34.5 per cent
Runner-up: Frank McAvennie (West Ham United), 26 goals
Everton finished runners-up in the First Division

Tottenham Hotspur
Season: 1989/90
Goals scored: 24 (out of 59); 16 home, 8 away
Percentage: 40.6 per cent
Runner-up: John Barnes (Liverpool), 21 goals
Spurs finished third

Gary Lineker was born on 30 November 1960 and joined his hometown club, Leicester City, on leaving school in July 1977, turning professional in December 1978. After some excellent performances in the intermediate and second teams, he helped Leicester win promotion to the First Division in 1980 before gaining a regular place in the Foxes' first team in 1981. Scoring at will, he netted nineteen goals in 1981/82 and twenty-six the following season when, once again, he had a big hand in helping the Foxes gain promotion for a second time in three years.

During his Filbert Street time, he twice finished amongst the top flight's leading strikers and in 1984-85 was the First Division's joint top scorer with twenty-four goals, sharing the honour with Chelsea's Kerry Dixon.

Lineker started Leicester's Centenary campaign with a brace in a 3-2 defeat at Newcastle, and after two goalless games he then struck once in each of the next three matches, a 1-1 draw with Watford and a 2-1 victory over Ipswich, both at home, and in the 2-2 draw at Stoke.

Partnering Alan Smith up front and with winger Steve Lynex supplying the crosses from the right, Lineker was on top of his game, and although he failed to find the net in any of the next five games, he stormed back with a stunning hat-trick in a resounding 5-0 home win over Aston Villa at the end of October.

He managed only one goal in November – in the 3-2 home defeat by Manchester United – but had a decent December, scoring five times in successive 4-0 wins, at home to QPR and away at Sunderland, twice in the 5-1 East Midlands derby demolition of Coventry City, and the winner in a 2-1 victory at Liverpool on Boxing Day.

At the halfway stage in the season, Lineker had netted 14 League goals, plus 2 in the League Cup, and he started 1985 with his second hat-trick, albeit this time in a 6-1 FA Cup win at non-League Burton Albion.

One goal (which secured at point against Chelsea) in two games in February was followed by three more in March, in wins over Sheffield Wednesday (3-1), Newcastle United (4-1) and West Ham (1-0). He then netted to no avail in a 2-1 reverse at Manchester United before rounding off the season with five goals in nine days – the winner against Nottingham Forest (1-0) and braces against QPR (lost 4-3) and Sunderland (won 2-0).

Between them, Messrs Lineker, Smith and Lynex scored forty-nine League goals during the season as Leicester stuttered along to finish fifteenth in the table.

It was not the best of campaigns, but Lineker's efforts in front of goal had attracted the attention of bigger clubs, and a move from Filbert Street duly came when he was transferred to League champions Everton for £800,000.

He made a terrific start to his career at Goodison Park, bagging forty goals in fifty-seven appearances in his first season. He was once again the First Division's leading marksman, this time with thirty goals, as he helped the Merseysiders claim second place in the League.

He also helped the Blues reach the FA Cup final for the third year in a row, but ended up losing 3-1 to double winners Liverpool, despite giving his side an early lead when he outpaced Alan Hansen to score.

Lineker scored three League hat-tricks for Everton in 1985/86: in the 4-1 home win over Birmingham City in August, in a 4-0 victory over Manchester City, also at Goodison Park, in February, and in the penultimate League game of that season, in May, when they kept their title hopes alive with a 6-1 home win over Southampton.

In his final League outing for the Goodison Park club, Lineker scored twice in a 3-1 home win over a West Ham side whose title hopes had just disappeared. However, he and his colleagues were denied the championship as Liverpool also won their final game of the season at Chelsea to pip Everton by two points (88–86).

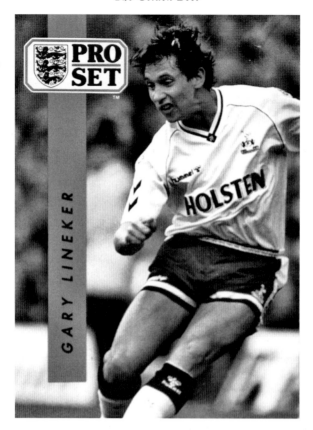

His other nineteen League goals in 1985/86 were scored as follows: one against Tottenham (away), won 1-0 ... two in a 5-1 walloping of Sheffield Wednesday at Hillsborough ... one in a 3-2 home defeat by near-neighbours Liverpool ... two in the 6-1 drubbing of Arsenal ... the opener in a 3-2 win at Southampton ... the last in a 3-0 win at West Brom ... two in the 3-1 victory at Coventry ... a fine effort when Manchester United were beaten 3-1 at home ... two more in another 3-1 win over Sheffield Wednesday 48 hours later ... a crucial one in the 4-3 victory over QPR ... both at Birmingham, where Everton won 2-0 ... clinchers in successive 2-0 victories over Liverpool (a) and Aston Villa (h) ... and the first in a 2-0 triumph at Watford.

Shortly after winning the 'Golden Boot' at the 1986 World Cup, Lineker left Everton to sign for Barcelona for £2.8 million. The Spanish giants were managed at the time by former Queens Park Rangers boss Terry Venables, who had also brought in Manchester United striker Mark Hughes.

Lineker did not disappoint the fanatical Barça fans, scoring twenty-one goals in forty-one games in his first season at Camp Nou, including three in a 3-2 win over bitter rivals Real Madrid. Barça won the Copa Del Rey in 1988 and lifted the European Cup-winner's Cup in 1989.
Manager Johan Cruyff then chose to play Lineker on the right of the midfield. He didn't like that position at all and this led to the striker moving back to England.

Manchester United chief Alex Ferguson attempted to sign Lineker to partner Mark Hughes in attack at Old Trafford, but Lineker spurned the Reds and instead signed for Tottenham Hotspur in July 1989.

During his three seasons at White Hart Lane, he scored 67 goals in 105 games and won the FA Cup. He was top scorer in the First Division in the 1989/90 season with twenty-four goals as Spurs finished third in the table. This feat also gave him the honour of being the only player to head the League charts with three different clubs.

Lineker played alongside Paul Stewart and Clive Allen in attack, and with Paul Gascoigne engineering openings from midfield Spurs looked a quality team. During the course of the season they produced some exciting football and finished third in the First Division.

Surprisingly, it took Lineker until the sixth game of the season to open his account for the London club, scoring his side's second goal in a 2-2 draw at Norwich. He then burst into action for the first time at home with a hat-trick in a 3-2 win over QPR, netted in a 3-1 victory at Charlton a fortnight later, and in late October bagged a couple in a 3-0 home success over Sheffield Wednesday.

However, for a short while after that, the goals dried up and, in fact, Lineker scored just once (a penalty in a 3-2 win at Crystal Palace) in the next six matches, but he had an excellent December, netting five times, starting with one in a 2-1 victory over his former employers Everton. He also struck the only goal of the game to see off Manchester United at Old Trafford, was on target in a 3-1 home victory over Millwall, and then scored twice in a 3-2 home defeat by Nottingham Forest.

Unfortunately, Lineker had a poor January (no goals at all) but he started February off in brilliant style, rapping in a hat-trick (including a penalty) as Spurs crushed Norwich City 4-0 at White Hart Lane. He followed up in the very next match with a second-half winner to beat Chelsea 2-1, but was goalless in three successive defeats before getting Spurs' second goal in a 3-0 home win over London rivals Charlton.

During the last seven weeks of the season Spurs completed nine matches, seven of which they won to rise from ninth in the table to third. Lineker scored in four of those victories, notching two against Sheffield Wednesday (4-2), claiming two more against Coventry City (3-2), poaching the winner at Millwall (1-0) and netting once against Manchester United (2-1). In between times, he also struck the woodwork four times and had three efforts cleared off the line, two in a surprise 1-0 defeat at Wimbledon.

In 1990/91, Lineker scored 19 goals in all competitions and followed up with another thirty-five in fifty outings in 1991/92, when he finished runner-up to Ian Wright with twenty-eight League goals to the Arsenal striker's twenty-nine.

He helped Spurs win the FA Cup against Nottingham Forest (2-1) in 1991, despite having the misfortune to miss a penalty in the final.

After three fine seasons at White Hart Lane, Lineker ended his career with an injury-plagued spell in Japan with Nagoya Grampus Eight, for whom he made twenty-three appearances in two seasons, scoring nine times, before announcing his retirement in the autumn of 1994.

During an illustrious career, Lineker was voted PFA Players' Player of the Year in 1986 and came third in the inaugural FIFA World Player of the Year in 1990 awards.

He was never cautioned by a referee for foul play (never once receiving a yellow or red card), and as a result of this accomplishment was honoured in 1990 with the FIFA Fair Play Award.

In his senior career, which spanned sixteen years and 568 club games, Lineker scored a total of 281 goals. He also scored forty-eight goals in eighty internationals for England between 1984 and 1992 and is currently England's all-time second highest scorer behind Bobby Charlton. His international goals-to-games ratio remains one of the best for the country and he is widely regarded as being one of England's greatest-ever strikers. He was top scorer in the 1986 World Cup and received the Golden Boot – the only time an Englishman has achieved this feat.

Following his retirement, he developed a career in the media, initially on BBC Radio 5, then as the anchorman for BBC football coverage, including their flagship football television programme *Match of the Day*. He was a team captain on the acerbic sports game show *They Think It's All Over* (1995–2003).

He followed Steve Rider as presenter for the BBC's golf coverage and also presented a six-part TV Series for the BBC in 1998 called *Golden Boots*.

In 2003, Lineker was inducted into the English Football Hall of Fame. Two years later, he was sued for defamation by Harry Kewell over comments made when writing in his column in the *Sunday Telegraph*. The jury failed to reach a verdict.

With Austin Healey in 2008, Lineker won £50,000 for the Nicholls Spinal Injury Foundation on the ITV1 programme *Who Wants To Be A Millionaire?*, and since 1995 he has advertised Walkers Crisps. He was awarded the OBE in 1992 for services to football.

LOFTHOUSE, NAT (BOLTON WANDERERS)

Season: 1955/56
Goals scored: 32 (out of 71); 22 home, 10 away
Percentage scored: 45 per cent
Runner-up: Charlie Fleming (Sunderland), 28 goals
Bolton finished eighth

Bolton's favourite son, Lofthouse was a hard-as-nails bustling centre forward whose aerial abilities were without parallel in the 1950s. Good with both feet, his cannonball efforts in an age when the ball was often rock-hard could frighten even the hardiest of 'keepers.

Due to the Second World War, Lofthouse had to wait until turning twenty-one before he made his full League debut for his hometown club. He'd already got on the scoresheet during the 1945/46 season by scoring twice in the FA second-round first leg against Liverpool, and against Chelsea in August 1946 he again scored twice. Over the next thirteen years, 253 more League goals were to follow before injury terminated his career.

Lofthouse missed out in the first game of the 1955/56 season in a 2-1 win away at champions Chelsea. He was on the scoresheet in the next, beating Charlton 'keeper Sam Bartram with a clever shot. A week later, another London side, Arsenal, were to find Lofthouse almost unplayable. With Bolton one down with just seconds to go before half time, the Bolton number 9 headed Ralph Gubbins's cross powerfully beyond Jack Kelsey, the Wales international 'keeper. On the restart, a Doug Holden cross was volleyed into the goal after first crashing off the inside of the post. Then, on 59 minutes, Lofthouse headed home his hat-trick goal from a Wheeler cross. With five goals in his next three matches, including a thunderous shot on 60 minutes at Portsmouth and two headers against Aston Villa, he was on nine by the end of September.

One month later, Luton travelled to play their first game at Burnden Park since March 1900. Leaving Lofthouse unmarked was never going to take the points back south, and on 45 and 82 minutes, he had the simple task of beating Ron Baynham from little more than 6 yards out.

Two weeks later, he grabbed another couple of goals. Manchester United was already looking a likely title contender when they visited Burnden Park. Making his debut was Eddie Colman, a marvellous player who sadly lost his life at Munich, as did Tommy Taylor, and it was Taylor who gave 'the Busby Babes' the lead. But when Gubbins delivered a high cross, Lofthouse soared above the United 'keeper Ray Wood and two defenders to again head home and make it 1-1. His second was a great effort; picking up the ball, he fed Gubbins, and on the return he breasted it down and drove a powerful shot past the 'keeper.

The Lion of Vienna pub in Bolton was named in honour of Lofthouse's most famous moment in an England shirt.

Sheffield United was next to find Lofthouse a real handful. Clean through after 2 minutes, he beat Alan Hodgkinson from 12 yards, and on 83 minutes he headed home Holden's cross to ensure a 3-1 victory.

In early December 1955, Lofthouse struck four in a 6-0 win against Birmingham City. There were only a couple of minutes on the clock when he scored his first. It would not be allowed today. Gill Merrick, a rival to Harry Hibbs as the Blues' greatest ever 'keeper, had caught Tommy Banks' cross, 'only to be hit at the same moment by Lofthouse's full weight and knocked into the net'. It was something Lofthouse did regularly throughout his career, including at Wembley in 1958, when he bundled Manchester United 'keeper Harry Gregg and the ball over the goal line for his second goal in that season's FA Cup final, which ensured Bolton captured the famous trophy.

When Bolton were 1-0 up against Birmingham, Lofthouse converted with his head two Gubbins crosses for his hat-trick before, in the final minute, he raced through to beat Merrick with a tremendous cross-shot for this twentieth goal of the season.

One week later, his record for the season had jumped to twenty-three. Chelsea was blown away by some exquisite Bolton forward play. Slick passing by Gubbins, Holden and Ray Parry repeatedly sliced open the London side's rearguard and when Lofthouse was offered a heading opportunity, he had no problems in making it 1-0. Then, on 52 minutes, Holden crossed perfectly – 'Lofthouse almost inevitably headed the perfect goal', reported *The Buff*. His hat-trick goal was the best of lot, sweeping home a long cross in a 4-0 win. It might even have been five, as Lofthouse also hit the upright with a header.

Lofthouse scored his twenty-seventh League goal at Molineux just before half time. On the restart he found himself donning the 'keeper's gloves when Joe Dean, at the time the youngest ever 'keeper in the First Division, was off the pitch for 10 minutes, receiving attention to a cut head. He did well to block a powerful Ron Flowers header to earn the cheers of the large crowd. Wolves won 4-2, but Bolton was back to winning ways when they beat Aston Villa, with Lofthouse's headed goal deciding the contest.

Having been so successful against sides from the West Midlands, WBA must have feared the worst prior to their game at Burnden Park on St Patrick's Day, 1956. The Baggies had new man Bobby Robson in their side, and he must have admired the way Lofthouse created the home side's first, a lovely cross swept home by Stevens. Lofthouse doubled the lead with a terrific shot. With nine games still to play, Lofthouse now had thirty-one goals.

Sadly, an injury saw him miss the two Easter games with Blackpool. The sides had played a fabulous game three years earlier at Wembley in the 1953 FA Cup final. Lofthouse had given Bolton an early lead, completing his record of at least one goal in each round, but with Mortensen grabbing a hat-trick and Stanley Matthews sublime it was the Tangerines who took the cup in a thrilling 4-3 victory. If there was any consolation for Lofthouse, he left the pitch knowing he had already been awarded the Footballer of the Year award.

Returning for the final two matches of the 1955/56 season, Lofthouse scored his final goal at Huddersfield Town. Appropriately, it was from another Gubbins cross, touching home after Harry Fearnley dropped – perhaps through fear of being barged over the line – the ball. Lofthouse had notched thirty-two League goals in thirty-six games, four ahead of his nearest rival, Sunderland's Charlie 'Cannonball' Fleming.

Lofthouse was to continue to score goals over the next few seasons, with twenty-eight in the League in 1956/57 and twenty-nine two seasons later. By ending up with 255, he stands in seventh place in the list of all-time scorers in England's highest leagues. No wonder he is still so revered in his hometown.

Lofthouse played thirty-three times for his country. It would undoubtedly have been more, if not for his late start caused by the war. In the modern-day era, his record of thirty goals is a better average even than Jimmy Greaves, who scored forty-four in fifty-seven. His most famous goal, and one still celebrated in the 'Lion of Vienna' pub named after him in Bolton, was the winning effort away to Austria in May 1952.

Played through the middle by Tom Finney, Lofthouse, with defenders hotly pursuing him, charged 50 yards and clattered into the 'keeper to ensure he missed seeing his effort entering the net, to the great joy of thousands of British soldiers watching in the crowd. Nat Lofthouse was a hard man in a hard era.

Nat Lofthouse died on 15 January 2011.

MACDONALD, MALCOLM (NEWCASTLE UNITED AND ARSENAL)

Newcastle United
Season: 1974/75
Goals scored: 21 (out of 59); 13 home, 8 away
Percentage: 35.6 per cent
Runner-up: Brian Kidd (Arsenal), 19 goals
Newcastle finished fifteenth

Arsenal
Season: 1976/77
Goals scored: 25 (out of 64); 14 home, 11 away
Percentage: 39 per cent
Joint top scorer with Andy Gray (Aston Villa)
Arsenal finished eighth

Despite having hit sixty-nine League and Cup goals for Newcastle in the previous three seasons, Macdonald had plenty to prove at the start of the 1974/75 season after his pre-match boasting that the Magpies would destroy opponents Liverpool in the 1974 FA Cup final had proven ill-founded. Inspired by Kevin Keegan and with Bill Shankly in charge for his final game, the Anfield side won one of the most one-sided finals ever 3-0. Macdonald had played poorly, but if anyone thought he would return the following season having lost his confidence, they were to be quickly disappointed.

With the bookies offering 5-1 that he would finish as the league's top scorer, he was quickly into his stride and after opening his account in the first match, which saw Coventry City beaten 3-2, he then bulleted home strike partner John Tudor's pass for Newcastle's second in the 2-2 draw with Sheffield United. Manager Joe Harvey had spent £170,000 on signing winger Micky Burns from Blackpool and Macdonald was confident he would ensure a regular supply of goal-scoring opportunities.

Against West Ham, Macdonald was again on the scoresheet, and might have had two, only for Tommy Taylor to prevent his goalbound effort with his hand, with Terry McDermott missing the resulting penalty. At the Baseball Ground, he netted his fourth goal of the season when he rose to meet a Burns free kick in a 2-2 draw with Derby County.

Seeking a quick return to Wembley, Newcastle faced QPR at Loftus Road in the League Cup. Macdonald scored a hat-trick, including a sensational opening goal in just 13 seconds. Pat Howard pushed the ball forward and he sliced through the home defence like a hot knife through butter to take the ball on his thigh, hold off Bob Hazell and with Terry Mancini rooted, he hit it first time into the far corner of the net. Seven minutes later, he headed on Irving Nattrass's free kick for Tudor to score, and then on 43 minutes a Terry Hibbitt ball saw him tear beyond Mancini to net. Restarting after half time, the former Luton man ran on to a 60-yard Alan Kennedy pass to beat Phil Parkes and complete one of his best ever performances in a black and white striped shirt.

Continuing his fine form meant a ponderous Chelsea defence were never going to be strong enough to stop him adding to his tally, and the Londoners returned south well beaten 5-0, with the former Fulham man scoring twice.

Against Manchester City, and with Mick Doyle at the unusual position of centre half, Macdonald had after 75 minutes done little to suggest he might be the answer to Don Revie's need for a new England number 9. He'd chested down the ball for Howard to open the scoring, but had otherwise been easily held; however, losing his marker, he headed home the winning goal just as Joe Harvey was looking to replace him.

At Upton Park, Macdonald scored a trademark goal, outpacing the West Ham defence and drawing 'keeper Mervyn Day before confidently blasting the ball past him for the only goal of the match.

His form brought praise from an unusual source. Bob Stokoe was a former Newcastle player, but was now in charge at Sunderland and said, 'He has blistering pace and frightens people. He has always had potential … now he has got his attitude right he has blossomed.' Burnley boss Jimmy Adamson agreed, saying, 'If there is a better centre-forward in the country, then I have yet to see one.'

Macdonald had scored in all four games against the side from East Lancashire in the previous season. These included a double in what is generally regarded as his finest game for Newcastle, the FA Cup semi-final at Hillsborough that was won 2-0.

Macdonald gained a small measure of revenge for the Cup final defeat on 12 February 1975, when he again scored twice as Liverpool were beaten 4-1 at St James' Park. This was one fewer than he had netted on his St James' debut in August 1971 against the same side.

Two more goals followed against Bobby Robson's Ipswich Town and as Tudor also grabbed two, it must have been a long ride home with the Newcastle defence having conceded five in an amazing match.

There were few highlights in the home game against QPR, a 1-1 draw being enlivened when a long David Craig ball saw Macdonald power through the inside right position, draw Parkes and flick the ball home with the outside of his foot.

Four days later was to be a very special day in Malcolm Macdonald's football career. He had played seven times for England before scoring in his eighth as world champions West Germany were beaten at Wembley in March 1975. Against Cyprus, the Newcastle striker became only the fourth and, to date, last player to score five times in a match for England. It was to prove by far the highlight of his time with England because another five games failed to produce a goal.

Macdonald ended his fine season by providing the only highlight of Joe Harvey's last game in charge at Newcastle when, on the final day of the season, against Birmingham City he powerfully headed home a Craig corner in a demonstration of the mark of a high-class striker. It was his twenty-first League goal of the season, two ahead of Arsenal's Brian Kidd in second place. And it was to be to Highbury that he journeyed, signing for £333,333.33 in 1976, where he was to go on and again finish as the Division One top scorer in 1976/77.

The first signing made by Arsenal manager Terry Neill, he made his Gunners debut on the opening day of the 1976/77 season, but in front of an expectant Highbury crowd of over 41,000, the whole team had an off-day as Bristol City upset the odds by winning 1-0.

Four days later, however, at Norwich, 'Supermac' struck his first goal in a red and white shirt in a 3-1 victory, and seventy-two hours after that he struck again in a 2-2 draw at Sunderland.

Not yet at his best, he missed the game at West Ham (lost 2-0) but scored in a 3-1 win over Everton, only to fire blanks in his next two outings before securing a 2-0 home win over Stoke City in mid-October, 'his second-half strike giving Peter Shilton no chance of saving.'

He thumped in a penalty in a 4-0 home win over Birmingham City three weeks later and a smartly-taken goal helped his colleagues beat Coventry 2-1 at Highfield Road before he became a hero by rattling in a hat-trick against his former employers, Newcastle United, as Arsenal won an eight-goal thriller at Highbury by 5-3 'Two of his efforts flew into the net before 'keeper Mick Mahoney could bat an eyelid,' wrote one reporter.

On song and seeking more goals, 'Supermac' scored twice in a 3-1 home win over Manchester United a week before Christmas, and a week later he did likewise in a 2-2 draw at Tottenham, following up with a point-saver in a 1-1 draw with Leeds United.

In January it was 'biff, bang, wallop' as he claimed his second treble for Arsenal in a 3-3 away draw with Birmingham City, for whom Trevor Francis also netted three times. This was the first time since April 1964 that a player from each side had scored a hat-trick.

After that impressive display at St Andrew's, Macdonald went five League games without a goal. Arsenal lost four and drew one of these fixtures and slipped five places down the table.

'Macdonald has lost his fire' was a heading on one newspaper, but he was soon back on the goal trail, scoring in each of the next three matches, all of which were lost!

He failed to find the net in his next three outings, and with Arsenal hovering in mid-table and looking an average side, it was apparent that another striker was required up front.

That was just paper-talk; nothing materialised on the transfer front and it was left to Macdonald, despite not being at his best – he admitted this – to battle on regardless. He did his best, rounding off the season with a flurry by scoring in wins over West Bromwich Albion (2-0),

Tottenham (1-0), Coventry City (2-0), Aston Villa (3-0) and Newcastle United (2-0). One of his strikes in the latter game was a stunning right-foot rocket past the hapless Mahoney (again).

Besides his twenty-five League goals, 'Supermac' also scored four more in Cup competitions. Annoyingly for him personally and certainly for the Arsenal supporters, he completed only one more season with the Gunners, topping the scoring charts with twenty-six League and Cup goals in 1977/78.

He scored once in the opening three League matches of the 1978/79 season before suffering a serious knee injury in a 2-1 League Cup defeat at Rotherham. Although he underwent lengthy treatment, 'Supermac' never recovered full fitness and despite a short loan spell with the Swedish club Djurgårdens IF, he officially announced his retirement at the end of August 1979, at the early age of twenty-nine.

After retirement, he returned to Fulham as commercial executive, taking over as manager in November 1980, becoming a director in August 1981 and resigning as manager in March 1984.

Next in charge of Huddersfield Town between October 1987 and May 1988, he assisted South Kinson FC (albeit briefly, in April 1990) and also played for FC Lusitano in South Africa before leaving football for good in 1991.

His time as manager at Craven Cottage was initially successful, with promotion being achieved in 1982, and the following season the London club looked nigh-on certainties for promotion to the First Division for the majority of the time, but a slump in the later stages of the campaign saw them wither away to finish fourth.

In 1983/84 Fulham finished in mid-table and as a result, 'Supermac' was subsequently replaced by Ray Harford.

His stay at Leeds Road was disastrous! The Terriers were thrashed 10-1 by Manchester City and suffered relegated from the Second Division in dismal fashion.

Turning his back on football, Macdonald was sadly declared bankrupt following a failed business venture. He divorced his second wife and after struggling with the aftermath of his injury, he became an alcoholic. He said in an interview that the pain from his long-standing knee injury led to his increasing dependence on alcohol. Thankfully, he eventually gave up drinking in 1997.

Since then, he has succeeded as a radio presenter on Real Radio's *Legends Football Phone-In*, alongside ex-players Bernie Slaven and Micky Horswill.

He also presents *Upfront With Malcolm Macdonald*, a 30-minute show consisting of interviews with ex-professional players across the Real Radio and Century Radio areas.

Born in Fulham on 7 January 1950 and initially a full-back, he played for Barnet, Knowle Park Juniors, Tonbridge and had a trial with Crystal Palace before signing as a professional for his local club, Fulham, in August 1968. Despite being converted into a striker by manager Bobby Robson, he failed to make headway with the Cottagers, and was sold to Luton Town for £17,500 in July 1969. Two years later, in May 1971, he moved to Newcastle United for £180,000.

A phenomenon of the '70s, and hero-worshipped at St James' Park, 'Supermac' scored 138 goals (95 in the League) in 258 first-team appearances for the Geordies, playing in the losing 1974 FA Cup and 1976 League Cup finals against Liverpool and Manchester City respectively, gaining fourteen England caps, plus two more at U23 level and representing the Football League. In fact, in his ninth international for England, in April 1975, he scored all five goals against Cyprus (won 5-0), becoming one of only four players to achieve this feat so far. Howard Vaughton (Aston Villa) was the first, against Ireland in 1882; the second was Steve Bloomer of Derby County against Wales in 1896; and the third was Tottenham Hotspur's Willie Hall, also against Ireland, in 1938.

MacDonald also played in Arsenal's 1978 FA Cup final defeat by Ipswich Town. He now lives in Jesmond, near Newcastle, and occasionally covers matches at St James' Park for a local radio station.

* In 1975, MacDonald took part in the Sports Superstars tournament and baffled everybody by clocking an amazing 10.9 seconds for the 100 metres. He held the European record for seven years until Des Drummond ran 10.85 seconds in the 1982 International Superstars in Hong Kong.

MACDOUGALL, TED (NORWICH CITY)

Season: 1975/76
Goals scored: 23 (out of 58); 12 home, 11 away
Percentage: 39.6 per cent
Runner-up: John Duncan (Tottenham Hotspur), 20 goals
Norwich finished tenth

It is not often that a player who won international honours and was ultimately remembered for his feats in the lower Divisions was also a leading goalscorer for one season in the Football League's top flight, but this is certainly the case with Ted MacDougall.

Having started his professional career with Liverpool, for whom he played only second and third-team football, MacDougall then spent two seasons with York City (1967–69) before scoring goals aplenty for Bournemouth between July 1969 and September 1972, banging in a record nine goals in an FA Cup-tie against Margate in November 1971.

From Dean Court, he moved to Manchester United, whose boss, Frank O'Farrell, paid out a record fee to a Third Division club of £200,000. Unfortunately, 'Super Mac', as he had been dubbed, was destined to spend only five months at Old Trafford, and when transfer-listed by newly-engaged manager Tommy Docherty in February 1973, domestic difficulties were said to be the main cause, his wife having failed to settle in Manchester.

A more apparent reason, however, was his lack of success on the field as the team, as a unit, failed to play to the opportunist's strengths! An early ball to the near post had generally seen MacDougall on hand to capitalize during his prolific spell with the Cherries, but sadly he netted only five times in eighteen League games for United, who sold him to West Ham for £170,000 three weeks after going on the list.

He was a 'Hammer' for just nine months, leaving Upton Park for Norwich City for £140,000 in December 1973, and over the next eighteen months became a star performer with the Canaries, notching a total of 66 goals in 138 outings.

Having been re-united with his former manager at Bournemouth, John Bond, he also linked up once again with his striker-partner Phil Boyer, who had played alongside him at both Bournemouth and York.

Unfortunately, at the end of the 1973/74 season the Canaries were relegated to the Second Division, although in the following season they not only regained their First Division status, but also reached the final of the League Cup.

In the semi-final, Norwich defeated MacDougall's former club, Manchester United, who were also spending a rare season in the Second Division. The final against Aston Villa was a tense, scrappy affair in which MacDougall had few scoring opportunities, with Villa winning by a single goal. It would be MacDougall's only Cup final appearance in his entire career.

In the 1975/76 season, Norwich were able to maintain their First Division place, with MacDougall – described by many as being a 'rough and ready centre-forward with an adventurous approach' – contributing twenty-three goals, making him the League's top scorer, three ahead of Tottenham Hotspur's John Duncan.

Highlights include two splendid hat-tricks in the space of four games. The first came in the third League match of the season, at home to Aston Villa on 23 August, when the Canaries gained sweet revenge for that League Cup final defeat by winning a thrilling contest 5-3. Two of his goals in this game were clinical finishes with his deadly right foot.

Two weeks later, 'Super Mac' bagged his second treble when Everton lost 4-2 at Carrow Road, and once again he let rip with two terrific drives after some smart work by Colin Suggett and Martin Peters. In his next two matches, MacDougall netted twice in each: in a rousing 4-4 draw with Burnley and a 2-0 win over Leicester. At this point in the campaign he was on fire, having netted fourteen times (in League and League Cup action).

Late in September he struck the winning goal at Sheffield United (1-0), but was then surprisingly quiet for virtually two months, mustering only one goal, in a 5-2 walloping at Newcastle.

However, MacDougall knew he wasn't playing badly and with a bit of luck could well have scored two or three more, twice grazing the woodwork in a 1-0 defeat against his former club, Manchester United, at Old Trafford on 1 November.

Norwich travelled to Anfield to play subsequent League champions Liverpool at the end of November and what a great day it turned out to be for the Canaries and their supporters as the Reds were beaten 3-1, with MacDougall scoring one of the goals and laying on another.

A week later, his effort beat West Ham (1-0) but his fine strike in the return fixture with Aston Villa proved fruitless as the Birmingham club turned things round to win 3-2.

Another five-match lean spell followed before MacDougall got back on the goal trail with a brace in a 3-0 away victory over Leeds United, knocking in another in a 3-1 win over Arsenal and doing likewise in a similar victory over Spurs.

Unfortunately for Norwich, MacDougall managed only three goals in the last eleven League games, scoring in away wins at West Ham (1-0) and Stoke City (2-0), and in the home victory over runners-up QPR (3-2).

Boyer (eleven) and Peters (ten) also got into double figures this season, but it was MacDougall who took the plaudits in the end – and who knows, if luck had been on his side in a few more matches, then he might well have topped the thirty-five-goal mark.

After spending the summers of 1974 and 1976 on loan with Jewish Guild (South Africa) and Weymouth respectively, he eventually left Carrow Road in September 1976 for Southampton for £50,000. A little over two years later, in November 1978, he re-joined his former club Bournemouth on a free transfer and later assisted, in turn, Detroit Express, Blackpool (as player-coach under Alan Ball, February 1980), Salisbury Town, Poole Town, AFC Totton, Gosport Borough, Floreaf Athena (Perth, Australia) and AFC Totton again and Andover (as player-coach), retiring in December 1983.

During his non-League days he had also run a string of south-coast sports shops and had been a licensee in Dunbridge, Hampshire, but that all changed in 1985, when he emigrated to Canada, where he entered property development, becoming a millionaire in a short period of time.

In June 1998, he came back to the UK and teamed up again with Alan Ball, this time as reserve-team coach at Portsmouth, but was sacked with Ball eighteen months later.

Now based in Atlanta, USA, where he was once the youth Director of Coaching with the Atlanta Silverbacks, in 2009 he actually created his own club, G.F.C Spurs, alongside Paul

Smith, who also played in England. One of MacDougall's youth teams, the U14 boys, won the Inter State Cup and made it to the regional finals, reaching the last eight.

During his adventurous career (at senior level) he netted well over 300 goals in more than 600 club games, including 256 in 535 League matches. He also scored three times in seven internationals for Scotland, starting with one fine effort on his debut against Sweden in Gothenburg in April 1975.

He was once keen to buy his former club, Bournemouth, who were £2.1 million in debt, but nothing came of his interest. MacDougall was born in Inverness on 8 January 1947.

Fact: Boyer and MacDougall when playing together for their various clubs, scored an aggregate total of 195 goals

McEVOY, ANDY (BLACKBURN ROVERS)

Season: 1964/65
Goals scored: 29 (out of 83); 14 home, 15 away
Percentage: 35 per cent
Joint top scorer with Jimmy Greaves (Tottenham Hotspur)
Blackburn Rovers finished tenth

Andy McEvoy was born in Dublin on 15 July 1938 and came to Blackburn from Bray Wanderers in October 1956. Originally an inside forward, he had been converted to wing-half and spent his early career in the Ewood Park reserves. As a result he did not make his first team debut until 20 April 1959, when he scored twice in a 3-1 home win against Luton.

Despite such success, he continued to be regarded as a backup for England skipper Ronnie Clayton and Irish international Mick McGrath at wing-half and never really threatened their positions in the team. Nevertheless, he was considered good enough to play for his country and made his debut against Scotland in 1961. It was to be the first of seventeen appearances, in which he scored six goals.

McEvoy's chance at Blackburn came when manager Jack Marshall decided to switch him back to inside forward to play alongside Fred Pickering in the 1962/63 season and he scored four goals in ten games.

The 1963-64 season saw the partnership blossom and if it had been allowed to stay together, there was a real chance McEvoy would have collected a League winner's medal, but when Rovers' directors, for reasons never properly explained, decided late in the season to let Pickering – who himself scored thirty-two League goals in 1963/64 – move to Everton, the east Lancashire side's challenge for the title inevitably faltered.

McEvoy was also pipped for top spot in the Division One scorers' charts, but with thirty-two in total he'd shown a knack for goals that only the great Jimmy Greaves had bettered with thirty-five. The two had faced each other early in the season, the winners of the European Cup-Winners Cup being hammered 7-2 at Ewood Park in a match in which Bryan Douglas at outside right was almost unplayable. Without a magnificent display between the posts by Bill Brown, the score would have been at least double. McEvoy grabbed two, his first of four doubles during the season.

There were also two hat-tricks, the first at the Hawthorns in a 3-1 success over WBA and the second on Boxing Day, when Upton Park witnessed Blackburn at their very best.

LANCASHIRE EVENING TELEGRAPH, Saturday, December 5, 1959

UICKSILVER ANDY CRACKS IN A BRILLIANT HAT-TRICK

By ALF THORNTON

ANDY McEVOY was back on the goals trail with a vengeance at Nottingham Forest today.

After the Rovers had gone behind in the fifth minute he popped in the equaliser from a Harrison cross and then rattled in two in two minutes early in the second half.

Byrom joined in the act ramming one home in the first half to help give the Rovers' score-line a healthy look.

Both teams were unchanged and at full strength.

NOTTS FOREST

THE GOALS:

WIGNALL (Forest) .. 5 min
McEVOY (Rovers) .. 23 min
BYROM (Rovers) .. 32 min
McEVOY (Rovers) .. 47 min
McEVOY (Rovers) .. 49 min
BYROM (Rovers) .. 73 min
CROWE (Forest) .... 83 min.

ing again with Douglas mesmerising Forest's defence by

Cycling

Liverpool keeper Lawrence cuts out a cross from Morgan to foil Lochhead.

Arriving as League leaders, they waltzed all over the Hammers to win 8-2 with Pickering and McEvoy, with goals on 40, 65 and 78 minutes, both scoring hat-tricks. Football, though, is a funny business and two days later West Ham got their revenge by winning 3-1 in the return fixture at Ewood Park.

McEvoy was also unable to beat Greaves in 1964/65, but with twenty-nine goals he did the next best thing by finishing alongside him at the top of the Division One scoring charts.

His first came in the third match as Rovers beat Champions Liverpool 3-2 in a thrilling Ewood Park match. Two doubles at home to Blackpool and away to Aston Villa showed that even without Pickering alongside him, McEvoy was still going to score regularly, especially when he had the likes of Douglas in his side; the England international ran riot when Wolves came north, creating McEvoy's first on the stroke of half time with a wonderful through ball. On 80 minutes the Irishman doubled his tally and might have had a hat-trick, only to be denied twice by Jimmy Barron, as Rovers ran off 4-1 winners.

Against Sheffield United, McEvoy took his total for the season into double figures when he notched his first hat-trick of the season as Blackburn won 4-0.

The following weekend at Goodison Park, Rovers suffered at the hands of his former teammate when Pickering scored on just eight minutes, with Alex Young making it 2-0 just 2 minutes later. There was therefore relief when McEvoy scrambled home to reduce the arrears on 21 minutes, and after half time the away side played some lovely football. It was no surprise when they equalised through McEvoy. New strike partner John Byrom pushed a lovely ball beyond Brian Labone for the Irishman to make it 2-2. Alan Bradshaw topped off the recovery with the winning effort on 70 minutes. McEvoy moved on to sixteen League goals for the season when he netted twice in a 4-2 home win over WBA.

Then, on 5 December 1964, he moved on to nineteen with a second hat-trick of the campaign. Nottingham Forest were leading when he got his first on 23 minutes, heading Mike Harrison's cross to the back post past Peter Grummitt's left hand. Shortly after, he hit the post from a lovely Douglas pass, but when the same player then cut open the home defence, Byrom pushed Rovers into the lead at half time.

On the restart McEvoy wrapped up his hat-trick, the supreme opportunist getting in front of everyone to head home Clayton's free kick before touching home a Douglas free kick to make it 4-1. Byrom got the fifth, one of twenty-five goals he contributed to the Rovers cause during the season, as Rovers ran out 5-2 winners. Byrom himself was to score two hat-tricks during the season, against West Ham and against Aston Villa on 2 January, when with two goals himself, McEvoy moved over the twenty-goal League barrier.

After such an exciting and successful first half of the season, he was unable to keep up the momentum in the second. Only one goal was scored in each of February and March. He was back on the mark in April with goals at Fulham and Spurs.

His final goal of the campaign then came in a remarkable contest at St Andrews, where relegation threatened Birmingham City and Rovers slugged out a 5-5 draw. The result did little for the home side, who were relegated. Joining them in Division Two at the end of the following season were to be their opponents, as with McEvoy picking up where he finished the 1964/65 season, Blackburn struggled in 1965/66 and went down with just twenty points. McEvoy scored ten goals in thirty-one League appearances. Relegation hit Andy McEvoy harder than most and he spent most of his time back in the reserves. He eventually returned to Ireland to play for Limerick in August 1967 and ended up driving a tram in the town. He went on to play for them into the early 1970s. He died in May 1994 in Bray, Ireland.

McEvoy's Blackburn Rovers career record reads: 183 League appearances, 89 goals; 17 FA Cup appearances, 10 goals; 13 League Cup appearances, 4 goals; with a total of 213 appearances and 103 goals.

McLEAN, DAVID (SHEFFIELD WEDNESDAY)

Season: 1911/12
Goals scored: 25 (out of 69); 17 home, 8 away
Percentage: 36 per cent
Joint top scorer with George Holley (Sunderland) and Harry Hampton (Aston Villa)
Sheffield Wednesday finished fifth

Season: 1912/13
Goals scored: 30 (out of 75); 18 home, 12 away
Percentage: 40 per cent
Runner-up: Charlie Buchan (Sunderland), 27 goals
Sheffield Wednesday finished third

Wednesday opened the 1911/12 season with just a point from the first five games, a 2-2 draw with Bury on 9 September in which McLean, signed in the summer from Preston North End, got his first goal.

In the sixth game they beat Spurs 4-0, with McLean one of the scorers. It was his first at 'Owlerton'. Surrounded by two defenders as he collected a Tom Brittleton centre, he manoeuvred the ball cleverly before driving home a powerful rising shot. Nevertheless, the new man continued to struggle, and his penalty against Newcastle United on 28 October was only his fourth of the season. It was a figure that hadn't risen when Wednesday played Bradford City on 25 November.

Fifteen minutes in, McLean's low drive beat Mark Mellors for the opening goal and he added his side's fourth when from George Robertson's centre, he 'crashed the ball into the net'. The following weekend at Plumstead Highbury, he pressurised Woolwich Arsenal's Percy Sands, blocking his clearance and picking up the rebound to put Wednesday ahead after 15 minutes. Continuing to look for every available opportunity, he wasn't going to miss when Manchester City's 'keeper Bill Smith dropped a simple cross, and he later added a second in a 3-0 win with a 15-yard shot. Two more quickly followed as WBA were beaten 4-1, the second completing a lovely move involving all the home forwards.

On Boxing Day, Sunderland travelled back home punch-drunk, hammered 8-0, with McLean getting four. The home side were helped by an injury to the Wearsiders' influential centre half Charlie Thomson, but it was still a fine all-round team performance. At 2-0 up, 'McLean slipped past the full backs and scored a brilliant 3rd goal' reported the *Newcastle Journal*. Before half time it was 7-0, with McLean completing the scoring in the 58th minute.

A (H)OWLING SUCCESS.

The Owl of Owlerton: "Fanny! None of my visitors seem to like this brand.
(On Monday, Sheffield Wednesday beat Blackburn Rovers 2—1.)

The score remains Sunderland's record equal defeat, with Wednesday's other goals coming that day from Sam Kirkman and Ted Glennon, both of whom scored twice.

Back on the familiar territory of Deepdale, McLean maintained his scoring form, playing a superb 1-2 with Robertson before netting and then hitting the winner with an unstoppable 25-yard shot after 80 minutes. Two more in a 3-0 home win against Notts County pushed Wednesday into fifth place. Albert Iremonger should have saved the first, described in the *Sheffield Telegraph* 'as not as severe as you expect when David deliberately lets drive', but the second was a wonderful effort, the centre forward shrugging off some heavy challenges before hammering a shot past the County 'keeper.

In February further efforts flew into the nets of Manchester United and Aston Villa, McLean sweeping home a left-wing cross in the former and pouncing on a lovely Kirkman centre before blasting the ball over Brendel Anstey's head against Villa.

Now playing the best football of his career, it was no surprise when McLean was given a first opportunity to play for his country. It could not have been a bigger game, Scotland versus England at Hampden Park with a world record crowd of 127,307. McLean joined his Wednesday colleague Andy Wilson, making his third of an eventual six appearances in the Scotland side. Also playing out wide was McLean's close friend, Jimmy Quinn from Celtic, with whom he enjoyed a marvellous two weeks in April 1909 when the Glasgow side swept to the Scottish title by collecting eleven points from the final games. Unable thereafter to find a regular place in the side, McLean moved onto Preston later that year.

Against England it was Wilson, a Wednesday legend who played more than 500 times and scored more than 200 goals for his club, who gave the home crowd something to really shout about on 7 minutes when he opened the scoring, only for Sunderland's George Holley to drive home the only other goal on 13 minutes. Sadly for McLean, he never got another chance to play for his country.

McLean wrapped up his season in fine form with all three of Wednesday's goals in a 5-1 final day thrashing of a WBA side still suffering from a shock FA Cup final defeat to Second Division Barnsley. He was helped by some poor refereeing, Mr Bullimore appearing to already be on his holidays by allowing two of his efforts from apparently offside positions, but his third was the result of a lovely left-foot shot following some fine forward line passing.

In a direct reversal of the previous season, Wednesday opened the 1912/13 season by losing just one point from the first five games. McLean was immediately up and running, hitting seven from five, including two against Middlesbrough – a first-half header and then, after hitting the crossbar, running through on 72 minutes to beat Tim Williamson. Injured in the 3-3 home draw with Manchester United, he still managed to score a penalty equaliser on 47 minutes. Wednesday's impressive opening start was to come to a shuddering half in the sixth game, hammered 10-0 at Aston Villa. Yet three consecutive victories, against Oldham, Chelsea and Arsenal, were enough to raise hopes of a third championship after previous successes in 1902/03 and 1903/04.

At Stamford Bridge, McLean was part of a superb all-round Wednesday forward line display. The crowning moment of a 4-0 victory came when McLean's pass out to Robertson saw the winger dash forward before pulling the ball back for the onrushing McLean to bury it deep into the corner of the net to end the scoring. By the end of December he had fourteen goals, with Wednesday in second place in the table.

Four more goals flew into opponents' nets in January, with his goal at Ayresome Park a remarkable effort in which he appeared to make the ball swerve in the air before beating Williamson.

Against Grimsby in the Cup, and on a snow-covered pitch, he once again scored four times in a match. Two of his efforts came from finishing off dribbling Glennon runs.

'As usual, he seldom looked to be doing much, yet you found in the end he was engaged in his favourite practice of scoring goals,' reported the *Sheffield Telegraph*. He did so in the next round as well, scoring another four in two matches against Chelsea.

At Anfield, McLean 'took a pass from Wilson, beat both backs, and went through to score with a shot which Campbell touched but could not stop.' Then, in the local derby against United, he hit an unstoppable shot from the corner of the area in a match won 2-0. Wednesday was now top of the league. Despite his form there was no second chance for Scotland, the selectors preferring Rangers' Bill Reid in a Scotland side that contained Wilson and Robertson from the Wednesday side.

Despite their absence, Wednesday still managed the same day to beat Bradford City 6-0. McLean grabbed the third after a brave, gutsy run and completed the scoring with a 30-yard shot. With four games remaining Wednesday were still top, but with just one point from four over Easter, they slipped behind Sunderland and Aston Villa and were to eventually finish third. McLean scored his final goals of the season in the penultimate match with WBA, failing to give Jesse Pennington time to clear and then netting after following up Robertson's saved shot in a 3-2 victory.

McLean's form was to dip the following season with just nine goals, but he returned with twenty-two in 1914/15. After the war, during which, by playing for Rangers, he became one of a select band of players to play for both Glasgow giants, he returned to play just three more times for Wednesday, taking his total appearances up to 147 appearances and 100 goals. Moving on to Bradford Park Avenue, he later enjoyed spells at Dundee and back at his first club, Forfar Athletic. He died in 1967.

MOIR, WILLIE (BOLTON WANDERERS)

Season: 1948/49
Goals scored: 25 (out of 59); 16 home, 9 away
Percentage: 42 per cent
Runner-up: Frank Bowyer (Stoke City), 21 goals
Bolton finished fourteenth

Willie Moir was a talented winger who was moved inside after Bolton started the 1948/49 season poorly and was thrashed 5-0 at home by Wolves in the third match. Two days later at Villa Park, Bolton were down 1-0 when 'Moir from just inside the box took a cross knee high first time and sent it hurtling under the Villa bar … for what was one of the best volleys by a Wanderer since the days of Joe Smith', reported the *Bolton Evening News*.

Moir, however, had only got started, and in the 52nd and 65th minutes of the game he found good positions to receive the ball from Harry McShane and Don Howe and smashed home two further goals. Then, on 70 minutes, the Scotsman who signed for Bolton after he was spotted playing for the RAF team by their chief scout, Bob Jackson, made it 4-1, converting Nat Lofthouse's cross to the congratulations of his teammates.

A few short weeks later, Moir took his total to six League goals by scoring both goals in a 2-0 away win at Huddersfield. First, on 57 minutes he superbly timed his header from Tom

Woodward's corner kick, and then, 7 minutes later, he was first on to a Harry McShane pass to push the ball home.

Moir then scored his first home goal against Blackpool. With Bolton 2-0 down, Moir shot out his leg to squeeze the ball past George Farm in a game that ended 2-2 and thrilled a large crowd. Moir was to score past Farm in a far more important encounter four seasons later, his effort putting Bolton back into the lead in the 1953 FA Cup final and seemingly setting them up for success when Eric Bell later made it 3-1. Blackpool, after finishing as runners up in 1948 and 1951, though, were not to be denied and, inspired by Stanley Matthews, roared back to win with Stan Mortensen scoring three times.

Sadly for Moir, that was his last chance to capture a winner's medal in League or Cup, because by the time Bolton was back at Wembley in 1958, he had retired. Moir did, however, play in the Bolton side that in 1944/45 beat Manchester United in the League North Cup final and then followed this up by beating the Southern League Cup winners Chelsea in the Cup Winners' Cup final. Sadly, with the war just over, no medals were awarded and he received some savings certificates instead.

Despite their fine play against their near neighbours, Bolton was struggling and scored just two, one from Moir, in the next six games. There was therefore an urgent need to collect two points when Manchester City visited Burnden Park. Moir got his side moving when he opened the scoring with an edge-of-the-box drive that beat City 'keeper Frank Swift and went into the net off the woodwork. Bolton's top scorer, though, was to be surpassed this particular day, with Malcolm Barrass rightly taking the plaudits with four goals in a welcome 5-1 victory.

With Lofthouse injured, the pair continued their partnership with devastating results. Stoke were unbeaten in seven games, but a goal apiece was enough for Bolton to win 2-1. Moir's effort was a piece of real opportunism as he turned Bradley's pass quickly into the net from 8 yards.

Preston North End arrived at Burnden Park in early December 1948, having avoided defeat there for twenty-four years. Bolton, though, was now in decent form after a poor start to the season, and the away side was thrashed 5-1. Barrass and Moir both scored, the latter heading home John Bradley's free kick for the third and then hitting a low shot on 75 minutes for his fourteenth League goal of the season. It was fifteen when he swept home a returning Lofthouse's cross against Sunderland.

Then, on 27 December, Moir scored four goals for the second time in the season. It was 0-0 at half time with Sheffield United, but on 48 minutes Moir, showing the sort of aerial ability more often associated with his strike partner Lofthouse, powered the ball into the net. Two well-placed fast shots ensured his hat-trick before a simple finish completed a fine afternoon's work as the Blades were beaten 6-1. Moir now had nineteen and it was just turned Christmas. Could he keep it going in the New Year?

In fact, he couldn't. Bolton managed to score in only two games out of the next ten. Fortunately, both were won, with Moir being among the scorers when Derby County lost heavily, beaten 4-0. Middlesbrough also suffered from conceding four at Burnden Park. Moir grabbed three. All came in the first 25 minutes. First, he followed up after Rolando Ugolini spilled a Lofthouse shot before then heading home from a corner, and then completing his scoring after some fine passing between him and Lofthouse carved open the Boro defence.

Moir hit his final goal of the season on the last day. With 21 minutes gone in the home game against Everton, he met a Woodward free kick to bullet a header past Ted Sagar.

There were only 22,725 present, but for Willie Moir it was a special moment: his twenty-fifth League goal of the season, ensuring he topped the First Division goalscoring table. His fine close control, good heading ability, improvisation in front of goal and an ability to find space around the box had all contributed to a remarkable achievement for a player more suited to playing out wide.

Moir scored 118 goals in 325 games for Bolton. Joining Stockport County in 1955, he hit another twenty-six goals in seventy appearances. He died in 1988. He was capped once for his country, playing against England on 15 April 1950 in a game Scotland lost 1-0.

MORRIS, FRED (WEST BROMWICH ALBION)

Season: 1919/20
Goals scored: 37 (out of 104); 26 home, 11 away
Percentage: 35.5 per cent
Runner-up: George Elliott (Middlesbrough), 31 goals
WBA were League Champions

In 1919/20, West Bromwich Albion set three League records – the first team to gain sixty points, the first to win more than twenty-five matches and the first to score over 100 goals in the top flight. Fred Morris finished up as the team's and the League's top marksman, with thirty-seven.

Congratulated, particularly on the 'clean and sporting manner' in which they won the First Division title, the Baggies showed such consistency that there was scarcely any doubt that they would become champions. In the end they outran their closest challengers, racing home nine points clear of Burnley.

There was a tremendous amount of experience in the team, which included five players who had helped the club win the Second Division in 1911 and reach the FA Cup final the following year.

Their defence was solid enough, with England international full-back Jesse Pennington an inspirational captain, while up front the king-pin was local discovery Fred Morris, a highly skilled inside-left with a powerful shot.

Morris, 5 feet 10 inches tall, was fast and alert, and a sharp-shooter of the highest calibre. An opportunist, willing to shoot on sight from any distance, he got his season off to a flier, scoring twice in an opening day 3-1 win at Oldham. His first was a beauty; receiving the ball at an awkward angle, he turned and flashed it into the net with a curving motion which left the Latics' 'keeper helpless.

Goalless in his next two games, Morris bagged his third of the campaign with a scrambled effort following a goalmouth melee to sew up a 3-0 home victory over Newcastle. In the next game, after edging Albion 2-1 in front just before half time, he laid on a second-half goal as the Baggies won a 'titanic contest' 4-3.

On target in a 4-1 home win over Bradford City when Albion centre-half Sid Bowser scored a hat-trick, and again in a 2-1 over Bolton, Morris became a 'national star' when he struck five goals (in the 9th, 40th, 47th, 75th and 77th minutes) when Notts County were hammered 8-0 at The Hawthorns on 1 November.

His first, fired low past Albert Iremonger after a precise cross from Claude Jephcott, was followed by a brilliant solo effort which saw him waltz past three defenders before sliding the ball home from 10 yards.

His third and fourth goals came as a result of some fine creative play by Tommy Magee, while his fifth came from a vicious right-foot drive after a clever dummy by Andy Smith.

Out of sorts in the return fixture with County (lost 2-0), and also in a 2-1 home defeat by Aston Villa, Morris was back to his best with a second-half brace in a 4-2 victory in swirling snow on a muddy Villa Park pitch. He put Albion 2-1 ahead 5 minutes into the second half with an 'easy' finish from Jephcott's cross before making it 4-1 after a 'beautiful piece of skill on the edge of the box'.

Between 29 November and 24 January, Albion played ten League games, winning nine, and hotshot Morris scored in every one. At this juncture he was at his peak, and after netting with a 'supreme individual effort' in a 3-0 victory at Sheffield Wednesday, he followed up with a brace in both games with Manchester City. He struck home two terrific right-foot rockets in 5 second-half minutes in a 3-2 win at Maine Road and amazingly netted twice inside the first 2 minutes of the return fixture at The Hawthorns (2-0) – a smart low from Howard Gregory's pass and a superb chip over the head of 'keeper Goodchild.

On fire and full of confidence, Morris rapped in three more twos in the next three matches – in wins over Derby County (4-0 home and 3-0 away) and Sunderland (4-0) in between. He bagged his first brace against the Rams in the space of 65 seconds halfway through the second half, converted two simple chances in pouring rain against Sunderland and got the ball rolling against County second time round with an opener after just 4 minutes.

Scoring in each of the next four games, including crucial ones in home victories over Blackburn Rovers (5-2) and Manchester United (2-1), Morris's effort in the latter was a fine, high drive past Jack Mew.

Goalless in home and away games against Sheffield United, Morris got back on song with two well-placed right-footed drives in a 4-2 victory away at Middlesbrough, his second being his thirtieth goal of the season. He then had a successful trial with England, which led to him gaining his first of two full caps later in the season when he scored in a 5-4 victory over Scotland.

Back in the fray and eager for more goals, the Black Country-born striker missed a couple of easy chances in the 2-2 top-of-the-table draw at Burnley before netting twice in a 4-1 victory in the return game, his second a clever chip over the grounded 'keeper.

With games fast running out and the League championship within their sights, Albion doubled up over Preston North End, Morris scoring twice in a 4-1 home win, and then thrashed Bradford 4-0 at Park Avenue, Morris again on target.

Closing in on the League scoring record, and with games fast running out, Morris now needed four goals to overtake Bert Freeman's tally of thirty-eight, set in 1908/09. He scored a 10th-minute winner against Arsenal (1-0), but owing to international duty (against the Scots in Sheffield) he missed the 3-1 home win over Bradford, the day the First Division championship was clinched. Then, after a subdued display at Liverpool (0-0), he netted in the return clash with the Merseysiders (1-1), which was also Albion's 100th League goal of the season.

This left Morris on thirty-seven goals and in the last game at home to Chelsea, all his teammates, even 'keeper Hubert Pearson with some over-elaborate clearances, tried to set up chances for their inside-left. He missed three easy openings, had two well-struck shots saved, and also shaved the woodwork in a 4-0 win. But who cared – Albion was champion of England!

Morris scored forty-six League goals over the next four seasons, becoming the first Albion player to reach the milestone of 100 goals in competitive football. He left The Hawthorns for Coventry City in August 1924, having netted career 118 times in 287 appearances for the Baggies. After a spell with Oakengates Town, he retired in May 1930.

Born in Tipton on 27 August 1893, Morris played initially for Bell Street Primitives, then Tipton Victoria and Redditch, before moving to The Hawthorns as a professional in May 1911. He guested for Fulham and Watford during the First World War and also represented the Football League.

Morris – master goalscorer – died in his native Tipton in July 1962.

MORTENSEN, STAN (BLACKPOOL)

Season: 1950/51
Goals scored: 30 (out of 79); 13 home, 17 away
Percentage: 38 per cent
Runner-up: Jackie Lee (Derby County), 28 goals
Blackpool finished third

Famous for scoring a hat-trick at the 1953 FA Cup final, Mortensen was the cutting edge of an exciting, entertaining forward line in which Stanley Matthews was the outstanding talent, with the Blackpool centre forward not too far behind.

Born in South Shields, Mortensen was lucky to survive the Second World War when his Wellington Bomber crashed, killing two of the four-man crew and leaving the other with just one leg. Signed by Blackpool in 1937, he had failed to make his first-team debut and his chances of doing so looked dim when the doctors told him the crash meant he should avoid heading the ball, as it could cause serious health problems. Ignoring this advice, soon afterwards he played with success for the RAF side before appearing in a number of friendly games for the Seasiders.

On the resumption of football in 1945/46, Mortensen scored on his debut away to Wrexham in the FA Cup. It was not going to be the last goal he scored in the famous competition, and in 1947/48 he scored in every round, including a blistering semi-final hat-trick to overturn a Spurs lead that lasted until the 86th minute of the match. Then, in the final, he put Blackpool back into the lead by converting a Hughie Kelly cross, only for Matt Busby's Manchester United to come out 4-2 winners at the end of a match many felt was the best FA Cup final ever seen at Wembley.

Blackpool had finished the 1949/50 season disappointingly. Seemingly set for a first ever Division One title success, only one game in the last ten was won, leaving Portsmouth to come through and retain their title. Spurs had gained promotion at the end of the season, and with their 'push and run' tactics were expected to do well in the top flight. So, a first-day encounter at White Hart Lane might have been something to avoid, yet with Matthews at his best, Blackpool stormed to an impressive 4-1 victory, Mortensen grabbing his first goal of the season.

At Burnley, Mortensen was so badly injured that the referee Bill Evans suggested he leave the pitch rather than limp out the remaining 20 minutes on the left wing. Refusing, he assisted his side to a 0-0 draw but suffered by being unavailable for the next two matches. There was further disappointment when he then learned he had been overlooked at centre forward for England in their subsequent international match against Northern Ireland. England had done badly at the 1950 World Cup finals, even losing 1-0 to the USA, and the selectors had decided to take a look at a new man in Derby County's Jack Lee. Mortensen had made his international debut in May 1947 when, in a match that Matthews rated as one of the greatest he had ever played in, England beat Portugal 10-0, with Mortensen grabbing four.

Mortensen grabbed his second goal of the 1950/51 season in Blackpool's tenth League game, yet according to Clifford Greenwood in the *Blackpool Evening Gazette*, he 'was still that half yard slower off the mark'. He then also played poorly against Chelsea, but with the game tied at 2-2 his non-stop effort paid off; when presented with a simple chance, he netted from 6 yards out for the winner. Continuing his bustling, battling performances, Mortensen managed a goal at St James' Park but should have done better, missing two golden chances that Greenwood reported showed 'that for now his old magic has forsaken him'. Yet with Alan Withers coming into the side and scoring five goals in his first four matches, Blackpool could afford to wait until Mortensen found his shooting boots.

When he did, he scored twice at Highbury in a 4-4 thriller. Then, at home to Liverpool, Allan Brown's perfect pass set up his first and he hit 'number two with all the old venom in the shot'.

With Blackpool nine points behind leaders Middlesbrough in early January, hopes of any success rested on the FA Cup. Mortensen managed four goals as Charlton and Stockport were beaten to put Blackpool in the fifth round. The goals seemed to kick-start his season, and at Aston Villa on 3 February 1951 he was one of the away side's three scorers in a match that had the whole crowd applauding Matthews as he left the field, so wonderfully had the wing-man played. Derby County then had to twice pick Mortensen's efforts out of the net – his second a blistering free kick – before he scored for the third consecutive game as Chelsea were beaten 2-0 at Stamford Bridge. It was an opportunist's goal, following up when Brown's shot got stuck in the mud.

There was now no stopping Mortensen, Portsmouth, Newcastle, Bolton and Everton all conceding goals to make it seven consecutive League games. In between, the north-east lad had also set up a place in the FA Cup final against Newcastle United by putting his side a goal up in the replayed semi-final with Birmingham City. 'Keeper Gil Merrick had got both hands to his shot, but the pace was simply too strong to prevent the ball rolling over the line as Blackpool advanced 2-1.

Mortensen made it eight scoring League games in a row when he struck at Burnden Park. It was a fierce encounter; Mortensen had deflected Bob Langton's shot into his own net and also scored Blackpool's goal when, with 2 minutes left, he followed up another Brown shot to give his side both points. It was his twenty-fifth League goal of the season.

Goals number twenty-six and twenty-seven weren't long in the making, Stoke suffering a 3-0 defeat that could have been much greater. Away at WBA, Mortensen made it ten scoring games in a row. He left it late, but after playing an important part in both Jackie Mudie's goals, the Blackpool centre-forward made it 3-0 with just 2 minutes remaining. Ten in a row then became eleven, but with Blackpool's players now doing their best to ensure they were fit to play at Wembley, Huddersfield won much more comfortably than the 2-1 scoreline suggested.

Next game up was Middlesbrough and Mortensen failed to score. Not that he ever had any chance of doing so as he was on England duty, earning high praise for ignoring a jaw injury to lead an ultimately unsuccessful fightback as Scotland won a fine match 3-2. However, his record of scoring in eleven consecutive games is a top-flight feat that remains unique.

One week later, and for his twelfth League game in a row, Mortensen was again on the Blackpool scoresheet as Sheffield Wednesday won 3-1 at Hillsborough. It was his thirtieth of the season, a brilliant effort, but one he might well have traded for just one match-winning effort at Wembley, but playing poorly, Blackpool lost 2-0 to two Jackie Milburn goals. Consolation for one of the losing side, captain Harry Johnston, came in the form of the Football Writers' Association Footballer of the Year Award.

Mortensen was, of course, to gain his FA Cup winner's medal just two seasons later when, inspired by Matthews, Blackpool recovered from being 3-1 down to Bolton to win 4-3. Mortensen, by scoring a hat-trick, became the first, and to date only, player to achieve the feat at a Wembley FA Cup final.

Mortensen also suffered further Wembley disappointment in 1953, playing alongside three of his Blackpool teammates as Hungary crushed the home side 6-3. It was to prove his final international match, leaving him with twenty-five caps and twenty-three goals. After leaving Blackpool in 1955, Mortensen played for Hull and Southport before spells with Bath and Lancaster City in non-League football. Returning to Bloomfield Road as manager in 1967, he was denied promotion on goal average in 1968. He died in May 1991 and the fine player that he was, it is entirely appropriate that a statue of him has been erected outside Blackpool's ground.

Tommy Lawton described Mortensen as 'the most dangerous attacker of his day. With that curious, energetic run he burst open more defences than any other man of his time, and I don't think I know a player who was faster off the mark than this Blackpool Bombshell was. Knocks and injuries meant nothing to Morty.'

NISTELROOY, RUUD VAN (MANCHESTER UNITED)

Season: 2002/03
Goals scored: 25 (out of 74); 16 home, 9 away
Percentage: 34 per cent
Runner-up: Thierry Henry (Arsenal), 24 goals
Manchester were Premier League Champions

Having seen his transfer from PSV Eindhoven to Manchester United delayed due to injury by nearly a year, the Dutchman arrived at Old Trafford in April 2001 for a fee of £19 million. He was quickly into his stride at the start of the following season, grabbing a brace on his League debut to overcome a spirited Fulham side 3-2 at Old Trafford. He was also on the score sheet in a sensational game at White Hart Lane when the away side came from three down at half time to win 5-3.

In December, van Nistelrooy began a remarkable run by hitting one of United's five goals against Derby. Then, after scoring the only goal in a 1-0 win at Middlesbrough, a hat-trick followed in a 6-1 Old Trafford demolition of Southampton. A single goal in each of his next five League games, plus two at Villa in the FA Cup, meant he had scored in eight consecutive League matches and nine in total. When he failed to hit the net, his partner up front, Ole Gunnar Solskjaer, was able to do so, scoring three at Bolton in a 4-0 win and twice at Elland Road, when Manchester United won a thriller 4-3.

However, with Arsenal in fine form, neither Solskjaer nor van Nistlerooy was able to score when the freshly crowned FA Cup winners came to Old Trafford in May, the Gunners leaving with all three points, the marvellous record of remaining unbeaten away in the League during the season and the Premiership Trophy. There was then further disappointment when Bayer Leverkusen managed to overcome Sir Alex Ferguson's side on away goals in the semi-finals of the Champions League. Nistlerooy had scored ten goals in Europe, more than anyone else, and was voted the PFA Players' Player of the Year.

Manchester United began the 2002/03 season slowly, with just eight points from six games. Plenty of chances had been missed in the seventh game when van Nistelrooy scored from the spot to win a tight game 1-0, after which his manger said, 'Ruud is scoring again and that's a good sign. His whole psyche is built around scoring goals.'

Kicking off early against Newcastle United, a large crowd inside Old Trafford and millions watching on TV witnessed a superb performance by Manchester United, capped by van Nistelrooy grabbing a hat-trick, his second in his Manchester career. Mikael Silvestre created the first, a simple header, and after Diego Forlán mis-kicked, the Dutchman had the easy task of knocking his second into an empty net. His third, on 53 minutes, was again from no more than a few yards out as the home side moved up the table with a 5-3 win. Only five points separated Ferguson's side from Arsenal at the top when 2002 ended.

Not that the Gunners were giving up their title without a fight and when Manchester United travelled to face Birmingham City in early February, three points were vital. In the 56th minute, van Nistelrooy showed why he had cost such a hefty fee. Receiving the ball with his back to the goal and seemingly no way through a packed defence, he swivelled before driving a low shot past Nico Vaesen in the home goal. A precious victory at 1-0.

Nevertheless, with nine games of the season left, Manchester United was still five points behind Arsenal. In March, though, the Gunners were to lose crucially twice to Blackburn Rovers. There was therefore real joy when David Beckham hit the only goal at Villa Park to set up the following weekend's home game with Fulham.

A fine 3-0 win duly saw van Nistelrooy grab all three. His first, a penalty, was easy enough, and his third enjoyed a touch of good fortune when his last-minute volley took a deflection to deceive Maik Taylor. His second, though, was a real cracker. Collecting the ball in the centre-circle, he shrugged off the challenge of Sylvian Legwinski before running clear of two defenders, jinking past Andy Melville and rifling a right-foot finish into the far corner of the net that those in the Stretford End behind greeted with universal approval. No wonder Sir Alex Ferguson said about it afterwards that the goal 'will be up there with the best goals in Old Trafford's history. It had courage, determination, drive and speed.' Only two points now separated Arsenal and Manchester United.

And when the United front-man hit two penalties as Liverpool were trounced 4-0, the gap was now just goal difference as Ferguson's side set off to face Spanish giants Real

Madrid in the Champions' League quarter-final. Three goals down, van Nistelrooy gave his side a possible lifeline with a 52nd-minute opportunist goal when Iker Casillas parried Ryan Giggs's shot. He also scored in the second leg and Manchester United won another thrilling game 4-3, going out 6-4 on aggregate.

The Dutchman had also played his part in another stunning performance a few weeks earlier. Newcastle were in third place before the match at St James' Park and victory would have taken them to within three points of the joint League leaders. There was therefore great joy when Jermaine Jenas opened the scoring on 21 minutes.

Shola Ameobi even grabbed a second in the last minute, but in between Manchester United ran riot to score six times. Van Nistelrooy got the final one, a penalty on 58 minutes, just 26 minutes after Solskjaer had scored the away side's first. For once, both forwards were outshone by Paul Scholes who, after hitting a wonderful volley, added two more. It was a fine achievement that took the midfielder's season's tally up to seventeen. United, said Ferguson, were 'awesome' as they roared into top spot. It was a position they maintained in a 2-2 draw at Highbury, in which van Nistelrooy opened the scoring with a fine finish after a surging run. Now all the away side had to do was keep winning and the Premiership Trophy was theirs. They did so, beating Blackburn 3-1 at Old Trafford and Spurs 3-1 at White Hart Lane, Nistelrooy scoring in both matches.

On the first Saturday in May Manchester United entertained Charlton Athletic, knowing that victory would put Arsenal under pressure in their final home game of the season the following day against Leeds United. The game was tied at 1-1 when on 32 minutes van Nistelrooy hit a beauty, swivelling to fire a volley into the net. Within 25 minutes he'd added another two, with his second settling any nerves for the Champions elect. And when Arsenal slipped up against Leeds the following afternoon, Manchester United were top-flight champions for the fifteenth time.

With the title in the bag, Manchester United made sure of finishing the season on a high, van Nistelrooy scoring a penalty to win 2-1 at Goodison Park. He thus became the first Manchester United player to have scored in ten successive matches, scoring a total of forty-four goals during the season. With twenty-five League goals, van Nistlerooy had also beaten Thierry Henry by one goal to finish as the Premier League top scorer.

'The title was a collective effort, but there can be no doubt that Ruud was a particularly inspiring figure,' said Sir Alex Ferguson.

The former PSV man was to enjoy further success with Manchester United before acrimoniously departing from Old Trafford in the summer of 2006. He scored twice, one a penalty, in a 3-0 victory against Millwall in the 2004 FA Cup final and although injury forced him to miss most of the 2004/05 season, he was still able to score eight times in the Champions' League. Back towards his best in 2005/06, when he collected a League Cup winner's medal, he netted twenty-one Premier League goals. When he departed Old Trafford, he did so having hit 150 goals in just 219 games. Since then he has enjoyed further success with Real Madrid and Hamburg.

OWEN, MICHAEL (LIVERPOOL)

Season: 1997/98
Goals scored: 18 (out of 68); 9 at home, 9 away
Percentage: 26.7 per cent
Joint top scorer with Dion Dublin (Coventry City) and Chris Sutton (Blackburn Rovers)
Liverpool finished third

Season 1998/99
Goals scored: 18 (out of 68); 12 home, 6 away
Percentage: 26.7 per cent
Joint top scorer with Dwight Yorke (Manchester United) and Jimmy-Floyd Hasselbaink
(Leeds United)
Liverpool finished seventh

Michael Owen has scored in every season except one since making his League debut for Liverpool in May 1997. And at the end of the 2010/11 campaign, his record in senior football was quite outstanding: 261 goals scored in 564 competitive matches at club and international level combined.

Born on 14 December 1979 in Chester, the son a former Everton footballer, Terry Owen, Owen junior attended Rector Drew Primary School in Hawarden, North Wales, and by the age of ten some of the nation's leading scouts were already monitoring his progress.

He represented the Deeside Primary School team, for whom he scored ninety-seven goals, beating the previous record held by Ian Rush (twenty-five). He also produced some excellent performances for Mold Alexandra Under-10s before attending high school where, as a thirteen-year-old, he became eligible to sign a schoolboy contract with a senior club.

He had talks with Chelsea, Manchester United and Arsenal before he eventually signed schoolboy forms for Liverpool, despite growing up as an Everton supporter!

Encouraged to attend the FA's School of Excellence at Lilleshall, from the age of fourteen Owen continued his studies at Hawarden High School and achieved ten GCSEs.

At the age of sixteen, he joined the Anfield youth training scheme and starred in the club's 1996 FA Youth Cup final victory over West Ham United, whose team included future England colleagues Frank Lampard and Rio Ferdinand.

Owen scored prolifically as he made rapid progress through the Liverpool ranks and soon after his seventeenth birthday he signed his first professional contract; six months later, he had the pleasure of scoring on his Premiership debut against Wimbledon in May 1997.

The following season – his first full one at Anfield – Owen top-scored and was also the Premiership's joint leading marksman (with Chris Sutton and Dion Dublin) with eighteen goals, the sixth Liverpool player to achieve this feat and the first for ten years, following John Aldridge in 1987/88.

Sharp, alert, and good on the ball with a strong shot, he started the season off with an equalising penalty to earn a 1-1 draw with one of his favourite opposing clubs, Wimbledon; he struck again at top-of-the-table Blackburn a fortnight later as Liverpool picked up another away point but then – and not for want of trying – he failed to score in his next eight Premiership games as Liverpool struggled to get any sort of rhythm into their overall play.

A late goal in a comprehensive 4-0 home win over Tottenham on 8 November saw Owen up and running again, but he was not firing on all cylinders and was goalless in his next three outings before slipping in Liverpool's second goal in a 3-0 win at Crystal Palace in mid-December, following up with a 14th-minute winner at home to Coventry City and the opener in a 3-1 Boxing Day home victory over Leeds United.

On his own admission, he was 'not at his best either side of the New Year', but after some more off-days in front of goal Owen netted the winner against Newcastle United (1-0) on 20 January and then had a superb February, scoring twice in a 3-2 home defeat by Southampton, grabbing the first hat-trick of his League career in a 3-3 draw at Sheffield Wednesday (Liverpool coming back from 3-1 down), and striking home a penalty in a 2-1 reverse at Villa Park.

At this juncture, Liverpool lay fourth in the table and Owen's winner against Bolton Wanderers (2-1) in early March saw the Reds edge up to second place, behind Manchester United.

The race for the Championship was on, and Liverpool was looking good. A point at Tottenham and a victory over Barnsley kept them in touch and Owen's 36th-minute equaliser at Old Trafford earned a vital point as the games started to run out.

By now, though, Arsenal were powering along and they took over from Manchester United at the top as Liverpool slipped down to third after a draw at Coventry (with another Owen goal) and a heavy defeat at Chelsea (a game which he missed).

Owen was then on target in brilliant wins over West Ham United (5-0) and the champions-elect Arsenal (4-0), but a last-match defeat at Derby meant that Liverpool would end up with nothing, as they finished thirteen points behind the Gunners and eight adrift of United.

Besides his eighteen Premiership goals, Owen also scored five 'Cup' goals to end 1997/98 with twenty-three to his name in forty-four appearances – an excellent start to his professional career.

And it continued in 1998/99, when once again – despite missing eight matches, including the last seven – Owen, still a teenager, finished up as the Premiership's joint top scorer on eighteen goals along with Dwight Yorke (Manchester United) and Jimmy-Floyd Hasselbaink (Leeds United).

As Brian Pead wrote in the *Football Factfile*, '1998–99 was yet another spectacular season by the boy genius. A brilliant hat-trick against Newcastle at St James' Park in only his third game of the campaign, augured well for the Reds and Michael. There is much more to come from thus young man, and he is surely destined, injuries apart, to re-write the record books.'

On target with a late winner at Southampton on the opening day of the season, Owen quickly followed up with a 15th-minute treble in a 4-1 victory at Newcastle, but then had to wait until the tenth Premiership game before scoring again! And it was worth waiting for when he put on a virtuoso performance with a four-timer, including a penalty, in a 5-1 demolition of Nottingham Forest at Anfield on 24 October.

Three successive defeats followed this rampant win over Forest, and after Aston Villa had been beaten 4-2 with a Robbie Fowler four-timer, Owen setting up two, Liverpool clipped Blackburn Rovers 2-0 at Anfield, with Owen sealing the points with his ninth League goal of the campaign.

Owen then went on to have a fine second half to December, scoring four goals – in 2-0, 3-1 and 4-2 wins over Sheffield Wednesday, Middlesbrough and Newcastle respectively. In fact, he struck twice against the Geordies, making it five for the season!

He netted Liverpool's sixth goal in their 7-1 thumping of Southampton in mid-January and followed up with strikes against West Ham (drew 2-2) and Chelsea (lost 2-1) before adding his eighteenth and last goal of another fine season in the 2-2 draw in the return game with Forest.

Injury then forced him to sit out the remaining four weeks of the season and Liverpool certainly missed him. They won three and lost three of their remaining seven games to finish a disappointing seventh in the table – their lowest position since 1993/94.

Owen once more added five Cup goals to his tally for an overall final total of twenty-three (in forty games).

In spite of a recurring hamstring injury, Owen was Liverpool's leading scorer seven years running, from 1997 until 2004. His first major club honours came in the 2000/01 season, when he helped the Merseysiders complete the treble of UEFA, FA and League Cup final victories. At the same time, he was the recipient of the Ballon d'Or.

Owen went on to score 158 goals in 297 first-class appearances for Liverpool before transferring to Real Madrid for £8 million in mid-2004. Unfortunately, he was never at his best at the Bernabeu, where he was frequently used as a second-half substitute, although despite all this, he managed to net thirteen times in La Liga and had that season's highest ratio of goals scored to number of minutes played.

He returned to England the following season, joining Newcastle United for £16 million, and made a promising start to the 2005/06 season before a spate of niggling injuries sidelined him on a regular basis over the next eighteen months.

On regaining full fitness, he was appointed team captain at St James' Park and was the team's top scorer in 2007/08 but then, when his four-year contract expired and Newcastle were relegated, Owen surprisingly moved to Manchester United as a free agent. However, with Messrs Rooney and Berbatov in the side he found it hard to gain a place in the first team and when the Mexican Javier Hernandez was recruited in 2010, Owen was basically listed as a full-time substitute, hardly getting a game as United went on to win a record nineteenth league title.

Internationally, Owen first played for England at senior level in February 1998, becoming his country's youngest player in the twentieth century and also the youngest goalscorer at the time. He was subsequently voted PFA Young Player of the Year and his performances at that summer's World Cup finals brought him to national and international prominence. He went from strength to strength, appearing and scoring in Euro 2000, the 2002 World Cup and Euro 2004 to become the only player ever to achieve the feat in four major tournaments for England.

Unfortunately, after suffering an injury in the 2006 World Cup, which took a year to mend, his international career eventually ended shortly afterwards, after he had struck forty goals in eighty-nine senior appearances.

Owen's long absence after the 2006 World Cup resulted in a dispute between FIFA, the FA and his club Newcastle United, which eventually resulted in an unprecedented £10 million compensation award to Newcastle and brought changes to the compensation arrangements between club and country regarding injuries sustained by contracted club players while on international duty.

PARKER, BOBBY (EVERTON)

Season: 1914/15
Goals scored: 36 (out of 76); 22 home, 14 away
Percentage: 47.3 per cent
Runner-up: Joe Smith (Bolton Wanderers), 29 goals
Everton were League Champions

Bobby Parker's story might have been one of the most sensational in even Everton's proud history of goalscoring heroes. Instead it was one of the most tragic. (David Prentice, *Liverpool Echo*)

Parker was a big, strong, robust centre forward who joined the Merseysiders from Glasgow Rangers in November 1913, signed as a replacement for Tommy Browell, who had been sold to Manchester City.

He immediately transformed the Toffees from nearly-men into League champions with one of the most prolific goals per game ratios in the club's history.

After proving his worth during the second half of the 1913/14 season, he followed up with an amazing tally of thirty-six goals in thirty-five League games in 1914/15, many of them created by right-winger Sam Chedgzoy, whose crosses at times were inch-perfect for the dynamic Parker as he bore down on goal.

Then along came the Great War, which turned out to be a horrifying experience for the Scotsman. Not only did it wipe out four years of his playing years, he also suffered a serious injury on the battlefield, and as a result he returned to Goodison Park with a German bullet in his back. He was never the same player again.

League runners-up in 1911/12, Everton slipped down to eleventh the following season and were struggling below halfway when they signed Parker.

He scored on his debut to earn a point from a 1-1 home draw with Sheffield Wednesday and celebrated his first hat-trick three weeks later, in a 5-0 Boxing Day drubbing of Manchester United. He ended that season with an outstanding record of seventeen goals in twenty-four appearances. And there was plenty more to come from the rampaging twenty-three-year-old Glaswegian.

What happened next was quite stunning; incredible really, as far as the Everton supporters were concerned.

Everton started the 1914/15 season relatively slowly, managing only two wins, over Spurs and Newcastle United, in their opening six games.

Then came the Anfield derby. Everton had not lost at home against their fiercest rivals since 1899 and on 3 October they extended that run with a brilliant 5-0 victory, Parker grabbing a hat-trick in front of a crowd of 32,000. Two of his goals were stunning right-foot shots and he also missed two other chances when only the goalkeeper to beat.

Victory took Everton above Liverpool for the first time that season – a position they did not relinquish.

Parker's most prolific spell of the campaign came in November. He fired in another hat-trick at home to Sunderland (won 7-1), followed up by bagging all four goals in a solid 4-1 win at Sheffield Wednesday, notched the winner in a 2-1 defeat of West Bromwich Albion and grabbed his fourth hat-trick when Manchester City were dispatched 4-1 at Goodison. Eleven goals in four games – he was on fire.

For a time, Parker's amazing goal-spree put Everton bang on target for the League and FA Cup double. They were leading the title race as they took on Chelsea in the Cup semi-final at Villa Park, but an early injury to another key player, Harry Makepeace, in the days before substitutes meant Everton had to play the majority of the match with ten men and subsequently lost 2-0.

Hotshot Parker hardly got a look-in but he was quickly back to his best, claiming his third treble of the season in a 5-3 home victory over Bolton Wanderers three days later.

With seven games remaining, there were at least ten clubs chasing the First Division championship. But Everton had Parker in their ranks and although he didn't score as often as he had done earlier in the season, he effectively saw them home with two goals in a 3-0 win over Sunderland and then exacted ample consolation for that semi-final defeat by clinching the Championship with an equalising goal in a last-match 2-2 draw with Chelsea at Goodison Park. Everton, unbeaten in their previous five matches, took the star prize with forty-six points, one more than runners-up Oldham Athletic.

Having seen Parker notch fifty-five goals in sixty-five games since arriving on Merseyside, all Evertonians, young and old, were licking their lips at the prospect of further successes. But the unwanted hostilities against the Germans quickly put an end to that.

Even the local *Football Echo* could barely muster any enthusiasm for Everton's title triumph. The front page was dominated by drawings of the front line at Ypres, with the Blues' triumph being pushed to the back pages.

Parker joined up and scored seven goals in seven regional games during the war. He then went overseas and was fortunate to return home again after the Great War, doing so with a serious injury.

He returned to action in the Anfield derby in December 1919 and scored in a 3-1 defeat. But it was plain to see he was not the player he was, as the *Liverpool Echo* commented:

> Whether the public was unaware of Parker's injury or whether it was felt public morale would suffer after the appalling losses sustained during the War, is unclear. But the press was hardly charitable when he made his long-awaited comeback four years later.

Despite scoring four goals in eight games in 1919/20 and twelve in eighteen the following season, to bring his overall and final record with Everton to seventy-one goals in ninety-two first-class appearances, Parker left Goodison Park for Nottingham Forest in May 1921. He retired two years later.

Everton never said a word about his injury, which brought his Goodison Park career to an abrupt end for certain. However, it later transpired that the club pensioned him for over thirty years – a good deed, done without stealth or advertisement.

There is no doubt that the First World War robbed Parker of his peak years – and with international football suspended, of any sort of international career too.

He ended his footballing career as manager of the Dublin-based club Bohemians, but Evertonians would always be left wondering what might have been.

Parker was born in Maryhill, Glasgow on 27 March 1891 and died in Liverpool in 1950.

PARKINSON, JACK (LIVERPOOL)

Season: 1909/10
Goals scored: 30 (out of 78); 22 home, 8 away
Percentage: 38.4 per cent
Runner-up: Albert Shepherd (Newcastle United), 28 goals
Liverpool finished second

A dashing, fearless forward whose effervescent style was laced with vigour and, at times, cunning, sharpshooter Jack Parkinson was a quality goalscorer and a huge favourite with the Liverpool supporters.

No relation to the player of the same name who was born in Blackpool in 1869 and played once for the Reds in September 1899, Parkinson was broken in gently by Liverpool. He played alongside some terrific forwards, including Sam Raybould, Robert Robinson, Ron Orr and Joe Hewitt, all of whom gave him great encouragement, before hitting the headlines in 1909/10 by scoring virtually a goal a game as Liverpool missed out on the League title by five points to Aston Villa.

Absent from the opening game of the season – a 2-1 defeat at Chelsea – he quickly found his feet by scoring in each half to earn the Reds a 2-1 victory at Bolton forty-eight hours later before following up by netting in the 75th minute to clinch a 3-1 victory over Blackburn Rovers at Anfield.

Bang in form, he struck a superb hat-trick in the fourth game of the season as Liverpool won 4-1 at Nottingham Forest, Jimmy Stewart and Artie Goddard assisting with two of his goals, while at the same time Parkinson had a helping hand with Orr's fine effort.

In early October, a crowd of 45,000 saw him net the winner in the Merseyside derby at Goodison Park (3-2) and a week later he opened the scoring in the 12th minute to set Liverpool on their way to a 3-2 home win over Manchester United.

Parkinson was on target again with two first-half goals in a 3-1 triumph over Sheffield Wednesday, netted after 8 minutes in a hard-fought 2-2 home draw with Bury and scored twice in a terrific 6-5 home win over Newcastle United in December.

On a muddy pitch, Liverpool found themselves 5-2 down at half time in this game. Then, after the break, the game changed completely. Newcastle were pegged back as wingers Goddard (right) and John McDonald (left) found more space and with Stewart, Parkinson and Orr bearing down on goal at every opportunity, the Reds stormed back to win an amazing eleven-goal thriller.

Parkinson, who had scored in the first half, made it 5-3 within four minutes of the restart and after that it was one-way traffic. Stewart added his second of the game, Orr netted twice and Goddard hit the other.

Parkinson and Stewart also scraped the woodwork and Lawrence, in the Newcastle goal, saved brilliantly from Orr and Jimmy Bradley.

Having taken over as the team's penalty-taker, Parkinson netted twice from the spot, in a 3-1 defeat at Villa Park and in a 3-0 home win over Bolton, before striking home an 80th-minute equaliser in a 1-1 draw away to Arsenal two days after Christmas.

The return game against the Gunners followed on New Year's Day and this time Parkinson whipped in a hat-trick, including another penalty, in a resounding 5-1 win.

A week later, he was twice on the mark in a 5-0 thumping of Chelsea at Anfield, but then surprisingly failed to score in any of the next four League and Cup games, was injured and out of the side for three of the next five, returning to score in the 11th minute in a 2-0 home win over Tottenham Hotspur in late March – his twenty-third goal of the season.

Only one player – Dugald Livingstone in 1902/03 – had scored thirty League goals in a season for Liverpool. So, with time running out and not 100 per cent fit, Parkinson had it all to do. He missed out in a 2-1 defeat at Sunderland and was sidelined for the clash with Preston at Deepdale, meaning he had to score seven times in the last five games to reach the thirty-goal mark.

While scoring in the 80th minute against Notts County (2-1) he took a knock and missed the next game at Newcastle, but returned in brilliant fashion against Nottingham Forest in mid-April, helping himself to a four-timer (two of his efforts being booming drives from outside the penalty area) as Liverpool roared to a 7-3 win. Now on twenty-eight goals, he had two games left and quickly reduced that by one with an 8th-minute strike in a 2-2 home draw with Middlesbrough before bagging his thirtieth and final goal of the season to clinch a 2-0 home win over the champions Aston Villa on 30 April.

It had been an outstanding campaign for Parkinson and one feels that if he had been fit and available for the seven games he missed, his overall tally of goals may well have been near the forty mark.

Born in Bootle, Merseyside on 13 September 1883, Parkinson began his Anfield career in September 1901. He turned professional in April 1903 and made his League debut six months later in a 2-1 victory against Small Heath at Muntz Street, scoring after 16 minutes. That season Parkinson netted six times in seventeen games, and in the following season he scored twenty-one goals in twenty-three appearances.

Unfortunately, injury often hampered Parkinson's career. He sustained a broken wrist against Woolwich Arsenal in Liverpool's championship-winning season of 1905/06. It meant he played just nine games (seven goals scored) – not enough to qualify for a medal.

After three moderate seasons, in which he scored just nineteen goals yet gained two full England caps, he hit top form in 1909/10 to top the charts. Over the next three campaigns he added a further forty-three goals to his tally, finishing up with 128 in 221 appearances for the Reds.

On leaving Anfield in July 1914, Parkinson joined Bury. He retired from the game during the war to become a newsagent and died in Liverpool on his fifty-ninth birthday in 1942.

PHILLIPS, KEVIN (SUNDERLAND)

Season: 1999/2000
Goals scored: 30 (out of 57); 13 home, 17 away
Percentage: 53 per cent
Runner-up: Alan Shearer (Newcastle United), 23 goals
Sunderland finished seventh
Partner Niall Quinn scored 14 times, the pair scoring 77 per cent of Sunderland's goals

When Sunderland roared to promotion to the Premier League with a then-record number of points in 1999, cynics such as Rodney Marsh scoffed at Wearside fans' predictions that twenty-six-year-old Kevin Phillips would repeat his goal scoring exploits of the previous two seasons, when he'd rammed home sixty goals in seventy-eight games.

Yet, with his quick feet, nimble skills, speed and an instinctive finish Phillips was always going to be a danger to even the toughest of defences. Especially as he had playing alongside him the experienced Niall Quinn who, supplied with a selection of superb crosses from wing-man Nicky Summerbee, could always be relied upon to pick out his partner in the box.

Phillips, capped the previous season for England, had never previously played in the top flight of English football and he, along with the rest of his team, was given a rude opening-day awakening when Chelsea thrashed Sunderland 4-0 at Stamford Bridge.

Three days later came a much easier challenge against another promoted side, Watford. A dubious penalty gave Phillips an early opportunity and then, 4 minutes from the end, he scored with a wonderful, curling 25-yard shot past Chris Day. Eleven days later, and the man

who had to drop down from Southampton to play for Baldock Town for two years before getting a second chance with Watford in 1994 had his third of the season, another penalty away to Leeds in a 2-1 defeat.

Four days later, Sunderland travelled to face local rivals Newcastle. Not having beaten 'the Mags' since 1979, the few hundred away fans allowed into a redeveloping St James' Park, engulfed by a torrential downpour that left them soaked through, feared the worst when half time arrived with the home side a goal to the good.

There was therefore ecstasy when Quinn headed the equaliser from a Summerbee free kick. With the ball by now hardly able to roll, Phillips then conjured a winner of real class when having seen his first shot saved by Tommy Wright, he spun backward towards the ball and clipped it over the 'keeper and beyond the retreating defenders before it dropped into the net. After that, it was a matter of Sunderland defending deeply to give their supporters local bragging rights.

There was no stopping Phillips after this goal. A cracking bicycle kick earning a 1-1 draw with Coventry came next, and when he was stopped from hitting the net in a 2-0 home victory over Leicester, it cost his marker, Foxes captain Gerry Taggart, two yellow cards and an early bath. On 18 September, the 5-foot, 7-inch forward grabbed his first Premier League hat-trick as Sunderland thrashed Derby County 5-0 at Pride Park. Bradford City at Valley Parade did slightly better, but with two goals in a 4-0 win, Phillips already had ten, to make him top scorer in a side second in the league. When two more followed in at home to Aston Villa, Phillips was already well on the way to achieving his personal target of twenty League goals come the season's end, especially as he scored another away goal in the following game at Upton Park in a 1-1 draw.

By now Phillips was becoming a Sunderland legend and even when he managed to miss a late penalty away to Middlesbrough, it mattered little, as Michael Reddy knocked in the rebound to give his side a point.

On 4 December 1999, Phillips and Sunderland provided a match that many of their followers still regularly recall. Generally agreed to be the best game ever staged at the

Stadium of Light since it opened in July 1997, it saw Chelsea, first-day conquerors, ravaged 4-1 after a sparkling first half display saw the hosts four to the good at half time. Quinn had opened the scoring on just 44 seconds, before, on 23 minutes, Phillips pounced on a loose ball around 30 yards out and with Chelsea 'keeper Edwin de Goey only just off his line, he belted a shot that flew beyond him for an absolutely stunning goal. Ten minutes later he'd added his second, a casual flick from 8 yards out.

Phillips was now an essential member of a side pushing towards the top of the League and when he missed the match at Goodison Park on Boxing Day, Sunderland slumped 5-0. Back in the side, he rattled home his twentieth League goal in the match with Leeds.

At home to Newcastle United, after the away side took a two-goal lead it was vital for Sunderland to get back into the game quickly. Phillips was the player who did it, slotting the ball under Steve Harper's legs to make it 1-2 at half time. Things still looked a little bleak when the scoreline remained the same with just 8 minutes remaining before, seizing on a loose ball inside the box, Phillips nutmegged the 'keeper for an equaliser that sparked a small pitch invasion amongst the delirious home crowd. Phillips now had twenty-two goals, eight more even than the legendary Alan Shearer in the black-and-white-striped opponents' shirts.

Despite the relief of a late point, Sunderland were now in free-fall, with the exciting attacking football they'd maintained following promotion making way for uncertainty at the back and in midfield. Phillips scored another goal at Highfield Road, but saw his side beaten 3-2 by Coventry City and when Emile Heskey and Stan Collymore ran riot at Filbert Street, Sunderland slumped 5-2. There was therefore relief when a late Phillips penalty at Anfield gave Peter Reid's side a point against the team he supported as a boy. Things looked even brighter when the former Evertonian saw the Toffees come unstuck when Phillips hit a late winner for Sunderland's first win of 2000. This renewed hopes of a European place, especially when it was followed by a 2-1 win at the Dell, where Phillips netted a penalty.

At Hillsborough, in front of a good number of travelling fans, Phillips, with just 4 minutes remaining, beat Sheffield Wednesday 'keeper Kevin Pressman with a curling 25-yard shot, and a minute later followed up with a neat, close-in finish to ensure a 2-0 victory.

However, when relegation-threatened Bradford City tore up the pre-match predictions by winning 1-0 at the Stadium of Light, it was clear that the form of the second half of the season was going to prevent Sunderland qualifying for the first time ever for Europe through a high-place League finish.

Not that the disappointment prevented fans celebrating wildly when, in the final home game of the season, Phillips hit his thirtieth League goal of the campaign. It came on 14 minutes, when he headed home a Nicky Summerbee cross in a mediocre match that finished 1-1. Among the first to congratulate him was Niall Quinn, who himself got fourteen Premier League goals in 1999/2000. This meant that between them, the two had scored forty-four of Sunderland's fifty-seven goals that season, exactly 77 per cent.

Phillips's thirty goals not only earned him the Premiership Golden Boot but also the European Golden Boot, awarded to the top scorer in the leading European leagues in a particular season. Despite this, Phillips was overlooked by England manager Kevin Keegan during the European Championship Finals matches in the summer of 2000. Phillips was to play eight times for his country, but failed to score on any occasion.

Following Sunderland's relegation at the end of the 2002/03 season, Phillips signed for Southampton, ending six seasons at the Stadium of Light that included 60 Premiership goals in 139 appearances.

RAYBOULD, SAM (LIVERPOOL)

Season: 1902/03
Goals scored: 31 (out of 68); 21 home, 10 away
Percentage: 45.5 per cent
Runner-up: Grenville Morris (Nottingham Forest), 25 goals
Liverpool finished fifth

Sam Raybould was twenty-five years of age when he joined Liverpool for £250 in January 1900.

Originally an outside right, he was switched to centre forward (in place of 'Sailor' Hunter) and became a highly successful marksman, being the first player to score 100 League goals for the Merseyside club, a feat he achieved in 170 matches covering a period of five years up to December 1905.

Top scorer with seventeen goals when the Reds won the League Championship for the first time in 1901, his most prolific period came two years later, when he set a new club record of thirty-one in the League. This stood until 1930/31, when the South African Gordon Hodgson broke it with a haul of thirty-six.

Not very tall, but solid in build, Raybould was always alert and lively in and around the penalty area and certainly proved a handful for opposing defenders.

He started the 1902/03 season with two goals in a 5-2 home win over Blackburn and followed up with penalties in 2-1 defeats at Sunderland and Everton before netting a brace, including another spot-kick, in a hard-earned 4-2 victory over Sheffield Wednesday at Anfield.

On target twice in a 2-1 win over West Bromwich Albion, he scored a fine second-half equaliser to earn a point at Bolton (1-1) and then claimed his first Liverpool hat-trick when Middlesbrough got thumped 5-0 on Merseyside.

Playing exceedingly well off his inside partners, 'Geordie' Livingstone and Edgar Chadwick, Raybould scored his thirteenth goal of the season in a 2-1 win at Newcastle, added another in a 4-1 triumph over Wolves (when all four Liverpool goals came in the first 11 minutes) and then helped tear Grimsby to shreds with a four-timer in a 9-2 win at Anfield, one of his goals, cracked in left-footed, almost tore a hole in the back of the net.

After striking the winner at Villa Park (2-1) and slamming in another penalty in the 5-1 home victory over Bolton, Raybould had a lean spell between the end of December and mid-February when he claimed only one goal, but he was soon back on track and scored in each of the next five League games, including two against Newcastle (3-0) and a second-half equaliser against Sunderland (1-1). He also passed George Allan's existing club record of twenty-five League goals in a season, set in 1895/96.

In the last month of the campaign, Raybould – who was lucky to avoid illness and injury – scored four more goals, two to see off Bury, and in the end Liverpool took fifth place in the Division, only four points behind champions Sheffield Wednesday. A poor run between 28 March and 18 April, when only one win was recorded in six games, ruined Liverpool's chances of winning the title.

A huge favourite with the Anfield fans, Raybould was born in Staveley, Derbyshire in January 1875 and played for a number of local sides before joining Derby County in 1894.

After scoring twice in five games for the Rams, he surprisingly returned to non-League football with Ilkeston. Then, following further spells with Poolsbrook United and Ilkeston Town and a few outings for Bolsover Colliery, he joined New Brighton Tower in 1899.

After netting ten times in thirteen League games, Raybould was signed by manager Tom Watson in January 1900. After his fine season in 1902/03, Raybould and his Anfield teammate Archie Glover were given a seven-month ban from football for agreeing in the summer of 1903 to 'financial inducements' to sign for Southern League Portsmouth. They were also given a lifetime ban on ever signing for Pompey.

Raybould's absence proved significant as Liverpool's form slumped dramatically as they battled against relegation. The ban was lifted on 31 December 1903 and he was selected for the first team virtually straightaway, but despite his four goals towards the end of the season, he couldn't prevent the dreaded drop into the Second Division.

Raybould scored 127 goals in 224 appearances for Liverpool, and on leaving Anfield in 1907 he moved to Sunderland, and after a season there finished his first-class career with Woolwich Arsenal. In 1909, he joined non-League Chesterfield and subsequently played for Sutton Town and Barlborough United before retiring in May 1915.

Raybould never gained international recognition, but he did represent the Football League against the Scottish League on three occasions. He died in Chesterfield in 1949.

RICHARDSON, BILLY 'W.G.' (WEST BROMWICH ALBION)

Season: 1935/36
Goals scored: 39 (out of 89); 22 home, 17 away
Percentage: 43.8 per cent
Runners-up: Raich Carter and Bob Gurney (Sunderland) and Pat Glover (Grimsby Town), with 31 goals each
WBA finished eighteenth

Centre forward Billy Richardson – nicknamed 'Ginger', but mainly called 'W.G.' to avoid confusion with his West Bromwich Albion teammate Bill Richardson – famously scored four goals in 5 minutes at the start of a First Division League game against West Ham United at Upton Park in November 1931, having netted twice in the Baggies' 2-1 FA Cup final victory over Birmingham just seven months earlier.

Richardson was a key figure in Albion's attack during that 1930/31 season, scoring a total of twenty-four goals while helping the Black Country team complete a unique double, that of winning the FA Cup and gaining promotion in the same season, a feat never achieved before or since.

On his day, Richardson had only a few equals and not too many superiors at snapping up half-chances, especially those inside the penalty area. He was quick, sharp and decisive, his anticipation was first-class and he was notably adept at deflecting low crosses, fired over by wingers Tommy Glidden and Stan Wood, and also Wally Boyes, past the opposing goalkeeper with the cleverest of touches. He also possessed good ball control and packed a strong right-foot shot, but rarely did he score a goal with his head.

Richardson spent a little over sixteen years as a player at The Hawthorns – from June 1929 until November 1945. During that time, he scored 328 goals in 444 first team matches, including a League return of 202 goals (in 320 games), a record that stood for twenty-one years, until bettered by Ronnie Allen in 1960.

He netted fourteen hat-tricks in major competitions (including four fours) and during the Second World War, when he helped Albion win the Midland Wartime Cup, his strike record was phenomenal – 100 goals scored in less than 100 appearances.

His best season with Albion, in terms of goals scored, came in 1935/36 when he netted a club record of forty, of which thirty-nine came in the League, making him the First Division's leading marksman.

Goalless in the opening two matches, he scored his first of the campaign to set up a 2-0 home win over Stoke City and found the net again, four days later, in a 6-1 thumping at Sunderland.

He missed one and failed to score in three of the next four games before having a tremendous six-match run in five weeks during October to November.

He stroked home the opener in a 4-1 win over Grimsby Town and earned a point with another fine finish at Leeds (1-1) before taking rivals Aston Villa apart with a four-goal blitz in the Baggies' emphatic 7-0 victory at a windy Villa Park.

His first came in the seventh minute, when he flicked Jack Mahon's low centre past 'keeper Fred Biddlestone. Fifty-five seconds later, he turned provider by setting up Stan Wood to net from close range, and on 25 minutes he made it 3-0 by whipping in another splendid ground pass from Mahon. After Mahon (40 minutes) and Jack Sankey (73) had increased Albion's lead to 5-0, Richardson cracked in two more to seal a famous victory. His hat-trick goal arrived in the 77th minute, after some excellent build-up play, and his fourth followed soon afterwards as Villa's defence disintegrated under severe pressure. Right at the death, Wood had a goal disallowed, Joe Carter hit the bar and Richardson missed two clear-cut changes. But who cared – the enemy from down the road had been well and truly hammered.

A week later, Richardson notched a close-range 33rd-minute equaliser – after Jack Mahon's shot had come back off the crossbar – to set up a 2-1 home win over Wolves, scored decisively in a thumping 5-2 victory at Sheffield Wednesday and then netted twice in a 2-0 triumph over Portsmouth.

After firing blanks in successive away defeats at Preston and Derby, he scored in a 2-1 home defeat by Huddersfield Town before netting twice in a resounding 6-1 rout of Everton at The Hawthorns; one of his efforts, a 20-yarder, flew hard and low into the net with Ted Sager, the England goalkeeper, left helpless.

After another lean spell in mid-December, he bounced back in style by scoring in each of the next seven games, starting with a four-timer in the 5-2 Boxing Day victory over Middlesbrough. That afternoon, he gave 'Boro's Scottish international centre-half Bob Baxter the runaround and all of his goals were finished with aplomb, two of them fizzing into the net with pace and direction.

Two days later, Richardson struck twice in a 5-1 victory over Manchester City at The Hawthorns and scored to no avail in defeats at Middlesbrough (1-3) and Stoke (2-3) before claiming hat-tricks in home wins over Blackburn (8-1) and Liverpool (6-1), ending his excellent run with a double in a 4-2 reverse at Grimsby.

He didn't have such an impact during the last third of the season, but still managed to score eight more times in fourteen appearances as Albion battled hard and successfully to pull clear of the relegation zone. He grabbed crucial goals in each of the last three games

– in the 2-2 draws against Bolton (home) and Brentford (away), and in a last-match victory at Birmingham (3-2).

His fortieth goal of the 1935/36 season came in a third round FA Cup victory over Hull City.

Richardson was born in Framwellgate Moor, County Durham on 29 May 1909 and died after collapsing in a charity football match in Birmingham in 1959. He was the nephew of England Test cricketer Tom Richardson and the great-uncle of the musician and writer Sarah Price.

* In 2004, Richardson was named as one of West Bromwich Albion's greatest-ever players.

ROBERTS, FRANK (MANCHESTER CITY)

Season: 1924/25
Goals scored: 31 (out of 76); 19 home, 12 away
Percentage: 41 per cent
Runner-up: David Jack (Bolton Wanderers), 26 goals
Manchester City finished tenth

When Frank Roberts insisted on becoming a pub landlord in October 1922, he was placed on the transfer list by Bolton Wanderers for breaking club rules. It was Manchester City who acted quickly to secure his services, paying a fee of £3,400 for a player who had notched 80 goals in 168 Trotters appearances either side of the First World War, in which he served in the North Lancashire Regiment.

Roberts opened his City account at Hyde Road in his fifth match, as his former colleagues were beaten 2-0. Not that Bolton lost out too much on his departure, as come the season's end they'd picked up the FA Cup after beating West Ham in the first Wembley final. Initially Roberts failed to hit the net with the same regularity as before, and he started the 1924/25 season with just twenty-four League goals in seventy-three matches for a City side now resident at Maine Road.

Two opening day goals in a 2-0 win at Bury were quickly followed by further goals in the matches against Nottingham Forest and Liverpool respectively. At Anfield, the home side, two up early on, were pegged back when Roberts scored two in 5 minutes, knocking home a Spud Murphy cross for the first before dribbling around two Liverpool defenders to beat Elisha Scott in a game the Merseysiders won with two goals in the final 3 minutes.

In the sixth game, it was again a double as Newcastle United were beaten 3-1 at Maine Road. Roberts made it ten goals in seven games in the following weekend's game at Sheffield United, which was won 5-0. On 46 minutes he headed home Murphy's cross to make it 2-0, and it was the same combination ten minutes later that produced the away side's third, Roberts beating Robinson easily. Six minutes later, after Robinson fumbled a simple cross, he had the third hat-trick of his career after previously scoring two for Bolton.

Continuing his fine form, Roberts again scored a double the following weekend in a 3-1 home win against West Ham. Playing at inside forward, he might have even have had the fourth hat-trick of his career, only to find, like the other City forwards, the West Ham 'keeper Tommy Hampson in brilliant form.

In early November, he rescued a point for his side in the home match against Everton, showing the instincts of a typical goal-poacher by being the first to react when Hunter Hart slipped and leaving debutant 'keeper Bob Jones with no chance after 84 minutes.

It was, though, the home match in January 1925 against the Toffees' neighbours Liverpool that saw Roberts at his peak. Moved to centre forward, with Tommy Johnson switched to inside right, he scored four times. Max Woosnam at centre half had opened the scoring before Roberts headed home a George Hicks cross for the second and made it 3-0 before half time with a low shot. His hat-trick saw him sweep beyond the Liverpool backs to beat Scott to the great cheers of the crowd, which had hardly died down before he made it 5-0 by heading home another George Hicks cross.

It was the culmination of a marvellous few weeks for the Sandbach man, who'd started his professional career at his local club, Crewe Alexandra. Only weeks earlier he'd made his England debut, aged almost thirty-two, in a 4-0 defeat of Belgium. Although he failed to score, that wasn't the case when he got his second chance. Playing against Wales in the Home Championships, he scored twice in a 2-1 victory at Swansea. Roberts was to make a further two final appearances for his country before the end of the season, suffering a 2-0 defeat in Scotland and enjoying a 3-2 success in Paris.

Arguably Roberts's finest effort of a very fine season came in a 1-1 draw at Leeds Road against the reigning champions, Huddersfield Town. Picking up the ball just inside the Terriers' half, Roberts made his way round Roy Goodall and George Shaw before sending a low, 20-yard drive beyond Billy Mercer into the far corner of the net.

Two days later, Roberts smashed home two more goals in a 2-1 home success against Sheffield United. Then, he scored another double as Notts County were beaten 2-1 at Maine Road. He now had thirty League goals and there were still nine League matches to play. In fact, Roberts was to manage just one more goal and in a disappointing end to the season, failed to score in the last six games. Yet with thirty-one goals, no one threatened his place at the top of the scorers' charts with former teammate David Jack back in second place with five goals fewer.

Jack had a measure of revenge the following season when City and Wanderers clashed at Wembley in the cup final, scoring the only goal. En route to the final, City had crushed Crystal Palace 11-4, with Roberts hitting five goals. Roberts's haul was part of nine he scored in the Cup that season, and although he also scored twenty-one League goals, and City eighty-nine in all, it was not enough to stop his side finishing twenty-first and being relegated.

He continued to score goals in Division Two, hitting thirty-four in the next two seasons as City returned to the top flight as champions at the end of the 1927/28 season. Now aged thirty-five, he made just fourteen appearances in the following campaign, hitting his final goal for City in a 5-1 thrashing at Villa Park in November. Without a contract at the end of the season, he moved to play for Manchester Central.

He left having scored 130 goals for Manchester City in 237 senior games, of which 116 came in 215 League appearances. He died in May 1961.

ROBLEDO, GEORGE (NEWCASTLE UNITED)

Season: 1951/52
Goals scored: 33 (out of 98); 17 home, 16 away
Percentage: 32 per cent
Runner-up: Ronnie Allen (West Bromwich Albion), 32 goals
Newcastle finished eighth

Robledo was the first man from outside the British Isles, and the only South American, to finish as top scorer when his thirty-three goals in 1951/52 made up a third of Newcastle's tally for the season, which at ninety-eight is the highest ever scored by the Magpies in a season. As Robledo also got six FA Cup goals, including the only goal in the FA Cup final against Arsenal, the Chilean ensured he remained a Geordie hero long after he joined his brother and Newcastle teammate Ted at Colo-Colo in his home country in 1953.

Signed in January 1949 from Barnsley for a fee of £26,500, the deal was only agreed on the understanding that Ted would join him from Oakwell. However, only George proved himself good enough to win a regular place over the next eighteen months and when Newcastle captured the FA Cup by beating Blackpool at Wembley in 1951, Ted failed to join him in the starting line-up.

By then, George had already formed a great striking partnership with Newcastle legend Jackie Milburn, and the pair were both on the scoresheet when the new man opened his account in a 2-1 derby match victory against Sunderland in March 1949. Five more League goals were to follow by the end of the season, with a further thirteen in 1949/50 and fourteen, including hat-tricks at home to Blackpool and away to Liverpool, in 1950/51. Robledo was to do considerably better in front of goal in 1951/52, although on the opening day of it he was outshone by Milburn, who notched three against his single effort, heading the opening goal from 10 yards out after he met Corbett's free kick. Newcastle's six goals, with Stoke failing to score, was an indication that goals were not going to be in short supply.

And so it proved on 1 September, when champions Tottenham, who'd hammered their opponents 7-0 at White Hart Lane the previous season, arrived at St James' Park. Newcastle ran riot to win 7-2, with Robledo hitting a hat-trick. Milburn was out injured with a calf injury and yet, even without their star man, the Newcastle forward line was almost unstoppable. They were already two up when Robledo got the third on just 17 minutes. Then, on 62 minutes, he swept home from close in a Tommy Walker cross before, 10 minutes later, sticking out a long leg to get between Ted Ditchburn and Bill Nicholson to push George Hannah's cross home.

The following weekend, in a much tighter, action-packed match away to Preston, Robledo made it nine for the season, when, after scoring twice in the mid-week game at WBA, he did it again. With his brother playing in defence, he scored from just 2 yards out for the opening goal on 42 minutes. Then, in the second half, he scored a great goal, Ernie Taylor's raking cross-field ball being half-volleyed home from the corner of the penalty area as Newcastle captured both points in a 2-1 win.

By the following Saturday, Robledo's total had risen to thirteen as Burnley's weak defence were ruthlessly exposed, especially by the sublime ball playing skills of Hannah. With Newcastle already a goal up, Robledo's first on 21 minutes was a simple tap-in from a Milburn pass; then, on 44 minutes, it was an even easier effort after Hannah beat three defenders before pulling the ball back. Heading home his hat-trick, the Newcastle striker scored his fourth on 62 minutes, both goals being made from him by Milburn. Both men were on the scoresheet in November at Blackpool, but inspired by the now ex-Newcastle man Ernie Taylor, the home side tore the away side apart to record a 6-3 victory that went some way to gaining revenge for what had happened at Wembley earlier in the year.

Another nine-goal thriller followed in mid-December, but this time, with five goals to their account, Newcastle just edged out Stoke City at the Victoria Ground. Robledo got two. His side were 3-1 up when he scored his first on 58 minutes. It was another great goal when, after brother Ted found Reg Davies, his fine through-ball saw George scamper away from John Kirton to leave Dennis Herod with no chance of saving. Twelve minutes later, John G. Duncan's fine forward pass was crashed home for his second. Ten days later he again scored twice, and as this helped Newcastle win 4-1 at Roker Park on Christmas Day, it thrilled the large away following in the 52,000-strong crowd.

Robledo continued his rich vein of away scoring with another effort at White Hart Lane, although it wasn't enough to prevent Spurs winning 2-1. However, after beating Charlton and Aston Villa in the FA Cup, Newcastle gained their revenge in the fifth round of the FA Cup. White Hart Lane was packed with 69,009 inside and they saw a marvellous all-round display from the Cup holders.

Robledo got the first on 13 minutes, but admitted afterwards he should have got at least a hat-trick as Newcastle won 3-0. Back in London the following weekend, he got his thirtieth League goal in a 1-1 draw at Fulham. Milburn might have been losing out, but the England international had also scored twenty and cut the gap by two with a subsequent hat-trick against Huddersfield as Robledo made it thirty-one for the season.

Both men were then on the scoresheet on consecutive weekend games against Portsmouth, Milburn again scoring three at Fratton Park in a 4-2 sixth-round FA Cup success before Pompey earned a point at St James' Park in a 3-3 draw.

Second Division Blackburn Rovers proved difficult to overcome in the semi-final, earning a 0-0 draw at Hillsborough. Robledo put Newcastle in the lead in the replay at Elland Road, and then, with the match tied at 1-1, his goal-bound shot was handled on the line by Campbell, leaving Bobby Mitchell to clinch the game and a place at Wembley from the penalty spot.

Rested for the games against Derby and Aston Villa, Robledo scored his final League goal of the season, his thirty-third, against Manchester City in a game in which all five goals came in a 20-minute period in the second half. It was Robledo who made it 3-1 for the away side when his 10-yard shot on the move had Bert Trautmann well beaten. With his five goals in the FA Cup, he now had thirty-eight in total during the season, just one behind Hughie Gallacher's record club total of thirty-nine in 1929/30.

Robledo took his chance to draw level when, with just 6 minutes remaining at Wembley, he was on the end of Mitchell's cross and although it wasn't the greatest header, it bounced off the post and into the net to ensure his side had retained the famous trophy. Arsenal had been forced to play much of the game without the injured Walley Barnes, but Newcastle had won the Cup.

The Chilean international, who'd scored twice in the 1950 finals in the game against the USA and went on to play thirty-one times for his country, was to score another sixteen League goals the following season to take his overall record up to 82 in just 146 games. Add in another nine in just eighteen FA Cup games and it was no surprise that many Newcastle fans were disappointed to see him leave in the summer of 1953. Back home, Robledo twice won the Chilean League and twice finished as the league's top scorer.

ROBSON, BRYAN (WEST HAM UNITED)

Season: 1972/73
Goals scored: 28 (out of 67); 23 home, 5 away
Percentage: 42 per cent
Runner-up: John Richards (Wolverhampton Wanderers), 27 goals
West Ham United finished sixth

An Inter-Cities Fairs Cup winner in 1968/69 with Newcastle United, Robson joined relegation-threatened West Ham for a fee of £120,000 in February 1971. He was immediately on the scoresheet with a debut goal as the Hammers beat Nottingham Forest 2-0 at Upton Park, the first home victory since October the previous year. Robson was to grab two more goals before the season's end, and both were priceless as they came in consecutive 2-1 home victories against Manchester United and WBA as West Ham rallied to finish in twentieth place, with Burnley and Blackpool relegated.

Despite his fine start, Robson struggled the following season and although he hit a hat-trick in the League Cup quarter-final to help dispose of Sheffield United 5-0, the outcome was ultimately bittersweet when he saw his penalty in the semi-final saved by Gordon Banks as Stoke moved on to Wembley and success there against Chelsea in the final. Playing in all fifty-six games that season, Robson managed just fourteen goals.

The following season would be considerably better, starting in the third game, when he scored twice as Leicester City were beaten 5-2 at Upton Park. Two more quickly followed in the game at Anfield, although Liverpool was the winner of a fine game, 3-2. Ron Lyall had decided to experiment by pushing forward Bobby Moore from the back, and with Trevor Brooking in fine form, Robson and his colleague up front, Clyde Best, could expect to receive a regular supply of the ball. Playing out wide, Tommy Taylor was also able to deliver the sort of crosses forwards thrive on.

In mid-September Norwich City were blown away, beaten 4-0 in a game that saw Moore at his very best. Robson scored the second and fourth, the latter a penalty. His success saw the following Monday's *Daily Mirror* start a theme that was to run throughout the season by stating Robson 'in England form'.

Crystal Palace were also beaten 4-0 at Upton Park, with Trevor Brooking, whose name had been extended in many papers to 'elegant Trevor Brooking', scoring twice and creating Robson's twelfth of the season.

Both men were again on the scoresheet in the following weekend's 2-2 draw with Wolves. Robson's had come in fortuitous circumstances when Bernard Shaw had deflected his effort into the goal. Strikers, however, are there to score goals no matter how, and that was certainly the case for Robson's next effort. Outplayed by title holders Derby County at Upton Park, the home side reduced the arrears to 1-2 when Robson's shot cannoned off the back of Roy McFarland to leave 'keeper Colin Boulton stranded. Robson now had thirteen League goals with well over half a season to run. By Boxing Day it was up to seventeen, with doubles against Stoke and Tottenham Hotspur.

His eighteenth seemed certain to ensure his side brought back both points from relegation-threatened Manchester United. With Best also scoring, West Ham were cruising at 2-0 with 'Robson in rip-roaring' form, reported the *Daily Mirror*, before a harsh penalty got the home side back into the game, which they rescued with a late goal. One week later he was up to twenty as WHU beat Chelsea 3-1 at home.

On 10 February it was twenty-one League goals, leading the *Daily Mirror* to headline its match report on the 12th 'How much longer can Ramsey leave out Robson?', with Nigel Clarke reporting that the goal 'merely confirmed that Robson is ready for England. He took his chance superbly, volleying home Billy Bond's back header from Trevor Brooking's corner to give West Ham victory.' Only some superb saves by 'keeper Kevin Keelan had prevented Robson at least equalling his previous highest total of twenty-two League goals.

He had to wait until injury time in the following match. West Ham was drawing 1-1 at home to WBA when they were awarded a free kick just outside the penalty area. Peter Latchford in the Baggies' goal was left helpless as the ball flashed beyond him for the winning goal. Three more followed as West Ham won three consecutive games which included a 3-1 away victory at Crystal Palace that pushed the Hammers into fifth place in the table.

Six days later, on Easter Friday, Robson scored his first League hat-trick for West Ham United. Having scored twice eight times during the season, it looked like he hated the figure three, but when who else but Trevor Brooking again curled in a perfectly weighted cross on 65 minutes, the man who was born only yards from Sunderland's old ground, Roker Park, met it superbly to glance the ball beyond 'keeper Eric Martin to put WHU 3-2 ahead. Robson had put the home side 2-0 ahead within 18 minutes of the start, finishing off a great Pat Holland run and pass for the first and then nodding home a shrewd Frank Lampard cross for the second. Carrying off the ball at the end of a game won 4-3 by the home side, Robson enjoyed a standing ovation from all those present.

Robson left WHU to join his hometown club at the end of the following season, helping Sunderland to promotion in 1975/76 before returning to Upton Park in October 1976, where he remained until the summer of 1979, when he moved back to Roker Park. Robson was voted Hammer of the Year by West Ham fans in 1973 and during his time at the club made 255 first team appearances, in which he scored 104 goals. Currently a chief scout for Chelsea, Robson's career aggregate of 264 League goals in 674 appearances for West Ham, Newcastle, Sunderland, Carlisle and Chelsea made him one of the outstanding goalscorers of his generation.

Robson, whose nickname 'Pop' derives from his schooldays, when friends gave him and his two close mates the nicknames from the Rice Krispies 'Snap, Crackle and Pop' advert of the time, never did get to play for England. 'Just to have played once would have been great,' he later said.

RONALDO, CRISTIANO (MANCHESTER UNITED)

Season: 2007/08
Goals scored: 31 (out of 80); 21 home, 10 away
Percentage: 39 per cent
Runners-up: Emmanuel Adebayor (Arsenal) and Fernando Torres (Liverpool), with 24 goals each
Manchester United were Premier League Champions

'There's only one Ronaldo' was the regular cry around Old Trafford during the Portuguese player's time there from 2003 to 2009. Ronaldo was just eighteen when Manchester United paid over £12 million to sign him from Sporting Lisbon at the end of the 2002/03 season, in which he had played twenty-five times in the green and white, scoring on his debut against Moreirense.

As a right-winger following in the footsteps of former number 7 greats such as Eric Cantona, George Best, David Beckham and Bryan Robson, it wasn't going to be easy. He started well, his 30-minute substitute appearance against Bolton Wanderers turning a 1-0 scoreline into a 4-0 one. Sir Alex Ferguson, though, was in no rush to play him regularly and by the season's end he had started fifteen Premier League games and scored four times. He played in the FA Cup final at Cardiff, where he scored with a header and largely ran the show in a one-sided match against Millwall that Manchester United won 3-0. His first major medal came a week after he had been sent off against Aston Villa in the Premier League.

Selected in that summer's Portuguese squad for the European Championships, he continued to build his reputation with some fine displays but had to settle for a runners-up medal after Greece surprisingly beat Portugal in the final.

Joining him at Old Trafford as the new season got under way was another youngster of considerable talent, Wayne Rooney, as Ferguson continued to refashion his side.

However, with Chelsea spending new owner Roman Abramovich's cash on some of the world's best players it meant that, for the first time in many years, Manchester United were looking distinctly second best and they finished a massive eighteen points behind the eventual champions. Ruud van Nistelrooy's absence through injury had been a big blow for a young side still finding its feet.

The gap was cut considerably in 2005/06, but Chelsea still won the Premier League by eight points. Ronaldo managed twelve goals. Consolation came in the League Cup final, where both Ronaldo and Rooney scored in a 4-0 demolition of neighbours Wigan Athletic.

The success boded well for the 2006/07 season, in which a maturing Ronaldo was expected to play a big part. He did not disappoint, overcoming in doing so some serious abuse from opposition fans for his part in Rooney's dismissal during the World Cup match between England and Portugal in the summer, not forgetting a feeling among many that he had a tendency to go down rather too easily when challenged for the ball. Ronaldo was good enough to make many pundits' team of the tournament and took his form from it into the new season.

The result was that he helped his side collect forty-four points from the first seventeen League games. Against Portsmouth in November he scored a wonderful free kick. On 15 February 2007, against Spurs, he hit his fifteenth goal of the season, a penalty after he had replaced the injured Louis Saha as United's spot kick taker. At Craven Cottage a draw seemed the most likely result as the match drew to its conclusion. Then, Ronaldo picked up the ball on the halfway line before surging forward, beating several defenders and hammering the ball into the net. It was a goal good enough to win any match and confirmed he had the ability to score from almost anywhere in the opposing half.

In Europe, Manchester United lost 2-1 away to AS Roma in the quarter-finals. The Italians could never have expected to be so easily thrashed at Old Trafford, trailing off beaten 7-1. On a night of so many stars, Ronaldo was undoubtedly the best and scored twice. AC Milan put paid to United's chances in the semi-final, with the World Player of the Year, Kaka, showing Ronaldo he still had some work to do if he hoped to take his crown.

Not that Michael Ball was going to be able to stop him as he raced towards the Manchester City goal. A flattened Ronaldo got back up to score his seventeenth Premier League goal of the season from the penalty spot and it was again Manchester United's title. José Mourinho's side, though, had just enough left to deny their northern rivals the double when a Didier Drogba goal at Wembley saw Chelsea beat Manchester United in the FA Cup final. Yet with Ronaldo and Rooney by now forming a formidable partnership, Paul Scholes and Ryan Giggs still performing with distinction in midfield and a defence that included Rio Ferdinand, Patrice Evra and Nemanja Vidic, it was clear there was still much to come from a maturing side.

Yet Manchester United started the 2007/08 season poorly. Ronaldo was sent off at Portsmouth. He hadn't scored in the League after seven games and must have been relieved to get his account under way by scoring in a 1-0 win at Birmingham City. Two more in the next match at home to Wigan Athletic were swiftly followed by all four goals in 2-0 home victories against Blackburn Rovers and Fulham, his first in the second game a wonderful volley that gave 'keeper Antti Niemi no chance.

Early in the New Year, he struck his first Manchester United hat-trick. Managerless Newcastle had held out to half time before Ronaldo broke their resistance with a low free kick before adding a second with a neat finish to a move involving Wayne Rooney and double-scorer Carlos Tevez. Another goal 2 minutes from the end by the number 7 completed the rout. Six weeks later, Newcastle was to again be on the end of some superb play by Manchester United, with Ronaldo scoring twice in a 5-1 away victory.

In the Champions League, Barcelona was United's semi-final opponent. Three minutes into the away leg Ronaldo had the chance to calm the nerves, but blazing his penalty kick high and wide wasn't to be expected. Fortunately, Paul Scholes repaired the damage in the second leg by scoring the only goal of two highly charged games.

Back in the Premier League, Ronaldo rewarded his manager for making him captain for the home game with Bolton by scoring twice. Having hit a scorching 25-yard free kick to

beat David James in the Portsmouth home game he did it again, a swerving dipping effort from even further out giving Ali Al Habsi no chance. At home to Aston Villa he was a lot closer to goal, but with Martin Laursen directly behind then, Scot Carson seemed unlikely to be beaten. Not so, however, as back-heeling the ball through the defender's legs left the 'keeper bamboozled and the home side surging to a 4-0 victory.

Wigan Athletic away in the season's final game stood in the way of another Premier League title. If Manchester United failed to win, Chelsea could pinch the title from under their noses. With 33 minutes gone, a penalty was awarded to the away side. Ronaldo tucked it away for his thirty-first Premier League goal and forty-first in all for the season. Ten minutes from the end, Ryan Giggs, equalling Sir Bobby Charlton's Manchester United appearance record, scored to ensure the title returned to Old Trafford.

Ten days later Ronaldo scored his forty-second goal of the season, heading home Wes Brown's cross to give Manchester United the lead against Chelsea in Moscow. Chelsea hit back through Frank Lampard and when the game ended 1-1, penalties were needed to settle the 2008 UEFA Champions League. Having enjoyed such a wonderful season, it looked like it might all end in tears for Ronaldo after he missed from 12 yards, but after John Terry missed the chance to win the Cup, Edwin van der Sar became the hero by saving Nicolas Anelka's spot kick.

Ronaldo had at times played brilliantly during the season and after rightly praising his whole squad, Ferguson said, 'It would be churlish not to acknowledge the forty-two goals scored by Cristiano Ronaldo, an incredible tally for essentially a wide player who can make goals as well.' The hope now was that Ronaldo would ignore the overtures from Real Madrid to go and play in Spain.

He did, but only for one season, departing for a record-breaking £80 million the following summer. Manchester United had won the Premier League, but Ronaldo had played poorly in the Champions League final against Barcelona that the Spanish side won comfortably. He left having scored 118 times for Manchester United from 244 starting and 48 substitute appearances.

ROOKE, RONNIE (ARSENAL)

Season: 1947/48
Goals scored: 33 (out of 81); 23 home, 10 away
Percentage: 40.7 per cent
Runner-up: Mick Fenton (Middlesbrough), 28 goals
Arsenal were League Champions

Twelve seasons after Ted Drake had become the first Arsenal player to end a season as the First Division's leading scorer, fellow centre forward Ronnie Rooke became the second, netting thirty-one of the Gunners' total of eighty-one as they lifted the League championship trophy for the sixth time.

Fitting admirably into a very effective front-line which included two high-quality forwards in Reg Lewis and Jimmy Logie, Rooke was extremely powerful physically, lethal with both feet and good in the air. He was a ruthless finisher who was an unmistakable figure on the pitch with his bandy legs, shirtsleeves flapping and black, wavy hair on top of a craggy face dominated by a 'Roman nose'.

A crowd of 60,000 saw him score on his Gunners debut in a 3-1 home win over Sunderland and after finding the net again in a 2-1 victory at Sheffield United, he grabbed a brace in his second outing at Highbury, when the FA Cup holders Charlton were clipped 4-2. Three days later he scored a spectacular goal that enabled Arsenal to beat Manchester United 2-1.

Receiving the ball in the inside right position, Rooke was looking to lay it off, but instead advanced forward, and from fully 30 yards out he let fly with a devastating left-foot shot. The ball ripped past United's goalkeeper Jack Crompton and into the top right-hand corner of the net. A brilliant effort – one of his best-ever goals for the Gunners. In his next outing, he slammed in a penalty to seal a 2-0 victory over Bolton.

After going four games without a goal Rooke netted in successive games against Midland opponents. He broke clear of his marker before flicking the ball over the head of advancing goalkeeper Jack Rutherford to win the game against Aston Villa 1-0 before driving home a low effort to earn a point at Wolves (1-1). He then cracked in another penalty as Blackpool succumbed 2-1.

Further goals followed in 1-0 and 2-0 wins over Blackburn and Huddersfield Town respectively before he hammered in another spot-kick to earn a point against Manchester City (1-1).

He was outstanding at Grimsby in mid-December, scoring twice in a resounding 4-0 victory, and on Christmas Day he struck home another brace, one a rasping right-foot rocket, as Liverpool were defeated 3-1 at Highbury.

Two of his three goals in January came in the 3-2 home win over Sheffield United, the other in a 3-0 victory over Preston, and he followed up by scoring twice in successive home wins over Burnley (3-0) and Wolves (5-2), while in between times his goal at Villa Park counted for nothing in a 4-2 defeat. He did, however, miss two easy chances in the latter game – much to his annoyance!

Also in mid-January, Arsenal's visit to Old Trafford was a real classic and attracted a crowd of 83,260 ... this still remains as the highest-ever attendance for a League game in England. Rooke was closely marked in this game, but he did find space to assist in the point-saving goal scored by Reg Lewis (1-1).

Games were fast running out, but Arsenal looked strong and confident as they marched on to glory. Rooke continued to plague and torment defenders, whipping in his first hat-trick for the Gunners in an emphatic 7-0 home win over Middlesbrough on Good Friday. One of his efforts almost ripped a hole in the net; another almost bent back the hands of nervous debutant goalkeeper Bob Anderson, while the 'Boro custodian also scuffed a goal-kick into the back of Rooke, who turned and duly banged the ball into the net.

His fine strike earned a vital point in the return game with Middlesbrough (1-1), and soon afterwards he secured a 2-0 victory over Blackburn with another extra-special effort.

Arsenal, easing towards the title, collected three points from their next four games to clinch the Championship. And with nothing at stake, their final game of the season, at home to Grimsby, was something of a celebratory party as well as being a personal triumph for Rooke, who scored four times in a magnificent 8-0 victory, Arsenal's biggest in the League since December 1934.

In fact, he scored one of the strangest goals of his career against the Mariners. He jumped to head a low goal-kick taken by Tweedy. The ball hit him flush on the chin and flew straight back into the net.

Thirty-three goals for a thirty-six-year-old, ever-present striker ... great stuff!

Born in Guildford, Surrey on 7 December 1911, Rooke had trials with Stoke City and played for his local club, Guildford City, and Woking before joining Third Division (South) side Crystal Palace in March 1933. He played in the Eagles' second XI for quite a while and made only eighteen League appearances (with four goals scored) between 1932 and 1936.

His main success came when he moved to Second Division Fulham in November 1936. He scored a hat-trick on his debut (against West Ham) and was the Cottagers' leading scorer for three consecutive seasons, notching a total of fifty-seven goals in eighty-seven competitive matches, including all six in a 6-0 FA Cup demolition of Bury in January 1939, which still stands as a club record.

The Second World War broke out at the peak of his career and Rooke immediately joined the RAF, although he still played in wartime matches for Fulham, scoring a staggering 212 goals in 199 regional fixtures alone. He also gained an unofficial England cap in a Victory International against Wales at Molineux in 1942.

The Football League programme resumed in August 1946 and despite being nearly thirty-five years of age and having never played in the top flight, Rooke, having notched a total of 77 goals in 110 League and FA Cup matches for Fulham, was signed by Arsenal in a package deal which saw David Nelson and Cyril Grant move to Craven Cottage.

The arrival of Rooke at Highbury surprised a lot of people, but the raven-haired striker made an immediate impact, scoring the winner on his debut against Charlton Athletic on 14 December 1946.

He went on to bag twenty-one goals in just twenty-four League matches that season before doing the business ten-fold in 1947/48, setting a post-war club record that has not been broken since.

After netting another fourteen goals in 1948/49 – to bring his tally with Arsenal to seventy in only ninety-four starts – he rejoined his old club Crystal Palace as player-manager. He had some initial success at Selhurst Park, guiding the Eagles to seventh place in Division Three (South) in 1949/50 ... but also blemished what had been a tremendous record in football by getting himself sent off in a tough encounter against Millwall in October 1949.

He left Selhurst Park in November 1950 and three months later became player-manager of Bedford Town, staying in that role until 1953. He joined the non-League club for a second spell in August 1959 and after playing in his last game when almost fifty, he retired from football entirely in October 1961. Later engaged as a porter at Luton Airport, he died in Bedford in July 1985 from lung cancer at the age of seventy-three.

ROSS, JIMMY (PRESTON NORTH END)

Season: 1889/90
Goals scored: 24 (out of 71) 15 home, 9 away
Percentage: 34 per cent
Runner-up: John Southworth (Blackburn Rovers), 22 goals
Preston finished as First Division Champions

Edinburgh-born Jimmy Ross was a talented inside forward who, along with his older brother Nick, joined Preston North End in 1883. Developing, in the years before the Football League got started, a good partnership with John Goodall, Ross scored his first goal in the FA Cup in January 1887, when PNE won a highly competitive match in Scotland against one of the game's great teams at the time, Renton.

It was during the following season's competition, however, that Ross put himself into the record books, hitting a then-record (since surpassed by Ted MacDougall – see page) eight as his side recorded a surely never-to-be-beaten biggest ever win in the world's longest running football competition, Hyde being thrashed 26-0.

Come the competition's end Ross had scored nineteen, a figure no one has come near challenging since. There was, however, major disappointment when WBA beat the Lilywhites 2-1 in the final before a record crowd of 19,000 at the Oval, South London.

Having enjoyed success in the race for the first League title, PNE found itself again facing a side from the Black County in the 1888/89 FA Cup final. Having made the fatal mistake of being over-confident the previous season, Preston having even asked to be photographed with the Cup the day before the final, this time there was no mistake against Wolverhampton Wanderers.

Such was Preston's reputation that the gates were closed an hour before kick-off with 23,000 inside the Oval. The League champions opened their account when a fine shot from Ross was punched out by Jack Baynton and when it landed at Fred Dewhurst's feet, he thumped it back between the posts.

Ten minutes later Ross, the smallest player on the pitch, dodged Harry Allen and Charlie Mason and hit a shot straight at Baynton. The ball slipped through the goalkeeper's fingers and behind the goal line. With a score of 2-0, and with Sam Thompson adding another on 70 minutes, 'the Invincibles' had done the first 'double' of League and FA Cup.

None of this was enough to keep Goodall at the club when he received a better offer from Derby, and although Jimmy Ross must have been sad to see him leave at the end of the season, there was also no doubt real joy when he then discovered that his older brother had agreed to return as captain after just one season on Merseyside with Everton.

Kicking off the 1889/90 season, PNE faced Stoke City. The Potters had finished at the bottom of the League in 1888/89, and in the two matches between the sides, PNE had scored ten times without conceding a goal. This time another ten goals were to be scored in just one game and PNE got all of them. Ross was bang on form with five goals. His first made it 3-0, and if the reports are accurate it was his only headed goal of the season, and he made it 5-0 with a fine low shot on 53 minutes. His hat-trick came on 65 minutes and he added the ninth and tenth of the match.

'All of them played well, Drummond, Thompson and Jack Ross particularly so. Stoke were quite baffled by the spending passing of North End,' said *Cricket and Football Field*.

There was then a major shock in the second game, PNE slipping to their first-ever defeat in League football. They went down fighting to the last. When they entered the final 10 minutes of the match away to Aston Villa 5-1 down, Ross then scored twice, his first a strong, low drive to the right of goalkeeper Jimmy Warner, and near the end he should have bagged his hat-trick but missed an easy chance from George Drummond's cross. Without Goodall Preston were no longer invincible, but they were still good and after beating Burnley 3-0, they were 4-0 up at home to WBA when Ross hit a strong right-footed shot on 75 minutes which 'flew past England goalkeeper Bob Roberts like a bullet fired from a gun'.

Preston had moved to within a point of leaders Everton prior to the sides' match on 16 November at Anfield. Such was the excitement in Liverpool that the ground was packed long before kick-off and when, early on, Everton appeared to take the lead, the crowd behind the goal swayed forward and the barrier behind it broke down. With a great mass of people lying on the ground, and with one boy severely injured, play was stopped for several minutes. When it resumed, it was the home side that took the lead through Fred Geary, which is how it remained at half time.

Ross and the other Preston forwards had spurned some good opportunities in the first period. They did not do so in the second, Dewhurst equalizing quickly. David Russell added a second, and with the away side swarming all over the Toffees, it wasn't long before Thompson made it 3-1. It was Ross who made it 4-1. 'The Preston boys were playing away with wonderful dash, their football showing what scientific football really was, and Jimmy Ross easily beat Smalley,' said *The Liverpool Mercury*. Having beaten its nearest rival 5-1, PNE was now again the favourite to win the title.

Jimmy Ross was clearly determined to play his part as he then hit four goals, including a point-saver at home to Blackburn Rovers, in the next three games. Then, on Christmas Day 1889, Ross hit all three of his side's goals against Aston Villa, following this up with both of Preston's goals at WBA. Top of the League in mid-January, there were real hopes of another double when the FA Cup got started. Ross scored twice in the first two rounds, but in the third Bolton sprang a surprise by putting out the holders 3-2 at Deepdale.

With three League games remaining, PNE struggled to overcome Notts County at home, winning by a single goal in seven, with Ross getting one of them. Two weeks later he was again on the scoresheet, helping his side to a precious point in a 2-2 draw at Accrington, which, with Everton then subsequently failing to win their final game of the season, confirmed Preston had retained their title.

After previously narrowly losing out to Johnny Goodall, Jimmy Ross had finished the season as the Football League's top scorer with twenty-four goals.

Ross was to remain a good scorer of goals over the next eleven seasons, ending up with sixteen League goals in 1891/92 and seventeen in 1893/94, after which he joined Liverpool. Over the following two seasons he scored thirty-seven goals in seventy-three games, earning the popular nickname of the 'Little Demon'. Later, he enjoyed success at Burnley, scoring twenty-nine times in fifty-one games to assist the Clarets to promotion.

Towards the end of his career he joined Manchester City, where he played alongside fellow trade union stalwart Billy Meredith. Ross was one of many top players who, upset at the setting of a maximum wage of £4 a week when he knew he could get £10, helped form the Association Footballers' Union in February 1898. Others who joined included the Villa striker John Devey.

Ross retired from the game at the end of the 1900/01 season and died just a year later, aged thirty-six.

RUSH, IAN, MBE (LIVERPOOL)

Season: 1983/84
Goals scored: 32 (out of 73); 23 home, 9 away
Percentage: 43.8 per cent
Runner-up: Gary Lineker (Leicester City), 22 goals
Liverpool were League Champions

Ian Rush, the greatest goalscorer in the history of both Liverpool and the FA Cup in the modern era, was admired by Kenny Dalglish, who played with him and then managed him. The Scottish international said:

> Rushy was the best striker I've ever saw. A deadly finisher, they used to say it was my vision that opened up the chances for Ian to put away. But really, it was his vision, his knowing when to run and where to run. That was the vital ingredient. I would just hit the ball into space, knowing that he would have the pace and the instinct to be moving there. A player of his qualities could turn a hopeful pass into a great one.

Shy, introverted and insecure as a teenager, the Welshman would emerge as an instinctive predator in front of goal, notably in the 1983/84 season, when he won the coveted 'Golden Boot' award as the leading goalscorer in European football.

The statistics say it all. In a total of 659 first-team appearances for Liverpool, Rush scored an amazing 346 goals, 229 in the Football League and 44 in the FA Cup, including five in four Wembley finals.

His tally is all the more impressive because so many of his goals were scored in important matches with trophies at stake, a tribute to his temperament as well as his skill.

His goals – yes, his goals – earned Rush (and Liverpool) one European Cup, five League Championship, three FA Cup and five League Cup, four FA Charity Shield winner's medals … and a handful of runners-up prizes as well.

Surprisingly, in his early days at Anfield, an overawed Rush could barely find the net in the reserves! He publicly admitted that he didn't think he was good enough for Liverpool following his transfer from Chester in 1980 for a fee of £300,000. Alan Hansen wasn't impressed either, saying, 'I watched him in training and thought – no pace, can't head it, can't score. They'll get rid of him at the end of the season.' How wrong was he!

Frustrated by his lack of progress and upset at being the target of much dressing-room banter and ribbing, Rush was, at one point, prepared to leave Liverpool. Yet, when word leaked out, there was no interest from top-flight clubs. His career was clearly at a crossroads.

Around this time (1981), during a dispute over pay, a fateful meeting with Bob Paisley took place. 'We bought you to score goals, and you're not doing it,' the manager told him bluntly. 'You've got to be more selfish in front of goal.'

That blast at the striker proved to be the turning point. Rush, determined to play more for himself, suddenly sparked into life. His strike rate increased, as did his confidence.

'I always had faith in him,' Paisley said later.

Between 1981/82 and 1986/87, Rush's consistency was quite remarkable. He averaged roughly two goals every three games – a ratio unmatched by any rival forward in top-flight football. Nothing like this had been seen since the heyday of Jimmy Greaves, two decades earlier.

The high point for Rush came in 1983/84, which he described as being the 'greatest season of my life'.

He scored no less than forty-eight goals in all competitions, topping the First Division charts with thirty-two while also breaking the club record previously held by Roger Hunt. And this terrific achievement made him the obvious choice for the 'Footballer of the Year' for both his peers and the football writers.

Wiry, tall and whippet-quick, Rush, who worked tirelessly on behalf of his team, relentlessly foraging for possession when the opposition had the ball, scored on the opening day to salvage a point at Wolves. A week later, he netted a late winner at home to Nottingham Forest and three days after that, he was on target in the 1-1 home draw with Southampton.

A priceless 79th-minute winner followed in mid-September to see off Aston Villa 2-1 but then, surprisingly, he was goalless in the next four games before becoming the first Liverpool player to score five goals in a League game since John Evans against Bristol Rovers in 1954 in a 6-0 home thrashing of Luton Town. He netted twice in the first 5 minutes and may well have struck twice more, but the woodwork intervened each time.

A 16th-minute effort against Everton helped set up a 3-0 win in the Merseyside derby early in November, while his next three goals earned a point at Tottenham (2-2) and narrow victories over Stoke City and Birmingham City.

His fourteenth League goal of the season was a real cracker in a 5-0 win over Notts County a week before Christmas, and he ended the year by scoring a late equaliser at home to Leicester (2-2) and the winner at Nottingham Forest (1-0).

After a slow start to the New Year, Rush tucked away his second hat-trick of the campaign in a competent 3-1 win at Villa Park, scored the opening goal in a 3-0 Anfield win over Watford and was on target in a 2-0 home victory over QPR before scoring again against arch-rivals Everton in a 1-1 draw at Goodison Park.

At this juncture – 3 March – Liverpool were right on course for the League title and Rush played a massive part during the run-in with important goals at Watford (won 2-0), at Leicester (3-3), at home to Ipswich (2-2) and Norwich City (1-1), while also scoring twice in a resounding 6-0 drubbing of West Ham and a four-timer in the 5-0 home demolition of Coventry City.

He also had a fine season in the League Cup (eight goals) and European Cup (six goals) as Liverpool won both tournaments to complete the treble.

After two more excellent seasons, Rush – perhaps surprisingly to many supporters – left Anfield for Juventus in July 1986 for a fee of £3.2 million, but was allowed to remain 'on loan' with Liverpool for the whole of the 1986/87 season before going to Italy in the summer of 1987. However, a year later, after just one term in Serie A, Rush was re-signed by Liverpool boss Kenny Dalglish for a fee of £2.8 million.

His second spell at Anfield last until May 1996, when he moved to Leeds United on a free transfer. Twelve months later, he switched his allegiance to Newcastle United and then gradually wound down his career with spells at Sheffield United (on loan), Wrexham and Sydney Olympic (Australia). He retired in May 2000 and was out of football for four years before becoming manager of Chester City in August 2004, a position he held until May

2005. After that, he was engaged as Liverpool's Academy coach, worked in the media and was also an advisor to Northwich Victoria before returning to Anfield in April 2010 as the club's Soccer Schools Ambassador, working with the Commercial team to help develop and support partnerships with other global sponsors and brands.

During his playing career Rush scored 425 goals in 900 appearances at club and international level. He was capped seventy-three times by Wales (1980–88) and netted twenty-eight times for the Principality.

Born on 20 October 1961 in St Asaph, Denbighshire, Rush played for Deeside Primary and Flint Comprehensive Schools and represented Flintshire U19s before joining Chester City as an apprentice in April 1978, turning professional in September 1979.

Rush's autobiography was published on 21 August 2008 – *Rush: The Autobiography*.

SETTLE, JIMMY (EVERTON)

Season: 1901/02
Goals scored: 18 (out of 53); 11 home, 7 away
Percentage: 34 per cent
Runners-up: Jasper McLuckie (Bury and Aston Villa), 17 goals
Everton finished runners-up

Jimmy Settle, who could easily have been a champion sprinter if he had not taken up football, was born in Millom, Cumberland, in June 1875. He played for his hometown club Bolton Wanderers (1894/95), non-League side Halliwell FC (until January 1897) and Bury before joining Everton for £400 in April 1899. After spending nine years at Goodison Park, he assisted Stockport County and announced his retirement in May 1909.

An FA Cup winner in 1906 (against Newcastle United) and loser in 1907 (against Sheffield Wednesday), he finished as the First Division's top goalscorer in 1901/02 with eighteen goals – the joint lowest of the highest totals achieved in the English top-flight to date.

He also represented England on six occasions between 1899 and 1903, playing twice against Ireland, Scotland and Wales. He netted six times, including a hat-trick against the Irish in February 1899, and also represented the Football League.

One of the game's most instinctive finishers during the early part of the twentieth century, fair-haired Settle was lightning-quick inside the penalty area, and one journalist wrote, 'Few are more dangerous near goal, often scores when the goalkeeping isn't looking.'

A fleet-footed inside or outside right who required little or no space in which to execute his trickery, he was also a fine passer of the ball and frequently carved out openings for his colleagues with a flat and precise 20–30-yard pass which measured nigh-on inch-perfect.

A shade lethargic and indeed selfish at times, he scored on his debut for Everton in a 2-1 home defeat by Sheffield United in September 1899 and ended that season with ten goals to his credit, following up with eleven the following season before bagging eighteen in 1901/02 to top the League charts.

Playing inside to right-winger Jack Sharpe, Settle cracked in a hat-trick in the second game of the season when Wolverhampton Wanderers were hammered 6-1 at Goodison Park, one on his goals flying 'high and wide past Wolves 'keeper Tom Baddeley with great power.'

He was on target in his next game – a 2-2 draw in the Merseyside derby – and in early October netted the winner to beat Sheffield United 2-1.

He had now been joined in the Everton attack by Alex 'Sandy' Young, who took over at centre forward, and the pairing quickly blended together, although Young was far more of a schemer than goalscorer, but was the perfect foil for Settle.

A smart goal by Settle salvaged a point against his former club Bury while braces brought successive away victories at Grimsby (2-0) and top-of-the-table Sunderland (4-2). He was then, stated one reporter, 'on fire' as he struck twice more in a 5-0 home battering of Sheffield Wednesday in early December.

In the game against the Owls, Settle also hit the woodwork and missed two easy second-half chances, but also set up goals for Sharp and Young.

A week later he netted again at Notts County (won 2-0) before knocking in the winner against Bolton Wanderers (1-0) as the championship race gained momentum. At this juncture, Sunderland topped the Division ahead of Everton, with Newcastle United and Blackburn Rovers also in the chasing pack.

After being eliminated in the first round of the FA Cup, beaten in a replay by arch-rivals Liverpool, Everton immediately gained revenge over their Merseyside rivals by battering the Reds 4-0 to register their first League win of 1902, Settle scoring twice.

Unfortunately, after this superb victory Settle and his teammates lost their way, recording only one more win in the next eight League games (2-1 at Stoke).

The reporter in the *Liverpool Echo* wrote: 'The Everton team has lost confidence. Even Settle and Young are looking very tame.'

In fact, Settle failed to find the net in any of those six games. The title was slipping away and with games and time fast running out, it would require something special if the Blues wanted to overtake Sunderland and win the championship.

In a crucial game at Goodison Park in mid-March, Everton beat League leaders Sunderland at home 2-0, Settle helping set up a goal for Walter Abbott, but defeat at Manchester City in their next game meant that it was going to be tough for the team to overhaul the Wearsiders.

Results improved as the season drew to its close, but as for Settle, he continued to struggle in front of goal and added only one more to his tally (in a 2-0 home win over Derby County in late March) as Everton ended up as runners-up, beaten by three points (44–41).

Having notched thirty-nine goals in his first three full seasons with Everton, Settle managed just fifty-eight in his next six campaigns, leaving Goodison Park with a record of 97 goals in 269 senior appearances.

It is believed that Settle died in 1950, aged seventy-five.

SHEARER, ALAN (BLACKBURN ROVERS AND NEWCASTLE UNITED)

Blackburn
Season: 1994/95
Goals scored: 34 (out of 80), 25 home, 9 away
Percentage: 42.5 per cent
Runner-up: Robbie Fowler (Liverpool), 25 goals
Blackburn were the Premier League Champions

Blackburn
Season: 1995/96
Goals scored: 31 (out of 61) 22 home, 9 away
Percentage: 51 per cent
Runner-up: Robbie Fowler (Liverpool), 28 goals
Blackburn finished seventh

Newcastle United
Season: 1996/97
Goals scored: 25 (out of 73); 20 home, 5 away
Percentage: 34 per cent
Runner-up: Ian Wright (Arsenal), 23 goals
Newcastle finished second

Kenny Dalglish signed Shearer from Southampton for a British record transfer fee of £3.3 million (along with David Speedie) in July 1992. Newly promoted Blackburn was in the market for top players, courtesy of millions from local benefactor Jack Walker, and making his debut against Crystal Palace on the season's opening day, Shearer scored twice. By Boxing Day he was runaway leader, with sixteen goals, at the top of the Premier League scorers' chart.

However, a serious knee injury, eventually diagnosed as a snapped right anterior cruciate ligament, was to bring his season to an early end. It seems certain that had he remained fit, he would have ended up with a lot more than Teddy Sheringham, whose twenty-two goals for Nottingham Forest and Spurs were enough to see him finish as the 1992/93 top scorer. Without Shearer, Blackburn finished fourth in the League and was knocked out in the last four and last eight of the League and FA Cups respectively.

The following season Dalglish waited for him to return to full fitness but once he was back playing regularly, the goals flowed again. His first hat-trick came in a 3-3 draw at Leeds and during a purple patch at the start of the year, Shearer scored nine goals in six games as Blackburn made up ground on runaway leaders Manchester United. Shearer also scored two goals against United in a 2-0 win at Ewood and Blackburn eventually got to within touching distance of them before United went on to regain the Premiership crown.

Shearer was to finish with thirty-one Premier League goals, just three behind top-scoring Andy Cole. Having missed eight games, it was a remarkable record and Shearer was rewarded with the Football Writers' Footballer of the Year award.

When the 1994/95 season got under way, Shearer was soon back hitting the net with Rovers' goal in a 1-1 opening day draw against his former side Southampton.

He had a new strike partner after Rovers again broke the transfer record to sign Chris Sutton from Norwich for £5 million. 'SAS', as the newspapers called them, created havoc throughout the Premiership as Rovers won the top-flight Championship for the first time in eighty-one years.

The pair combined brilliantly in the first home game of the season against Leicester City, Shearer producing a wonderful chip into the box that Sutton headed bravely home before his partner set Robbie Slater through and when the ball rebounded from the post, Shearer was on hand to score the second goal in a game Rovers won 3-0. All of which had the *Daily Mirror* suggesting that the Premier League race might be a lot tighter than the previous season.

For once, Shearer was to be outstaged in front of goal in the next game with Sutton scoring three times as Coventry were easily beaten 4-0. And it was Sutton, scoring with his only chance at Stamford Bridge, who again took the plaudits in a 2-1 success against Chelsea.

Against Aston Villa both men were again on the scoresheet, with Shearer adding to an early penalty by running onto Sutton's flick on 74 minutes to make it 3-1, with his defending marker Paul McGrath later praising both men, but adding that 'Shearer is as strong as Mark Hughes.' With Sutton scoring twice, Rovers beat Liverpool 3-2 at Ewood Park to maintain their challenge for the title. And when Shearer's 53rd-minute goal at Sheffield Wednesday proved the only goal of the match, Dalglish's side had risen to second in the table. Ipswich were plummeting down it and with a goal apiece, Sutton and Shearer helped win all three points in a 3-1 win at Portman Road.

The following weekend it was more of the same, QPR being well-beaten 4-0. Sutton opened the scoring on 16 minutes, but it was Shearer who had opposition 'keeper Sieb Dykstra clutching fresh air with three efforts for his hat-trick. First, he powered his way through to net, and then doubled his tally with a penalty kick before hitting an unstoppable 30-yard shot for his third goal. His good form continued as he netted his seventeenth of the season in a fine 3-0 win at Wimbledon.

Against Southampton, Ewood Park saw one of its greatest ever goals when Matt Le Tissier beat Tim Flowers from 35 yards, but with another two goals, including scoring after Bruce Grobbelaar had first saved his penalty, Shearer ensured a 3-2 home success.

Defenders' hopes of a quieter New Year were ruined just two days into it. Struggling West Ham played decently, but with a second hat-trick of the season, including two penalties and a fine finish when sent clean through by Jason Wilcox, Shearer sent Harry Redknapp's side back south beaten 4-2. Little more than three weeks later, Shearer had made it three hat-tricks at Ewood Park in the last five games, Ipswich losing out 4-1 and Rovers consequently moving four points clear at the top of the table.

Continuing to net regularly, Shearer was on the scoresheet against Sheffield Wednesday and Wimbledon. It was Colin Hendry, though, who got the all-important only goal at Aston Villa to keep Rovers out in front. Against Arsenal at home, Shearer gave marker Andy Linighan a torrid time, losing him for the opener on 4 minutes and adding his second from the penalty spot after Linighan had brought him down. The Rovers man then scored again as Chelsea was beaten 2-1 at Ewood Park. And with both Shearer and Sutton on the scoresheet in a 2-1 victory at Everton, the way was now open for Blackburn to take the title, with Manchester United five points behind and having played a game more.

Returning three days later from Loftus Road with all three points courtesy of a 67th-minute Sutton winner, Blackburn seemed unstoppable. Two dropped points in a 1-1 draw with Leeds did, though, cut the gap with United to six points. There was therefore relief when Alex Ferguson's side could only draw at home to Chelsea on a day when another Shearer goal wasn't enough to stop Manchester City winning 3-2 at Ewood Park. There was relief all round when Crystal Palace were beaten 2-1, with Rovers' second coming from Kevin Gallagher, later stretchered off with a broken leg.

However, when defeat at Upton Park followed, the gap over Manchester United was down to just five points, with United having played a game fewer. And knowing that their rivals had beaten Sheffield Wednesday twenty-four hours earlier, Dalglish's side ran out at Ewood Park on Monday 9 May knowing that victory against Newcastle United was vital. With Tim Flowers playing probably his best game between the sticks during his time at Blackburn, it was left to Shearer to knock home the only goal of the game. His thirty-third Premier League goal of the season came on 28 minutes, when he headed Graham Le Saux's cross home and ensured that his side would win the title as long as they avoided defeat at Anfield the following Sunday. Failure would set Manchester United up for the title, as long as they won at Upton Park.

Everything looked rosy when Shearer put his side ahead after 20 minutes, playing a one-two with Stuart Ripley before blasting the ball home. With virtually everyone in the ground willing Rovers to hang on, the only ones not prepared to throw in the towel – the Liverpool players – produced a wonderful second-half recovery and when Jamie Redknapp blasted the winner with only seconds remaining, it seemed that the way might be open for Manchester United to snatch the title, especially as their game still had 4 minutes remaining. However, when Andy Cole missed a late chance, it was time for celebration and as extra reward for his Championship-winning efforts, Shearer also collected the PFA's Footballer of the Year for 1995.

The 1995/96 season was to be Shearer's last at Ewood Park. It was to be filled with controversy. Kenny Dalglish resigned and there was to be Champions League failure, during which David Batty and Le Saux fought on the pitch during a game in Moscow.

There were also rumours about Shearer that eventually led to his status going from hero to zero. First, there was new manager Ray Harford switching Chris Sutton to centre-half, reputedly at the request of Shearer, as they didn't 'get on' and he was jealous of the striker's popularity with the fans. Sutton eventually only made nine League appearances plus four as a sub and scored only once all season.

Despite the furore Shearer continued to do the business on the pitch, scoring thirty-one League goals in thirty-five appearances. Just under half came from five hat-tricks. Four came at Ewood against Coventry, Nottingham Forest (in a 7-0 rout), West Ham, for the second season running, and Bolton. The fifth was enough to see Rovers win 3-2 at Tottenham.

His last goal was his second in a 3-2 win against Wimbledon on 17 April. He then went into hospital for an operation to make sure that he was fit for Euro96. In the two remaining games, Rovers drew 1-1 with Arsenal and won 3-2 at Chelsea, despite which European football was missed by one point. Rovers fans began to question Shearer's loyalties as his England career suddenly became more important than Rovers' quest for European football next season, especially as the striker was receiving criticism from the press for his lack of goals for England. However, he stated before the tournament that he was staying at Ewood but during Euro96, where he was top scorer, his thoughts clearly drifted to a future elsewhere.

As rumours again circulated, he repeated, not only to Rovers but also to Jack Walker himself, that he was going to stay, posed in the new kit for the forthcoming season and organised a book signing at Ewood. Then he suddenly changed his mind and joined Newcastle United, after, as it was uncovered later, at one time agreeing to join Manchester United.

The betrayal sent shockwaves throughout Blackburn. Not just the usual 'Judas' stuff, but because he may not have played the role he did at Euro96 if he had put Rovers first and helped them get into Europe beforehand. It was the beginning of the end for the Jack Walker era, as without Shearer, who during his four seasons had become the first striker to net more than 100 goals in the Premier League, Rovers fell down the table and were to be relegated in 1999.

Brave and strong, superb in the air, Shearer was the complete striker; he could shield the ball for others and was almost impossible to dispossess once he was bearing down on goal.

After finishing as leading scorer at the 1996 European Championships that summer. Alan Shearer resisted overtures from double winners Manchester United to instead join his hometown club for a world record fee of £15 million. Ironically, his first game was when the sides met in the Charity Shield curtain-raiser to the season. Heavily beaten 4-0, Newcastle then played poorly at Goodison Park in the first League game of the season to lose 2-0.

Four days later, the nerves of a packed St James' Park crowd were calmed by an early David Batty effort against Wimbledon. Then, with just 2 minutes of the match remaining, Alan Shearer scored his first of many subsequent goals in a black and white shirt. Neil Sullivan had repeatedly denied the Newcastle number 9, but the Dons 'keeper was left helpless on 88 minutes when Shearer drove an unstoppable 20-yard free kick for a goal he described post-match as 'a dream come true'.

Having lost out so agonisingly at the end of 1995/6 season to Manchester United for the title, Newcastle needed a good start. With Shearer quickly forging a fine partnership with fellow England International Les Ferdinand, and ably supplied with the ball by Colombian Faustino Asprilla and Frenchman David Ginola, goals were a certainty. Both front men were on the scoresheet as Shearer's former team Blackburn Rovers were beaten 2-1 at home before a single effort at Elland Road from the ex-Rover helped push his new side to the top of the table.

They stayed there after a great game against Aston Villa, Ferdinand scoring two and Shearer getting the third goal from a Ginola corner in a 4-3 win. Derby had strengthened their defence by signing Irishman Paul McGrath and he had a fine match when Newcastle played at the Baseball Ground. However, one moment of indecision on 76 minutes proved fatal, Shearer powering home what was in truth not even a half chance.

Eight days later, with millions watching around the world on TV, Newcastle thrilled their supporters with one of the finest performances ever seen at St James' Park. Manchester United were thrashed 5-0; it was Alex Ferguson's heaviest defeat in twenty-two years of management and it could have easily been more. Shearer got the fourth, his seventh League goal of the season so far. Beating Middlesbrough at home saw Newcastle rise to the top of the League, a position they maintained when Shearer struck at Stamford Bridge to ensure a 1-1 draw.

December proved to be a bad month. Shearer scored in both matches, against Coventry and Liverpool, but they were Newcastle's only goals in four matches and with just two points gathered, victory at home to Spurs on 28 December was vital if a Premiership title bid was to be maintained. It was again Shearer who got his side moving, opening the scoring on 20 minutes before adding his second on 82 minutes in a 7-1 hammering of the Cockneys. Four days later, he again grabbed a pair as Leeds United returned south beaten 3-0

Both goals came from Peter Beardsley corners with Shearer finishing off headers from Ferdinand, who himself grabbed the third late on.

After the match both managers were full of praise, with Keegan saying, 'He's world class when it comes to sticking chances away. He's the best in the world – no doubt about that,' and George Graham saying, 'Ferdinand and Shearer were unplayable.'

Kevin Keegan, though, was on his way out of St James' Park, sensationally quitting his post on 7 January, saying he felt he 'had taken the club as far as I can'. He'd offered to stay until the end of the season but the Newcastle directors, after failing to persuade him to change his mind, decided it would be better if he left immediately.

Despite the disappointment, Newcastle continued to push up the League with five points from the next three games, with Shearer scoring a penalty during a magnificent last 20 minutes that saw Everton beaten 4-1 after leading for much of the game.

Things looked even bleaker in the next home game, with Leicester City 3-1 up with just 13 minutes remaining. Shearer then blasted a 20-yard free kick past Kasey Keller before, 8 minutes later, squeezing a shot past the 'keeper. One minute from time, he rose superbly to power home Robert Lee's cross for his hat-trick, with the new man in charge, Kenny Dalglish, saying afterwards that 'I'm lost for words in describing Shearer's achievements.'

Walking off the pitch at the end, Shearer was given the match ball by referee Mike Reed who said, 'Yours, I think.' Newcastle were now just five points behind leaders Manchester United, although a poor March in which only two points from four games were gathered scuttled any prospects of winning the title.

Shearer scored his side's equalizing goal in the Tyne-Wear derby in April before scoring twice in a 3-1 home win against Chelsea. On 12 minutes, when Frank Leboeuf left his clearing header short, Shearer was onto it like a flash to drive home past Froda Grodas. Then, after Asprilla got the second, Shearer added his twenty-third of the season from the penalty spot. Three days later, he got his twenty-fourth as Derby was beaten 3-1 at St James' Park. On the final day of the season, Newcastle's record signing hit his twenty-fifth Premier League goal of the season as Nottingham Forest were beaten 5-0, thus ensuring that the following season St James' Park would witness Champions League football for the first time after Liverpool failed to beat Sheffield Wednesday and dropped to third.

As local rivals Sunderland had also lost at Wimbledon that afternoon to suffer relegation, Tyneside was in party mood as in addition to Shearer recapturing his spot at the top of the

Premier League scorers' charts, Les Ferdinand's double saw him join his strike partner as the only players to have notched 100 Premier League goals.

Alan Shearer continued to score regularly for Newcastle United over the next decade and although he failed to add to his triple appearance as the Premier League top scorer, he did come second twice. It all meant that when he retired in 2006, he left behind a magnificent scoring record that included 283 top-flight goals in 559 appearances for Southampton, Blackburn Rovers and his beloved Newcastle United. This puts him in fifth place in the list of top division English scorers since 1888, behind Jimmy Greaves, Dixie Dean, Steve Bloomer and Liverpool's Gordon Hodgson. In more modern times, only Ian Rush comes near with 232.

Despite his incredible achievements at Newcastle, they were never enough to help his side capture either the League or a major Cup, although Newcastle did twice finish as runners-up in the FA Cup.

SHEPHERD, ALBERT (BOLTON WANDERERS AND NEWCASTLE UNITED)

Bolton Wanderes
Season: 1905/06
Goals scored: 26 (out of 81); 16 home, 10 away
Percentage: 32 per cent
Runners-up: Billy Jones (Birmingham City) and Wattie White (Bolton Wanderers), with 25 goals each
Bolton finished sixth

Newcastle United
Season: 1910/11
Goals scored: 25 (out of 61); 16 home, 9 away
Percentage scored: 41 per cent
Runners-up: Billy Hibbert (Bury) and Tim Coleman (Sunderland), with 20 goals each
Newcastle finished eighth

Born in Great Lever, Shepherd signed professionally for his hometown club only weeks after Bolton had lost to Manchester City 1-0 in the 1904 FA Cup final. Wanderers were a team too good for the Second Division but not quite good enough for the First, and between 1899 and 1911 they were to be relegated four times and promoted on three occasions. Bolton were to gain a measure of revenge the following season when, with Shepherd scoring his second FA Cup goal, they knocked out Manchester City 2-1 in a fine match at Maine Road. Put out by Newcastle in the following round, consolation came in the form of promotion behind Liverpool, with Sam Marsh the top scorer with twenty-seven goals.

Initially, at least, it looked like Shepherd and Bolton would struggle in the top flight. Five games in and with only two points gathered from a couple of drawn games, fans must have been deeply concerned. In a tough encounter with near neighbours Blackburn, it was Shepherd who provided the only goal of the game when on 32 minutes he got on the end of a Marshall McEwan header to powerfully head the ball, and even though Bob Evans got a fist to it, he couldn't stop it entering the net.

The following weekend, when David Stokes pulled back a cross, Shepherd was onto it like lightning to lash it beyond Sunderland 'keeper Tom Naisby, adding a second in the second half in a 3-3 draw at Roker Park. However, when Bolton then crashed at home to Birmingham in the next match, 'The Tramp' in the *Cricket and Football Field* was in no doubt what was needed, starting his comment section with the headline, 'WANTED, A GOAL SCORER!' Bolton had failed to take their chances during a game they dominated.

Shepherd gave an indication that Bolton might just have a goalscorer on their books already when in the next home game, against Derby County, he took advantage of a moment's hesitation in the Rams' defence to race onto the ball and dribble it around Jimmy Methven before sending the ball into the corner of the net with just 30 seconds on the clock. Inspired, Bolton went on to win 5-0, with Sam Marsh hitting a hat-trick. Shepherd, reported the Tramp, was now 'showing his real capabilities'.

Two weeks later, Shepherd played possibly his finest game for Bolton. Nottingham Forest arrived at Burnden Park with a poor away record, having gained just a single point from five matches. Heavy fog had made the game uncertain, and with money tight, many spectators were seen outside the ground deciding whether to risk their 'tanner' and face seeing the game being abandoned later. In the event, the crowd was down to around a quarter of what might have been expected at just 5,000.

There was a great opening goal when Shepherd beautifully controlled David Stokes's pass and despite an acute angle, his shot carried such power that it flashed past Harry Linacre. The Forest 'keeper was, though, in fine form, twice denying the Bolton centre forward with fine saves. Two barnstorming runs by Shepherd were then ended with fouls as the away side fought to stay in the match.

However, on 55 minutes, Shepherd could not be denied, brushing 'aside all opposition, Fullerton, Craig and Dudley failing in turn to shake him off the ball, which he drove all along the ground at lightning speed out of the reach of the watchful Linacre' (*Cricket and Football Field*). Two minutes later, McEwan's accurate centre was well controlled and Shepherd curled home his third to the great cheers of the small crowd that could just about see what was going on. Within a minute Shepherd had scored again, touching home Wattie White's header. Victory by six goals to nil pushed Bolton five points clear of the relegation zone.

When Bolton travelled to play Middlesbrough in mid-December, there was even a chance of moving into the top half of the table. After falling behind early on, the away side roared into the lead with goals from Shepherd on 30 and 31 minutes, rounding England international 'keeper Tim Williamson for the first and then blasting a 30-yard shot for the second. An exciting encounter was to end in a 4-4 draw.

Against 'Boro's near neighbours Sunderland in February, Shepherd did even better, putting his side 2-1 up after beating Dusty Rhodes for pace before tucking the ball beyond Naisby. Then, in the second period, his close control saw him dribble round virtually the whole of the Wearsiders' defence, only to be foiled by a fine Naisby save. The 'keeper, though, had no chance when, soon after, a long ball over the top saw Shepherd dash through to give 'the oncoming Naisby absolutely no chance of dealing with a sharp low shot'. Stokes then centred accurately to give the Bolton centre an easy finish for his hat-trick, Bolton going on to win 6-2.

Such fine form was bound to attract the England selectors' attentions and Shepherd was chosen to lead the line against Scotland at Hampden Park in April 1906.

Not yet twenty-one, Shepherd scored his side's only goal, his 81st-minute effort giving England a chance to recover from two earlier James Howie efforts that had thrilled a then-world record crowd of 102,741. Despite his success, it was to be another five years before he got another chance to play for England. When he did so, he again scored! His goal at Hampden had in fact come during a period when Shepherd had struggled to score for his club, and when Bolton faced Liverpool, already confirmed as League Champions, on 16 April, he had gone two months without scoring.

Absent for a number of games through injury, his place at the top of the scorers' charts was under threat from his teammate Wattie White – in fact, come the season's end, the *Cricket and Football Field* recorded the latter as top scorer, with two more league goals. White had scored in five consecutive matches to take his total to twenty-four, exactly the same as Shepherd.

In Alex Raisbeck Liverpool had a fine captain and stalwart defender, while behind him in goal was Sam Hardy, one of the game's greatest ever 'keepers. Shepherd had scored twice at Anfield earlier in the season, in a 2-2 draw on Christmas Day. He got another two at Burnden Park: 'The 25,000 who were privileged to see the Bolton youth shoot his second goal will remember it for seasons to come,' reported the *Cricket and Football Field*. Victory by three goals to two helped push Bolton to their highest position ever, sixth, with Shepherd finishing on twenty-six goals from thirty-one matches, just one ahead of White and Birmingham's 'Tipton Slasher', Billy Jones.

Shepherd was to remain at Bolton until November 1908, when after scoring 90 goals in 123 senior games he cost Newcastle United £850.

Shepherd's arrival at St James' Park in November 1908 was not an immediate success as despite scoring on his home debut, Newcastle suffered their record defeat, thrashed 9-1 by local rivals Sunderland. However, a further ten League goals, including a hat-trick against Notts County, were enough to help his club capture the League title for the second time in three years.

Success continued the following season, when with twenty-eight goals, including a hat-trick against Bolton and four against both Preston and Liverpool (in an amazing game that Newcastle lost 6-5), he finished just two goals behind Liverpool's Jack Parkinson at the end of the season. However, with three FA Cup goals, Shepherd outscored the Liverpool man in all games. More importantly, his two efforts in the replayed FA Cup final against Barnsley had

ensured the Geordies' everlasting affection as after three previous defeats, it meant Newcastle had won their first FA Cup final.

Come the start of the new season, Newcastle made the short journey to Roker Park and although his side lost 2-1 to Sunderland, Shepherd opened his own goal account with a penalty. Two more followed at Boundary Park, where the Oldham backs could hardly hold him in check, and after a simple finish from 6 yards in the first half, he blasted home in the second to seal the match.

Against Notts County, he scored a great goal. Receiving the ball from Wilf Low, he ran wide of John Montgomery before sending Arthur Griffiths the wrong way and with Albert Iremonger narrowing the angle, he curled the ball into the corner of the net to the open the scoring. All to the huge cheers of the 30,000-strong St James' Park crowd.

Then, for the second consecutive season, he hit four against Liverpool as Newcastle won 6-1. On 27 minutes, he was quickest to the loose ball to give Sam Hardy no chance. Adding his second just before half time, he added a further two in the second period after fine wing play by Jock Rutherford and Andy Anderson had left him with simple chances from a few yards out.

Continuing his fine form, Shepherd hit a hat-trick in a 6-1 demolition of Bradford City, his second a shot that flashed past Harry Maskrey. Two weeks later he went one better, scoring all four of his side's goals in the 4-1 defeat of Nottingham Forest. Losing 1-0 on 53 minutes, he produced a good shot for the equaliser and by the time another 20 minutes had gone, he'd scored with an easy chance made for him by Anderson, squeezed the ball from a tight angle past Hazell for his third and beat Ginger Maltby for pace before racing clear to beat the 'keeper.

With Newcastle seeking to defend the FA Cup, Shepherd came to his side's rescue when, 1-0 down at home to Bury in the first round, he scored twice in 3 minutes. With the pressure off, Shepherd completed his hat-trick as Newcastle waltzed to a 6-1 victory. His first was well made for him by his striking partner Jimmy Stewart, but the second was the result of a powerful shot that Jim Holt could hardly have seen as it flashed into the net.

With his form being so good, the England selectors decided to give him a second chance in his country's colours and so nearly five years after his scoring debut, Shepherd was again picked to play, this time against Ireland at the Baseball Ground. He opened the scoring, but played poorly as England stuttered to a 2-1 win. Fans argued that if he was going to be selected, it should be as part of a pair alongside his club colleague Stewart. Come the Scotland game later in the season, though, it was Stewart who found himself facing the old enemy, with Shepherd on the sidelines.

Over 46,000 watched Shepherd score twice as Hull were beaten 3-2 in the FA Cup; sweeping home Rutherford's cross, he then combined superbly with Sandy Higgins before finishing confidently. Facing Chelsea in the semi-final, Shepherd grabbed the second in a 3-0 win, finishing off a precise pass from Sandy Higgins.

The previous weekend against Aston Villa, he had scored his twenty-fifth goal of the season, George Wilson pushing the ball inside the full-back for Shepherd to power through and stab the ball past Brendel Anstey for the only goal of a competitive encounter.

One week before the cup final, tragedy was to strike. Dashing through in an attempt to reach the ball, he collided with the Blackburn 'keeper Jimmy Ashcroft. Immediately attended to by trainers and directors, he left the field on a stretcher in obvious pain and clearly out of the big match. 'A mad rush,' he called it. Without him, Newcastle struggled and after a 0-0 draw, lost the cup final replay 1-0 to Bradford City.

Ironically, when Shepherd did leave Newcastle in July 1914, it was to play for the Bantams. He'd made 123 first team appearances for the Magpies, in which he had scored 92 goals. In later life he became the landlord at the Crown and Cushion public house in Bolton, where he died in 1929.

SHERINGHAM, TEDDY (TOTTENHAM HOTSPUR)

Season: 1992/93
Goals scored: 22 (out of 60); 14 home, 8 away
Percentage: 36 per cent
Runner-up: Les Ferdinand (QPR), 20 goals
Tottenham finished eighth

Sheringham joined Tottenham Hotspur within weeks of the start of the 1992/93 season. His one-year spell at Nottingham Forest had been a success, with his goals taking Brian Clough's side to eighth position in Division One and a place at Wembley in the League Cup final.

The former Millwall man had scored Forest's first Premiership goal, and the first ever live goal shown on Sky Sports, in the opening day's success against Liverpool. Scot Gemmill's first-time ball had given him possession on the flank, the striker cutting inside to blast the ball beyond David James into the top corner. It was justification, it seemed, for Clough's decision to reject a £2 million bid from Spurs, even if post-match the scorer confirmed he 'still wanted to move'.

In the event, when he did move soon after, the transfer proved one of football's most controversial ever, bringing in its wake bung allegations against Terry Venables and Clough, with the former later losing a highly publicised case after he was dismissed for his business dealings by Spurs chairman Alan Sugar.

The £2.1 million man made his home debut against Sheffield United, and poached a 43rd-minute goal with a close-in finish. With his strike partner Gordon Durie grabbing the second in a 2-0 success, the Spurs joint coach Ray Clemence was confident enough to say post-match that 'the two can form a great partnership.'

Nevertheless, Spurs struggled to score goals and win points and with another £2 million signing, Portsmouth's Darren Anderton, struggling to demonstrate the form he had shown at Portsmouth, it was left to teenager Andy Turner to grab the all-important last-minute winner against Everton.

Blackburn away became an opportunity for Sheringham to show both his goal making and scoring qualities, threading an astute pass for David Howells to open the scoring before hitting home a late penalty in a 2-0 success. Nevertheless, by Christmas there looked little likelihood of Sheringham finishing anywhere near the top of the scorers' charts come the season's end, as with just five he was a long way behind Alan Shearer on fourteen goals.

Sheringham, though, was only getting started, while Shearer was to get stuck on sixteen when, after snapping his right anterior cruciate ligament against Leeds United in December, he missed the remainder of the season.

Sheringham was on the scoresheet as Spurs set off in search of a place in the FA Cup final with a 5-1 win at non-League Marlow. The fourth round was much tougher, but away at table topping Norwich City he swept home both goals just before half-time, the first from teenager Nick Barmby's cross and the second a header from an Anderton free kick. The following weekend, he then inspired fourteenth-placed Spurs with another double in a 3-1 win away at Crystal Palace, silencing those Lilywhites fans who had got on his back for failing to hit the net regularly, and leading to him to state afterwards that he felt he 'had turned the corner'.

Coming into February Sheringham continued his rich scoring vein, hitting two in a remarkable game against Southampton. With Spurs 1-0 down with 55 minutes gone, his equalising goal from another Anderton free kick was one of four in just 4 minutes.

Sheringham had signed for Spurs soon after they had been thrashed 5-0 at Elland Road. Revenge was in the air at White Hart Lane and after opening the scoring by eluding his marker to head Anderton's free kick past John Lukic, he then finished off Neil Ruddock's through ball to make it 2-0, completing his hat-trick with a second-half penalty in a 4-0 home win.

The previously misfiring Spurs front line had been turned into a potent force by the discovery of Barmby, the return to form of Anderton and Sheringham's finishing skills.

One week later, it was another two for Sheringham as QPR left White Hart Lane narrowly beaten in a fine game 3-2, and although he then missed a penalty at Maine Road, it mattered little as with Nayim grabbing three, Spurs beat Manchester City 4-2 to advance to the Cup semi-final. Any hopes, though, of winning the trophy for the second time in three seasons were to be lost when Arsenal won a tight game 1-0.

With little to play for, Spurs were in relaxed mood when Norwich City came to White Hart Lane searching desperately for all three points to give themselves a chance of winning the Premier League. The Canaries were walloped, beaten 5-1; Nayim scored the goal of the day with a superb solo effort, but Sheringham took the plaudits with another pair of goals.

Celebrating his first call-up to the England squad, Sheringham then slotted home two penalties and also made Spurs other goals in a 4-1 defeat of Oldham Athletic. He now had twenty in the league. Nineteen had come with Spurs and as he had also scored seven goals in the Cup competitions, his total of twenty-six meant he had equalled the first season record of the man whose boots he had been signed to replace, Gary Lineker. Praise came from another former England man, with Clemence saying, 'Teddy is the coolest customer I've ever known. It doesn't matter how many times he might miss, he'll still get into the box and have a go at goal.'

Sheringham continued to have a go, although his effort at Anfield mattered little as Liverpool won 6-2. Then, with George Graham choosing to select a reserve side in the week before the Gunners' cup final date, he helped himself to his twenty-second League goal of the season as Spurs won 3-1 away. After a difficult start, no one was now complaining that Sheringham wasn't worth the money paid for him as he had finished at the top of the scorers' chart, and also helped bring on a number of the Spurs' younger players with his enthusiasm and intelligent use of the ball.

Having failed to adequately replace him, Nottingham Forest were relegated, a sad end to the managerial career of Brian Clough.

Sheringham was to continue to score regularly for Tottenham for the next four seasons, with his and Jurgen Klinsmann's partnership fashioning some great goals in 1994/95, but when given the chance to move to Old Trafford in June 1997, there was no holding him back.

Although he was by then thirty-one, he had never relied on pace or dashing around and he went on to become a firm favourite with the Manchester United supporters. This was never more so than when he scored his side's equalising goal in the 1999 European Champions' League final before making the winner for Ole Gunnar Solskjaer. In 2000/01, Sheringham was to be voted as the Football Writers' and PFA Player of the Year.

Having won three Premier League titles and one FA Cup winner's medal, Sheringham returned to White Hart Lane for the start of the 2001/02 season. Later spells with Portsmouth, West Ham United and Colchester United followed prior to retirement in 2008 at age forty-two. Sheringham enjoyed a lengthy spell in the England side, hitting eleven goals in fifty-one appearances and forming a fine partnership with Alan Shearer that peaked during the 1996 European Championships in England. Under Terry Venables' leadership the host nation almost made it to the final, only to lose out to Germany on penalties in the last four of the tournament.

SMITH, ALAN (ARSENAL)

Season: 1988/89
Goals scored: 23 (out of 73); 10 home, 13 away
Percentage: 31.5 per cent
Runner-up: John Aldridge (Liverpool), 21 goals
Arsenal were League Champions

Season: 1990/91
Goals scored: 23 (out of 74); 14 home, 9 away
Percentage: 31 per cent
Runner-up: Lee Chapman (Leeds United), 21 goals
Arsenal were League Champions

After a 'bedding in' season with Arsenal when he netted sixteen times (in all competitions), tall striker Alan Smith became the toast of Highbury when, in 1988/89, he struck twenty-three goals in the First Division as the Gunners became English champions for the ninth time in the club's history and lifted the trophy the first time since their double-winning campaign of 1970/71. He also bagged a couple more in the League Cup, one on the final defeat by Luton Town.

Playing up front with Paul Merson, Smith began the campaign with a bang, scoring in each of the first eight League games.

He smacked in a hat-trick in an opening-day 5-1 win over the FA Cup holders Wimbledon at Plough Lane. Everything went right for Smith – four attempts, three goals, two made by Brian Marwood.

He then netted in a disappointing 3-2 home defeat by Aston Villa a week later, grabbed the winner in the North London derby against Tottenham in game three, slipped in the second-half equaliser (2-2) against Southampton in mid-September and was on target in a 2-1 loss at Sheffield Wednesday, a defeat which sent the Gunners slithering down the table to seventh.

Perry Groves came in for Merson (injured) for the sixth game of the season, at home to West Ham. Right away he and Smith linked up superbly; the Gunners won 4-1, Smith netting twice.

Following up with the winner against QPR (2-1) and the opener at Luton (1-1), Smith – who had Merson back alongside him – then missed out in a 2-0 home victory against

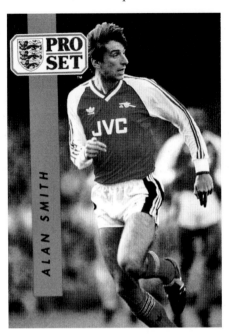

Coventry City, but was back on track with a strike in the 4-1 win over Nottingham Forest and in the 1-1 home draw with Liverpool.

However, he only managed to find the net six times in seventeen League games between mid-November and the end of February, but was still a key figure in Arsenal's attack as the team held on to the number one spot in the Division.

Even as the fixtures started to run out, Smith remained prominent, laying on chances for his fellow front men. He scored himself – albeit only occasionally – including two in a 5-0 home victory over Norwich City before heading Arsenal in front with a splendid 52nd-minute glancing header from Nigel Winterburn's free kick in the end-of-season championship decider against Liverpool at Anfield on 26 May.

Arsenal HAD to win this game by two clear goals to become champions. And they did just that thanks to Michael Thomas's late, late goal from Smith's inch-perfect pass. This denied the Merseysiders back-to-back title wins; it also ended the Reds' twenty-four-match unbeaten run and it was Arsenal's first League win at Anfield for fifteen years.

After a lean season in 1989/90, with only ten League goals scored as Arsenal finished fourth, Smith was back to his best in 1990/91, netting another twenty-three in the First Division as the Gunners regained the title from their arch-rivals Liverpool.

Like he had done two years earlier, Smith scored against Wimbledon in the opening game, but this time it was only one strike in a 3-0 win.

He was then injured soon afterwards and missed a 4-1 home win over Chelsea before returning as substitute in a 2-0 victory at Nottingham Forest. Thankfully for his manager George Graham – and the fans – he remained in the team until the season's end, although, perhaps surprisingly, he found it hard to get the ball into the net, failing to score in seven outings before striking twice in the second half of a 4-0 win over Southampton in mid-November.

He then scored in each of the next three games, a 3-1 win at QPR, a 3-0 home victory over Liverpool and a 1-1 draw at Luton, before striking five times immediately after Christmas, twice in successive home wins over Derby County (3-0) and Sheffield United (4-1), and in the New Year's Day winner at Manchester City.

As the games rolled on, the race for the championship hotted up, but Smith was still finding it hard to breach opponents' defences, scoring only two goals in six games up to 23 March. But then all of a sudden, things changed – for the best.

He netted twice in a 2-0 win at Derby which sent Arsenal to the top of the League with eight games to play, followed up with another brace in a resounding 5-0 home victory over Aston Villa, clinched a 2-0 win at Sheffield United and earned a point from a 1-1 draw at Southampton.

Unbeaten since 23 February and only defeated once all season, by Chelsea three weeks earlier, Arsenal were now in the driving seat. And after drawing with Manchester City and Sunderland and beating QPR, they saw Liverpool lose their penultimate game at Nottingham Forest, thus handing Arsenal the title – before they took on Manchester United.

With the pressure off the Gunners played some lovely football, Smith scored a hat-trick, including a penalty, in a 3-1 victory over Alex Ferguson's men. And then it was celebrations all round on the last day of the campaign when a Highbury crowd of 41,039 saw Coventry walloped 6-1, with Smith notching his twenty-third League goal in the process.

Smith also netted five Cup goals in 1990/91, to finish with a total of twenty-eight.

Born in Bromsgrove on 21 November 1962, Smith had attempted to start his career with Birmingham City in 1978, but was rejected by the Blues after a trial. A year later he joined non-League side Alvechurch, and in June 1982 moved into the Football League with Leicester City for £22,000. He spent five years at Filbert Street, playing alongside Gary Lineker, before transferring to Arsenal for £800,000 in March 1987, being loaned back to the Foxes for two months.

Having averaged almost a goal every three games for Leicester, he went on to enjoy a very successful career with Arsenal, with whom he won all three major domestic trophies – two League Championships, the FA Cup and the League Cup – and also helped the Gunners win the European Cup-winner's Cup.

He scored Arsenal's opening first goal, a dramatic League Championship-winning victory over Liverpool at Anfield in May 1989, and struck the only goal in the 1984 ECWC Cup final victory over Parma.

Smith, who was Arsenal's top scorer for four consecutive seasons, retired due to a niggling injury at the end of the 1994/95 season. Only thirty-two years of age, he had scored 84 goals in 217 senior appearances for Leicester City and 115 in 346 outings for Arsenal.

He was also capped three times as a semi-professional (while with non-League side Alvechurch) before adding four B and thirteen full caps to his wardrobe as an Arsenal player.

'Smudger' Smith was a well-disciplined player, receiving just one yellow card throughout his entire career.

SMITH, BOBBY (TOTTENHAM HOTSPUR)

Season: 1957/58
Goals scored: 36 (out of 93); 18 home, 18 away
Percentage: 38.7 per cent
Runner-up: Tommy Thompson (Preston North End), 34 goals
Spurs finished third

Season: 1958/59
Goals scored: 32 (out of 85); 22 home, 10 away
Percentage: 37.6 per cent
Joint top scorer with Jimmy Greaves (Chelsea)
Spurs finished eighteenth

When it came to toughness, nobody surpassed flint-hard Bobby Smith. He was burly, robust, brave, had a strong right-foot shot, could head a ball with power and above all, he was never afraid to go in where it hurt, often taking a heavy knock to ankle, shin, knee, thigh, back or head!

Born in Lingdale near Middlesbrough on 22 February 1933, he played for Redcar Boys' Club and Redcar United before joining Chelsea on schoolboy forms in 1947, taking amateur status in 1949 and turning professional in May 1950. He spent the next five-and-a-half years at Stamford Bridge, during which time he scored thirty goals in eighty-six senior appearances, acting as deputy to Roy Bentley for a number of seasons.

In December 1955, Tottenham's manager Jimmy Anderson paid £18,000 for Smith. When he arrived at White Hart Lane, Spurs lay just one place off the bottom of the First Division table, but Smith scored the necessary goals to dispel the threat of relegation and thereafter went on to play a major role in the London club's glory years.

Initially Smith played inside-left, with Len Duquemin leading the attack and Johnny Brooks on the right, and in 1955/56 he scored ten vital League goals and, after switching to centre forward, he followed up in 1956/57 with another eighteen before netting thirty-six in 1957/58 to equal Ted Harper's 1930/31 club record for most in a season.

By now he had alongside him Tommy Harmer, who was one of the finest passers of the ball in the English game and could split open the tightest of defences with one magical touch! Spurs also had some exceptionally fine wingers in Terry Medwin, George Robb and Terry Dyson, with Cliff Jones ready in waiting.

Smith scored twice in the first four games of the season, both to no avail as Spurs lost 5-1 at Portsmouth and 3-1 at Newcastle. He was injured in the return game with Pompey and missed the next three matches before returning for the home clash with Birmingham City in mid-September.

Spurs crushed the Blues 7-1, but amazingly Smith failed to get on the scoresheet, Bobby Stokes weighing in with a five-timer!

However, three days later Smith scored twice in a 4-2 home win over Sheffield Wednesday, giving the Owls' defence a tough time as he bustled and barged his way into the penalty area at every opportunity.

Absent from the next game (against Manchester City), Smith was completely out of sorts in a 4-0 defeat by Wolves at Molineux and he didn't fare much better in the next game, which Spurs lost 4-3 at home to Nottingham Forest. But after netting a 'real beauty' in a 3-1 North London derby win over Arsenal, he never really looked back.

He found the net at Bolton (lost 3-2), did likewise in successive home wins over Leeds United (2-0) and Everton (3-1), and struck a decisive blow to earn a point at Villa Park (1-1).

He had a few off-days, but was at his brilliant best at Old Trafford on 30 November, grabbing a hat-trick in an excellent 4-3 victory. This was his first treble for Spurs and in fact, he could well have scored five or six goals had not United's 'keeper David Gaskell been in such good form.

Smith weighed in with five goals during December, scoring braces in wins at Blackpool (2-0) and against his former club Chelsea (4-2), as well as sliding in the winner to beat champions-elect Wolves at White Hart Lane in front of almost 59,000 spectators.

On target twice in a third round FA Cup-tie against Leicester City (won 4-0), Spurs went out in the next round and, in fact, January was a disappointing month with only two League games being played, Smith scoring in a 3-3 home draw with Preston but having a poor game in a 2-0 defeat at Burnley.

On 8 February, he did what very few players have done over the years – he scored a hat-trick against the other Manchester club, City, as Spurs cruised to a 5-1 home win, gaining sweet revenge for a same-score drubbing at Maine Road earlier in the season.

Two weeks later, Smith netted twice in a thrilling 4-4 draw at Highbury, bagged both goals in a 2-1 win at Leeds and struck his third hat-trick of the season in a 4-1 home win over Bolton.

At the end of March he was rampant against Aston Villa and gave Jimmy Dugdale a roasting as he scored four times in a splendid 6-2 victory. A week later, he notched a couple in a 4-3 win at Everton and ended the season with singles in 3-1 and 2-1 wins over Leicester City (away) and Blackpool (home).

Spurs, who scored a total of ninety-three League goals in the season, finished third in the First Division – a massive thirteen points behind Wolves and eight adrift of runners-up Preston.

In 1958/59, Smith was once again the leading scorer in top-flight football, sharing the honour this time with Jimmy Greaves (Chelsea), both players notching thirty-two League goals. In fact, Smith and Greaves had been together briefly at Stamford Bridge (1955) and would team up again when Greaves joined Spurs in 1961.

Scorer of one goal in each of the first two games – both defeats, at the hands of Blackpool at home (2-3) and Chelsea away (2-4) – he was off target in the next three before netting in the 1-1 draw at Nottingham Forest. At this juncture, Spurs were not playing well. In fact, they won only two of their first ten League games and were well down the table.

After netting twice in a 2-2 draw with Manchester United in front of 62,277 fans at Old Trafford and banging in the opener in a 2-1 home win over Wolves, Smith missed two sitters and hit the woodwork in a 1-1 draw at Portsmouth before scoring four times in a record 10-4 home victory over Everton on 11 October.

On the morning of the Everton game it was announced that Bill Nicholson had been appointed as Spurs' new manager – and in the afternoon he looked on as the team selected by his predecessor, Jimmy Anderson, walloped the Merseysiders in front of almost 38,000 spectators at White Hart Lane.

The goals started to flow as early as the third minute when Alf Stokes fired Spurs ahead. Everton equalised through Jimmy Harris on 11 minutes, and on the quarter-of-an-hour mark Smith rose unchallenged to nod home Tommy Harmer's delightful cross to make it 2-1 before Danny Blanchflower sent George Robb through to score a third for Spurs.

In the 31st minute, outside-right Terry Medwin flew down past Bramwell and his cross was met square on by Smith (4-1). Medwin then found space to score twice before half time to virtually see off the Merseysiders at 6-1.

Harris reduced the deficit soon after the break, but Blanchflower quickly set up Smith, who completed his hat-trick with a great finish … 7-2 to Spurs. There was a lull in proceedings between the 60th and 80th minutes before the game exploded into life once again. Harmer belted in a rocket from 15 yards (8-2) … Harris replied (8-3), Smith put away Stokes's corner (9-3), Bobby Collins made it 9-4 and the injured Johnny Ryden nipped in with a later tenth to seal a memorable victory.

Smith maintained his form by scoring in each of the next four matches – a 4-3 victory at Leicester, a 2-3 home defeat by Leeds, a 1-5 drubbing at Manchester City and a 1-1 draw with Bolton at White Hart Lane. He then struggled in the 2-1 win at Luton and the 4-0 home reverse against Birmingham before scoring twice in a seven-goal thriller at West Bromwich, which Spurs lost 4-3.

Smith scored in two of the five League games played in December – in 2-1 defeats by Preston and West Ham – before starting the New Year with a smart effort in a 3-1 victory over Blackburn. He then netted in successive FA Cup-ties against West Ham (won 2-0) and Newport County (won 4-1), scored in a disappointing 4-1 home defeat by Arsenal and struck twice in a hard-earned 4-4 home draw with Portsmouth towards the end of February, but was then sidelined for three games at the start of March.

Returning for the home visit of Manchester City, he scored in a 3-1 win, netted again six days later when Aston Villa were beaten 3-2 and was on target in the 3-0 win over FA Cup finalists Luton Town during the first week of April.

He then went out and ended the season in style, grabbing both goals in the 2-2 draw with Burnley (one a fierce drive from outside the area), cracked in his second four-timer of the campaign when West Brom were battered 5-0 on a barren White Hart Lane pitch (he could have had six or seven in this one-sided game if Baggies' goalkeeper Ray Potter had not been at his brilliant best) and netted the opener in a last-day 2-2 draw at Preston.

After two wonderful campaigns, during which time he scored seventy-three goals in competitive football and twelve more in friendlies, Smith followed up in 1959/60 with another twenty-five in the First Division, plus five more in the FA Cup, four of which came in a 13-2 fourth-round replay victory over Crewe Alexandra.

He then added thirty-three more to his tally in 1960/61 (twenty-eight League, five FA Cup) when, of course, Spurs completed the double. After that, he struggled with injury problems for long periods and managed only twenty-seven more League goals in the next three seasons before transferring to Brighton & Hove Albion for £5,000 in May 1964. His record with Spurs was superb – 208 goals in 317 first-class appearances. He gained League, European Cup-winner's Cup and two FA Cup winner's medals, scoring in the 1961 final against Leicester, and against Burnley a year later with his socks rolled down to his ankles. He also won fifteen England caps, scoring thirteen goals, including two in the 9-3 drubbing of Scotland at Wembley in April 1961.

Smith, who helped Brighton win the Fourth Division championship in 1965, remained at The Goldstone Ground until October 1965, when he moved to Hastings United, later assisting Leyton Orient (on trial) and Banbury United. He retired in May 1969 to become a painter and decorator and as the years passed by he became a cripple, the legacy of his footballing career. Sadly, Smith died after a short illness in Enfield, Middlesex on 18 September 2010.

Shortly after his death, the Tottenham Hotspur manager Harry Redknapp paid tribute to Bobby Smith as both a player and a person. 'I loved Bobby. A proper character, and what a player,' said Redknapp. 'He was a larger-than-life character and I am sorry to see him go. I remember seeing him terrorize goalkeepers in those days of European football, battering the ball into the back of the net, but not only that, he could play as well. He was a real top centre forward and a great, great character.'

SMITH, JOE (BOLTON WANDERERS)

Season: 1920/21
Goals scored: 38 (out of 77); 29 home, 9 away
Percentage: 49.4 per cent
Runner-up: Tommy Bromwell (Manchester City), 31 goals
Bolton finished third

More widely known as the manager behind Blackpool's 1953 cup final success, Joe Smith was a prolific scorer for the Tangerines' defeated opponents, Bolton Wanderers. In the four seasons prior to the First World War, he notched eighty League goals for the Burnden Park side. Having lost some of the best years of his life on active service, Smith, despite being thirty, soon resumed normal service in front of goal with eighteen in the League in 1919/20.

The following season was to be his best as Bolton, under his leadership on the pitch as captain, began to build a fine side that would go on to capture the FA Cup on three occasions, all played at Wembley, over the next decade. Smith's partnership with Ted 'the Wizard' Vizard on the Bolton left was to be key to the Trotters' success.

The 1920/21 season started away to Manchester United. Centre forward Frank Roberts was quick off the mark, scoring twice in a 3-2 victory. Seven days later, in the return fixture, Smith got on the scoresheet for the first time in the season. Bolton was 1-0 down when he superbly chested down an Alec Donaldson cross and with his marker Jack Silcock thrown off balance, he hit a neat, low shot that deceived Jack Mew as it flashed into the corner of the net. Smith had caused something of a controversy by appearing in shorts that failed to reach at least the knee, and so it must have been a pleasure to find his name in the papers for doing what he knew best – scoring goals.

He was widely praised in the Bolton sports paper, *The Buff*, with 'the Tramp' writing, 'Joe Smith – there are few men who can claim great reputations for individual achievement, but do you know any man who works harder for his pals? I don't.'

On 11 September, Bolton faced League champions WBA. Not long after kick-off, 'when Donaldson beat Cook to land a precise pass Smith beat Pennington for pace to rap it into the net' (*The Buff*). After Roberts doubled the lead on 75 minutes, Smith headed home the third. A crowd of 41,584 saw the action and roared their approval and with eight points from the first six matches, Bolton had given themselves a title chance.

Intense interest for the home game with Manchester City saw the Bolton directors erect seats around the Burnden Park running track. Smith headed home on 15 minutes and then scored from a re-taken penalty in the second period. City went home beaten 3-0, but had their revenge a week later when, despite another Smith goal, Bolton lost 3-1.

On 30 October, Smith grabbed his first hat-trick of the season. Tim Williamson is probably Middlesbrough's greatest ever 'keeper, and he made two fine saves to deny the Bolton inside forward before Smith put his side back into the lead on 37 minutes, then made it 4-2 just after half time. Vizard then left a spell on the Boro defence and his partner, in a game Bolton won 6-2, swept his inch-perfect cross home.

Smith was to go one better against Sunderland. It might have been Christmas Day, but he was clearly in no charitable mood and notched up four in another 6-2 victory.

Having scored twenty-three goals, any hopes defenders might have entertained of him losing his touch when the New Year got under way soon ended when he scored the only goal from the penalty spot on New Year's Day as Spurs went back south defeated. Bolton were now second in the League and although defeat against leaders Burnley a few weeks later put paid to any realistic title chances, it was nevertheless proving a successful season.

Hopes were high for the future, especially as it was clear that a new player, signed by manager Charles Foweraker, was going to be really special. David Jack was the son of a Bolton lad. He'd started out at his father's club, Plymouth Argyle, and now back home, he and Smith set out to form a formidable inside forward partnership that saw both of them play important roles in Bolton's capturing of the FA Cup in 1923 and 1926.

Having hit a hat-trick against Middlesbrough and four against Sunderland, Smith hit another hat-trick on 9 April, completing a north-east treble as Newcastle went home beaten 3-1.

The Geordies had Bill McCracken playing at the back. Noted for using the three-man offside rule then in place to his advantage by stepping up to catch the attacker offside, he was coming towards the end of a long, distinguished career. Asked to look after Smith, he struggled, and when Roberts found the Bolton inside forward on 15 minutes, it was 1-0. Having seen Newcastle equalise, Smith, on 41 minutes, worked a neat position and hit a low, left-foot drive to make it 2-1. Then, on 70 minutes, Jack, with a great run to the penalty spot, then 'pushed the ball beautifully forward for Smith to come galloping in and beat Lawrence all the way … Master McCracken followed the referee to the goal-line evidently protesting Smith was offside.' (*The Buff*) Smith now had thirty-five for the season.

Having hit the only goal in the final home game against Liverpool, Smith took his grand total to thirty-eight in the return at Anfield. With Bolton 2-0 down, Smith headed home on 53 minutes. Then, after Jack made it 2-2 and with just 5 minutes remaining, he scored the winner with a beautiful shot from just inside the area for a victory that helped Bolton finish in their highest ever League placing, third.

Smith had equalled Bert Freeman's record of thirty-eight goals in a season, and he was to continue to score goals over the next few years. Eighteen arrived in the following season, although Jack was to outscore him with twenty-four. The two continued to fight it out for top spot over the next few seasons, and in 1924/25 Jack had twenty-six, just two in front of Smith. Together, it was exactly two-thirds of the goals Bolton scored that season. Smith eventually left Bolton in 1927. He had scored 254 League goals, and with 243 of them coming in Division One, he stands at number ten in the list of English all-time scorers at the highest level. Playing for Stockport in Third Division North, he scored sixty-one goals in sixty-nine League appearances.

Retiring from playing full time, he took on the role of player-manager at Darwen. After success there and four years in charge at Reading, Smith began a long association with Blackpool. Building a side around greats such as Harry Johnston, Stan Mortensen and Stanley Matthews, he took Blackpool to three FA Cup finals between 1948 and 1953. He died in 1971 aged eighty-two.

Smith played five times for England. He scored his only goal for his country against Wales in March 1914.

SOUTHWORTH, JACK (BLACKBURN ROVERS AND EVERTON)

Blackburn Rovers
Season: 1890/91
Goals scored: 26 (out of 52); 13 home, 13 away
Percentage: 50 per cent
Runner-up: Fred Geary (Everton), 20 goals
Blackburn finished sixth

Everton
Season: 1893/94
Goals scored: 27 (out of 90); 19 home, 8 away
Percentage: 30 per cent
Runners-up: Jack Devey (Aston Villa) and Jimmy Millar (Sunderland), with 20 goals each
Everton finished sixth

Southworth was Blackburn's first truly prolific goalscorer. Born in the town in 1866, he initially turned down Rovers' request to join them and remained with local rivals Blackburn Olympic, the 1883 FA Cup winners.

And when he then suffered a serious career-threatening knee injury while playing as a guest for Accrington, it appeared that his football career was over. Switching his attentions to playing between the posts, Southworth showed his all-round sporting instincts by becoming Olympic's first team goalkeeper and helping his side to win the Lancashire Cup final against Rovers in 1885.

In 1886, he then left football for a time and, as he was a keen musician, joined a theatre in Chester. Returning home, he began playing again at centre forward for the Olympic before, at the start of the 1887/88 season, finally succumbing to the Rovers' charms and signing for them.

He made his debut for the Rovers, ironically against Olympic, on 5 November 1887, in an FA Cup tie. As the Rovers then began their new Football League adventure he captained the side and became a prolific goalscorer. He scored twenty-two goals in twenty-two League appearances in 1888/89 and five goals in five FA Cup ties as the Rovers won the FA Cup in 1889/90 and finished third in the League.

His best season was the 1890/91 season, when he was the League's top scorer with twenty-six goals from just eighteen appearances, missing the final four games as Rovers rested players prior to the cup final against Notts County. Nearly half his goals came from four hat-tricks, starting on the opening day of the season in a remarkable game that Rovers lost 8-5 at Derby County.

In early October, one down at home to new boys Sunderland, Rovers equalised when Southworth leapt high to plant a firm header from a Jimmy Forrest cross past Ted Doig. Then, after Joe Lofthouse had put Rovers a goal ahead, Southworth 'beat Doig with a splendid shot', reported the *Newcastle Daily Chronicle*. He had seven goals in six games, a figure that rose to nine in seven the following weekend as local rivals Burnley were crushed 6-1 at Turf Moor. He then scored the crucial goal which gave his side a priceless 1-0 home win against two times champions Preston North End, raising Rovers fans' hopes of a first ever championship. And when Everton's Bob Smalley allowed Southworth's tame effort to beat him in the next home match, the victory put Rovers top of the table.

In the return fixture at Anfield, Southworth gave his side an early lead when, showing the pace with which he had become famous, he dodged past the Everton half and full backs to hit a shot that the home side believed had gone over the bar rather than under it. This, in the absence of goal nets until the start of the following season, left the referee to decide. On this occasion, he agreed with the view of the Rovers players that it was a goal and the Everton debutant in goal, David Jardine, had conceded his first goal.

The following weekend, Southworth grabbed his second hat-trick of the season as Aston Villa were heavily beaten 5-1, adding three more in the return at Villa Park and at home to WBA. Revenge for the opening day's heavy beating arrived when Derby journeyed north and were thrashed 8-0. On a heavy pitch, Southworth scored three times. He also scored three times in the next League fixture, but in an age where the FA Cup was the most important football competition in the world, it was two months later as the fixtures were suspended to allow the knockout competition to proceed.

When it did, Southworth again scored a hat-trick as Chester were thrashed 7-0 in the second round. On semi-final day, he was one of three Rovers scorers as WBA were beaten 3-2 to set up a final against Notts County. A few days later he was back on form in the League, scoring three times as Accrington were beaten 4-0. As he was hitting the net regularly, there was no surprise when he was called up for this second England cap on 7 March 1891. The match against Wales was almost a repeat of his debut two seasons earlier, England again winning 4-1, with Southworth scoring in both. He was to make one further appearance. It came the following season at Hampden Park, where, in a thrilling start, England raced into a 4-0 lead after 20 minutes. Southworth scored the third.

Southworth had scored in the previous season's Cup final. Rovers had won 6-1 against [Sheffield] Wednesday, during which William Townley became the first player to record a hat-trick in the final. The 1890/91 final was a lot closer, but Rovers retained the Cup in a 3-1 success, with Southworth hitting his side's second.

Southworth was transferred to Everton for £400 in 1893 and when his football career ended, he turned to his other passion, music, and became a professional violinist. He appeared with the Hallé Orchestra, the BBC Northern Orchestra and the Liverpool Philharmonic. His musical skills were such that he played the trombone, euphonium, tuba and violin. His brother James also played for the Rovers at the same time and John, who had a reputation for speed, always maintained his brother was the faster.

Costing £400 in August 1893, Southworth made a goalscoring Everton debut in a 7-3 defeat away to Derby County. The England international was also among the scorers in Everton's next game, but his opening goal on 15 minutes in the game at Villa Park proved mere consolation as the away side slumped to a 3-1 defeat.

There was much more to Everton's play the following weekend when champions Sunderland came to Goodison Park, Everton having moved across to Stanley Park from Anfield at the start of the previous season. At 1-1, some fine passing between Alex Latta, John Bell and Edgar Chadwick opened up the Wearsiders' defence to allow Southworth to run the ball beyond Ned Doig and into the net. Buoyed by their success, Everton thrilled a huge crowd of 30,000 by going on to win 7-1.

Against Darwen in an 8-1 thrashing, Southworth struck twice. He opened the scoring on 5 minutes but it was his second that took him into the Everton record books, when just before the end Orr was penalised and Southworth stepped up to become the club's first ever scorer from the penalty spot. Two more goals then followed against PNE at Goodison that the home side, despite a well-hit shot from distance for their second, lost 3-2. Southworth now had eight goals in just eight games.

Away to Sheffield United, it took him just 15 minutes to open the scoring. Everton had started briskly and it was no surprise when they took the lead through a well-hit shot and Southworth might have made it two shortly after, but his shot crashed back into play from the crossbar. Alf Millward got Everton's second before Southworth got his side's third in a 3-0 win.

The Merseysiders also struck three times when they travelled to play at Ewood Park – Southworth got one. Everton were 2-1 down, when 'Southworth flourished off a smart movement by scoring a neat goal' reported the *Liverpool Echo*. In the end, Blackburn did just enough to win a fine game 4-3. With Everton lying in ninth place and opponents Wednesday back in thirteenth in a sixteen-team table, there were fewer than 10,000 in the Goodison crowd for the match played on 23 December 1893.

The away side started in fine form and Fred Spiksley gave them the lead. Southworth then equalised almost immediately, and by half time he'd added two more and Everton ran off leading 4-1. It was, though, his fourth of the game and Everton's fifth that was the highlight of a game that finished off 8-1 in favour of the home side.

'Southworth gave a splendid display in every respect, the manner in which he commanded his wings and worked the ball being of an ideal character,' said the *Liverpool Mercury* in its match review of 25 December 1893.

There were 5,000 more in the crowd for the following weekend's match with WBA and they witnessed one of the greatest displays ever by an Everton player. Bell gave the home side an early lead before the Baggies 'keeper Joe Reader did well to keep out a Southworth effort. The Everton centre forward was not to be denied for long, though, and when Latta crossed, he headed powerfully home. And when Reader could only push out Bell's effort, Southworth was on to the loose ball to make it 3-0 before grabbing his hat-trick shortly afterwards.

Just after half time, Bell again turned provider to set up Southworth for his fourth, Everton's fifth of the match. WBA were still battling though, and reduced the arrears through Owen Williams only to find Southworth in an unforgiving mood as he rattled home his fifth and sixth in quick succession to make it 7-1. He was the first, and to date only, Everton man to hit six in a single match. Incredibly, it might even have been seven as just before the end, he hit a shot that hit Latta on the way into the net, the effort being disallowed for offside.

Two days later, the record scorer was again doing what he knew best: scoring. It was, however, only the once in a 3-3 draw at Darwen, and just to prove that he was after all human, he then missed a penalty as Newton Heath lost 2-0 at Goodison Park. He did, however, get the second and followed this up by hitting one of Everton's goals in a 4-2 win at Deepdale.

On Easter Monday he again hit the net when Bolton were beaten 3-2 before a 25,000-strong holiday crowd. It was his twenty-seventh League goal of the campaign and ensured, despite missing the final two League games of the season, that he ended, for the second time in his career, as top scorer in the First Division.

Jack Southworth was well on his way to finishing top scorer again in the following season. Having hit hat-tricks against Small Heath and Nottingham Forest, he ran out at Ewood Park on 20 October 1894 with eight goals in seven games, all of which Everton had won to race to the top of the League, giving rise to great expectations of a second title success in five years.

Southworth was tightly marked by Anderson who, the *Liverpool Mercury* reported, 'stuck to him like a leech' and although he managed to net his ninth goal in eight League goals, Everton lost their first match of the season 4–3.

The following weekend the Toffees faced Sunderland and with the sides tied at the top, there was a crowd of 25,000 at Goodison Park. With five minutes remaining, Everton were 2–1 down, but they equalised when Southworth's free kick was headed home by Dickie Boyle amid great enthusiasm. The Everton centre forward had again been tightly marked, this time by McCreadie. Sadly, it was to prove his final game. Injured, he never recovered, and the loss of such a fine footballer also crippled Everton's League chances. Seventeen out of twenty points had been gathered in the first third of the season and thirty-five goals had been scored. Twenty games later, Everton had scored another forty-seven and taken twenty-five points. Sunderland had done better, and finished five points clear of the Toffees.

During the First World War he played for Falkirk in Scotland, but returned to appear for the Rovers once more in 1916. His Rovers record reads: 108 League appearances, 97 goals; 25 FA Cup appearances, 25 goals; the total was 133 appearances with 122 goals. He died in Wavertree, Liverpool on 16 October 1956.

STEELE, FREDDIE (STOKE CITY)

Season: 1936/37
Goals scored: 33 (out of 72); 22 home, 11 away
Percentage: 45.8 per cent
Runner-up: Dave McCulloch (Brentford), 31 goals
Stoke finished tenth

Freddie 'Nobby' Steele was described by Stanley Matthews as Stoke City's greatest centre forward.

A prolific marksman, he netted a total of 159 goals in 251 first-class games plus another eighty-one in ninety-five wartime fixtures for the Potters during his sixteen-year professional career at The Victoria Ground, and was certainly very effective and mightily successful in the late 1930s.

Born in Hanley, Stoke-on-Trent on 6 May 1916, Steele signed for Stoke as an amateur in the summer of 1931 but was told by manager Tom Mather that he would be working in the club's offices and playing for the club's nursery side, Downing Collieries, 'to gain experience' at a higher level.

Mather was clearly confident of Steele's ability, and in June 1933 offered him a professional contract, which Steele accepted without any hesitation.

He made his Football League debut in a 4–1 home victory over Huddersfield Town in December 1934 and it wasn't long before he struck his first senior goal, in a 3–0 Boxing Day victory over West Bromwich Albion.

The following season he scored eleven goals and then, in 1936/37, he bagged a total of thirty-six, of which thirty-three came in the Football League, when he was the First Division's top marksman.

He actually missed seven League games (through injury and illness) during the course of the season, and in his absence the team managed just five goals.

He was effectively a 'one-man' attack in terms of goalscoring. His left-wing teammate Joe Johnson netted thirteen times in the League, while the next best tally came from Matthews.

Arguably Steele's finest performance for the Potters, in any game that season, came in February 1937, when he scored five times in a record-breaking 10-3 home League victory over one of his favourite teams, West Brom.

His first goal was smashed home off a post from 12 yards in the 10th minute following a Matthews corner. His second arrived 10 minutes later, a crisp, low drive from Matthews' right-wing cross, the ball taking a slight deflection off George Shaw. His hat-trick goal made it 4-1 just before half time, when he stroked the ball home from 8 yards after some fine approach work by George Antonio and Jock Kirton.

His fourth, and Stoke's sixth, arrived in the 62nd minute after another mazy run and pass from the brilliant Matthews, and goal number five was claimed just 5 minutes later when he barged past the Baggies' centre half, Bill Richardson, to score with a powerful right-foot cross-shot from the edge of the penalty area.

With time running out, Steele almost made it a double hat-trick with a low shot that clipped the outside of an upright.

Besides his goal feast against Albion, he notched four more hat-tricks – in the 4-2 away win at Birmingham and in 6-2, 5-3 and 5-1 home victories over Middlesbrough, Sunderland and Brentford respectively.

He also scored twice each in the 2-0 home and 3-1 away wins over Grimsby, secured the winners at Preston (1-0) and at home to Wolves (2-1), netted in draws with Charlton (1-1), Manchester City (2-2), Derby County (2-2) and West Bromwich Albion (2-2), netted twice in a 4-2 defeat by Portsmouth and weighed in with extra goals in 2-1 losses against Manchester United, Derby, Wolves and Huddersfield Town.

He actually scored nine goals in five games in three weeks between 12 September and 3 October, while twenty of his thirty-seven League goals came in the last sixteen matches, from 4 February to 1 May. And besides his exploits in the League, he also fired in a hat-trick in a 4-1 FA Cup win over Birmingham.

Steele's splendid all-round performances in 1936/37 caught the attention of the England selectors and in October, he made his international debut in a 2-1 defeat by Wales at Ninian Park, Cardiff. The following month he played well and set up a goal in the 3-1 win over Ireland on his home ground at Stoke and in April 1937, playing alongside his club-mates Stanley Matthews and Joe Johnson, he scored in a 3-1 defeat by Scotland in front of almost 150,000 spectators at Hampden Park. This, in fact, was the first time since 1892 that three Stoke players had lined up together in the same England team.

On England's end-of-season tour to Scandinavia, Steele added three more caps to his tally, scoring twice in 6-0 and 8-0 wins over Austria and Finland respectively and achieving a first-half hat-trick in a 4-0 victory in Sweden.

In 1937/38 he reaped fifteen goals in twenty-three League games and in 1938/39 struck twenty-six in thirty-one, but then, out of the blue, just as the Second World War started, he shocked fans by announcing his retirement, stating that he was suffering from depression.

However, after treatment Steele made a successful recovery, and he became a star performer during the hostilities, when he also appeared as a guest for several clubs including Arsenal, Leeds United, Leicester City, Nottingham Forest and Sheffield United.

Unfortunately, the war robbed Steele of his prime playing years. Not perturbed by this long absence, though, he came back stronger than ever for the transitional 1945/46 campaign, in which he netted forty-three goals in forty-four appearances. The following season he scored thirty-one times in League and Cup action, despite suffering a serious knee injury against Charlton Athletic in September 1947 when he collided with goalkeeper Sam Bartram. This threatened to end his career, but once again he bounced back and ended the season with twelve goals to his name. However, 1948/49 proved to be his last season with Stoke – and he said farewell with a flurry, notching another nineteen goals before becoming player-manager of Mansfield Town in June 1949. Switching to Port Vale in the same capacity for £1,500 in December 1951, he retired as a player in January 1953, but remained as manager until January 1957, leading the Valiants into the FA Cup semi-finals and to the Third Division (N) Championship in 1954. Five years later he returned for a second spell as manager at Vale Park, eventually leaving the club by mutual consent in February 1965.

Matthews said that Steele was one of the few footballers he knew who could genuinely use both feet, and not only could he score with his feet, but he also racked up an impressive tally of headed goals, too.

His technique was described as 'receiving an invisible punch'. At 5 feet 10 inches tall, Steele would spring into the air, tilt his shoulders and head backwards before steering the ball goalwards at lightning speed. Many goalkeepers felt he could head the ball harder than some could kick it.

He also boasted a tremendous turn of pace. His speed over 10–15 yards was uncontested and took him away from struggling defenders.

At the peak of his fitness Freddie Steele also hurdled for Staffordshire, as well as competing in the 4x100-yards relay.

Stoke's greatest ever goalscorer died in Newcastle-under-Lyme on 23 April 1976.

SUTTON, CHRIS (BLACKBURN ROVERS)

Season: 1997/98
Goals scored: 18 (out of 57); 10 home, 8 away
Percentage: 32 per cent – Kevin Gallacher also scored 16, the partnership thus contributing 60 per cent of Blackburn's goals.
Joint top scorer with Michael Owen (Liverpool) and Dion Dublin (Coventry City)
Blackburn finished sixth

When transferred from Norwich City to Blackburn Rovers in 1994, Sutton became the most expensive footballer in English football at £5 million. Jack Walker's money was allowing the small east Lancashire town to dream of a first League championship since before the First World War when, ably led by captain Bob Crompton, Rovers had twice captured the title.

Sutton had initially started out as a centre half, but there was never any question he would play up front with Alan Shearer. SAS, as they became popularly known, although not among defenders, scored freely in the 1994/95 season; Sutton scored an early season hat-trick as Coventry were heavily beaten 4-0. By the season's end, Shearer had scored thirty-four and Sutton fifteen as Blackburn pipped Manchester United for top spot.

No-one really knows how they might have combined if they'd stayed together because by the time Sutton had recovered from a series of niggling injuries, Shearer had moved on during the summer of 1996 to play for his beloved Newcastle United.

Sutton was back to his best in the 1997/98 season, partnering Kevin Gallacher up front. An opening day success in which the latter scored the winner at home to Derby County was followed by a mid-week away 4-0 walloping of Aston Villa in a game in which Sutton put his miserable two years behind him with the second Rovers hat-trick of his career.

His first, on 21 minutes, saw him take Stuart Ripley's long throw on his chest before swivelling and volleying past Michael Oakes from close in. Four minutes later, he collected Gallacher's pass before hitting an unstoppable 25-yard shot, and then on 41 minutes Sutton swept Jason Wilcox's cross home.

Two games later, under new manager Roy Hodgson, Rovers were top of the League when Sheffield Wednesday were thrashed 7-2 at Ewood Park, Sutton's two goals taking him up to five in just four games. It was six in five the following weekend, when Rovers then won 2-1 away at Crystal Palace. And it was then seven in six when Leeds came to east Lancashire, although it was the away team that took all three points in a 4-3 win.

Sutton's scoring run continued at Leicester and although his single effort was pegged back by the home side, a 1-1 draw at Filbert Street wasn't a bad result as Rovers stayed in third place in the table. And they stayed there when returning with three points from Selhurst Park, where Sutton scored his ninth goal to beat Wimbledon 1-0.

On 30 November, Sutton blotted his record by being sent off at Old Trafford, earning a second yellow for a late lunge on Nicky Butt as Rovers tumbled 4-0. He was in better form the following weekend as he scored one of Rovers' three goals in a narrow 3-2 home defeat of Bolton before Sutton and Gallacher combined perfectly on 27 December to hit two goals apiece in a 4-2 victory at Ewood Park against Crystal Palace. Sutton now had thirteen League goals, although in January it was Gallacher who showed his class by ramming home a hat-trick as Villa were again heavily beaten, this time 5-0.

Rovers remained in third place, but a February run saw them drop down to sixth. As this would still ensure a place in the UEFA Cup, there was relief when Sutton got his fifteenth and sixteenth League goals in a 5-3 victory against Leicester City.

His seventeenth came against Manchester United and it capped a marvellous first half for the Rovers forward, who was almost unplayable during it. Certainly United centre-backs Gary Pallister and Ronny Johnsen must have been glad to go in at half time with their side just a penalty goal down, allowing Alex Ferguson's team to recover to win 3-1 in the second. Only weeks earlier, Sutton had argued with England manager Glenn Hoddle about his lack of opportunities at international level. He'd made his debut in November 1997, but when he refused to play for England B side there was no way back for him. On this performance, it seemed a shame that he would miss out on the chance to travel to the World Cup in France in the summer.

With just 2 minutes of the season remaining, Rovers too looked like they would miss out on playing in Europe the following season. At 0-0 with Newcastle, Blackburn were set to finish in seventh place, a point behind the Villa side they had twice thrashed during the season.

Elected as the Rovers player of the year, Sutton strode forward to take an edge-of-the-area free kick. Newcastle's ex-Rovers man David Batty had been sent off on 65 minutes but the Geordies, under ex-Rovers manager Kenny Dalglish, were hanging on to a point.

With another ex-Rovers man, Alan Shearer, also looking on, Sutton sent his right-foot shot round the Newcastle wall to leave ex-Rovers 'keeper Shay Given helpless. Chris Sutton had booked Blackburn's place in the following season's UEFA Cup, and in doing so taken himself to eighteen Premier League goals – joint top with Michael Owen and Dion Dublin (who scored at Everton for Coventry at exactly the same time as Sutton's effort against

Newcastle). With Gallacher getting sixteen, the Blackburn front two had formed the most deadly partnership in the top League.

Chris Sutton was unable to replicate such form in England from then on, managing just seventeen League games and three goals in the 1998/99 season as Rovers were relegated. Joining Chelsea in the summer of 1999 for £10 million, he did badly, scoring just once before trying his luck in Glasgow with Celtic a season later. He did well, forming a formidable partnership with Swede Henrik Larsson to help Celtic win three Scottish Premier League titles, three Scottish Cup finals and one Scottish League Cup final. Celtic also made it through to the 2003 UEFA Cup final, where they lost a thrilling game 3-2 against Porto.

Later in his career Sutton played for both Birmingham City and Aston Villa, but an eye injury saw him retire in July 2007, since when he has remained in the game with a year-long spell which ended in September 2010 as manager at Sincil Bank with Lincoln City.

TEVEZ, CARLOS (MANCHESTER CITY)

Season: 2010/11
Goals scored: 21 (out of 60); 13 home, 8 away
Percentage: 35 per cent
Joint top scorer with Dimitar Berbatov (Manchester United)
Manchester City finished third

Carlos Tevez joined Manchester City in the summer of 2009. He had played and won two Premiership titles, the League Cup and the UEFA Champions League, while on loan at Manchester United for the previous two seasons but, frustrated by starting matches on the bench, he was unwilling to extend his contract. This allowed City to secure his services from the company that owned his rights, Media Sports Investments. Both parties denied rumours that the transfer fee was £47 million.

He'd managed nineteen Premier League goals for United, but in 2009/10 he rammed home an impressive twenty-three as City grabbed a place in the Europa League with a fifth place finish during a season when Mark Hughes had been replaced as manager by Roberto Mancini. City's wealthy foreign owners allowed the Italian to invest heavily in new players during the close season as the club geared itself up to challenge for a place in the UEFA Champions League. Leading the charge was to be a new captain, with Tevez taking over the armband from Kolo Touré.

The former West Ham United man had spent the summer representing his country at the South Africa World Cup. He scored twice in the 3-1 victory against Mexico in the last sixteen, but failed to add to his overall total of eleven as Germany hammered Argentina 4-0 in the quarter-finals. Tevez started his career at Boca Juniors, where he made his first-team debut at age seventeen. A record South American transfer fee of around £14 million saw him move to Brazilian side Corinthians before he joined teammate Javier Mascherano in moving to Upton Park in August 2006.

Tevez scored his side's winning goal at Old Trafford on the final day of the season, West Ham's victory pushing Sheffield United into English football's second tier. The Blades' revenge – of a sort – came later, when the Hammers were found guilty of breaking 'third-party' League rules over the signing of Tevez and Mascherano and forced to compensate the Steel City club to the tune of £20 million.

Tevez was quickly on target at the start of the 2010/11 season, hitting two in the first home game as Liverpool were beaten 3-0. The first saw him glance Micah Richards's header past Pepe Reina and he scored the third from the penalty spot.

Travelling north to face Sunderland, Tevez then produced his own entry for the miss of the season. Yaya Touré had torn open the home defence before squaring the ball to Tevez who, with an open net in front of him, somehow scooped the ball over in a game City subsequently lost 1-0.

Much better was his match-winning effort at home to unbeaten Chelsea, where he burst from halfway before curling the ball through Ashley Cole's legs and in off the post. The following weekend, his second penalty of the season helped City to beat Newcastle 2-1 and move into second place in the table. His scoring run continued with two in the next match away to Blackpool, forcing home David Silva's cross from close in and then rifling home after the Seasiders had equalised in a game City won 3-2. Two more away goals, this time in a 4-1 thrashing of Fulham, pushed the Argentine up to eight League goals for the season.

On Boxing Day, Tevez reached double figures. He had already created Gareth Barry's 1st-minute opener when he scored to make it 2-0 after 5 minutes. Nine minutes from the end, his deflected effort helped ensure six points for the season from Newcastle United in a 3-1 win. A further double in a 4-3 victory at home to Wolves made it twelve for the season.

On 5 February 2011, Tevez celebrated his twenty-seventh birthday by keeping Manchester City on course for a Champions League spot with a first-half hat-trick in the 3-0 win against West Brom. It was the striker's third treble of his City career, his first coming against Blackburn Rovers in January 2010 during a 4-1 success. Two were penalties and the third a lovely finish after a 1-2 with David Silva had carved open the Baggies' defence. He had now scored eighteen League goals. A further penalty, this time against Sunderland, moved the total on by one, although there was disappointment when a hamstring injury ruled him out of the FA Cup semi-final success against Manchester United. He was, though, fit enough to play in the final and proudly hoisted the famous trophy aloft after a 1-0 success against Stoke City.

City had already qualified for the Champions League in the lead up to the Cup final and when finalists met in City's final home match of the season, Tevez was in superb form in a 3-0 success. After beating two men he hammered home, before later curling a spectacular free kick for a goal that took him level with Dimitar Berbatov on twenty-one Premier League goals for the season. Tevez thus became the third Manchester City player to top the goal scorers' charts at the end of the season, a fitting end to a fine season for the blue half of Manchester.

TROTTER, JIMMY (SHEFFIELD WEDNESDAY)

Season: 1926/27
Goals scored: 37 (out of 75); 26 home, 11 away
Percentage: 49 per cent
Runner-up: Hughie Gallacher (Newcastle United), 36 goals
Sheffield Wednesday finished sixteenth

County Durham-born Trotter's finest football season was without doubt 1926/27. He'd spearheaded Wednesday's promotion challenge the previous season, scoring thirty-seven times, twice what he'd notched during the previous three seasons. Almost a quarter had come from just two September games, with nine goals entering the nets of Preston and Stockport County. Trotter's five against the latter was the second time he had achieved such a feat, the Wednesday centre forward having hit all his side's goals in a 5-2 beating of Portsmouth in December 1924.

Pitched against local rivals United in the first match of the 1926/27 season, Trotter showed signs that his fine form of the previous campaign was going to continue. He equalised just before half time. Timing his run perfectly, he met Jack Wilkinson's cross, and soon after the restart he put his side ahead with a shot from the edge of the area. The Blades, though, had their own danger man and two goals from Harry Johnson proved just enough to give them a narrow 3-2 victory.

Trotter then scored in the following two away games, but even though Wednesday managed three goals at Spurs and Leicester City, his goal at Filbert Street coming after Wilkinson found him with a fine through ball, it was not enough to collect even a single point in 7-3 and 5-3 defeats. There was therefore real relief when Trotter scored the only goal as West Ham was beaten at Hillsborough.

Trotter then scored for his fifth consecutive game as Everton went back over the Pennines well-beaten 4-0. With Wednesday already leading 1-0, 'Trotter received the ball on the left of the penalty area. He was tackled by two men but held on and in spite of Baker rushing out and others closing in the centre-forward scored with a beautiful oblique drive to the far corner.' Another powerful shot and a late header rounded off the scoring for his first hat-trick in Division One. He might even have had another five, but Ben Howard Baker in the Toffees goal had a fine game, preventing his side being much more heavily beaten.

Having missed out in the sixth game, a 0-0 draw, Trotter then bagged three in his next two matches. Two came at Ewood Park, a 32nd-minute shot, and then one on 56 minutes that seemed certain to give the away side both points. Ted Harper, though, hadn't finished top scorer in the previous season for nothing, and after scoring a penalty, he forced a late Blackburn equaliser. Back at Hillsborough, Trotter hit a well-directed shot out of Huddersfield 'keeper Billy Mercer's reach in a 1-1 draw. It meant he had scored ten times in eight games.

After two matches without a goal Trotter hit his eleventh goal of the season, a rising shot from a Wilkinson pass on 38 minutes that helped Wednesday win a thrilling game 3-2 against WBA. Against Derby County, a fierce cross drive on 74 minutes was enough to see Trotter's side home in a 2-1 victory.

In early December, Wednesday beat leaders Newcastle 3-2 at home. Trotter got two, heading into an empty net on 12 minutes, and then seizing on a mistake by Joe Wilson to push the loose ball beyond the 'keeper before sliding the ball home to make it 3-1. At Leeds the following weekend he scored again, his last-minute effort reducing the arrears to 1-4. On 28 December, he scored his nineteenth and twentieth League goals as Spurs were beaten 3-1 at Hillsborough. It was, though, to be almost two months before he next scored in the League.

Championship-chasing Sunderland was the side to suffer as Trotter raced to twenty-three League goals. Wednesday roared into a three-goal lead in just 20 minutes and dominated throughout in a 4-1 success. 'Their flank men finessed cleverly especially Wilkinson and Trotter's leadership was excellent with first-time and accurate shooting,' reported the *Newcastle Journal*. Trotter's hat-trick goal came 'with a great shot on the run', reported the *Journal*.

Two more flashed into opponents WBA's net on his next appearances, heading home Hooper's high dropping cross for the first and then using every ounce of his 12 stone 6 pound frame to muscle his way to a second to put his side 2-0 up in the second half. However, hopes of a first away victory of the season were dashed as the Baggies rallied to grab a point.

On 12 March, he scored his third hat-trick of the season as Arsenal was beaten 4-2 at Hillsborough. First, he dived bravely to head home Wilkinson's cross before then scoring on the rebound after Dan Lewis had saved his shot, adding his third with a close-in shot. Goal of the game, however, came from Tony Leach, whose shot from 40 yards sailed beyond the 'keeper and into the net to the tremendous cheers of the 21,252 spectators.

There were ten thousand fewer spectators for the game with Manchester United, and they missed a rough match in which a number of players were to be issued with cautions from the referee. Trotter scored both the goals, hooking home the first as he fell backwards and then, after forcing Alf Steward into making two fine saves, beating the 'keeper when Wilkinson cut the ball back to him. 'The irrepressible Trotter gives Wednesday another win,' reported the *Sheffield Saturday Sports* paper.

He got another two against Bolton Wanderers at Burnden Park, but the away side continued to struggle on their travels, losing 3-2. Back home, Trotter hit a great drive to open the scoring in a 3-1 success against Aston Villa. He got two more against Villa's great rivals Birmingham City in a thrilling 4-4 game before hitting his thirty-seventh and final goal of the season against Leeds United on the season's final day. He had hit the crossbar in the first half before scoring the only goal of the game on 77 minutes. The victory was enough to push Wednesday up to sixteenth place.

The Owls had scored seventy-five times, with Trotter getting almost half of his side's efforts. No wonder the local paper, in its review of the season, reported that, 'Trotter's goalscoring abilities have been a godsend. This hard and enthusiastic worker is to be complimented on his distinction and his skill.'

Wednesday continued to struggle the following season. Trotter did well by scoring sixteen times, but was overtaken as the club's highest scorer by Mark Hooper with twenty-one. The Owls looked doomed as the season entered March, but a magnificent seventeen points from the last ten matches helped pull off 'the Great Escape', in which Spurs 'reject' Jimmy Seed scored in both matches against his former club to help send them down.

Twice capturing the title, 1928/29 and 1929/30 were to be the best seasons in Wednesday's history. Key to the success was the form of Jack Allen, previously an inside forward who took over at centre forward when Trotter was injured for the game at Portsmouth. Having scored at Fratton Park, Allen then hit a hat-trick against Birmingham and four against Bury and after fourteen games in his new position, he had scored twenty-two times from it. It was the beginning of the end for Trotter and his final game came in a 1-1 draw against Sheffield United in February 1929.

After 160 first team appearances from which he scored 114 goals, Trotter moved on to Torquay United, where he continued to regularly hit the net, scoring twenty-six times in his first season. A spell at Watford was ended when a knee injury forced him to retire from playing, after which became trainer at Charlton Athletic for over two decades before taking over for a five-year spell as manager.

VIOLLET, DENNIS (MANCHESTER UNITED)

Season: 1959/60
Goals scored: 32 (out of 102); 17 home, 15 away
Percentage: 31 per cent
Runners-up: Jimmy Greaves (Chelsea) and Jimmy Murray (Wolves), with 29 goals each
Manchester United finished seventh

Dennis Viollet holds the Manchester United record for the most League goals in a single season. It would have been more, but he missed six of the last seven games of the 1959/60 season with a knee injury. Even more remarkably, Manchester-born Viollet achieved his feat in a season in which he played in four of the five forward positions, and also wore the number 4 shirt in the game at Preston, during a campaign in which Manchester United scored 102 goals and conceded eighty.

Viollet was a 'Busby Babe', one of a group of youngsters brought through the youth and reserve teams in the years following the Second World War. Selected six times for England Schoolboys, he turned down City to sign for United, learning quickly under the inspirational Jimmy Murphy, Matt Busby's second-in-command and trainer at the club.

He made his debut in April 1953, playing at outside right and in the same forward line as a record new signing, and a man with whom he was to subsequently form a fine partnership, Tommy Taylor. Newcastle was beaten 2-1 and Taylor scored both. The following weekend Viollet played his first game at Old Trafford, taking just 29 minutes to score the first of his 159 league goals for United. Playing at right wing, he beat two men in a style reminiscent of one who played there later on, George Best, before squeezing his shot into the corner of the net.

Retaining his place in the first team for much of the following season Viollet, scored eleven goals in twenty-nine games. Busby was refashioning a side that had won the FA Cup in 1948 and the League four seasons later, and Viollet was being groomed for a regular spot.

His first hat-trick came in one of the greatest games ever seen at Stamford Bridge, when Chelsea scored five times on 16 October 1954. Manchester United won the game by scoring six, with John Berry rightly earning the man of the match award by creating five of them. Viollet was to end the season with twenty goals from thirty-four League games.

His importance was underlined to his side when he missed four games at the start of the following season, Manchester United losing three of them. At Christmas, Viollet scored another hat-trick as WBA was beaten 4-1 at the Hawthorns. In early April, a late goal by Tommy Taylor was just enough to beat second-placed Blackpool and give Viollet his first championship medal during a season in which he again scored twenty goals in thirty-four League games.

Favourites to retain their title, Manchester United started the 1956/57 season in fine form, none more so than Viollet, who scored a magnificent hat-trick to overcome Preston 3-1. With Eddie Colman and Duncan Edwards providing the United front five with the ball, goals were a certainty and United literally blew the other sides away to win the Championship by a distance. Real Madrid had, though, put paid to their chances of a first European Cup success by beating Manchester United in the semi-final. With Old Trafford still without floodlights, 'home' games had been played at Maine Road and the first was to prove one of the most exciting, with Anderlecht being hit for ten with Viollet scoring four times.

Speaking years later, Sir Bobby Charlton had this to say:

Dennis's movement both on and off the ball was a sight to behold. The intelligent way he linked up with the wing-halves and his crisp, inch-perfect passing to his forward colleagues was stamped with class while his unique partnership with Tommy Taylor was something special.

Losing out to Aston Villa in the 1957 FA Cup final, Viollet was back at Wembley to face Bolton the following season. Alongside him were just two players from twelve months earlier, Bill Foulkes and Bobby Charlton. The Munich air crash had robbed Manchester United of some of its finest stars, including Taylor and Edwards.

Denis Viollet had survived, thrown, like Bobby Charlton, from the aircraft strapped to his seat. Taylor had scored twenty-two times before the tragedy in February and although Viollet had sneaked past him to finish as the club's top scorer with twenty-three by the season's end, no one was celebrating, especially as Bolton won the Cup final 2-0.

Refashioning the side saw Viollet pushed back to outside right after nine games of the 1958/59 season. Starting slowly, Manchester United ran into fine form when winter kicked in, and when they beat leaders Wolves in February, courtesy of a last-minute goal by Charlton created by Viollet, it meant twenty-three of a possible twenty-four points had been gathered from twelve games. Even defeat in the next game seemed to be shrugged off as the next five were won. Against Leeds, Viollet scored another hat-trick, swivelling to score the first with a rising shot that left former Sheffield United 'keeper Ted Burgin cursing his luck.

Inside forward Albert Quixall had joined for a British record fee of £45,000 and with Viollet now at centre forward, there was a real chance of Matt Busby's side winning the title. In the end, though, their poor start was to prove their undoing, Wolves making it two in a row with six more points. Viollet had managed twenty-one League goals, second in the United scorers' chart, eight behind Bobby Charlton.

Viollet scored Manchester United's first League goal of the 1959/60 season, taking just 18 minutes to open his account at WBA. After four games his total had risen to six but with Manchester United struggling, Busby had even tried playing him at right-half again at Preston. With United beaten 4-0, the experiment was never repeated.

Back at centre forward, Viollet scored a marvellous goal at Molineux, hammering home a right-foot drive worthy of many similar ones associated with Bobby Charlton. On 14 October he scored two more, this time against Sheffield Wednesday. As he was also being praised for his ability to bring other players into the game, it was no surprise that demands for a first England cap were growing. In fact, Viollet only played twice for England, his first match coming against Hungary at the end of the 1959/60 season.

Viollet took his goal total to twenty-one in early December in a 5-1 thrashing of FA Cup holders Nottingham Forest. Albert Scanlon ran the away side ragged to set up his teammate for a hat-trick. Combining perfectly, the pair scored a double each as Burnley, eventual Champions come the season's end, were thrashed 4-1 at Turf Moor. Not that United were ever in the running for the title, four days later being battered 7-3 at Newcastle. They were, though, proving an entertaining side to watch, with Blackpool torn apart at Bloomfield Road in a 6-0 victory in which Viollet scored another double, with Charlton grabbing three.

Manchester United scored a goal fewer at Craven Cottage shortly after, winning comfortably 5-0, and with Viollet again scoring twice, it took him above United's previous record holder, Jack Rowley, and up to thirty-one League goals. He scored his final goal at Hillsborough in a 4-2 defeat before injury brought his season to a premature end. With thirty-two League goals, he had, though, already ensured he would finish at the top of the scorers' charts come the season's end.

Viollet was to play at Manchester United for another full season before departing in January 1962 to Stoke City. Although he was in his thirteenth season at Old Trafford, he was only twenty-nine. Yet Matt Busby was already looking to younger players and when his form dipped at the start of the 1961-62 season, Viollet found himself in the reserves. Signed by Tony Waddington for £25,000, Viollet helped Stoke City win the 1962/63 Second Division championship, getting on the end of many of Sir Stanley Matthews's crosses to hit twenty-three goals in thirty-seven matches. Viollet died on 6 March 1999.

WARING, TOM 'PONGO' (ASTON VILLA)

Season: 1930/31
Goals scored: 49 (out of 128); 32 home, 17 away
Percentage: 38.2 per cent
Runner-up: Jimmy Dunne (Sheffield United), 41 goals
Villa finished second

Tall, long-striding, six feet of sinew, muscle and bone, Tom 'Pongo' Waring – the 'Gay Cavalier' – was a wonderfully consistent goalscorer, supremely confident in his own ability, who battered defences up and down the country in 1930/31 while scoring a total of fifty goals, forty-nine in the League, to set a new and still existing record for Aston Villa.

A colourful character, the stories about him, apocryphal or otherwise, are legion.

A former teammate of his at Villa Park, the ex-England international Billy Walker, wrote in his autobiography, published in 1959:

> There were no rules for 'Pongo.' Nobody knew what time he would turn up for training – ten o'clock, eleven o'clock, twelve o'clock, it made no odds. Nobody on the staff at Villa Park could do anything with him, although I think I can claim, as his team captain, to be the only person able to handle him. He was a funny lad indeed. We started the week's training on a Tuesday morning and every time he followed a habit which he could never break. He would go round all the refreshment bars on the ground and finish off the lemonade left in the bottles! Then he would start a little of his training – but that seldom lasted very long.

Waring wasn't the sort of bloke who enjoyed jogging around the pitch or running up and down the pitch in straight lines. He simply wanted to get hold of the ball and shoot, even at a wall if need be. He always looked fit and was one of the finest goalscorers of his era.

Born in Birkenhead on 12 October 1906, Waring – who, as a youngster, sold chocolate outside Prenton Park on match days – signed professional forms for his local club, Tranmere Rovers, in February 1926 and after taking over from Dixie Dean, became a star performer.

Several big-name clubs sent scouts to watch him and shortly after seeing him score six goals in an 11-0 victory over Durham City in a Third Division (North) game, Aston Villa moved in and secured his services for £4,700 in February 1928.

As well as playing football, Waring also worked for the Hercules Motor and Cycle Company in Aston, but that was just to boost his income – bear in mind he was paid just £8 a week during the football season, and £6 a week in the summer!

Eager to see their new 'man' in action, a crowd of 23,440 saw him make his Villa debut in a reserve game against local rivals Birmingham a few days after signing – and what a start he made, cracking in a hat-trick in a 6-3 victory.

That performance set the pattern. He never yielded after that – he became as popular as the Prime Minister – and went on to score 167 goals, including ten hat-tricks, in 226 senior appearances over the next seven-and-a-half years for Villa, and he also gained five England caps (scoring four goals).

He started his record-breaking season of 1930/31 in magnificent style, scoring all of Villa's goals in a 4-3 victory over Manchester United at Old Trafford, two of them made by winger Eric Houghton, who was to play a major role in Waring's record-breaking campaign, assisting in more than twenty of his goals.

A week later, West Ham suffered at the hands of the 'Gay Cavalier', who cracked in another four-timer in a resounding 6-1 win at Villa Park, two of his goals this time being set up by Walker.

In the first seven games of the season, Waring netted thirteen times as Villa, who dropped only one point, stormed to the top of the First Division table. In October, the irresistible Waring scored in three of Villa's four games before having a quite brilliant November and December, bagging twelve goals, including a stunning winner at Sheffield United (4-3) and two stunning strikes (one blasted into the net from 35 yards) in a 5-2 home victory over Blackburn. And he even missed the 7-0 rout of Manchester United in the return fixture, with his deputy George Brown scoring twice!

Waring ended the year with twenty-eight goals to his name (in twenty-two starts) and after missing another two matches at the start of 1931, things seemed to get better and better!

He netted once against Bolton (won 3-1), twice – although he missed three easy chances – in a resounding 8-1 home win over Middlesbrough, did likewise when Huddersfield were battered 6-1 a week later, and scored all four goals when Sunderland were overpowered 4-2 at Villa Park in mid-February.

The goals continued to come in 4-2 and 2-0 wins over Leicester City and Blackburn before he scored twice in the top-of-the-table encounter with Arsenal, which Villa won emphatically by 5-1.

Another hat-trick – his fourth of the season – followed against Blackpool (won 4-1) and after that he finished off a brilliant season by scoring in successive wins over Newcastle (4-3), Sheffield United (4-0), Leeds (2-0) and Manchester City (4-2), his effort against the latter being his fiftieth of the season.

Unfortunately, for all Waring's bold and brave efforts and of course his goals, forty-nine out of an amazing total of 128 scored by the team, Villa finished runners-up to Arsenal in the League, beaten by seven points (66–59).

Waring was sent off for the first and only time in his career playing for Villa against Tottenham at White Hart Lane in January 1934. As he walked from the pitch, head bowed, he received a bigger cheer than the whole team would have got if they'd won the FA Cup!

On leaving Villa Park in November 1935, Waring joined Barnsley. He moved to Wolves a year later, played next for his first club, Tranmere, whom he helped win the Third Division (North) title, and before the war assisted both Accrington Stanley and Bath City. A guest player for New Brighton, Wrexham, Everton, Crewe Alexandra and even Aston Villa during the hostilities, he ran down his career in non-League football in the Merseyside area, eventually retiring in 1950.

Waring was seventy-four when he died on 20 December 1980.

WAYMAN, CHARLIE (PRESTON NORTH END)

Season: 1952/53
Goals scored: 23 (out of 85); 13 home, 10 away
Percentage: 27 per cent
Runners-up: Doug Lishman (Arsenal) and Peter Harris (Portsmouth), with 22 goals each (Some record books show Harris scored 23)
Preston finished second

Charlie Wayman was twenty-nine when promotion-seeking Preston paid Southampton £10,000 for him in September 1950. It proved money well spent as he bashed home twenty-seven goals in thirty-four matches as the Deepdale side captured the Second Division trophy. A seventh-place finish the following season demonstrated PNE could compete in the higher League. That was certainly true in 1952/53 and with Tom Finney at his best, and Wayman in sparkling form in front of goal, Preston were to remain in the title hunt until the very end.

Wayman started in fine form, hitting both of his side's goals in 1-1 draws with Liverpool and Blackpool before notching the only goal at home to WBA. In early September, he hit a wonderful free kick to level the scores at St James' Park in a marvellous game that Newcastle won with two late George Robledo goals. Against Sunderland in mid-November, he opened the scoring as Preston beat the Wearsiders 3-2, a result that sparked a run up the table with fifteen points from eight games. At home to Charlton and losing 1-0, Wayman scrambled a vital equaliser in muddy conditions before Finney headed a late winner.

On 26 December, Manchester City was easily beaten 6-2 at Deepdale. Already a goal up, Wayman showed his creative abilities with a fine pass that Jimmy Baxter swept past Bert Trautmann, and when the two again combined, it was Wayman who added the third. Then, just before half time, he picked out Derek Lewis, who was to tragically die of a brain haemorrhage in July 1953 at the age of twenty-four, to make it 4-0. On 68 minutes he scored his second, and with Finney scoring the sixth, it meant all five home forwards had scored in a game in which Preston's teamwork was at its greatest.

Five days later, local rivals Blackpool were next to suffer as with Wayman again on the score-sheet, Preston won a thrilling game 4-2. Two days later, Middlesbrough was crushed 3-0, with Wayman scoring all the goals. On a frosty pitch, Finney twice picked him out with fine crosses, his second header showing that even at just 5 feet 6 inches, he could head with deadly accuracy. It was his first hat-trick in almost a year. His next took a lot less time arriving – the following weekend, in fact. This was an FA Cup game at home to one of the favourites, Wolves, who returned beaten 5-2.

He put his side back into the lead on 38 minutes, and notched his second and third goals in similar fashion by running into open space before receiving a neat pass and beating Bert Williams with a fine shot. No wonder the *Lancashire Evening Post* waxed lyrically that, 'Wayman gave an impressive exhibition of effective leadership, rounding off intelligent constructive play with deadly opportunism. He took all his chances well in recording another popular success that was partly due to his shrewd positional play.'

It was Wayman's second FA Cup hat-trick of his career, his first coming for his first club, Newcastle, in a 3-1 success against Southampton in January 1947. Three months earlier, the County Durham lad had played his first game at centre forward, playing alongside debutant Len Shackleton against Newport County. The pair scored ten times, with Shack scoring a double hat-trick as the Football League record victory of 13-0 was equalled.

Wayman scored his fourth Cup goal of the 1952/53 season against Spurs, but the Cockneys won out at home 1-0 after a 2-2 draw away. Preston did a lot better the following season, earning a place in the final, with Wayman having scored in every round, including a plunging diving header to open the scoring in the 2-0 semi-final victory against Sheffield Wednesday.

In the final, Wayman became only the tenth player to score in every round by putting his side ahead 2-1 on 51 minutes. WBA recovered to win 3-2 with a late Frank Griffin winner that disappointed the nation, which was desperate to see Tom Finney win the FA Cup.

Having scored once in February, Wayman was back in goal-scoring mood in early March. His two goals at Old Trafford weren't much consolation, however, as inspired by Tommy Taylor, Manchester United won 5-2. Much better was another double in a 4-0 home hammering of Portsmouth that pushed Preston to within two points of leaders Burnley, and when Bolton were subsequently beaten 3-0 away, the Deepdale side moved to the summit.

A disappointing 3-1 defeat against Aston Villa at home failed to still the title challenge and with four games remaining, Preston and Arsenal were locked in a battle for the Championship Trophy. On 18 April, a tricky contest at Charlton Athletic was made more so by the absence of Finney, playing at Wembley for England the same day against Scotland.

Wayman again scored, his twenty-first League goal of the season, but a 2-1 defeat put the Gunners in pole position. The sides locked horns in their penultimate match and Wayman scored with a glorious left-foot shot on 67 minutes in a 2-0 win.

Four days later, Preston completed their fixtures with a 1-0 win against Derby courtesy of Ton Finney's seventeenth goal of the season. It meant that Arsenal had to win two days later, when they faced Burnley at home. The away side took the lead through Roy Stephenson and although the Gunners replied with three quick efforts, there were still 15 minutes remaining when Billy Elliott reduced the arrears. In a frantic finish, 'somehow Arsenal held out and won', reported Bob Ferrier in the *Mirror*. Preston had to make do with the runners-up spot.

Wayman left Deepdale to move to Middlesbrough in autumn 1954. Manager Frank Hill felt that at thirty-three he was past his best, but having already notched six goals in six games, that wasn't the view of Preston's followers. He scored thirty-one more League goals over the next couple of seasons before playing for Darlington in Division Three North, where a knee injury ended his professional career in 1958 after 382 League appearances in which he notched 255 goals.

Charlie Wayman died in February 2006.

WATSON, VIC (WEST HAM UNITED)

Season: 1929/30
Goals scored: 42 (out of 86); 24 home, 18 away
Percentage: 49 per cent
Runner-up: Jimmy Dunne (Sheffield United), 36 goals
West Ham United finished seventh

The Hammers' record scorer, Watson arrived at Upton Park in March 1920 after manager Syd King paid Southern League Wellingborough Town £25 for a player he felt would make perfect cover for local hero Syd Puddefoot.

On 4 October 1920, during his third game, he scored his first goal in a 1-0 away win at Coventry City. After making nine appearances in his first season he became a regular in the second, scoring thirteen goals in forty matches. Second Division West Ham then enjoyed a wonderful 1922/23 season, winning promotion and fighting their way to the first FA Cup final held at Wembley. Watson scored two hat-tricks in the League, including hitting four at Crystal Palace, and he also struck five times in the FA Cup. Despite his best efforts at Wembley, West Ham lost out 2-0 to Bolton Wanderers before a crowd estimated to have exceeded 200,000.

His fine form had attracted the England selectors' attentions and he made his international debut in March 1923, scoring as England drew 2-2 with Wales in Cardiff. Retained in the side for the match in Glasgow, he again scored in another 2-2 draw.

Despite his successes, it was to be another seven seasons before he collected the third of his five caps when, unable to ignore his goal scoring exploits, the selectors picked him to play against Scotland at Wembley in early April 1930. He scored twice as Scotland were crushed 5-2 at Wembley, but after failing to score against Austria and West Germany on an end of season continental tour, Watson was never again selected.

Watson's first season in Division One wasn't a great success and he scored just three times, but he then scored 111 League goals in the next five. He also scored three great FA Cup goals

in the match against Spurs in January 1927, helping West Ham squeeze home 3-2 before their second highest ever gate of 44,417. In February 1929, he'd become the first Hammer to hit six goals in a game as Leeds was thrashed 8-2 at Upton Park.

On the first day of the 1929/30 season, Watson was quickly into his stride, hitting his side's second in a thrilling 3-3 draw at Blackburn. Playing for the first time at home, West Ham and opponents Middlesbrough provided thrilling fare for the 35,000-strong crowd, with Watson heading his side's fifth in a 5-3 win. Two days later, West Ham again scored five against a side from the north-east, Newcastle being easily beaten 5-1, with Watson again scoring his side's fifth. Winger Tommy Yews, who in addition to scoring twice constantly bamboozled the Geordies, made it for him.

Despite five goals from his first five matches, there was criticism of Watson in the *Liverpool Echo* the following weekend, where despite scoring his sixth of the season in a 3-1 defeat at Anfield, the local reporter felt he 'had grown big and rather heavy moving'.

He certainly wasn't slow when Everton came south and returned beaten 3-1. Watson, praised for his 'energy and deft work at centre-forward' by the *Liverpool Echo*, opened the scoring when he again reacted quickly to a loose ball in the box to beat 'keeper Arthur Davies.

At Elland Road, he continued his personal crusade against Leeds United by again scoring twice in a 3-1 away success. In early December, he scored his fifteenth goal of the season in a 1-1 draw at home to Sunderland. In truth, a single goal was poor reward as West Ham should have won by a large margin, but for once Watson was guilty of some poor finishing. He was in better form in the following home game, scoring his first hat-trick of the season as Aston

Villa were beaten 5-2. It could have been more, as he also hit the post and bar.

Against Notts County in the FA Cup, Watson scored twice in a 4-0 victory, setting up a tie with Leeds United. Poor Leeds – they played well, but found Watson at his very best. Well fed by Yews, Jimmy Ruffell and John Ball, he crashed four goals into the net, making it twelve in the last three matches against the Yorkshire side. Returning to Upton Park in March, things got slightly easier for Leeds, Watson managing to hit only three into their net in a 3-0 victory. It meant that in four games in little more than a year, Watson had scored fifteen times against the Elland Road side.

Victory in the Cup resulted in a fifth round tie at near neighbours Millwall of Division Two. Four first-half goals for the away side showed there was a real gulf in class. Watson got the second and fourth during a 3-minute spell in which West Ham scored three times. First, he diverted a Jim Barrett centre home, and then for his second he rose beautifully to head Yews's cross beyond Joe Lansdale. West Ham's assault on Wembley was to come to a shuddering halt, however, when they were heavily beaten 3-0 at home by Arsenal in the last eight. Revenge, of a sort, came the following weekend when Watson netted twice in a 3-2 home win against the Gunners.

Over Easter, Watson took his tally up to thirty-nine League goals with the only goal of the game against Sheffield United, and two in a 5-3 victory against Bolton Wanderers. He then added three more in the match at Villa Park, opening the scoring on 21 minutes with a low drive. In the second, a header from a Yews cross made it 2-1 and after Villa again equalised, he scored a 70th-minute winner when left unmarked in the box. It was his second hat-trick of the season against his opponents and it his raised his total to fifty for the season, forty-two in the League and eight in the FA Cup – all from just forty-four games.

Watson was to continue scoring for West Ham for the next five seasons, although his twenty-three League goals in 1931/32 couldn't prevent relegation. Hitting fifty League goals in the next two seasons, Watson left West Ham in March 1935. With 326 goals he had established himself as West Ham's record goalscorer, and in addition to his six against Leeds United, he also hit four goals on four occasions and recorded thirteen hat-tricks. Playing for Southampton for one season before retiring, he was the Saints' top scorer with fourteen goals in thirty-six appearances. Returning to his birthplace, Girton in Cambridgeshire, he lived a long life, dying aged ninety in 1988. In June 2010, a plaque honouring Watson was unveiled in Girton.

WEST, ENOCH (NOTTINGHAM FOREST)

Season: 1907/08
Goals scored: 26 (out of 59); 19 home, 7 away
Percentage: 44.6 per cent
Runners-up: Sandy Turnbull (Manchester United) and Albert Shepherd (Bolton Wanderers), with 25 goals each
Forest finished ninth

Enoch 'Knocker' West was born in Hucknall Torkard, Nottinghamshire on 31 March 1886. He worked as a coal-miner and played for Hucknall Constitutionals until signing for Sheffield United in November 1903. He failed to make the first team at Bramall Lane and returned to the Constitutionals until June 1905, when he joined Nottingham Forest.

In his first two seasons at The City Ground, utility forward West scored a total of twenty-eight goals, playing an important role in helping Forest win the Second Division championship.

In 1907/08, he was quite outstanding while occupying all five front-line positions and besides being Forest's leading marksman again, he also topped the First Division scoring charts with twenty-six goals in thirty-five games.

Powerful in all aspects of forward play, his total included four goals in a 4-1 home win over Sunderland in November, and hat-tricks in a splendid 6-0 victory over Chelsea and in the 3-3 draw at Blackburn Rovers.

Forest fielded an unchanged team in their first eight games of the season, winning three of them, including a 3-1 opener against Liverpool and the demolition of hapless Chelsea in late September.

West, in fact, occupied the left wing position in all of these games. Arthur Green led the attack, and Tom Marrison and Grenville Morris were the inside forwards, with Bill Hooper on the right.

It was the dashing Hooper who helped set up two of West's three goals against the London club, but after that each of the other forwards and more assisted West on his quest for goals.

After scoring against Blackburn Rovers (won 3-2) and Birmingham (1-1) West, who had by now been switched to inside left, was in great form with a booming four-timer against Sunderland, two of his goals being struck with deliberate right-foot drives after some smart build-up play involving Morris and left-winger Alf Spouncer, who had returned to the side following a lengthy injury.

After a goal in each of his next two games – in a 3-1 defeat at Arsenal and a 2-2 home draw with Sheffield Wednesday – West missed two easy chances in a 3-0 defeat at Bristol City before scoring in a 2-0 win over arch-rivals Notts County. He took a battering from some sturdy defenders in a 4-2 defeat at Manchester City, but his well-taken effort against Preston in the next game helped salvage a point from a 2-2 draw.

Out of sorts in a 4-0 drubbing at Villa Park on Christmas Day, West netted both goals in the return fixture twenty-four hours later, which finished 2-2, but then he was rather frustrated as he failed to hit the net in four of the next five matches, owning up to missing three clear-cut chances in a 0-0 draw at Anfield.

That disappointing display against Liverpool was soon forgotten, however, as West returned to form with a wonderful treble against Blackburn in early February, one of his shots almost ripping a hole in Rovers' net!

During the last months of the season West suffered a few injuries, missing three games. He scored only five goals in his last nine outings, two coming in a 3-1 home win over Bristol City and a beauty in a 2-0 win against Manchester United.

Despite West's bold efforts, Forest managed only ninth place in the First Division – reasonable enough, one felt – but over the next two seasons they slipped even lower, finishing fourteenth both times.

During the 1908/09 and 1909/10 campaigns, West netted forty-four goals for Forest, ending his five-year stay at The City Ground with exactly 100 to his credit in 183 competitive games. He was one of three players who scored hat-tricks in a record-equalling First Division victory of 12-0 over Leicester Fosse in April 1909, and he also represented the Football League.

In June 1910, West, who was still only twenty-four, moved to Manchester United to replace Jimmy Turnbull. He had a great first season, scoring nineteen goals in thirty-five games. He formed a terrific partnership with Sandy Turnbull and they netted more than half of the team's goals.

On the last Saturday of the season, League leaders Aston Villa lost at Liverpool while with West outstanding, United thrashed Sunderland 5-1 to clinch the title.

In the 1911-12 season, West was once again leading scorer with twenty-three goals. However, his fellow strikers, Sandy Turnbull and Harold Halse, were disappointing and Manchester United finished thirteenth.

West again topped the scoring charts in 1912/13 with twenty-one League goals. However, he lost form in 1913/14, scoring just six times, and was under par again in 1914/15 with just nine goals.

After Manchester United had defeated Liverpool 2-0 on 2 April 1915, certain bookmakers claimed they had taken many bets on the 7-1 odds offered on a 2-0 United victory. They suspected the game had been fixed and pointed out that late on, Liverpool's Jackie Sheldon had missed a penalty. The bookmakers refused to pay out and offered a £50 reward for information that would unmask the conspirators.

The *Sporting Chronicle* newspaper took up the story and claimed to have discovered evidence that players on both sides had combined to concoct a 2-0 scoreline. The newspaper argued that some of the players had large bets on the result.

The Football League investigation that followed reported in December 1915 and concluded that, 'A considerable amount of money changed hands by betting on the match and ... some of the players profited thereby.'

Three Manchester United players were banned for life, including West who, in fact, was the only one to play in the match. Sandy Turnbull and Arthur Whalley were the others. The same sentence was imposed on four Liverpool players – Jackie Sheldon, Tom Fairfoul, Tommy Miller and Bob Pursell. An eighth player, Laurence Cook, who played for Stockport County, was also convicted of being a member of the betting ring.

It was suggested that if the men joined the armed forces, their punishment would be rescinded. All the men, except West, who protested his innocence, signed up. After the war, six of the men were allowed to continue playing in the Football League. The exception was Sandy Turnbull, who had been killed on the Western Front in 1917. Arthur Whalley was seriously wounded at Passchendale, but recovered to play in twenty-three games in the 1919/20 season.

West contested the sentence several times in court, but the ban was only lifted in 1945 as part of a general amnesty, by which time he was fifty-nine years old. He eventually died in September 1965.

NB: An accomplished sportsman, West also won medals as a track athlete and at billiards, finishing runner-up in the Professional Footballers' Charity Billiards tournament in 1915.

WESTCOTT, DENNIS (WOLVERHAMPTON WANDERERS)

Season: 1946/47
Goals scored: 38 (out of 98); 23 home, 15 away
Percentage: 38.7 per cent
Runners-up: Doug Reid (Portsmouth, Reg Lewis (Arsenal) and Freddie Steele (Stoke City), with 29 goals each
Wolves finished third

Dennis Westcott was born in Wallasey, Lancashire, on 2 July 1917. He represented England schoolboys and had an unsuccessful spell as an amateur with Everton before joining New Brighton in 1932, turning professional at the age of seventeen.

He then had a two-week trial with West Ham United before Major Frank Buckley signed him for Wolverhampton Wanderers in February 1937. He became a hero at Molineux and went on to serve the Black Country club for eleven years.

Initially an outside right, Westcott made his first-team debut for Wolves five days after joining the club and celebrated the occasion by scoring in an emphatic 6-0 victory over Grimsby Town in a fifth round FA Cup replay. In the team that day were star players such as Stan Cullis, Alex Scott, Tom Galley and Welshman Bryn Jones, who would soon move to Arsenal for a record fee of £14,000.

Westcott kept his place on the wing for the next two games before switching to centre forward in place of Gordon Clayton (sold to Aston Villa) for a game against Portsmouth. He played well, assisted in Harry Thompson's goal in the 1-1 draw and never looked back, finishing the season with six goals in ten League appearances.

Westcott made the centre forward position his own three weeks into the 1937/38 season, and immediately hit the goal trail with a brace in a 4-0 win over the FA Cup holders Sunderland at Molineux. He netted ten times before Christmas, and early in the New Year struck his first hat-trick for the club in a 4-0 FA Cup win over Swansea Town.

As the season drew to a close, he fired in seven goals during April, including a splendid four-timer in a club record 10-1 home League victory over Leicester City.

Westcott ended the season as top scorer with twenty-two goals (nineteen in the League) as Wolves settled for the runners-up spot behind Arsenal.

Then, with war clouds gathering over Britain, Westcott and Wolves finished runners-up again in 1938/39 (this time behind Everton), and also reached the FA Cup final.

Westcott was brilliant throughout the campaign, bagging a club record of forty-three goals (thirty-two in the League, eleven in the Cup – netting in every round except the final) to finish as the First Division's third top marksman.

He scored hat-tricks in successive home League wins over Grimsby Town (5-0) and Brentford (5-2), netted another treble in a 3-1 win at Chelsea and slammed in four goals in a runaway 5-0 FA Cup semi-final victory over his favourite team, Grimsby, in front of a record crowd at Old Trafford of almost 77,000.

Unfortunately, Westcott failed to find the net in the final, when Wolves were defeated by underdogs Portsmouth 4-1. Afterwards, it was discovered that the Pompey players, like those of Wolves, had also been injected with a so-called 'monkey gland drug'.

In the summer of 1937, Wolves boss Buckley had been approached by a chemist called Menzies Sharp who claimed he had a 'secret remedy that would give the players confidence'. It is believed that Sharp's ideas were based on the experiments of Dr Serge Voronoff, a Frenchman who had been born in Russia. Between 1917 and 1926, Voronoff carried out over 500 transplantations on sheep and goats, and also on a bull, grafting testicles from younger animals to older ones. His observations indicated that the transplantations caused the older animals to regain the vigor of younger animals.

Sharp's 'gland treatment' involved a course of twelve injections. Buckley later explained:

> To be honest, I was rather sceptical about this treatment and thought it best to try it out on myself first. The treatment lasted three or four months. Long before it was over I felt so much benefit that I asked the players if they would be willing to undergo it and that is how the gland treatment became general at Molineux.

Westcott scored in twenty of the thirty-seven League games he started in 1938/39. He had a wonderful strike-partner in Dicky Dorsett, who weighed in with twenty-nine goals, and between them the 'deadly duo' netted 72 of the club's 108 competitive goals.

The outbreak of the Second World War in 1939 brought to an end League football for seven years and during the hostilities Westcott was brilliant, scoring ninety-one goals in seventy-six appearances, helping Wolves win the Wartime League (North) Cup in 1942.

He continued to disrupt defences when League football resumed in 1946/47, scoring another thirty-eight League goals, including two fours, against Liverpool and Bolton, to head the First Division charts, nine more than his nearest challengers.

This tally remains a club record to this day.

Jesse Pye started the 1946/47 season alongside Westcott in the Wolves attack, and he celebrated his debut with a hat-trick while Westcott netted twice in a thumping 6-1 home win over Arsenal.

After this brilliant start, Wolves struggled on the pitch over the next sixteen days, failing to win in five League games. Westcott scored just one more goal, in a 2-1 home defeat by Brentford, but after that, he and Wolves played some superb football.

He scored in four of the next five League games and although sidelined for a fortnight in late October/early November, he stormed back to net fourteen times before Christmas, including successive four-timers in a 5-1 win over Liverpool at Anfield and a 5-0 slaughter of Bolton at Molineux. He was on a 'high' after this and who knows, he may well have scored four more against Chelsea at Stamford Bridge on 21 December, but missed the train to London!

Wolves, in fact, went to the top of the First Division table in early December and they remained in touch with the leaders right through to the final day of the campaign, thanks mainly to Westcott's goals. He scored in fourteen of the sixteen League games played by Wolves from 4 January to 17 May inclusive but annoyingly, right at the death, when he was needed most, he was injured and missed the last two games, at Huddersfield and at home to Liverpool.

Wolves beat Huddersfield 1-0 and this left them needing a point against the Merseysiders to clinch their first-ever League championship success. Unfortunately, a shot-shy forward line fumbled along without Westcott and the Reds won 2-1 to pinch the title by a point (57-56), with Manchester United edging Wolves into third place, also on 56 points.

The game against Liverpool was Stan Cullis's last ever appearance on a football pitch.

In the 1947/48 season, Westcott netted fourteen times, bringing his overall total with the club to 215 in just 220 appearances in all competitions.

Sold to Blackburn Rovers in April 1948, he added thirty-seven League goals to his collection in two years at Ewood Park, tucked away another thirty-seven in two seasons for Manchester City and then scored twenty-one for Chesterfield in 1951/52.

Westcott ended his career with Stafford Rangers in May 1956, having scored exactly 200 goals in 300 League appearances for four clubs in almost twenty years.

He also played in five wartime internationals for England between 1940 and 1943, scoring five goals. He died from leukaemia on 13 July 1960, aged forty-three.

Acknowledged as being one of the best centre-halves in the Football League, perhaps in Europe, during the late 1930s, Wolves and England skipper Stan Cullis said this about his teammate Westcott, a champion marksman:

> He was a great centre-forward of immense physique, as strong as an ox, afraid of no-one, a player who simply loved to score goals, and above all, a player totally committed to playing football. He was terrific at times, certainly in the late 1930s. I was glad to be playing behind him and with him, rather than against him.

NB: Westcott's tally of forty-three senior goals in 1938/39 stood as a Wolves record for forty-nine years, until Steve Bull bettered it with a haul of fifty-two in 1988/89.

WHELDON, FRED (ASTON VILLA)

Season: 1897/98
Goals scored: 23 (out of 61); 16 home, 7 away
Percentage: 37.7 per cent
Runner-up: Fred Spiksley (Sheffield Wednesday), 17 goals
Villa finished sixth

One of the select band of men who have won fame both at cricket and football, Fred Wheldon had a long and brilliant sporting career.

As a footballer, his services would have been accepted by any club in the country. When at his best, he was undoubtedly the finest inside left in England, possibly Scotland as well.

His command of the ball, his adaptability to prevailing conditions, combined with his dodging, his swerving, and his deadly shooting, made him a great player in the highest company. Superb with both his head and feet, he often demoralised many a defence with his intricate play and not only did he score plenty of goals, but he created chances galore for his colleagues.

One of the few players to serve three clubs within a 10-mile radius – Small Heath (now Birmingham City), Aston Villa, and West Bromwich Albion – Wheldon, known as 'Diamond', certainly had an eye for goal and during his fourteen-year career at senior level (1890–1904), he scored over 200 goals (for club and country).

Born deep in the heart of the industrial Black Country, at Langley Green, Oldbury on 1 November 1869, Wheldon, the youngest of ten children, played for several local teams and had an unsuccessful trial with West Bromwich Albion in October 1888 before joining Small Heath of the Football Alliance in February 1890.

During the following six seasons he missed only one League game and in 1892/93, the inaugural season of the Football League Second Division, he scored Small Heath's first ever goal in that competition (against Burslem Port Vale) and finished the campaign with twenty-five goals in twenty-two appearances as the Blues won the Championship. Unfortunately, they failed to gain promotion, losing out in the Test Match system that was then in operation. He scored over twenty goals again the next season, and this time the club was promoted.

On Small Heath's relegation in 1895/96, Wheldon – having bagged a total of 84 goals in 134 games – joined reigning First Division champions and near-neighbours Aston Villa for a fee of £350.

In his first season he was Villa's leading scorer, with twenty-two League and Cup goals, as the Birmingham club emulated Preston North End's feat of winning the double, and then, in 1897/98, he topped the League's scoring charts with a total of twenty-three goals as Villa slipped down to sixth in the table.

Wheldon, in fact, make a sensational start to the season, netting a hat-trick in each of the first two games, which resulted in home victories over Sheffield Wednesday (5-3) and rivals West Bromwich Albion (4-3). His treble against the Owls included one stunning drive from fully 20 yards, while two of his efforts against the Baggies were executed with 'precision and exquisite skill'.

The reporter covering this local derby for the *Sports Argus* wrote:

> Wheldon was the only Villa player who looked like scoring. He posed a threat throughout the game and besides his two goals, had two more efforts saved by the Albion custodian Joe Reader. He also failed with what looked like two easy close range headers following deep crosses from the right by Charlie Athersmith.

Goalless in the third match, against Notts County, he stroked home his seventh goal of the campaign in a 3-1 win over Bury before bagging a couple (one a penalty) in a 4-3 defeat at Blackburn.

Another blank afternoon followed in the return fixture with Sheffield Wednesday (lost 3-0) but he was back on track in the next game, scoring a decisive goal in a hard-earned 3-2 home victory over Bolton Wanderers.

After netting in 4-2 and 3-1 wins over Notts County and Liverpool at Villa Park during the second half of October, Wheldon weighed in with two more braces in successive homes wins over Everton and Sunderland in November, and then ripped in a beauty when Blackburn were thrashed 5-1 at the start of December.

Unfortunately, Villa slipped off the pace from mid-December to late January, failing to win a single League game and also suffering first round FA Cup elimination at the hand of Derby County.

Besides the team struggling on the pitch, Wheldon was also 'off form', scoring just twice in six games before regaining his touch in early February with a fine goal against Preston North End (won 4-0). Absent for two games in March due to international calls, he scored the winner at Bury (2-1) and also netted in defeats at Nottingham Forest (3-1) and at home to Wolves (2-1) to finish the season with twenty-three goals in twenty-six appearances, twelve more than runner-up Jack Sharp.

Over the next two seasons Wheldon scored a further twenty-nine goals, ending up with a total of 74 goals in 140 senior appearances in four years with Villa. He helped the team win two more League titles, in 1899 and 1900, gained four caps for England, scoring six goals, represented the Football League on four occasions and also played four times for an England XI.

In August 1900, Wheldon moved to nearby West Bromwich Albion for £100 and played in the first-ever game at The Hawthorns (against Derby County, and his England colleague Steve Bloomer). He scored just three times in twenty-nine starts for the Baggies and after spells in the Southern League with Queens Park Rangers and Portsmouth, plus a brief sojourn with Worcester City, he retired from football in January 1907 at the age of thirty-seven. He subsequently became a licensee of a Worcester pub, a job he held until the outbreak of the Great War.

As a cricketer, Wheldon, a right-hand batsman, scored 4,938 runs for Worcestershire, whom he served from 1899 to 1906. He averaged 22.50 per innings, notched three centuries and also claimed ninety-three catches, some as a wicketkeeper. He also played for Carmarthenshire CCC (1910/11).

His brother, Sam, played for West Bromwich Albion in season 1891/92, his son, Norris, assisted Liverpool, and his grandson, John Spilsbury, played once for Worcestershire CCC in 1952.

Wheldon died in Worcester on 13 January 1924.

WILSON, ANDY (MIDDLESBROUGH)

Season: 1921/22
Goals scored: 32 (out of 79); 18 home, 14 away
Percentage: 40 per cent
Runner-up: David Jack (Bolton Wanderers), 24 goals
Middlesbrough finished eighth

Scotsman Wilson returned to Ayresome Park after restarting his career back home following the end of the First World War, during which a shell fragment shattered his left hand and he was invalided home from the battlefields of France. Having played nine times for them during the 1914/15 season, Middlesbrough held on to his Football League registration while he played first for Heart of Midlothian and later Dunfermline Athletic.

Rejoining Middlesbrough, he quickly found his shooting boots. He might have opened his account on the opening day's fixture away to champions WBA, hitting two powerful drives – 'like projectiles from a gun', reported the local *Gazette* – from over 30 yards that George Ashmore did well to keep out in a game that ended 0-0.

Back home, he hit four in two games, opening his account with an 87th-minute equaliser against Oldham Athletic in the first. Injured in the first half and largely anonymous thereafter, he hit a remarkable goal when, on 'receiving the ball with his back to the goal he swung round to screw the ball past two defenders and against the underside of the bar.'

Six days later, he scored his first hat-trick of the season, against WBA at home in a remarkable game in which both sides led before Middlesbrough ran out 3-2 winners. His first two efforts were powerful blasts, rocketing home from 25 and 30 yards respectively. He then eluded his marker to head home Tommy Urwin's cross for the only goal of the game in the return fixture with Oldham Athletic.

He continued his fine form with another two goals in the following fixture as Cup holders Spurs were beaten 4-2 at White Hart Lane. After just 14 minutes the away side were 3-0 up, but were pegged back to 3-2 when, with just 5 minutes left, Wilson scored a remarkable goal. It came when Jackie Mordue's cross hit him smack bang in the 'middle' and as he sank to the floor in agony, the (foot)ball rocketed into the net. It was probably appropriate that such a goal came against a side whose nickname is, of course, the Cockerels!

Agony of another sort came in the return fixture the following weekend. Sent off, Wilson added himself to the record books by disappearing down the tunnel for the second time after an earlier dismissal playing against Liverpool in March 1915. Not until Jimmy McClelland in January 1928 did another Middlesbrough man join Wilson on the list of those sent off playing for the club. Back after a short suspension he again scored, this time against Bradford City.

He was also on the scoresheet at Old Trafford in a fine 5-3 success that caused 'Pathfinder' in the *Gazette* to remark afterwards that ' Middlesbrough provided one of the most sparking exhibitions of forward craft seen at Old Trafford in a long time.' Wilson was particularly praised for his unselfishness. Back home, Boro beat United 2-0, with Wilson's neat piece of opportunism opening the scoring in another display in which Pathfinder praised him for 'picking up long balls and finding his wingers'.

Victory against leaders Liverpool pushed 'Boro to just two points off the top; Wilson got the third in a 3-1 success, a clever low shot doing the damage. However, despite notching two against Burnley in a 4-1 win, nodding George Elliott's cross past Jerry Dawson for the first and hitting a wonderful drop shot for his second, he remained four goals behind Sunderland's Charlie Buchan in the scoring charts.

The gap was to be reduced when Manchester City travelled north, Wilson's second hat-trick of the season being a fine reward for a polished performance in which he constantly brought wingmen Urwin and John Carr into action during a 4-1 success.

And when Wilson outscored by four to one the Sunderland man in the double-headed Tees-Wear derby matches that saw 'Boro take three points, it was clear the Scottish international had his heart set on a place in the record books. At Roker Park he opened the scoring in a 1-1 draw, fastening on to a loose ball to finish from 4 yards out. Back home at Ayresome Park, he scored twice in a 3-0 win. On 55 minutes he hit a free kick from a good 35 yards that Willie Harper was unable to keep out and when the chance of hitting it past the 'keeper from 12 yards arrived in the 90th minute, he sent the Sunderland man the wrong way.

It wasn't just his efforts in front of goal that were noted, with the reporter in the *Newcastle Daily Chronicle* effusive in his after-match praise, writing:

> Wilson's inspired leadership was a feature of the game and he seemed to be here, there and everywhere but almost always seemed to be in the right place at the right time. He certainly succeeded in puzzling the Sunderland halfback line many times and gave their rearguard endless trouble with his indefatigable efforts and brainy methods.

Huddersfield arrived possessing one of the best defences in the League and took an early lead. Yet with Wilson and Elliott combining brilliantly to 'play their best ever football together', and with John Carr in sparkling form, the Terriers left well beaten 5-1, with Wilson grabbing a couple.

Wilson then equalised with a header from Urwin's cross on 51 minutes in the 1-1 draw with Birmingham City before his low drive put his side ahead at Preston in another drawn match.

He'd missed the previous home match with Arsenal. Having played and scored twice for Scotland against newly formed Northern Ireland in early March, he turned out for his country against England. Drawing 0-0, he lashed home the only goal at the appropriately named, for a Scotsman, St Andrews. Wilson was to make another three appearances for Scotland during his Middlesbrough career and by scoring three more times, it meant that in six games he had scored seven times. Adding in his record at Hearts and Dunfermline, it's a pretty impressive one with seventeen goals in just fifteen games.

Single goals in three consecutive games followed, with his final League goal of the season coming against Bolton Wanderers in a 4-2 home victory, in which George Carr scored three times. Wilson's thirty-two goals also helped his side finish as the League's highest scorers, Middlesbrough's seventy-nine being seven more than next highest, Burnley.

Wilson was to leave Middlesbrough in late November 1923, signed for £6,000 by Chelsea as the Pensioners sought, ultimately unsuccessfully, to avoid relegation. Joining them in Division Two was Middlesbrough, for whom he played ninety times and scored fifty-seven times. He had also, of course, been sent off twice! He went on to make over 250 appearances for Chelsea before joining neighbours QPR. He died in October 1973.

WITHE, PETER (ASTON VILLA)

Season: 1980/81
Goals scored: 20 (out of 72); 11 home, 9 away
Percentage: 27.7 per cent
Joint top scorer with Steve Archibald (Tottenham Hotspur)
Villa were League Champions

For Aston Villa, the 1980/81 season was something of a throwback to the nineteenth century. The claret and blues won the Football League for the first time since 1910, using only fourteen players, of whom no less than seven were ever-present.

Villa and Liverpool were joint top at the end of December, with Ipswich Town just a point behind with games in hand. After some hard-earned displays which brought a handful of important victories, Villa finally edged clear of the pack on 4 April and although Ipswich remained in with a shout right to the death, Villa hung in thanks mainly to an impressive home record.

Striker Peter Withe – manager Ron Saunders' final piece in his jigsaw, signed for a club record fee of £500,000 in the summer of 1980 from Newcastle United – was the team's top scorer with twenty League goals. He also finished as the leading marksman in Division One, the first time a Villa player had achieved this feat since 'Pongo' Waring fifty years earlier in 1930/31.

The much-travelled Withe, who during the previous twelve years had played, in turn, for the amateur club Skelmersdale, Smith Coggins FC (Liverpool), Southport, Preston North End (briefly), Barrow (trial), Port Elizabeth and Arcadia Shepherds in South Africa, Wolves, Portland Timbers in the NASL, Birmingham City, Nottingham Forest, with whom he won the First Division championship in 1978, and, of course, Newcastle, was twenty-nine when he moved into Villa Park.

He adapted to his new surroundings like a fish to water and quickly drew up a fine understanding with fellow striker Gary Shaw. He also had Tony Morley flying down the wing and sending over quality crosses for him to get on the end of, and with the hard-working and highly skilful trio of Des Bremner, Dennis Mortimer and Gordon Cowans carving out openings from midfield, Villa were a strong unit. And so it proved.

He didn't exactly fly out of the blocks, however, scoring only three goals in the opening ten League games – all against the Manchester clubs! Two salvaged a point at Manchester City (2-2), while the other earned Villa a share of the spoils at Old Trafford.

He managed one in the League Cup, but was out of sorts along with his teammates as lowly Cambridge United dumped Villa out of the competition in the third round.

In League game number twelve Morley, with two goals, and Withe, with the other, eased Villa past Spurs by 3-0 and four days later the big striker helped himself to the team's second goal in a 4-1 victory at home to Brighton before winning the points against Southampton with a second-half net-buster at The Dell.

Surprisingly, perhaps, during the month of November Withe failed to score in six League games, only one of which was won. He then missed four matches in December (David Geddis taking over), but after his Boxing Day winner against Stoke City he hardly looked back in anger during the second-half of the campaign.

After seeing Villa eliminated from the FA Cup by Ipswich in the third round, Withe netted in the 2-0 and 2-1 home away wins over Liverpool and Coventry City respectively, struck both goals when Crystal Palace were defeated at Villa Park, bagged the winner against his former club, Wolves, at Molineux at the end of February and scored twice in another thrilling 3-3 home draw with Manchester United.

At this stage of the season – 14 March – it was tight at the top, with Villa, Liverpool, Ipswich, Midland rivals West Bromwich Albion and Liverpool all in with a chance of taking the title.

A 1-0 defeat at Spurs interrupted Villa's momentum slightly, but they responded magnificently with successive wins over Southampton 2-1, Leicester 4-2 and West Brom 1-0. Withe netted a late winner against the Baggies when he latched onto a weak back-pass from the full-back Brendon Batson to gain all three points in a tight Midlands derby in front of a mid-week crowd of almost 48,000, the biggest of the season at Villa Park.

Four days later, Ipswich put a spanner in the works by winning 2-1 at Villa Park. It was stunner, but two victories and a draw in their next three games, Withe scoring in each one against Nottingham Forest (won 2-0), Stoke City (1-1) and Middlesbrough (won 3-0), effectively clinched the title as Bobby Robson's Ipswich dropped crucial points, including a 2-1 defeat at Middlesbrough on the same day Villa lost their final game of the season 2-0 at Highbury.

In the end, thanks to Withe's twenty goals, plus eighteen from Shaw and ten from Morley, Villa finished four points ahead of Ipswich (60–56), with Arsenal third (53) and West Brom fourth (52).

For his bold efforts as leader of the attack, Withe gained the first of his eleven full caps for England, making his international debut in a 1-0 defeat in Brazil in mid-May. He continued to play for his country, off and on, until November 1984.

A year after helping Villa win the League Championship, he had the pleasure of tapping in the winning goal from Morley's left-wing cross to win the European Cup at Bayern Munich's expense in Rotterdam. He remained at Villa Park until July 1985, when he was transferred to Sheffield United, having netted 92 goals in 233 appearances during his five-year association with the Birmingham club.

Over the next four years Withe also played for Birmingham City (on loan, September-November 1987) and was player-coach at Huddersfield Town (July 1988-January 1991) before returning to Villa Park as assistant-manager/coach. In October 1991 he was appointed manager of Wimbledon but stayed at Plough Lane for only four months, taking over as Port Vale's Football in the Community Officer before acting as Villa's Chief Scout for two years, 1997–99. From April 2000 to October 2003 he was national team coach/advisor to the Thailand national team.

Withe was born in Liverpool on 30 August 1951 and during his extensive career scored 210 goals in 609 club appearances at various levels while serving with fifteen different clubs.

His brother, Chris, played for Bradford City.

WORTHINGTON, FRANK (BOLTON WANDERERS)

Season: 1978/79
Goals scored: 24 (out of 54); 14 home, 10 away
Percentage: 44 per cent
Runner-up: Kenny Dalglish (Liverpool), 21 goals
Bolton finished seventeenth
Partner Alan Gowling also scored 15 goals

Frank Worthington netted on his Bolton Wanderers debut against Stoke City in October 1977. After two seasons of near misses, manager Ian Greaves hoped his arrival would help ensure promotion into the top flight. The England international, signed at just £90,000 from Leicester City, where in the 1973/74 season he had ended up just behind Southampton's Mick Channon at the top of the First Division scorers' chart, did not disappoint and on 26 April 1978, his goal away to Blackburn Rovers won the Wanderers the two points they needed to confirm promotion.

Back in Division One after a fifteen-season absence, Worthington's goal threat and ability to bring others into the game with his sublime passing skills were going to be important if Bolton were to stay there. Joining him up front was former Newcastle United man Alan Gowling, and the two were to form a fine partnership. And it was the latter who struck the opening goal against Bristol City on the season's first day, only for the Robins to recover to win 2-1.

There was therefore relief when a point was earned from a hard fought 2-2 draw at the Dell. Worthington scored two and after a summer in which some great free kicks had been scored at the World Cup finals in Argentina, the man who started his career at Huddersfield was clearly determined to show he had his own special ways of hitting the back of the net from a dead-ball situation. He did so twice, leading Greaves to comment afterwards that 'he loves skill and if he comes across someone who can bend a free kick 4 feet he will always want to do it better'.

Worthington's next League goal was also a free kick, his 49th-minute shot finding the back of the Birmingham net. Then, on 70 minutes, he sent 'keeper Neil Freeman the wrong way from the penalty spot for his third double of the season after two goals had put Chelsea out of the League Cup.

Another goal of real quality came against Leeds United at home. The away side were pushing forward in search of an equaliser when Willie Morgan sent Worthington free, and he beat David Harvey with a fierce low drive to make it 3-1 on 87 minutes. Interviewed later for an article in the *Bolton Evening News*, Worthington was at pains to play down his goalscoring achievements saying, 'Really I think like a midfield player as I am constantly trying to help the players around him.'

On 7 October 1978, the Special Correspondent for the *Bolton Evening News* wrote, 'Quality is the feature that runs through Worthington's play. His subtle touches and high entertainment value have not been lost to supporters of other clubs.'

Gowling too was also hitting the net, and when he and Worthington both netted for the third consecutive match in a 2-2 draw with Manchester City, the two established a reputation as 'goal twins'. Come the season's end, the pair were to have hit thirty-nine.

Three of these came in a fine 3-1 win at QPR. Worthington had a magnificent match and scored twice, one of which was a marvellous solo effort. At the same time he was also accused of spitting at Ernie Howe and John Hollins and when the former committed a bad foul on him, the Bolton centre forward was fortunate to stay on the pitch after throwing a retaliatory punch. Fortunately, it wasn't as good as his shooting, as he missed! 'If I had connected he would have been flat out,' said Worthington later.

He scored another double as Bolton thrilled their fans with a 3-0 demolition of Manchester United just before Christmas. Almost inevitably, it was Gowling who got the other goal.

Bad weather in January and February meant it wasn't until March that Worthington was back finding the net. His curling free kick to beat Joe Corrigan wasn't enough to prevent Manchester City winning 2-1.

Playing so well, it was no surprise that Worthington was in demand. Attempts to rebuild the USA Soccer League saw Philadelphia Fury offering him big money to play there during

the summer. He was determined to go. Greaves didn't want him to, but had to concede, telling Bolton fans he had no choice 'because with his contract expiring at the end of the season I'd have probably lost Frank for good if I refused to let him go.'

Worthington, at thirty, was looking to the future, but nevertheless was clearly enjoying himself at Bolton as Gowling and he both bagged a pair of goals in a 4-2 beating of Arsenal. Continuing their double act, both players scored as QPR were beaten 2-1 in a fine game.

Bolton also won the next match 2-1 and as it was at Old Trafford, it ensured a famous 'double' against Manchester United. Worthington grabbed both in front of the Stretford End. Martin Buchan had given the home side a 1-0 half-time lead and then, after Worthington had equalised, Gordon McQueen missed a penalty.

Bolton, though, remained under considerable pressure, but with little more than a minute to go, a fine Brian Smith run and pass was flicked beyond the 'keeper for the winning goal to the delight of the Wanderers fans in the crowd.

At Ipswich Town on 21 April 1979, Frank Worthington scored the goal of the season.

In front of the TV cameras Worthington scored a goal fit to grace any occasion. He was on the edge of the box, back to goal with the Ipswich defenders snapping at his heels. Calmly he flicked the ball up twice, lifted it over his head and turned to fire a shot past Cooper's left hand into the corner of the net. (Gordon Sharrock, reporting in the *Bolton Evening News*)

Worthington netted his final goal of the season against Tottenham Hotspur. For once, he was outshone by the all-round abilities of Argentine Osvaldo Ardiles. Few, though, were the players in 1978/79 who could say they'd played better than Frank Worthington. Yet within months he'd departed Burnden Park when, after arriving back late from America, he failed to produce anything like the form he had previously displayed. He was quickly sold to Birmingham City. Three seasons at St Andrews were quickly followed by a tour of the country, with spells at a host of clubs before he finally finished playing in 1991, a quarter of a century after his first appearance for the Terriers.

WRIGHT, IAN (CRYSTAL PALACE AND ARSENAL)

Season: 1991/92
Goals scored for Crystal Palace: 5 (out of 16); 3 at home, 2 away
Percentage: 31.2 per cent
Goals scored for Arsenal: 24 (out of 81); 14 at home, 10 away
Percentage: 29.6 per cent
Runner-up: Gary Lineker (Tottenham Hotspur), 28 goals
Palace finished tenth
Arsenal finished fourth

Ian Wright entered professional football relatively late. Despite having trials with Southend United and Brighton & Hove Albion as a teenager, he was unable to attract sufficient interest to earn a professional contract offer and reverted back to playing for amateur and non-League teams. He was left disillusioned about his chances of a career in football and actually spent two weeks in Chelmsford Prison for driving without tax or insurance.

Then, out of the blue, a Crystal Palace talent scout, Peter Prentice, saw him score hat-tricks for Greenwich Borough and Dulwich Hamlet within a fortnight and immediately invited him for trial at Selhurst Park. He then impressed manager Steve Coppell, who signed him as a full-time professional in August 1985, just three months short of his twenty-second birthday.

Wright quickly made his mark in his first season at Selhurst Park, netting nine goals to finish as the Eagles' second-highest scorer. When Mark Bright arrived on the scene the following year, he and Wright quickly established themselves as a lethal and successful striking partnership ... and it was largely due to the goals they scored between them that Palace gained promotion to the top flight via the play-offs in 1989.

Wright was called up for England 'B' duty in December 1989, but a twice-cracked shin bone reduced his initial impact in the First Division. However, after recovering from the injury, he made a dramatic appearance as a 'super-sub' in the 1990 FA Cup final against Manchester United. He equalised for Palace almost immediately to force extra-time. Then, with the tension building, he put his side ahead, but United hit back to force a 3-3 draw and then won the replay 1-0.

The very next season, 1990/91, Wright gained full international honours and reached a hundred goals for Palace, also scoring twice in the Zenith Data Systems Cup final victory over Everton at Wembley. He ended that campaign with a total of nineteen goals and then bagged five more at the start of the next season before transferring to reigning League champions Arsenal in September 1991 for £2.5 million.

He said farewell to the Palace fans by netting the winner in a 3-2 derby win over Wimbledon, secured a 2-1 victory over Sheffield United, won the game 1-0 at Villa Park, scored in a 3-2 home defeat by West Ham and ended his Palace career with a smartly-taken goal in a 3-2 win at Oldham.

Overall, he notched 117 goals in 277 senior appearances for Palace, making him the club's record post-war goalscorer and the third in the club's history.

Going straight into the team alongside Alan Smith in Arsenal's attack, Wright made a terrific start as a Gunner, firing a hat-trick on his debut in a League Cup win over Leicester City and then following up soon afterwards with a second-half treble in his first League start for the club in a 4-0 win at Southampton. 'Everything I tried came off,' he said as he clutched his second match ball.

He was then on target in his second game – a 3-2 win over Chelsea – but missed out in a 1-1 draw with Manchester United before securing a 2-0 home win over Notts County in his fourth game.

The Highbury faithful had gained a new hero and Wright responded in style with a point-saver at Oldham (1-1) and a 'sweet finish' to set up a 2-0 home victory over Spurs before going off injured.

After sitting out a 3-2 defeat at Nottingham Forest, he returned in style by blasting a four-timer into the Everton net to earn an early Christmas present as Arsenal retained sixth place in the Division with a 4-2 win.

Unfortunately, the team – and Wright – lost momentum from Boxing Day through to early February, failing to win any of seven League games and slipping embarrassingly out of the FA Cup to lowly Wrexham.

But after a scrappy 1-0 win at Notts County and a scrambled draw at home to Norwich, the Gunners started firing on all cylinders again with an outstanding performance at home to Sheffield Wednesday. They won 7-1, with Wright scoring his first goal since his epic spree against Everton.

He then netted in four of the next five games, including a couple in a 2-0 victory at West Ham and a clever effort in the 1-1 draw with Spurs. Soon afterwards, he struck twice when

Arsenal defeated Norwich 3-1 at Carrow Road, scored twice in a brilliant 4-0 home victory over Liverpool and ended the season with his third hat-trick for the Gunners in a 5-1 home win over Southampton to become the first Arsenal player to score a hat-trick in home and way games against the same club in the same season since Jack Lambert achieved the feat against Middlesbrough in 1930/31. His last two goals against the Saints came in injury time.

Wright continued to score on a regular basis for Arsenal. In fact, he was the club's top scorer six seasons running, and when he eventually left Highbury for West Ham United in a £750,000 deal in July 1998, he had netted 185 goals in 288 appearances.

He broke Cliff Bastin's club scoring record with a hat-trick against Bolton Wanderers in September 1997, and his final tally of 185 stood for seven years until Thierry Henry toppled it in October 2005.

He had also taken his tally of full England caps to a healthy thirty-three, scoring nine goals – four coming in a 7-1 win over San Marino. He helped the Gunners win the 'Cup' double in 1993 and reach the European Cup-winner's Cup final in 1994, but missed Arsenal's charge towards the League and Cup double in 1998 through injury.

This, coupled with the fact that Dutchman Dennis Bergkamp had by now arrived at Highbury - signed by manager Bruce Rioch in July 1995 - led to him leaving the club. He spent only fifteen months with the Hammers, during which time he was loaned out to Nottingham Forest. In October 1999, he signed for Celtic on a free transfer and after assisting Burnley (February–May 2000) he retired with a quite remarkable record to his credit – 333 goals in 661 appearances (all competitions, all levels). He was awarded the MBE for services to football (on his retirement) and since then has been a soccer pundit, presented his own chat show on TV, captained a team on a BBC game show, penned a regular column for *The Sun* newspaper and has been inducted into the English Football Hall of Fame.

While at Arsenal, Wright wrote his autobiography, *Mr Wright*. It was first published in hardback in 1996 by Collins Willow and reprinted in paperback a year later, including a new, updated chapter.

In 1993, he compiled and released a single called 'Do The Right Thing'. The song was co-written and produced by Chris Lowe (of Pet Shop Boys) and reached No. 43 in the UK Singles Chart.

Now patron of the African-Caribbean Leukaemia Trust, Wright was born in Woolwich, North London, on 3 November 1963.

YORKE, DWIGHT (MANCHESTER UNITED)

Season: 1998/99
Goals scored: 18 (out of 80); 8 home, 10 away
Percentage: 22.5 per cent
Joint top scorer with Michael Owen (Liverpool) and Jimmy Floyd Hasselbaink (Leeds United)
Manchester United were Premier League Champions

Yorke immediately established with Andy Cole the most deadly partnership in Europe when, after months of speculation, he moved to Old Trafford from Aston Villa for £12.6 million at the start of the 1998/99 season. The result was that Manchester United not only won the Premier League and FA Cup, but also conquered Europe, with the deadly duo scoring sixty-three goals between them, with Yorke only just out-scoring, by eighteen to seventeen, his teammate and good friend in the League.

It meant that for most of the season Teddy Sheringham and Ole Gunnar Solskjaer, who remarkably struck four goals in 10 minutes against Nottingham Forest as a late substitute, largely kept the bench warm. Not, of course, that it did the latter two any harm, as they were to both score, as substitutes, very late goals to win their side the UEFA Champions League Final 2-1 against Bayern Munich at Camp Nou. No one, though, outscored Yorke in the Champions League during the season, his eight goals ensuring he finished joint top scorer.

Yorke scored in his first match at Old Trafford, the first of two against Charlton Athletic seeing him head home a David Beckham free kick in a 4-1 win. With two games in a week at home and abroad, he reached eight in total by October, when he opened the scoring at Goodison Park in a match the away side won comfortably 4-1. There was nothing spectacular about a simple tap-in after Cole and Paul Scholes had set him up.

Against Brondby in the UEFA Champions League, he turned provider to set up Cole, who finished with a superb chip over 'keeper Emeka Andersen. Some delightful interplay between the pair helped Yorke equalise away at Sheffield Wednesday, but it still failed to prevent the away side going down 3-1.

Alex Ferguson's side had enjoyed a thrilling 3-3 draw in Europe with Barcelona at Old Trafford earlier in the season, and in a remarkable return match the sides again shared the goals in another six goal thriller, in which following a lovely run by Jesper Blomqvist, Yorke drilled home an early equaliser from the edge of the area.

With Manchester United stuttering over the Christmas and New Year period, Yorke helped his side get back to winning ways when just 10 minutes into the match with West Ham on 10 January, he hit a savage drive that his good friend Shaka Hislop had no chance of saving in a game the home side won 4-1. Six days later, at Filbert Street, Leicester were swept away in a marvellous second-half Manchester United display in which Yorke scored his first hat-trick for the club, hitting his third by popping home the rebound after Cole had rapped the bar.

Two weeks later, the former Villa man helped push his side to the top of the Premiership table with a last-minute winner when he rose to head substitute Nicky Butt's header beyond Charlton 'keeper Simon Royce. And it was the same two players who did the damage the following match, at home to Derby County, Yorke finishing off Butt's weighted pass with a clipped shot that Russell Hoult could only admire.

Inter Milan had clearly failed to do their homework on Yorke when they travelled to play the first leg of the UEFA Champions League quarter-final in early March, the man from Tobago combining superbly with Beckham to get on the end of the England international's trademark free kicks to head home twice.

The following Wednesday, Manchester United were leading 1-0 at Stamford Bridge in a sixth round FA Cup replay match when Yorke scored his best goal of the season. He'd already scored on 4 minutes when he received the ball from Cole and instantly chipped Ed de Hoey with the outside of his right foot. It was a goal of stunning brilliance, but was later forgotten when Ryan Giggs danced 70 yards down the Arsenal right to leave five defenders trailing before beating 'keeper David Seaman to ensure Manchester United won their replayed FA Cup semi-final match.

United had drawn 1-1 at home with Juventus in the first leg of the Champions League semi-final and were in crisis when they fell two goals behind in the Stadium Delle Alpi by 11 minutes. Yet within 23 minutes they were level, when, after Roy Keane headed

Beckham's corner beyond Angelo Peruzzi, Yorke neatly beat the Juve 'keeper with a header from a Cole cross. Then, on 71 minutes, the favour was returned when Cole hit the winning goal after Yorke's dart into the box set up a chance the former Newcastle man took with glee.

It took Yorke only 5 minutes to open the scoring at Anfield in the League, but with Liverpool leaving it late to grab a draw, Manchester United were under pressure to ensure all three points in the next game at the Riverside Stadium against a Middlesbrough side that early in the season had won 3-2 at Old Trafford. It was the tightest of games, but just before half time Yorke headed the match's only goal; Sheringham headed Butt's cross back across goal for his fellow striker to head home as Middlesbrough appealed for offside. It was his eighteenth and final Premier League goal of the season, but it had ensured a vital three points which, with Manchester United gaining four points from the next two games, proved just enough to give Alex Ferguson his fifth Premier League title and Manchester United their twelfth top-flight success.

Further success soon followed with Newcastle United beaten 2-0 in the FA Cup final before Bayern Munich were beaten in Barcelona, Yorke watching on as two Beckham corners set up a dramatic finish.

Dwight Yorke was to score 64 goals in 188 appearances for Manchester United, adding to his Premier League medal in 1998/99 with two more, in 1999/2000 and 2000/2001. Spells with Blackburn Rovers, Birmingham City, Sydney FC and Sunderland followed his transfer from Old Trafford in 2002, during which he collected a Second Division winners' medal with Sunderland in 2006/07. Earlier in his career, Yorke had twice won the Football League Cup with Aston Villa. Yorke made nineteen international appearances for Trinidad and Tobago.

YOUNG, ALEX 'SANDY' (EVERTON)

Season: 1906/07
Goals scored: 28 (out of 70); 19 home, 9 away
Percentage: 40 per cent
Runner-up: Arthur Bridgett (Sunderland), 25 goals
Everton finished third

Alex 'Sandy' Young was a golden-haired aristocrat among footballers with his subtleties and grace, a Scottish international capped twice, against England in 1905 and Wales in 1907. He was Everton's top-scorer in five successive seasons, 1903–08, and was leading marksman again in 1910/11.

In between times, in 1906/07, he netted more goals than any other player in the First Division (28) and during his ten-year association with the Goodison Park club, he claimed a total of 125 goals in 314 appearances, striking the winner for the Blues in their 1906 FA Cup final victory over Newcastle United. The reaction that this goal received was likened by one newspaper to the San Francisco earthquake, which had happened a week earlier.

An imposing, muscular centre forward, who in later years appeared in the inside left position, Young had a heart of gold and an engine that seemed to roll along forever.

He was born in Slamannan, Stirlingshire on 23 June 1880 and played for Paisley, St Mirren and Falkirk before joining Everton in July 1901. He made his debut for the Merseysiders against Aston Villa three months later and remained in the team, injuries, illness and international call-ups apart, for a decade.

He only managed seven goals in his first season and five in his second, but after that he became a more frequent marksman, and in 1906/07 Young was quite brilliant in a fast-raiding forward line which also included wingers Jack Sharp (right) and Harold Hardman or George Wilson (left), with fellow Scot Hugh Bolton and Jimmy Settle as the inside players.

After scoring a point-saver in a 2-2 draw at Middlesbrough on the opening Saturday of the season, he tore the Manchester City defence apart in Everton's first home match forty-eight hours later, cracking in four goals in an emphatic 9-1 victory. He twice found the net with vicious low drives and was unlucky not to grab a fifth goal when his header struck an upright.

His next goal salvaged a point from another 2-2 draw, this time against Notts County, and then in the Merseyside derby he struck twice, a real beauty, in Everton's 2-1 win at Anfield.

Over the next four weeks he grabbed the winner in the return fixture with Notts County, netted twice in a 4-2 home win over Sheffield United and was on target in 3-1 and 3-0 victories at Bolton and at home to Manchester United respectively.

In mid-November, despite taking a buffeting from a couple of tough-tackling Blackburn defenders, his fine strike settled the game at 2-0, and two weeks later he bagged a couple when Birmingham were defeated 3-0 at Goodison Park.

During the period from 22 December to 19 January, Young scored seven goals, including home and away winners against Bury and a brace in a competent 3-0 home victory over League leaders Newcastle. He also scored and helped set up two goals for his colleague Bolton in the 5-1 demolition of Middlesbrough.

At this stage of the season Everton were still in with a fighting chance of winning the First Division championship and also the FA Cup (as were Newcastle), but unfortunately Young, due to various reasons, missed five of the last eleven League games.

During his absence, Everton played well below par, losing 4-1 at Sheffield United, 2-1 at Blackburn and 5-2 at Derby, and although his presence may have made some difference, those three defeats and a poor away record of twelve defeats proved costly in the end as Everton finished in the third place, six points behind Newcastle!

It was also disappointment for Young and his teammates in the FA Cup as Everton, the holders of course, lost 2-1 in the final to Sheffield Wednesday.

On leaving Goodison Park in the summer of 1911, Young moved south to Tottenham Hotspur. He started well with the London club, scoring three goals in his first two games, but failed to find the net in his next three and was left out of the team. Somewhat peeved, Young immediately demanded a transfer, which was granted, and in the November he signed for Manchester City, staying at Hyde Road until the end of the season, when he returned to Merseyside to play for South Liverpool, and then briefly for Port Vale. He retired in May 1914, and two months later emigrated to Australia.

Young had been living and working in Tongala, Northern Victoria for eighteen months when, in December 1915, he was arrested and charged with the murder by shooting of his brother John, a farmer, following an argument over money.

At his trial in Bendigo Supreme Court near Melbourne, evidence was produced from football officials in England revealing that during his playing days he had been subject to fits of temporary insanity.

Young was subsequently convicted of manslaughter in June 1916 and sentenced to three years' imprisonment. After his release Young worked as a sheep-rustler before returning to

Scotland early in his sixties. He died in an asylum in Portobello, Edinburgh on 17 October 1959.

* The Edinburgh-born forward Alex Young who played for Everton between 1960 and 1968 is not an ancestor of Sandy.

APPENDIX 1

Complete list of top scorers from 1888 to 2011

FOOTBALL LEAGUE

1888/89 John Goodall (Preston North End)	20
1889/90 Jimmy Ross (Preston North End)	24
1890/91 John Southworth (Blackburn Rovers)	26
1891/92 John Campbell (Sunderland)	32

FIRST DIVISION

1892/93 Johnny Campbell (Sunderland)	30
1893/94 John Southworth (Everton)	27
1894/95 John Campbell (Sunderland)	21
1895/96 John Campbell (Aston Villa)	26
1896/97 Steve Bloomer (Derby County)	24
1897/98 Fred Wheldon (Aston Villa)	23
1898/99 Steve Bloomer (Derby County)	24
1899/1900 Billy Garraty (Aston Villa)	27
1900/01 Steve Bloomer (Derby County)	24
1901/02 Jimmy Settle (Everton)	18
1902/03 Sam Raybould (Liverpool)	31
1903/04 Steve Bloomer (Derby County)	20
1904/05 Arthur Brown (Sheffield United)	22
1905/06 Albert Shepherd (Bolton Wanderers)	26
1906/07 Sandy Young (Everton)	28
1907/08 Enoch West (Nottingham Forest)	26
1908/09 Bertie Freeman (Everton)	38
1909/10 Jack Parkinson (Liverpool)	30
1910/11 Albert Shepherd (Newcastle United)	25
1911/12 George Holley (Sunderland), Harry Hampton (Aston Villa), David McLean (Sheffield Wednesday)	25
1912/13 David McLean (Sheffield Wednesday)	30
1913/14 George Elliott (Middlesbrough)	31
1914/15 Bobby Parker (Everton)	36

First World War 1915–1919

1919/20 Fred Morris (West Bromwich Albion)	37
1920/21 Joe Smith (Bolton Wanderers)	38
1921/22 Andy Wilson (Middlesbrough)	32
1922/23 Charlie Buchan (Sunderland)	30
1923/24 Wilf Chadwick (Everton)	28
1924/25 Frank Roberts (Manchester City)	31
1925/26 Ted Harper (Blackburn Rovers)	43
1926/27 Jimmy Trotter (Sheffield Wednesday)	37
1927/28 Dixie Dean (Everton)	60
1928/29 David Halliday (Sunderland)	43
1929/30 Vic Watson (West Ham United)	42
1930/31 'Pongo' Waring (Aston Villa)	49
1931/32 Dixie Dean (Everton)	44
1932/33 Jack Bowers (Derby County)	35
1933/34 Jack Bowers (Derby County)	34
1934/35 Ted Drake (Arsenal)	42
1935/36 Ginger Richardson (West Bromwich Albion)	39
1936/37 Freddie Steele (Stoke City)	33
1937/38 Tommy Lawton (Everton)	29
1938/39 Tommy Lawton (Everton), Mick Fenton (Middlesbrough)	34

Second World War 1939–1946

1946/47 Dennis Westcott (Wolverhampton Wanderers)	38
1947/48 Ron Rooke (Arsenal)	33
1948/49 Willie Moir (Bolton Wanderers)	25
1949/50 Dickie Davis (Sunderland)	25
1950/51 Stan Mortensen (Blackpool)	30
1951/52 George Robledo (Newcastle United)	33
1952/53 Charlie Wayman (Preston North End)	23
1953/54 Jimmy Glazzard (Huddersfield Town)	29
1954/55 Ronnie Allen (West Bromwich Albion)	27
1955/56 Nat Lofthouse (Bolton Wanderers)	32
1956/57 John Charles (Leeds United)	38
1957/58 Bobby Smith (Tottenham Hotspur)	36
1958/59 Jimmy Greaves (Chelsea), Bobby Smith (Tottenham Hotspur)	32
1959/60 Denis Viollet (Manchester United)	32
1960/61 Jimmy Greaves (Chelsea)	41
1961/62 Ray Crawford (Ipswich Town), Derek Kevan (West Bromwich Albion)	33
1962/63 Jimmy Greaves (Tottenham Hotspur)	37
1963/64 Jimmy Greaves (Tottenham Hotspur)	35
1964/65 Jimmy Greaves (Tottenham Hotspur), Andy McEvoy (Blackburn Rovers)	29
1965/66 Roger Hunt (Liverpool)	30
1966/67 Ron Davies (Southampton)	37
1967/68 George Best (Manchester United), Ron Davies (Southampton)	28

1968/69 Jimmy Greaves (Tottenham Hotspur) — 27
1969/70 Jeff Astle (West Bromwich Albion) — 25
1970/71 Tony Brown (West Bromwich Albion) — 28
1971/72 Francis Lee (Manchester City) — 33
1972/73 Bryan Robson (West Ham United) — 28
1973/74 Mick Channon (Southampton) — 21
1974/75 Malcolm MacDonald (Newcastle United) — 21
1975/76 Ted MacDougall (Norwich City) — 23
1976/77 Malcolm McDonald (Arsenal), Andy Gray (Aston Villa) — 25
1977/78 Bob Latchford (Everton) — 30
1978/79 Frank Worthington (Bolton Wanderers) — 24
1979/80 Phil Boyer (Southampton) — 23
1980/81 Peter Withe (Aston Villa), Steve Archibald (Tottenham Hotspur) — 20
1981/82 Kevin Keegan (Southampton) — 26
1982/83 Luther Blissett (Watford) — 27
1983/84 Ian Rush (Liverpool) — 32
1984/85 Gary Lineker (Leicester City), Kerry Dixon (Chelsea) — 24
1985/86 Gary Lineker (Everton) — 30
1986/87 Clive Allen (Tottenham Hotspur) — 33
1987/88 John Aldridge (Liverpool) — 28
1988/89 Alan Smith (Arsenal) — 23
1989/90 Gary Lineker (Tottenham Hotspur) — 24
1990/91 Alan Smith (Arsenal) — 22
1991/92 Ian Wright (Crystal Palace/Arsenal) — 29

PREMIER LEAGUE

1992/93 Teddy Sheringham (Nottingham Forest/Tottenham Hotspur) — 22
1993/94 Andy Cole (Newcastle United) — 34
1994/95 Alan Shearer (Blackburn Rovers) — 34
1995/96 Alan Shearer (Blackburn Rovers) — 31
1996/97 Alan Shearer (Newcastle United) — 25
1997/98 Michael Owen (Liverpool), Dion Dublin (Coventry City), Chris Sutton (Blackburn Rovers) — 18
1998/99 Dwight Yorke (Manchester United), Michael Owen (Liverpool), Jimmy Floyd Hasselbaink (Leeds United) — 18
1999/2000 Kevin Phillips (Sunderland) — 30
2000/01 Jimmy Floyd Hasselbaink (Chelsea) — 23
2001/02 Thierry Henry (Arsenal) — 24
2002/03 Ruud van Nistelrooy (Manchester United) — 25
2003/04 Thierry Henry (Arsenal) — 30
2004/05 Thierry Henry (Arsenal) — 25
2005/06 Thierry Henry (Arsenal) — 27
2006/07 Didier Drogba (Chelsea) — 20
2007/08 Cristiano Ronaldo (Manchester United) — 31
2008/09 Nicolas Anelka (Chelsea) — 19

2009/10 Didier Drogba (Chelsea) 29
2010/11 Carlos Tevez (Manchester City), Dimitar Berbatov (Manchester United) 21

MAJOR RULES CHANGES THAT MADE AN IMPACT ON GOALS SCORED

1891: Goal nets and penalty kicks introduced.
1912: Goalkeepers restricted to handling the ball in their own penalty area.
1925: Offside rule changed from three to two players.
1965: Substitutions introduced into league football.

APPENDIX 2

Records

Highest scorer in a single season
Dixie Dean (Everton): 60 goals in 39 League games in 1927/28.

Top scorer with the lowest number of goals
Jimmy Settle (Everton) in 1901/02 (a 34-game season); Michael Owen (Liverpool), Dion Dublin (Coventry City) and Chris Sutton (Blackburn Rovers) jointly in 1997/98; and Dwight Yorke (Manchester United), Michael Owen (Liverpool) and Jimmy Floyd Hasselbaink (Leeds United) jointly in 1998/99. All scored 18 goals.

Finished top with more than two clubs
Gary Lineker: Leicester City 1984/85, Everton 1985/86, Tottenham Hotspur 1990/91.

Finished top with two clubs
Jack Southworth (Blackburn Rovers and Everton); Bill Shepherd (Bolton Wanderers and Newcastle United); Jimmy Greaves (Chelsea and Tottenham Hotspur); Malcolm Macdonald (Newcastle United and Arsenal); Alan Shearer (Blackburn Rovers and Newcastle United); and Jimmy-Floyd Hasselbaink (Leeds United and Chelsea).

Finished top on six occasions
Jimmy Greaves

Finished top on four occasions
Steve Bloomer and Thierry Henry

Finished top on three occasions
John Campbell (Sunderland); Alan Shearer; and Gary Lineker.

Top marksman twice
Bowers; Dean; Ron Davies; Didier Drogba; Jimmy-Floyd Hasselbaink; Tommy Lawton; Malcolm Macdonald; David McLean; Michael Owen; Alan Smith; Bobby Smith; Southworth; and Shepherd.

Highest percentage of his team's goals
Dean, with 59 per cent in 1927/28 for Everton.

Players with 50 per cent or more of their team's goals
Southworth (Blackburn Rovers), 1890/91
Bowers (Derby County), 1934/35

Ron Davies (Southampton), 1966/67
Shearer (Blackburn Rovers), 1996/97
Kevin Phillips (Sunderland) 1999/2000
* Joe Smith (Bolton Wanderers) had a 49 per cent rate in 1920/21

Highest percentage partnership
Phillips and Niall Quinn (Sunderland), 77 per cent in 1999/2000
Frank Worthington and Alan Gowling (Bolton Wanderers) 75 per cent in 1978/79

Scored most goals without ever finishing top
Gordon Hodgson (Liverpool, Leeds United, Aston Villa), 287

Top ten scorers of all-time in top-flight football
Greaves, 357; Dean, 310; Bloomer, 309; Hodgson, 287; Shearer, 283; Buchan, 258; Lofthouse, 255; David Jack (Bolton Wanderers and Arsenal), 255; Joe Bradford (Birmingham), 248; and Hughie Gallacher (Newcastle United, Chelsea, Derby County) 247.

Highest still playing
Michael Owen (Liverpool, Newcastle United, Manchester United), 148

Finished top scorer when in relegated team
Mick Channon (Southampton), 1973/74

Finished top scorer when side won the title
John Goodall (Preston North End), 1888/89; Jimmy Ross (Preston North End), 1889/90; Johnny Campbell (Sunderland), 1891/92, 1892/93, 1894/95; Johnny Campbell (Aston Villa), 1895/96; Billy Garraty (Aston Villa), 1899/1900; Fred Morris (WBA), 1919/20; Dixie Dean (Everton), 1927/28, 1931/32; Ted Drake (Arsenal), 1934/35; Tommy Lawton (Everton), 1938/39; Ronnie Rooke (Arsenal), 1947/48; Ray Crawford (Ipswich Town), 1961/62; Ian Rush (Liverpool), 1983/84; Alan Smith (Arsenal), 1988/89, 1990/91; Alan Shearer (Blackburn Rovers), 1994/95; Dwight Yorke (Manchester United), 1998/99; Thierry Henry (Arsenal), 2001/02, 2003/04; Ruud Van Nistlerooy (Manchester United), 2002/03; Cristiano Ronaldo (Manchester United), 2007/08; Didier Drogba (Chelsea), 2009/10; and Dimitar Berbatov (Manchester United) 2010/11.

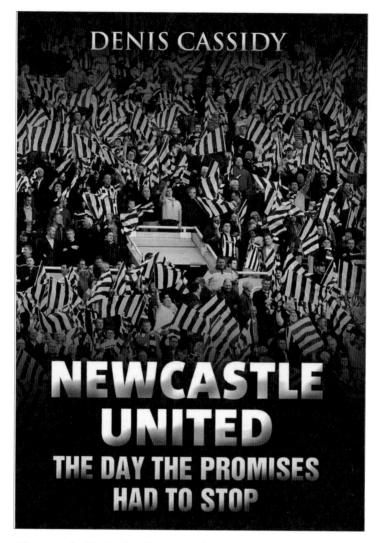

Newcastle United: The Day the Promises Had to Stop

Denis Cassidy

The story of a great club's history and a fascinating glimpse behind
the scenes of top-flight football.

978 1 4456 0059 8

192 pages

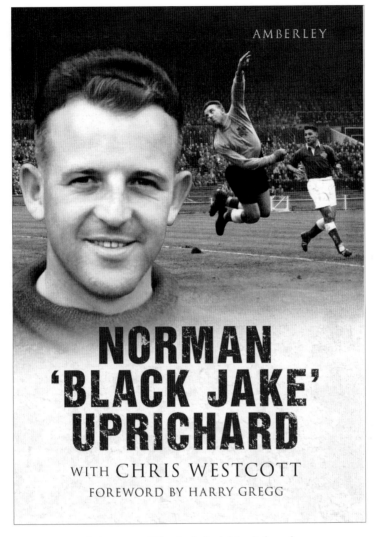

Norman 'Black Jake' Uprichard

With Chris Westcott

The fascinating tale of a young lad from Lurgan who played for the most famous English club of his day, Arsenal, and was capped 18 times for Northern Ireland.

978 1 4456 0088 8
128 pages

Thank You, Hermann Goering: The Life of a Sports
Writer

Brian Scovell

An entertaining and hugely readable autobiography of one of sports
journalism's most famous names.

978 1 4456 0174 8
192 pages

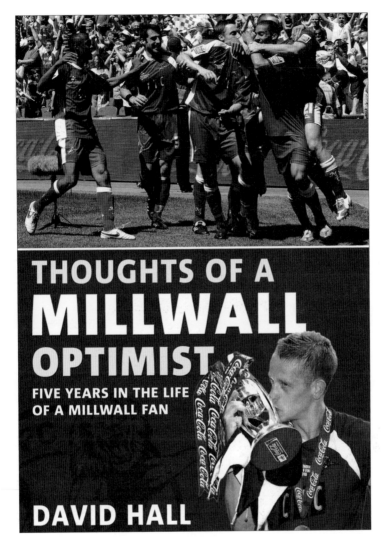

Thoughts of a Millwall Optimist
David Hall

A fascinating insight into life as a fan of one of London's most
enduring clubs.

978 1 4456 0220 2
192 pages

ALSO AVAILABLE FROM AMBERLEY PUBLISHING

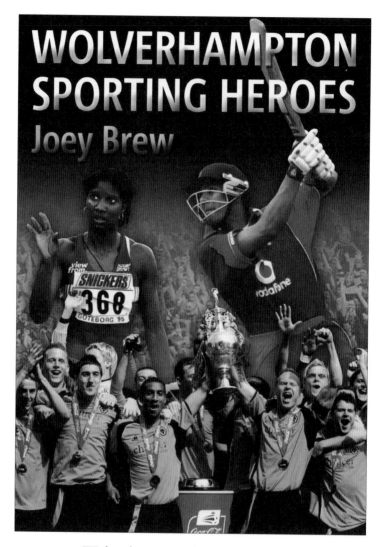

Wolverhampton Sporting Heroes

Joey Brew

The fascinating story of Wolverhampton's rich sporting heritage.

978 1 84868 485 0

96 pages,

Available from all good bookshops or order direct
from our website www.amberleybooks.com